China

Urban Land Management in an Emerging Market Economy

The World Bank
Washington, D.C.

Copyright © 1993
The International Bank for Reconstruction
and Development/THE WORLD BANK
1818 H Street, N.W.
Washington, D.C. 20433, U.S.A.

World Bank Country Studies are among the many reports originally prepared for internal use as part of the continuing analysis by the Bank of the economic and related conditions of its developing member countries and of its dialogues with the governments. Some of the reports are published in this series with the least possible delay for the use of governments and the academic, business and financial, and development communities. The typescript of this paper therefore has not been prepared in accordance with the procedures appropriate to formal printed texts, and the World Bank accepts no responsibility for errors.

The World Bank does not guarantee the accuracy of the data included in this publication and accepts no responsibility whatsoever for any consequence of their use. Any maps that accompany the text have been prepared solely for the convenience of readers; the designations and presentation of material in them do not imply the expression of any opinion whatsoever on the part of the World Bank, its affiliates, or its Board or member countries concerning the legal status of any country, territory, city, or area or of the authorities thereof or concerning the delimitation of its boundaries or its national affiliation.

The material in this publication is copyrighted. Requests for permission to reproduce portions of it should be sent to the Office of the Publisher at the address shown in the copyright notice above. The World Bank encourages dissemination of its work and will normally give permission promptly and, when the reproduction is for noncommercial purposes, without asking a fee. Permission to copy portions for classroom use is granted through the Copyright Clearance Center, 27 Congress Street, Salem, Massachusetts 01970, U.S.A.

The complete backlist of publications from the World Bank is shown in the annual *Index of Publications*, which contains an alphabetical title list (with full ordering information) and indexes of subjects, authors, and countries and regions. The latest edition is available free of charge from the Distribution Unit, Office of the Publisher, Department F, The World Bank, 1818 H Street, N.W., Washington, D.C. 20433, U.S.A., or from Publications, The World Bank, 66, avenue d'Iéna, 75116 Paris, France.

ISSN: 0253-2123

Library of Congress Cataloging-in-Publication Data

China : urban land management in an emerging market economy.
        p.   cm. — (World Bank country study, ISSN 0253-2123)
    ISBN 0-8213-2395-4
    1. Land use, Urban—China. 2. China—Economic conditions—1976–
I. International Bank for Reconstruction and Development.
II. Series.
    HD926.C474   1993
    333.33'713'0951—dc20   93-543
                                                                       CIP

CURRENCY EQUIVALENTS

Currency = Renminbi; Currency Unit = Yuan = 100 fen

$1.00 = Y 5.46
Y 1.00 = $0.19

FISCAL YEAR

January 1 - December 31

WEIGHTS AND MEASURES

Metric System

ACRONYMS AND ABBREVIATIONS

CABR	-	China Academy of Building Research
CASS	-	Chinese Academy of Social Sciences
CSCEC	-	China State Construction Engineering Company
CSHREDC	-	China State Housing and Real Estate Development Company
CAUPD	-	China Academy of Urban Planning and Design
CBD	-	Central Business District
CBTDC	-	China Building Technology Development Center
DPA	-	Development Permission Area
DSL	-	Da-She Lan District, Beijing
FAR	-	Floor Area Ratio
GDP	-	Gross Domestic Product
GIS	-	Geographic Information System
KLDC	-	Korea Land Development Corporation
LAB	-	Land Administration Bureau
LDC	-	Land Development Corporation, Hong Kong
LIS	-	Land Information System
MoA	-	Ministry of Agriculture
MoC	-	Ministry of Construction
MOF	-	Ministry of Finance
NBSM	-	National Bureau of Surveying and Mapping
NEPA	-	National Environmental Protection Agency
O&M	-	Operations and Maintenance
PC	-	Portable Computer
PCBC	-	People's Construction Bank of China
REAB	-	Real Estate Administration Bureau
REDC	-	Real Estate Development Company
SHCLAB	-	Shanghai County Land Administration Bureau
SHMLAB	-	Shanghai Municipal Land Administration Bureau
SIS	-	Strategic Information Systems
SLA	-	State Land Administration
SMG	-	Singapore Municipal Government
SPC	-	State Planning Commission
SREC	-	Shanghai Real Estate Company
SUCF	-	Shanghai Urban Construction Fund
TMG	-	Tianjin Municipal Government
TREDC	-	Tianjin Real Estate Development Company
TVE	-	Township and Village Enterprise
TVIE	-	Township and Village Industrial Enterprise
URA	-	Urban Redevelopment Authority, Singapore
ZGC	-	Zhong-Guan-Chun District, Beijing

ACKNOWLEDGEMENTS

This report was written on the basis of a preparation mission, undertaken during July/August 1991, and a main mission, which took place in January/February 1992. The report was discussed with local and national authorities in August/September 1992 and revised in response to comments made at that time. Mission members, some of whom participated in only one mission, included: Andrew Hamer (EA2EH), task manager; Alain Bertaud (INURD); Paul Stott (RMC); Nena Manley (LEGEA); David Dowall, Peter Fong, Daniel Lam, and Youxuan Zhu (Consultants); as well as local consultants Wang Yukun, Ren Zhiyuan, and Sun Chongwu. The report was prepared by Hamer and produced by Meredith Dearborn (EA2DR), who also provided valuable editing assistance.

The team's work would have been impossible to accomplish without the help of over 100 Chinese colleagues, working within central agencies and in the cities of Shanghai, Guangzhou, Chengdu, Hangzhou, Fuzhou, and Shenzhen. The team extends its gratitude to Vice-Minister Zhou Ganshi, Ministry of Construction; Director Wang Xiangjin, State Land Administration; and Director Zhu Fulin, Ministry of Finance; for facilitating the mission's access to information and advice. At the central level, grateful thanks go to the State Land Administration team organized by Deputy Director Zou Yuchuan and led by Sun Yinghui, Qi Mingshen, and Li Huanjun. Within the Administration's working-level group, special thanks are due to He Zhan, Zhao Long and Li Ling. At the Ministry of Finance, Xu Fangming and Chen Zhigang provided valuable logistical support, information, and advice. The Ministry of Construction's Deputy Directors of the City Planning Department and the Real Estate Department (Zou Shimeng and Gu Guangcheng, respectively) helped to clarify many issues and provided early reaction to preliminary mission findings.

At the local level, special thanks go to the late Vice Mayor Ni Tianzeng (Shanghai), and to Vice Mayors Shi Anhai (Guangzhou), Shu Luanyi (Chengdu), Li Zhixiong (Hangzhou), and Lin Zhongxion (Fuzhou). In each of those cities, along with Shenzhen, the directors or bureau heads in charge of the local Construction Commission, State Land Administration Bureau, and Finance Bureau were very supportive. Important information was also provided by the City Planning Bureaus, Real Estate Management Bureaus, Environmental Protection Bureaus, and the Housing Reform Groups in the various cities.

In Hong Kong, Singapore, and Seoul, local government authorities dealing with urban land use management patiently accommodated the demands of team members.

In addition, special acknowledgement should be made of the role played by Bank staff, including Shahid Yusuf (EA2DR), Paul Cadario (EA2CO), Anthony Ody (EA2EH), Bertrand Renaud (EMTIN), Gregory Ingram (RAD), Stephen Mayo (INURD), Michael Rutkowsky (EC3HR), Natalie Lichtenstein (LEGEA), Songsu Choi (ASTIN), William Dillinger (INURD), Catherine Farvarque (INURD), Johannes Linn (FPRVP) and

Fitz Ford (INURD). The Urban Management Program, locally administered by Mr. Ford, provided critical financial support to the project; his United Nations' Nairobi-based colleague, Patrick McAuslen, also assisted the mission members with very useful advice.

As always, Professor Lin Zhiqun, at the Ministry of Construction, deserves special acknowledgement for providing the team with unstinting advice and data. The team also benefited greatly by previous work done on the subject, particularly by the Chinese Academy of Social Sciences and by Chreod Consultants, working in Shanghai.

Several individuals played "supporting roles" that nevertheless deserve acknowledgement. Wang Yuan (RMC) proved an invaluable source of advice, while Wu Zhiyong and Sok Lee deserve special thanks for translating otherwise unpenetrable written materials in Chinese and Korean. Anthony Yeh, at the University of Hong Kong, and Edwin Leman, head of the Chreod consulting firm, proved generous with their advice. Although already acknowledged as part of the sector study team, researcher Youxuan Zhu's contributions in the field and at headquarters deserve reemphasizing. He personally prepared several annexes. Without his help, bookshelves full of Chinese-language journals and unpublished information obtained from continuous personal contact with local officials would have been unavailable to the sector team.

CONTENTS

TEXT BOXES

EXECUTIVE SUMMARY

Background: What Drives Urban Land Reform: The Chinese Rationale

During the 1980s, economic activity within China's cities and statutory towns, which accounts for more than half of the gross domestic product (GDP), grew at well over 10 percent per annum. In addition, the urban population grew at a rate of 5 percent per year between the census of 1982 and that of 1990. By 1990, 26 percent of China's population, or 301 million, lived in urban areas. *In absolute terms, China now has the world's largest urban population.* Urban employment rose at roughly similar rates. The size of the urbanized, built-up areas of cities and towns expanded at 4 to 5 percent a year in the aggregate. The scale of urban residential and nonresidential investment grew at equally dramatic rates, adding 6 percent to the existing stock each year and accounting for 10 to 15 percent of urban GDP.

In spite of this vigorous expansion, the built-up areas of cities total only 13,000 square kilometers (km^2), with another 9,000 km^2 under development in statutory towns. By contrast, total cultivated land in China totaled at least 1 million km^2 and the built-up area of rural villages and townships occupied an additional 140,000 km^2 (1985). Cities and statutory towns cover an area equivalent of only 2 percent of China's cultivated land area. This corresponds to the experience of other Asian countries, as well as land-abundant North America and Western Europe.

This report's main theme is that though the land area involved is small, urban land management reform is required to accelerate the efficient expansion of a regulated market economy, where land is treated as any other commodity, and where many complementary measures involving planning, legal and regulatory institutions, taxation and information infrastructure are in place. As Chapter VI makes clear, that is now emerging as a view at the central and local level. However, during the first 6-7 years of overall urban reform, beginning in 1984, the central and local authorities often viewed *reform* as a set of disarticulated *changes* that did not have a comprehensive content or an ultimate objective of promoting the development of land market transactions. The initial rationale was to either increase administrative controls over land or generate some revenue from its use.

For example, because of a national commitment to maintain highly localized urban foodstuffs self-sufficiency, the perceived need to control urban spatial expansion became paramount by the mid-1980s. That urge to control expressed itself at the macrospatial and project level as different tiers of government, particularly the central authorities, tried to limit the overall expansion of localities, while eliminating "wasteful" and "unnecessary" allocation of land to individual urban investment projects. *Control, rather than the introduction of market mechanisms, became a primary driving force behind urban land "reform."* That limited objective was quickly achieved.

Revenue-generation concerns, as well as a desire to assert control over wasteful urban land uses, encouraged government at the central and local level to charge domestic land users for the use of land, beginning as early as 1982. Yet this initiative was tempered by an overriding concern that introducing market "prices" would prove "unaffordable" to state-owned enterprises.

The pressure for change derived further impetus from the reintroduction of foreign investments into China. Between 1979 and 1991, 15,000 foreign-funded firms invested $22 billion in China. These investors, accustomed to well-defined rights over property, found prevailing arrangements unsatisfactory. For example, land contributed by Chinese partners as equity proved hard to value, impossible to use as collateral to obtain loans, and subject to unreasonable occupancy time limits. Local governments, especially after 1988, adopted a pragmatic attitude, realizing that, in return for selling long-term use rights, they could raise convertible currency revenues while improving the local business climate. In this regard, the examples of Hong Kong and Singapore proved instructive. But, as discussed below, the actual introduction of leases proved inconsequential in scope and did little to create competitively determined market prices.

A Review of Experiments to Date

Beginning largely in 1984, China's cities embarked on land use management changes across a broad front and have few if any peers among cities in post-command economies. These changes are proceeding at a different pace in different cities. Southern and central coastal provincial cities as well as the "Special Economic Zones" are well ahead of their counterparts in the interior of the country and even northern coastal cities. However, in every city visited by the sector team during preparation missions, the absence of a clear vision of the end-objective—to create a regionally, nationally, and/or internationally competitive city—meant that these changes lacked coherence, and the critical need to create a land market, governed by price signals and guided by appropriate planning and regulatory mechanisms, was unfolding too slowly. In retrospect, it was only during the latter half of 1992 that evidence emerged of an acceleration in reform efforts, with land leasing being adopted at an unprecedented scale in selected cities. Among the changes undertaken, whose adequacy is discussed below, the following are the most significant:

- creation of profit-oriented real estate development companies (REDCs), mostly with public sector equity, with a mandate to develop commercial estates or properties, and sell these at prices that include land location premiums;

- promotion of economic development zones, though often far from the city center, to attract foreign investors;

- selective use of land use lease mechanisms, giving users certain ownership rights in return for paying land use premiums;

- introduction of land use development fees, taxes, and other exactions;

- promotion of spot redevelopment of inner-city areas, with occasional recourse to "value added" strategies linked to a change in land use;

- greater sensitivity by planners and developers alike, prompted by rising implicit or explicit land prices, to the need to increase land use efficiency at the project level, promoting densification previously blocked by adherence to centrally supplied guidelines concerning "norms and standards";

- reintroduction of land and building registration cadasters, carefully defining the dimensions, uses, and occupancy rights involved.

Urban Land Management Goals and Overall Restructuring: What Should Drive Land Reform?

Like the typical factory in the state-owned sector, large areas of China's cities are still obsolete, i.e., saddled with inadequate infrastructure, housing and nonresidential facilities. Two thirds of their output is generated by the industrial sector, utilizing equivalent proportions of the labor force and occupying up to 30 percent of the built-up area of the central city when warehouses are included (with higher amounts in the high-accessibility old-city core areas). Using indicators from comparator cities in Asia and among developed countries, *all those proportions should be cut in at least half.* And, if the core areas of the old industrial cities are to shift from industrial to commercial uses, investments in infrastructure will have to vastly increase the amount spent in upgrading the central core area "carrying capacity." Road space, for instance, will have to be increased by a factor of two. This will require a rationalization of land use.

Such a transformation would allow major Chinese cities (particularly those wishing to be internationally competitive) to shift to a focused development strategy. The economy of the future must rely more heavily on information services to generate competitive manufacturing products in selective categories of goods. The successful, international competitive cities of the twenty-first century will have vibrant producers' services sectors, employing up to 40 percent of the local labor force. The structural transformation to such a knowledge-based economy will require an accompanying unprecedented revolution in urban land management practices. The old city, full of factories and warehouses located in inappropriate locations, cannot be modernized by administrative fiat and the moving of 30 or 40 facilities per year. Little will be achieved unless incentives to move are greatly sharpened and occupants of sites having high implicit values are allowed to undertake land transactions that yield substantial financial rewards and permit new investments by the original occupants, who would retain the bulk of the earnings from any such transaction. In some cities, including Guangzhou and Shanghai, this message has been accepted in principle.

Towards a Comprehensive Urban Land Systems Reform Strategy

To achieve these sector goals, a multifaceted strategy is needed to enable urban land use rights to be obtained and exchanged on commercial terms. Government must craft a plan that (a) allows for the expansion of *land price reforms*, in place of administered allocation practices; (b) develops a *legal framework* that reintroduces the full range of property rights, with the coordinated registration of all property rights related to a single parcel of land, in a manner consistent with best international practices, and transparency in both the mechanisms and rules for property dispute resolution; (c) institutes a *local planning framework* that helps extend serviced land development in an affordable manner, while promoting infill development, upgrading, and redevelopment in core areas of cities; (d) creates *land-based revenue generation mechanisms* that provide a return to a very valuable state asset, while requiring identifiable beneficiaries of government investments in local infrastructure to pay a "fair share" of the costs of construction and maintenance; and (e) provides adequate *incentives and guidelines that give high priority to historic preservation objectives and ensure that land-related environmental degradation is first contained and then reversed.*

The transition, implementing this multifaceted strategy, should begin with all new investments that involve land acquisition. All new industrial, commercial, residential and nonprofit activities should be subject to the full impact of this strategy, even if some differential policies are adopted, varying according to the sector involved. *The coverage of the prevailing, traditional system must be progressively diminished in size according to a time-certain schedule for the introduction of new rules.* Every opportunity should be taken to accelerate the pace of reform among existing urban land users, by moving some into the new system ahead of others, while ensuring a rapid convergence in outcomes on the basis of objective definitions of "affordability."

Because the required reforms are interrelated, and market forces must be guided by planning and regulation, it is important to follow an integrated strategy. This is because *what is traded on the market is not land but a bundle of rights and obligations which provide for control over particular parcels of property, including stratified interests in buildings, land use rights, mineral rights, and easements, each of which yields possibilities for generating income.* In addition, by announcing the overall strategy simultaneously, the impact of the reform can be brought forward in time, particularly if that time horizon is short enough to force all users to internalize quickly the implications of that reform.

Given the multifaceted nature of the reform, Government should consider creating a Real Estate Sector Reform Group. Eventually, a new Ministry, able to deal with property markets in a comprehensive fashion, should be established, replacing existing entities with more narrowly focused mandates and agendas.

First Things First: Prices and Property Rights

Since rural land converted to urban uses will continue to supply the bulk of land utilized for new construction, one of the first issues to be faced is who will undertake land requisition in suburban areas and on what terms. Here, international experience provides a range of models, from one-to-one negotiations between users or developers and rural occupants, to a largely centralized requisition of land by public authorities. In most countries, the process of rural-to-urban land conversion is bedeviled by the fact that the "announcement" effect of impending urban development, and the introduction of the infrastructure required for intensive urbanization, will drive prices to a level that is a significant multiple of its value in agricultural use, because the marginal productivity of land has increased dramatically. *It is not unusual for the price of rezoned, serviced land at the urban fringe to exceed the cost of farmland by a factor of 15 to 20 times. This price differential is not due to a lack of inadequate land supplies in any one category but by the fact that each is a recognizably different product, carrying different locational advantages, property rights, etc.* Flooding the market with greater supplies of the "higher-value" land, disregarding the rates of return of such actions, merely to "flatten" the price gradient, would obviously narrow the differential but is inefficient and not in line with practice followed even in "developer-friendly" market economies.

The rising cost of suburban and peri-urban land may encourage agricultural land preservation, *assuming hard budget constraints prevail.* Urban land buyers would face an increasingly expensive input, whose price would help contain demand for land. *But the prospect of significant revenue windfalls also creates an incentive for rural dwellers to extend negotiations with prospective urban users until they can capture a significant portion of the increased market value, even though they contribute little to the revalorization taking place. The bargaining process may create supply-side bottlenecks and inequities.* This is particularly so since, at present, there is no effective income tax system in place to capture part of any "windfall gains" obtained by the rural communities. And, since hard budget constraints among urban consumers of land are only just emerging, one-on-one land negotiations, without State Land Administration (SLA) mediation, could lead many urban bidders to "cave in" and allow rural dwellers to reap large capital gains. During the transition to the market economy, some form of local government oversight is needed to keep the process from generating politically dangerous charges of runaway "speculation."

Under the 1982 constitution, as amended, rural communities own rural land, while the state owns all urban land. The state has the right to acquire land from rural communities and may trade use rights in the market. *Local government should consider taking complete control of the suburban land requisition process, expropriating rural land for all urban conversion purposes, including those that promote economic development, in a manner that is transparent, in terms of compensation rules, as well as equitable.* Compensation amounts could be subject to appeal before regulatory bodies, but not the requisition itself. The actual location and use of the land would be market-driven, and SLA would only be involved in a technical function, attempting to restrain the length of requisition bargaining and moderating the monetary demands of farmers, who have an incentive to seize as much of the future appreciation of land value as possible, as conversion occurs. Occupants could continue to use the land until actual urban development became necessary. When urban construction would begin, compensation would be paid, based on the value established at the announced requisition date, adjusted only to cover inflation. Government would then lease the remaining land, through auction, negotiation, or grant, to urban users, including land development companies who could transfer leases to plots of serviced land to smaller private, cooperative or state-sponsored developers. The medium-run goal should be the creation of an effective income and capital gains tax system, as well as reforms that force all enterprises to operate under hard budget constraints, limiting and finally eliminating the need to use administrative requisition mechanisms.

Such a strategy would have to be matched by a reform of prices and use rights over existing urban land. *Vacant serviced plots should enter the new system immediately, with new occupants signing leases regardless of user category.* As much as possible, sites should be leased in a publicly advertised and competitive manner, to allow market prices (and property valuation data) to emerge spontaneously. Regulatory mechanisms should be in place to ensure the fairness with which lease bids are evaluated and awards are made. Institutional nonprofit users (hospitals, research institutes, schools and universities, libraries, government offices) should only receive land grant leases after a high-level review of any proposed use to ensure that the opportunity cost of relinquishing the particular site to nonprofit use is justified by the benefits involved and that alternative, lower-value sites have been considered. In addition, all users favored by such a land grant policy should be subjected to minimum floor to land area ratio restrictions, so that the density of the development reflects the implicit, shadow price of the land area. Institutional users wishing to transfer their lease rights to profit-making users would be subject to capital gains taxes or other forms of revenue sharing with the land-owning authority.

Developed land has occupants who must suffer the effects of price changes that are retroactive in character. This will force them, in many instances, to recycle a repriced product rather than simply worry about how to use "future inputs" more efficiently. Nonresidential occupants of existing, developed sites should be given the option to lease or rent, with rent rates set high enough to provide a competitive rate of return on the implicit lease value of the property. Lease and rent levels would be set with regard to market-value data in locations and corridors that are self-evidently choice sites. In those areas, the number of market-value data points could be increased by ensuring that redevelopable sites vacated through relocation would be made available to new users through a properly monitored competitive bidding process. Relocated users would retain the bulk of the capital gains involved, as an incentive to move. Price signals from regularized "black market" transactions should also be allowed to guide the process. Elsewhere, occupied sites should be leased or rented at levels no lower than the prices of comparable suburban, serviced sites, and again be subject to the market test provided by emerging implicit and explicit rents and prices. Residential users of land should be incorporated into a system of rental reform, aimed at full cost recovery, as expeditiously as possible, following the recommendations of the earlier Bank report on housing reforms, and discussed further below.

The issue arises: how to deal with the political opposition to such a move to a regulated market, assuming regulatory mechanisms are set in place to deal with issues of transparency and fairness, and the possibility exists of appeals to impartial bodies in cases where corruption of the process is suspect? For users of new sites, affordability should not be a major impediment to reform, since the potential occupant could move to any one of many locations or simply not bid for a new site. Industrial enterprise should include likely land values in feasibility studies. All owners of housing estates and individual units would be expected to compensate the state through the signing of a negotiated lease. Commercial activities should not take place on new leasable space if the activity proves unprofitable when land prices are factored in. Furthermore, since there is no compelling economic reason to maintain state control over most commercial operations, these should be privatized as expeditiously as possible, making market real estate transactions possible. Institutional, nonprofit users could be taken care of on an exceptional basis, as already discussed.

For existing occupants, annual market rents would provide an alternative to buying a lease. Those rents could be phased in over three to five years. *Existing users occupying valuable real estate within the existing built-up area and not willing to pay such rents would be given the opportunity to relocate to suburban locations, in return for signing a lease for the new site, with the added incentive of receiving a significant percentage of any new lease income obtained from the old site.* This particular option can be defended as promoting the overall goal of introducing a land market, even if the income obtained is, in a strictly legal sense, unearned, because the original occupant did not have legal rights to dispose of the administratively allocated sites. As noted, this view has now been accepted, in principle, by national and selected local authorities. Much is made of the weakness of the state-owned enterprises in China and for the need for enterprise restructuring. Land reform could provide an unexpected tool in this process because, fortuitously, many urban loss-making enterprises are located on valuable sites whose sale could generate resources that would allow the management or its workforce to begin new ventures elsewhere. Because Government has allowed occupants to develop implicit "ownership" rights in the past, it must now adopt some formula to deal with the issue during the transition period. And the dislocations created by a transition to a regulated market economy are too far-reaching to correct by administrative fiat alone; incentives are needed.

This price reform for present occupants of developed sites would be facilitated by several factors. Industrial income tax reform now under way will reduce statutory tax rates for state-owned enterprises from 55 percent to 33 percent. Taxable income will exclude land costs, making them directly deductible or treated as part of depreciation allowances shielded from taxation. With deductibility taken into account, prices or rents can be a multiple of that which would otherwise prevail, and thus not affect retained earnings significantly. Commercial activity is now increasingly disciplined by market forces and able to avoid price controls and to maximize profits. As one indication of this, evidence already exists of a lively trading of urban use rights. Desirable real estate in favorable locations, regardless of formal ownership, is being transferred to other users at very high explicit or implicit prices.

After a decade of rapid increases in real household income, and in the wake of forthcoming housing rent reform with compensating wage adjustments, *it is not unreasonable to ask residents of existing housing units to pay land rents*. Since these rents will be phased in over several years, and since the massive housing construction effort of the past decade can be expected to continue, there should be little hardship involved because relocation to lower-cost sites will be a realistic option. "Grandfather" clauses could allow long-term residents to live out their lives in such areas, under rules and conditions not applicable to others, and revocable if they agree to "buy-out agreements" that provide generous relocation incentives. But all other residents should be subject to market rules, including relocation. Households affected by redevelopment projects would receive cash compensation for the depreciated value of the structure occupied and the pro-rata value of the land involved or, alternatively, the prevailing price for comparably located commodity housing. Additional hardship cases could be dealt with through "safety net" programs that provide housing allowances to the certifiable needy. Government workers, whose pay scales lag behind those of comparably experienced workers in the for-profit sectors, could be included in the "safety net" program. Perhaps, however, it is time to include government wage-scale restructuring into the overall reform agenda; there is little justification, political sensitivities aside, for paying government workers wages that are clearly inequitable (and inefficient) when compared to pay scales prevailing elsewhere in the economy.

The development of the legal framework and institutions will have to be accelerated in order to clarify rights and obligations of owner and occupant alike, as well as to establish an ordered and publicly accessible system for recording such rights and obligations. Fortunately, the issue of state ownership per se appears to pose no problems in terms of efficient occupant behavior. Those who obtain leases can be expected to behave in roughly the same manner as landowners in other systems, if the leases are long-term (50+ years), renewable well ahead of the lease expiration date, and provided leaseholders can easily transfer use rights while retaining attractive after-tax capital gains. Developing this framework for a leasehold system should continue to be the responsibility of the central government.

In addition, *the emerging property market requires changing a perception that the established conflict-resolution and court system fails to protect property rights.* It should be presided over by judges who can quickly hear disputes, issue and publish rulings to protect the rights of borrowers and creditors in foreclosure proceedings in accordance with published laws, rules, and regulations. The courts should have enforceable powers of eviction where land users operate under land rental agreements and fail to meet the obligations defined in those agreements. Any political interference with court decision-making should be eliminated.

Property markets also require that all land holdings be registered and, thus, that any potential buyer of a leasehold be able to establish whether or not the title to be transferred is subject to any obligations to third parties, including those created when land is used as collateral in obtaining loans. The precise definition of the boundaries of each and every parcel and the nature of interests in each property must be very clearly defined.

The state should retain expropriation rights within the urban built-up area parallel to those exercised in the periphery. Local government can designate any property as subject to expropriation if the site is needed for approved public works such as a transportation project requiring additional rights-of-way. *"Excess condemnation" (i.e., additional expropriation) of high-access nodes created by new transport investments should be encouraged. Similarly, areas designated as priority redevelopment zones should be subject to expropriation if the occupants, through private arrangements, fail within a time certain to assemble sites and provide for the prescribed redevelopment investments.* This measure is made necessary by the fact that, particularly in older "downtown" areas, the fragmentation of land use may make redevelopment financially unattractive and encourage certain occupants to "hold out" for remunerative or noneconomic reasons. The example of Singapore's laws, which facilitate redevelopment, can be cited in this regard. Compensation criteria must be carefully spelled out, avoid inclusion of any opaque in-kind rewards, with any compensation package (but not the expropriation itself) subject to appeal through some impartial judicial mechanism. Unfortunately, the ability to challenge administrative resolutions and decisions in a Chinese court of law and the ability to utilize the Chinese court system for the protection of property interests by foreign investors is perceived by investors as untested. Problems encountered include the inability to obtain applicable laws, regulations and rules of court procedures. Neglecting this strand of the reform could prove to be a major impediment to fulfilling the agenda defined in this report.

Reinventing the Chinese City: Planning and Regulating Development with Property Markets in Mind

Any municipal or metropolitan government has a limited capacity to add to trunk infrastructure within a medium-term horizon, say between now and the year 2000. Where that infrastructure is located will determine what options will be available to investors and consumers. The redevelopment of the old core areas of the cities, in particular, cannot be accelerated at a sustainable rate without a redirection of infrastructure investments from peripheral locations to the CBD. *Furthermore, the supply of serviced land developed during any given time period should be employed to its highest and best use, unless welfare, health, safety, historic preservation, and environment considerations, codified in the form of "performance indicators," dictate otherwise and, in the short to medium term, unless infrastructure capacity cannot sustain the scale of investment involved.* In this latter case, planners should examine ways to accommodate user-led trends, identified by an adequate monitoring system, by modifying trunk and connective infrastructure plans.

Planners should forgo the temptation to endorse a "blank sheet" approach, whereby redevelopment is viewed as too messy, and "orderly" greenfield development is systematically preferred. In core areas of the city, this approach has yielded to ad-hoc approval of spot redevelopment which, cumulatively and over time, will force infrastructure investments to be refocused and recentered geographically, regardless of any current strategy of denial. Planners should internalize the implications of limited infrastructure expansion options by restricting the number of new spatial priority zones. Trunk infrastructure investments are both costly and a function of distances involved; compact development is therefore to be promoted, all other things being equal. *A metropolis cannot, in a financially sustainable fashion, simultaneously create a large number of satellite cities, industrial and residential suburbs, and major, new special economic development zones 20 to 40 kilometers from the city center, while accommodating redevelopment of the historic core area.* A more compact development strategy, promoting redevelopment, would also be more consistent with strategies that discourage unnecessary conversion of agricultural land to nonagricultural uses.

The potential to redevelop the existing core area deserves reemphasizing. Even though reuse is dictated by the need to adapt urban areas to accommodate the shift from industrial- to commercial-led development, and from welfare- to market-oriented housing solutions, observers standing at the top of the tallest buildings in any city will notice that such redevelopment has been exceptional. In some areas, like Guangzhou, which is at the forefront of market experiments, completed redevelopment often rings the core rather than tackling the center. Similarly, Shanghai's leasehold experiments through mid-1992 were usually located outside the old (pre-1949) city boundaries. Why? The answer lies in the past absence of forceful public sector leadership. High value-added opportunities have been forgone because the profitability inherent in redevelopment was diminished by (a) limits on use and density options; (b) limited commitment to new, facilitating infrastructure investments; (c) associated, wrong-headed citywide dedensification strategies; and (d) a failure to tackle the excessive entitlement demands of existing occupants of redevelopable sites. These obstacles to financially feasible redevelopment can be removed, following suggested options detailed in this report, but they will require political action to bring them about.

There are many legitimate reasons for a local government to have plans governing property markets. Open space and its distribution, the placement and scale of public facilities, and the location of public infrastructure, over the medium term and governed by a comprehensive framework, all require macrospatial plans. The preservation of environmentally sensitive areas and historic preservation districts is another responsibility of the public sector. *In China, planners at the macro and micro level already exercise enormous urban planning control. They specify macrospatial plans and related infrastructure and they provide for detailed district-level land use and building plans.* Unfortunately, master plans in China have been developed as rather abstract, architectural exercises without the use of analytical tools to test alternatives in terms of costs and consequences. And the cumulative effects of district-level permits for land development are usually not monitored and reflected in revised macrospatial infrastructure plans. *The issue is thus not omission of planning, but the need for more informed planning, taking into account feedback gathered by monitoring indicators and common-sense economics.*

Mayors and city councils should be presented with costed alternative analyses that document the amount of potential development made possible per unit of infrastructure investment, under various scenarios. These should reflect the shadow value of land. Planners must also internalize the concept of consumer sovereignty, unless there is a clearly articulated public purpose for not doing so. Thus, if what is happening on the ground is very different from what is projected by the master plan, then the objective of monitoring and planning is not to identify departures as delinquent events but to assist governments to revise the scale and location of public investments.

Risk Assessment. Bold reforms may produce unanticipated side effects. For example, will land reform create a surge in retail prices? Will workers faced by the resulting reuse of land be forced to undertake onerous additional commuting journeys to work? The Bank's previous work on relative price adjustment reform suggests that retail price inflation can be contained if central monetary policy follows its current, conservative course and if new price signals yield additional supplies of inputs, moderating price inflation. That conclusion is assumed to be applicable in this case. That is, a gradual decontrol of land prices with adequate development of market institutions should minimize the risk of price spirals. As for the commuting-related consequences of land use changes led by market reform, the answer lies in the results of costly simulation exercises. Consider, however, that large numbers of workers have been moved to residential locations, including Pudong, relatively distant from their CBD-located factories. Reform may well decrease unnecessary commuting. The best advice is to monitor trends and develop remedial measures as necessary. Coordinated policies at the central and at the local level would then follow.

The Equity Issue

Equity concerns have to be suitably defined, where China's cities and towns are concerned. A "level playing field" must be provided for newcomers who engage in activities involving real estate development or its use. Though local, state-sponsored entities have been favored in the past, the future should prove different, if events in late 1992 are taken as a guide. Any remaining formal or de facto barriers to real estate developers from other countries, provinces, counties or from the private/cooperative sector should be reexamined and removed. If the less well-regarded can outperform their rivals, including those with local state-owned credentials, so be it. Outcomes, not ownership composition, should be what matter.

Sooner or later, Government must also face up to the inherent inequity involved in the treatment of the increasing number of temporary residents. On an experimental basis, temporary residents who have lived in a city or town for more than a certain period of time should be granted the rights to purchase or develop real estate. The barriers imposed on such residents to buy or lease property are counterproductive and should be reversed, even if Government wishes to maintain strict controls over population movement in general.

Sitting on Golden Stools? Land-Based Revenue Mobilization and Reform

The primary objective of reform should be the establishment of explicit land price signals to govern land use behavior choices. Land should be priced like any other productive input, at rates set by the market. Then land users will treat land more efficiently. Distributional issues, dealing with who gains from land price reform, and creates what some might perceive as "windfall profits," are best dealt with by a revised tax system, which is not a major focus of this report. *The issue of unfair individual gains, revenue generation and the question of how revenues are split between local and central governments should not obstruct the achievement of that primary objective.*

The People's Republic, as a sovereign state, has the status under international law to act as a "legal person." Nevertheless, the state must clearly designate an institution (or lower-level government to act for it) as the titleholder and there must be clear rules involving revenue assignment.

The revenue issue would then be reduced to who would receive the benefits from rents, leases, property taxes, and capital gains or transfer taxes. At present, this may be an academic question in most cities, since relatively little revenue has been generated by urban land. In the exurban counties of the Pearl River Delta, however, the issue must already be faced. If urban land reform, as defined in this report, is to become a reality, incentives should be in place to encourage those price signals to grow rapidly. Furthermore, the variation in revenues per square meter (m^2) within a city, and the variation in average revenues across cities, must be allowed to emerge spontaneously. This argues for local-level incentives and limited central interference. *Finally, international experience with urban land revenues suggest that, even under different political systems and different levels of economic development, local appropriation is the norm.* This leads to the following recommendation: *all land-related revenues should be assigned to local governments.*

Having said that, the fact remains that China's cities are expanding their expenditures at a rapid rate, and using off-budget, nontax sources to finance these to an increasing degree. Whether or not land revenues prove a significant contributor to local revenue generation, the increased reliance on loans means there is an urgent need to identify clear sources of loan repayment, linked to the beneficiaries. User charges for public utilities will have to increase significantly during the next decade, since there is little likelihood that central or provincial authorities will provide grants as substitutes. And budgets overseen by local finance bureaus must be made more comprehensive in nature, to allow such documents to be used for management purposes.

There are other issues to be tackled. In cities like Hong Kong and Seoul, as a matter of deliberate policy, government has set limits on the number of hectares leased per year. Resulting land revenues can provide a significant source of income, when combined with other land-related taxes and fees. However, where such very restrictive policies are pursued, development may be handicapped, and the availability of affordable housing may be compromised. Given the overwhelming fear of "unaffordable" reforms, it seems sensible to set aside strategies that promote revenue generation rather than accommodating user demand for serviced urban land.

The issue of real estate development company exactions, for the purposes of promoting infrastructure development, is more complicated to resolve. These companies, given managerial autonomy during the last half-decade, often control land resources for which no lease price was paid; occasionally, the requisition cost required to free up the land was also shouldered by the government. Furthermore, companies have usually benefited from temporary tax exemptions; in some cases, the companies have been classified as nonprofit institutions. Under these circumstances, and given the apparent profitability of their operations, it is not unreasonable to require that they pay for more than the costs of servicing the land they occupy. The question is how. Here, the rule should be: transparent regulations fairly applied. Exactions should be replaced by land lease arrangements, openly arrived at and supervised by appropriate regulatory bodies.

Information as Infrastructure

Proof of title is fundamental to the exercise of property rights, including the use of land as loan collateral and the ability to transfer land use rights for profit. The new registration system intended to establish proof of title is based on a meticulous process of examination and field work. The separate building registration process is also very thorough, and includes an examination of the structure to ascertain its conformity with existing building controls. This latter anomaly was brought about by the fact that, at the national level, land use rights were, and continue to be, the purview of SLA, while building rights are registered by the Ministry of Construction (MoC). The land and building cadasters are kept separately. There is no compelling justification for such practices.

One important reform initiative, the full regularization of transactions between individual land users, is likely to be stymied by this fragmentation of responsibility. The transfer of uses will be restricted to those holding registered land use certificates, who are generally also the "owners" of any associated structures. But the regulations are conspicuously silent concerning the rights of public housing tenants to rent or sublet the rights to space they now occupy, particularly attractive ground-floor residential space located on commercial streets. This is the major source of "black market" activity. Rents or sublease values reflect *land-related* location factors, while what is actually traded is *building space*. Both MoC and SLA will have to cooperate to solve the problem, by taxing a portion of the monthly or yearly payments in return for a guarantee of "regularization."

Aside from the inefficiency associated with the maintenance of separate records, the key problem to date is the incomplete coverage of the registers. Progress has been greatest in the newer built-up areas of cities and in the suburban counties under the municipalities' jurisdiction; elsewhere, the process is ad-hoc. Furthermore, in some cases, real estate occupied by public agencies has been ignored.

The cadastral maps and associated topographical base maps represent a source of fundamental physical information. Other important data, including land uses, land values, demographic and economic information, and infrastructure network location, when overlaid onto the fundamental information, can provide a comprehensive and coordinated database that can be used to monitor urban development. The advent of digital database technology now allows storage of information in a form suitable for convenient manipulation. Thus, planners, administrators, and those seeking title information, can make projections or display results quickly. Information can be used, for example, to forecast where people will live and work in the future, the problems they will face, the services they will require and can afford, as well as the public revenues that can be expected. These data can help select and appraise investment projects, as well as manage related operations and maintenance (O&M) programs.

Unfortunately, within China, the self-evident advantages of automated Geographic Information Systems (GIS) have led to a set of narrow bureaucratic responses. The economies of scale and advantages of integrated planning have not emerged, because each agency or bureau has attempted to develop its own independent GIS. Furthermore, the technology is currently in the hands of information engineers who do not place consumer requirements high on their agenda. Finally, GIS cannot really flourish and maximize its potential impact while the urban planning system remains rooted in a traditional static mode that allows for little feedback. As always, urban land management reform requires a multifaceted response.

Urban Environmental Strategies

Industrial redevelopment is of critical importance in China's large urban areas not only in terms of potential industrial productivity gains, but also in terms of urban environmental pollution. Industrial pollution in urban areas has created dangerous conditions—houses next to polluting factories, chemical spills, noise pollution, vibrations, dust, congested alleys and lanes. Many of the polluting firms that are left behind in the urban areas are the least profitable ones and financing their relocation is difficult. One means of moving such firms out is to ensure that they receive adequate compensation for relinquished land. Therefore, urban land market reforms can also create important environmental benefits.

Initial concerns about land use sprawl and the poisoning of agricultural land in *peri-urban areas* were motivated by satellite images that revealed uses unanticipated by master planners and by vocal Government concerns about the adverse environmental impact of township and village enterprise activity. The transfer of polluting enterprises from central to peripheral locations also raised doubts about the degree to which relocation merely exported pollution. In general, these concerns have proved somewhat overstated, but not unwarranted. Aside from insisting that an environmental impact statement accompany all new factory and storage plans, and that enterprises, existing and proposed, have budgets to deal with effluent disposal, rural areas must move quickly to introduce elementary "township" zoning or planning procedures, creating industrial zones, providing for areawide effluent disposal solutions, and tackle the issue of "township" budget and financing sources associated with such measures. In this process, *there is a need for municipal authorities to extend the coverage of the controlled "urban planning area" to cover peri-urban areas, curbing the autonomy of township authorities to dispose of land in an unplanned manner.*

Summing Up

The transformation of formerly centralized, command economies is now a worldwide phenomenon, with very few exceptions. *In both the rural and urban sector, China is a pioneer and, in assessing economic achievements to date, has few peers.* While generally preserving macroeconomic stability, Government has encouraged localities to experiment on a wide range of changes and then internalized that experience and applied the lessons nationwide. In the final analysis, though any sector report embodies a critical assessment of unfinished tasks, note should be taken of overall achievements to date. China's future urban development will be far smoother than that of its post-Socialist counterparts. Government must now begin to measure its progress not by that standard, but by that of the newly industrialized countries and those on the verge of achieving that status. They are the wave of the future. They will be China's key competitors in the export market. With trade liberalization, they will provide the stiffest competition for domestic market shares. Bolder reforms must follow.

The main message of the report bears repeating. The key objective of the reform is to create property markets, where land and structures are traded at prices set competitively. This will improve the efficiency with which a key input of production is used and promote the emergence of internationally competitive cities. This will require a complementary set of legal, fiscal, planning and institutional reforms. The reform cannot be driven by mere administrative means; incentives are needed to encourage individuals to buy and sell land use rights. Regulatory mechanisms must be set in place to ensure the public of the inherent fairness of the process. Distributional concerns, encouraging authorities to tax away substantial portions of the gains involved, should be moderated by the need to "lubricate" the land market transaction reform. Planners must become more "developer-friendly" and accommodating to land use demand regarding the location, density, and building use desired. The legal system, now viewed as weak in this area, must be reviewed and strengthened, as necessary, to guarantee property rights and resolve property disputes. And a macroeconomic environment that sustains rapid growth while maintaining low inflation is also necessary, as the negative experience of other post-command economies in transition makes clear. All these strands hang together. Neglect any one and the reform will fail, if any reasonably short time horizon is envisioned to accomplish the reform.

I. THE RATIONALE FOR URBAN LAND MANAGEMENT SYSTEMS REFORM

Creating Competitive Cities: Objectives of Urban Land Management

With barriers to trade and economic activity falling dramatically in recent years, and the scope of market forces rapidly expanding, urban land management in China should increasingly seek to establish and preserve well-functioning land markets, as part of a larger strategy to create regionally, nationally, or internationally *competitive cities*. At least four objectives for urban land management can be set forth; they can easily work at cross-purposes with one another if policymakers pursue any one of them in a single-minded fashion. Trade-offs, based on the analysis of costs and benefits, are essential tools in resolving debates and reaching decisions on urban land policy.

One objective is to promote land conservation and control the length of trunk infrastructure investment by promoting compact cities. Such cities would contain a substantial proportion of residents and jobs within a "reasonable" distance from the identifiable Central Business District (CBD). The radius involved will clearly be positively correlated with city size. It is, however, *not* the case that larger cities are, per se, more wasteful in their use of land than smaller urban and rural centers, as China's national urban planners assume, discouraging the growth of metropolitan areas in favor of towns and smaller cities (Box 1.1).

Box 1.1: LAND USE PER CAPITA, BY SIZE OF URBAN SETTLEMENT

The Center for Policy Studies, within the Ministry of Construction, revealed in 1992 that *large cities are far more efficient users of land than smaller towns or peri-urban townships and villages*. Using 1990 data, gross per-capita land consumption per "nonagricultural resident" rises from 61 m²/capita for cities with more than one million persons, to 80 m²/capita for smaller cities with populations exceeding 500,000; and 86 m²/capita for those cities with 200,000 to 500,000 residents. The smallest cities consume 103 m²/capita. Bank mission estimates suggest that examining the built-up area of towns and rural settlements adds further evidence of how land use/capita increases drastically with decreasing settlement size. Designated towns require, on average, 135 m²/capita, while rural townships and villages occupy 152 m²/capita and 144 m²/capita, respectively.

Source: Lin Zhiqun, "The Development of Land for Urban Development in the 1980s," Beijing, Center for Policy Studies, Ministry of Construction, 1992, processed; and mission estimates.

A second objective stresses the need to expand serviced land development, and promote redevelopment of existing urban areas, so that land inputs are available at "affordable prices," or prices perceived to match the "real" marginal value product of land. In the simplest possible terms, there is no obvious reason that the internal rate of return of redeveloping urban land or rezoning and servicing greenfield plots should exceed substantially the internal rate of return of comparable investments. An adequate supply of appropriately priced land is a key component of a broader strategy for achieving urban competitiveness. Quite obviously, though, the goals of achieving compact development and of maintaining a steady supply of "affordable" land can come into conflict (Box 1.2).

Box 1.2: INTERNATIONAL URBAN DEVELOPMENT DENSITIES

Seoul, Korea is a model of compact development (especially if the "need" to build distant satellite cities and the related connective trunk infrastructure to accommodate vast greenbelt reservations around the city is temporarily ignored). Compared to a set of similar market- and nonmarket-economy cities, Seoul manages to accommodate 6 million people within 10 kilometers of the city center, while Paris requires a radius of 14 kilometers to achieve the same objective, and is outperformed only by Shanghai, which has one of the densest "old cities" in the world, where 6 million people live within a 7-kilometer radius from the CBD (Figure A1.1).1/ Yet, Seoul has achieved that first objective at an extraordinary cost.2/ This is because the city planners have systematically withheld more than half of the total area within Seoul's boundaries from development, while allowing very little land zoned residential to remain vacant (5 percent) and ensuring that new large-scale suburban residential districts achieve relatively high gross floor to land area ratios, averaging 2.3 for walk-up apartments and 3.5 for high-rise apartments (Figure A1.2). By contrast, cities that have treated land as an input with only nominal value (Warsaw, Poland; St. Petersburg and Moscow, Russian Federation) exhibit a degree of sprawl that can be traced directly to planner-led decisions, and appears to have little to do with the implicit value of land, however roughly calculated. Warsaw's population of 2.5 million requires an urban area 40 kilometers in radius from the CBD, while Paris accommodates that many people within a radius of 5 kilometers, without resorting to Seoul's extreme planning practices. Warsaw's extraordinary sprawl is due quite simply to a set of regulations and planning practices, backed by massive transport investments, that have forced development along five radial corridors, and encouraged fragmented development, as communities "leapfrog" across greenbelts, and individual projects make lavish use of land, with gross floor to land area ratios well below 1. In addition, large tracts of land are zoned for agricultural and open space uses, even near the city center (Figure A1.3).

1/   Figures can be found in Annex 1.

2/   In Korean cities, up to 60 percent of the value of a housing unit is accounted for by land costs, while in the more land-abundant, relatively deregulated US markets, 20 percent is the norm. (B. Renaud, "Confronting a Distorted Housing Market: Can Korean Practices Break with the Past?," World Bank, June 1992, processed.)

A third objective is a more subjective one: to build a "city beautiful," creating a mix of green space and amenities that are both attractive to "footloose" businesses and skilled workers, and otherwise intrinsically appealing (Box 1.3). Pushing this objective without regard to the economic costs involved, however, can quickly overwhelm attempts to meet the first two objectives.

Finally, and often harder to quantify, are the costs and benefits of promoting conservation and preservation. Few would dispute that cities have entire neighborhoods or groups of neighborhoods which have great historic value, and which, by their very fabric of narrow streets, examples of vernacular architecture, and numbers of cultural monuments, are irreplaceable. Central Paris and Amsterdam, in the Netherlands, along with Venice and Florence, in Italy, are four examples. Neighborhoods in United States cities, like Georgetown

Box 1.3: THE REDEVELOPMENT OF BALTIMORE'S INNER HARBOR

Properly conceived, "city-beautiful" objectives can prove extremely beneficial to a city. Many cities have high-access areas formerly devoted to port and warehouse activities outmoded by changes in transport technologies and locational choices. Baltimore, Maryland, United States, transformed 121 ha of "Inner Harbor" land into a vibrant office, commercial and entertainment center that created a "living room" for the city while attracting 25 million tourists annually, where few existed a decade ago. A public-private partnership has created a real estate bonanza involving 100 buildings and $1.8 billion in investments. Conscious of conservation and preservation, blocks of older buildings surrounding the Inner Harbor have been saved from "urban renewal" (i.e., destruction) and have added to the amenity value of the area.

(Washington, DC), the North End (Boston, Massachusetts), and the newly restored shophouse areas of Singapore, fit this category, though they were all once viewed by urban planners as prime targets for wholesale demolition and "modernization." Interestingly enough, conservation objectives can also make good economic sense and, as such, can be fully compatible with an urban competitiveness strategy (Boxes 1.4 and 1.5). The locations just cited are immensely desirable as business and/or residential locations, and have very high market values, precisely because they have been preserved and upgraded rather than destroyed. Until very recently, this

Box 1.4: SINGAPORE: TANJONG PAGAR HISTORIC PRESERVATION PROJECT

Singapore's Government commitment to historic preservation and conservation evolved only during the last decade, and moved from the preservation of individual structures to renovating entire neighborhoods. The best example of this new approach can be found in Tanjong Pagar, on the western edge of Chinatown. It covers over 200 shophouses on five streets. Units have been renovated with "adaptive reuse" in mind, promoting commercial occupancy (restaurants, shops, offices). The buildings and land involved were compulsorily acquired by the Urban Redevelopment Authority, and then leased. The first shophouses were put up for tender in 1987, and the process continued through 1991. The tender offers stress the fact that, though usually only three stories high, the structures are "rich in architecture and history" and "strategically located" to subway stations and nearby commercial and financial activities in Shenton Way. The government invested funds in upgrading infrastructure "by building an electric substation ...; construction public amenities like water, telecommunication mains and modern sanitation; improving the physical environment by planting trees and creating sidewalks." Tender offers were publicly advertized, and required successful bidders to "conserve [the structures] and to restore and preserve the same according to the architectural design and concept of their original construction, within a period of 35 months from the date of the Authority's acceptance of tender." Lease periods were granted for 99 years, with rights to mortgage and sell or sublease, under conditions spelled out by the Authority.

Bids have far exceeded what the Authority expected, and the restoration effort has proved to be a "value-added" exercise, generating such a high rate of return that commercial developers have begun to enter the conservation market, notably in the case of Clarke Quay, which involves the renovation of several hundred warehouses and shophouses on the eastern bank of the Singapore River, and is slated for completion in 1993.

Source: Singapore Urban Redevelopment Authority.

- 4 -

Box 1.5: AMSTERDAM: REDISCOVERING THE VALUE OF HISTORIC PRESERVATION

The Structure Plan published in 1982 openly endorsed the concept of a *compact city*, with high population and construction densities. The land use policy underlying Amsterdam's development parallels China's chosen path in several respects; most (75 percent) of the municipality's land is available only on leasehold terms, with general conditions and inflation-adjusted lease rents subject to revision every 50 years. Earlier still, and building on legislation dating back as far as 1918, 7,000 buildings in the historic city center were slated in 1969 for protection and rehabilitation. As in Singapore, the strategy has proved economically viable:

"When existing houses are preserved and restored, there is a less drastic cut in the number of dwellings, and rents are usually lower than for new houses. There is a great demand for small, low-rent apartments. Businesses also profit from the preservation and restoration of old neighborhoods, especially the very many small businesses. Not only do these plans provide for maintaining the present population level, and thus the number of potential customers, but low-cost accommodation will also encourage new business developments, so that the whole city may benefit."

The same strategy was seen as providing valuable income from tourism, as Amsterdam became the fourth-largest tourist center in Europe.

Source: *Amsterdam: Planning and Development*, Amsterdam Physical Planning Department, 1983.

---

potential has received very little emphasis in China. In hindsight, who would not deplore the aesthetic and economic loss involved in the insensitive disregard of the historic core of certain Chinese cities where "urban renewal" wiped out much of the character that made them so distinctive only one-half century ago. Certainly the policymakers of the day would be hard-pressed to defend these measures today.

Conservation and preservation also covers the natural habitat. In some cases, the issue is clear-cut. Failure to protect the water catchment areas of a city, as Shanghai has discovered, leads to very costly and otherwise avoidable investments in substitute source development. Wetlands in and around urban areas can play a significant role in enabling nature to carry out functions otherwise requiring expensive capital investments. Ecologically fragile hillsides, if opened to development, can lead to man-made disasters (mud slides in the slums of Rio de Janeiro, Brazil) or require extravagant infrastructure retrofitting investments (Bogotá, Colombia). In such extreme cases, market demand or infrastructure costs are not really at issue. Case-by-case decisions need to be made. Decisions to remove potential urban land from development for ecological reasons must be soundly justified and accompanied by complementary measures to accommodate demand-driven pressures by providing attractive serviced land alternatives nearby, if the other goals of efficient urban land management are to be met.

All in all, urban planning raises critical choices. Decisionmakers face the challenge of creating cities that are nationally, and often internationally, competitive, as defined in economic terms. Yet professional urban planners in China, by training and experience, are often ill-equipped to face these choices and challenges, given a historic legacy emphasizing architectonic values, abstract planning exercises, and imported Soviet norms which were never exposed to hard-headed cost/benefit review and alternatives' analyses.

The Urban Sector's Decade of Achievement

During the last decade, particularly after 1984, China's cities and towns have undergone a series of policy and institutional reforms, as part of a larger, national transition to a regulated market economy. These reforms have been reviewed in a number of World Bank reports, including the 1991 Country Economic Memorandum and a variety of sector-specific studies on resource mobilization, financial intermediation and monetary policy, housing, social security, urban labor markets and industrial restructuring.[1] Within the context of shifting macroeconomic objectives, the reforms have sought to decentralize governmental power to lower-level authorities, particularly municipalities; differentiate the functions of government departments from those of business enterprises (granting the latter increasing autonomy in decision-making); increase the scope of market-guided prices and of profits in promoting economic restructuring and growth; shift resources to the household sector by rapidly increasing the size of the total wage bill (including wages, bonuses and a variety of monetary subsidies); and expand the scope of property rights for individuals, households, and cooperatives in and around cities and towns. Over the last decade, in response to the implementation of various changes and reforms, GDP has grown at an average real rate of 9 percent per annum.

These reforms, together with rapid growth, have led to a massive transformation of the urban landscape, particularly outside the "old" city, defined by its 1949 boundaries. Residential and nonresidential construction has flourished. Based on a 1985 end-year census of housing and nonresidential structures and estimates of additions to stock since then, it is clear that half of all the urban structures in China, measured in terms of square meters, were added during the last decade alone (Table 1.1). This can also be documented at the individual city level (Table 1.2). Annual investments in real estate accounted for approximately 10-15 percent of urban GDP, adding approximately 300 million m^2 of space in

---

[1] World Bank, *China: Country Economic Memorandum: Planning and Reform in the 1980s*, Report No. 10199-CHA, April 15, 1992; *China: Revenue Mobilization and Tax Policy*, Report No. 7605-CHA, 1989; *China: Reforming Social Security in a Socialist Economy*, Report No. 8074-CHA, June 25, 1990; *China: Industrial Policies for an Economy in Transition*, Report No. 8312-CHA, June 29, 1990; *China: Financial Sector Review: Financial Policies and Institutional Development*, Report No. 8415-CHA, June 29, 1990; *China: Urban Housing Reform: Issues and Implementation Options*, Report No. 9222-CHA, June 26, 1991; *China: Reforming the Urban Employment and Wage System*, Report No. 10266-CHA, March 1992; and *China: Industrial Restructuring: A Tale of Three Cities*, Report No. 10479-CHA, April 1992.

Table 1.1: 1985 END-YEAR HOUSING AND NONRESIDENTIAL STRUCTURE
CENSUS: VINTAGE OF EXISTING STOCK
(million m²)

Total	Before 1950	1950s	1960s	1970s	1980-85
		I. 323 Cities			
2,833.9 (of which 1,363.3 residential)	274.0	320.1	379.3	853.5	1,006.9
		II. 5,270 Statutory Towns			
1,842.8 (of which 927.8 residential)	167.3	104.4	222.8	654.4	693.8

Source: Ministry of Construction.

Table 1.2: SHANGHAI: CHANGING FLOOR AREA IN CITY DISTRICTS (1980-90)
(million m²)

	Land area (km²)	Building stock 1980	Building stock 1990	Floor/land area ratio 1980	Floor/land area ratio 1990	Building stock change (%)
City proper	748.71/a	91.34	172.56	0.12	0.23	88.9
Huangpu	20.46	8.30	13.39	0.41	0.65	61.4
Nanshi	27.92	7.84	14.23	0.28	0.51	81.6
Luwan	8.05	6.18	8.29	0.77	1.03	34.2
Xuhuei	46.64	11.05	18.81	0.24	0.40	70.3
Changning	28.82	6.38	13.88	0.22	0.48	117.5
Jingan	7.62	6.94	9.08	0.91	1.19	30.9
Putuo	29.88	8.71	16.73	0.29	0.56	92.1
Zabei	27.95	8.49	14.04	0.30	0.50	65.4
Hongkou	23.48	9.62	16.19	0.41	0.69	68.3
Yangpu	59.63	14.63	27.72	0.25	0.46	89.5
Minghang	43.08	n.a.	7.51	0.00	0.17	n.a.
Baoshan	425.18	3.21	12.69	0.01	0.03	295.6

/a Boundaries as of 1990.

Sources: *Shanghai Statistical Yearbook 1991*, p. 407; and *Shanghai City Proper Real Estate Statistical Material 1980.*

1990 alone.2/ The overall stock of urban residential and nonresidential space, at 6 billion m², has a replacement value of at least Y 5 trillion, and a depreciated value of at least Y 2 trillion.3/ By comparison, national GDP in 1990 was Y 1.8 trillion, while urban GDP totaled at least Y 1.1 trillion. This estimate seems consistent with evidence from other cities where such information is available;4/ in Hong Kong, where land is considered a relatively scarce good, the Government estimates that the market value of all property is equivalent to 3.4 times current GDP (Table 1.3).

China's remarkable record in urban construction stands in contrast with the relatively small proportion of China's population living in urban areas (26 percent) and the fact that the built-up area of China's cities and statutory towns amounts to only 20,000 km² (in turn, equivalent to only 2 percent of China's documented cultivable agricultural land area). These proportions should not, however, mask the fact that *China now has the world's largest urban population, 301 million people, which is growing at a rapid rate of 100 million persons per decade. Temporary residents swell these numbers by approximately 66 million on any given day (Box 1.6). China is undergoing the transition from a rural to an urban society rapidly enough that, by the start of the new century, policymakers will have to plan for the fast-approaching day when half of China's population will live in officially designed cities and towns.* That event, achieved in advanced countries like the United States 100 years ago, will come sooner than

---

2/   As a rule of thumb, total building space additions are roughly twice residential stock additions. The annual investment in urban construction, as a percent of GDP, is thus estimated at *at least* twice the size of annual investments in urban residential construction, which the Bank's housing sector report estimated at roughly 3.5 percent of GDP; thus, as a percent of GDP, urban building investments exceed 7 percent of GDP. *Urban* GDP is at least 50 percent of total GDP, when statutory towns are excluded. Actual urban GDP is probably equal to 65-70 percent of total GDP, even if town-level productivity is heavily discounted vis-a-vis city-level productivity. Thus, real estate investments as a percent of *urban* GDP can be set at 10-15 percent.

3/   The replacement value of different types of buildings is based on reports of average building costs for residential and nonresidential structures. The latter systematically exceed the former by about 25 percent. Mission estimates gathered on previous and current work in the housing sector suggest that total investment costs for average residential structures rarely fall below Y 600/m²; the estimated "average" for all space assumes that total investment costs for all building investments average around Y 800/m². The depreciated value estimates place an average value of Y 320/m², and give heavy implicit weight to the 50 percent of the existing stock added during this decade, particularly after urban growth accelerated dramatically in the period after 1984. These are obviously order-of-magnitude estimates. They do serve to underscore the importance of the real estate sector, no matter what sensitivity analysis may suggest as appropriate lower and higher bounds.

4/   Ingram, analyzing the fraction of nonagricultural land value in relation to nonagricultural output in the United States, *during the 1970s*, suggests that the value is approximately 0.62. If land values in urban areas represent no more than one quarter of real estate values, overall, then this example suggests that real estate stock as a fraction of local urban GDP equals 2.48 in the United States (G. Ingram, "Land in Perspective: Its Role in the Structure of Cities," in M. Cullen and S. Woolery, eds., *World Congress on Land Policy*, 1980, Lexington, Massachusetts: Lexington Press, 1982). Data for the United States, as a whole, as reported periodically by the US Bureau of Economic Analysis, suggest that the ratio of gross value of structures to GDP is approximately 2.74 (David Dowall, personal communication).

Table 1.3: HONG KONG: CURRENT VALUE OF PROPERTY AND
ITS RELATION TO GDP
(in 1992 Hong Kong dollars)

District	No. of assessments	Total rateable value
Hong Kong	377,102	67,988,027,660
Kowloon	206,255	31,340,973,040
New Kowloon	206,053	30,308,790,630
New Territories	409,162	47,957,524,560
Total	1,198,572	177,595,315,890

Notes: (1) Market value of all properties (residential, commercial, industrial) (including
buildings and land)
= Rateable value x 12
= HK$177.595 billion x 12
= HK$2,131 billion
(2) GDP at current market price (1991/92) = HK$633 billion
(3) Property + land value/GDP = 2,131/633 = 3.37

Source: Rating and Valuation Department, Hong Kong Government.

official statistics are likely to document because, fanning out from each of China's most vibrant
cities, in suburban areas, and along major interurban highways and waterways, a vast set of peri-
urban settlements is developing. There, township and village enterprises (TVEs), engaged
mostly in industrial activity, are already producing over one fifth of the gross value of industrial
production, while the state-sponsored urban enterprise sector now accounts for barely half of
national output.5/ *Despite the existing size of the urban population, China can still benefit
from being at a relatively early stage of the rural-urban transition, avoiding mistakes, at the
margin, and options not available to other, already largely urbanized, post-Socialist economies.*

The Challenge of Restructuring the Urban Economy

If one resorts to a set of stylized facts to describe a large nationally and
internationally competitive city in the late twentieth century, one would single out a few key
items. First, whether in the developed or developing world, the manufacturing sector's share
of output and employment ranges from 20 to 30 percent. Second, employment tends to

5/   The spatial distribution of TVEs is not known to Chinese authorities except on the basis of anecdotal
evidence. That evidence suggests that it is largely a suburban phenomenon, in terms of land occupied,
employment, and value added. This issue should become a high-priority research item among urban and
economic development planners in China, who alone can assemble the necessary corroborating evidence.

Box 1.6: SELECTED TIME SERIES FOR TEMPORARY RESIDENTS /a
IN EIGHT CHINESE CITIES
('000 persons)

	1984	1988	1989/b
Beijing	300	1,310	1,310
Tianjin	417 (1985)	813	612
Shanghai	750	1,246	1,260
Guangzhou	500	1,170	914
Shenyang	86 (1985)	-	328
Wuhan	350	-	745
Chengdu	270	-	420
Hangzhou	250 (1985)	295	358

/a Present for more than three days at the time of the survey.
/b Recession year. Temporaries were often involuntarily repatriated.

Source: M. Rutkowski, "China's Floating Population and Labor Market Reforms,"

concentrate in particular subsectors, rather than range across all output categories. Third, these activities operate in a relatively fast-paced environment, as product life spans are progressively shortened, competition increases, and quality and price depend increasingly on an evermore complex, interrelated strategy that works to improve efficiency at the physical plant level and within executive and financial management operations, while giving greater prominence to marketing research.

In this process, information-intensive inputs have grown enormously (whether provided "in-house" or through the use of external suppliers). In highly urbanized Singapore, where manufacturing accounts for 29 percent of GDP, financial and business services total 30 percent of GDP. And there, as elsewhere among advanced Asian cities, services are the key generators of GDP and employment. In Hong Kong, 66 percent of employment is in the services sector, while 80 percent of Seoul's employment is tertiary in nature. By contrast, in those cities, manufacturing accounts for 34 percent and 19 percent of all jobs, respectively.[6]

For a highly urbanized country like the United States, the story is much the same. Manufacturing accounts for 25 percent of employment in a typical large city, government takes up another 5-8 percent, as does construction. The remainder involves transportation and

[6]   Information derived from local annual statistical yearbooks issued by each city.

business and personal services. Business services alone may now account for as much as 40 percent of city employment.7/

The driving force behind these figures can best be described by the following quotation:

> "The developed world at the end of the twentieth century is still in transition from an industrial to an information economy where information becomes the most important, indeed all-pervasive commodity. This does not mean that manufacturing industry will atrophy or that the demand for goods will diminish; on the contrary, there will almost certainly be massive increases in demand for manufactured products. But it does mean that various complex substitutions will take place. One involves the introduction of ever more powerful information technology into the manufacturing process, hence the substitution of this technology—based on robotics and automation—for labor and traditional energy-intensive capital. Another is the substitution of knowledge and intelligence for some material and energy resources, thus achieving the more efficient design of products, greater knowledge of their markets, and tighter, more robust planning and operation of their production and distribution processes. These two changes are also facilitating the shift to increased quality, diversity, and 'personalization' of the products involved.
>
> The mass markets of the industrial age are evolving into smaller, more specialist niche markets, offering the consumer specialized services and products which in the past were assumed to be totally inconsistent with traditional manufacturing."8/

By contrast, for all 467 cities of China, taken as a whole, 56 percent of municipal GDP is still derived from the secondary sector; and in cities like Shanghai, the number rises to 65 percent. Among major cities surveyed by the mission, the lowest percentages were found among the "southern" cities considered the most advanced in reforming

---

7/   This includes engineering, legal, real estate brokerage, telecommunications, finance, accounting, consultants, insurance, and marketing, as well as nongovernmental quaternary services such as research and development.

8/   "Epilogue," in J. Brochie, M. Barry, P. Hall, and P. Newton, eds., *Cities in the 21st Century: New Technologies and Spatial Systems*, New York: Halstead Press, 1991.

their economy. Even there, the proportion contributed by the secondary sector totaled or exceeded 40 percent.9/

Furthermore, China's cities typically produce every conceivable manufacturing product, revealing little selectivity or specialization, while operating with plants that are, by almost any measure, generally obsolete in layout, technology, inventory management, quality control, labor efficiency and raw material utilization rates.

Worse still, as documented below, much of this industry is located in the built-up areas of the city, often within the boundaries of the 1949 city, utilizing 20-30 percent of the land.10/ In Hong Kong, by contrast, industry utilizes only 6 percent of the built-up area, while in Seoul, the proportion is 9 percent. In North America, the norm is 10 percent or less.11/

At a small-area level, the situation is even worse. Shanghai's port authority, for example, controls 229 hectares of prime real estate along the Puxi side of the Huangpu River, along the Bund and on either side of that center. This land is typically devoted to low value-added activities, such as warehouses. That amounts to 2.5 percent of the area of the old (pre-1949) city, and obviously a much higher percentage of its land value. If freed up, much of this area could potentially be transformed into a much higher-value mixed-use commercial and entertainment center, following examples set by such cities as Boston and Baltimore in the United States.

In places like Shanghai, *restructuring will involve important land use readjustments, and infrastructural investments to accompany them.* These investments will be massive in scope within any one sector, and may require significant spatial targeting, directed at the densely populated old core areas of the city. To cite but two examples. First, in the competing Asian cities like Singapore and Hong Kong, there are approximately 45-50 telephones per 100 persons; in London, Paris, and New York, the number of phones per capita is greater than 1. In Shanghai, there are only 6 telephones per 100 persons. Second, within Shanghai's

---

9/ State Statistical Bureau, *China Statistical Yearbook-1991*, Beijing, 1992. Ironically, when Shanghai was one of the premier urban centers of China, and a contender for Pacific Rim leadership in international trade, in 1952, 42 percent of GDP originated from tertiary activities such as commerce, finance, communications, science and technology research and development, education, and "culture." Today that proportion has fallen to 30 percent. (K. Fung, Z. Yan, and Y. Ning, "Shanghai: China's World City," in Y. Yeung and X. Hu, eds., *China's Coastal Cities: Catalysts of Modernization*, Honolulu: University of Hawaii Press, 1992.

10/ According to Lin Zhiqun ("The Development of Urban Construction Land in China During the 1980s," Beijing, Ministry of Construction, 1992, processed), the percentage of built-up area land devoted to industrial uses in the sector study cities varies from 18 percent in Shenzhen to 27 percent in Guangzhou. An additional 3 to 6 percent is taken up by warehouses. The same phenomenon emerged in Soviet cities. Approximately 30 to 40 percent of the inner areas of Soviet cities are occupied by industry (G. Andrusz, *Housing and Urban Development in the USSR*, London: Macmillan, 1982).

11/ Ibid.

inner-ring road area, equivalent to the 1949 city boundaries, only 10 percent of land is used for transportation, whereas the norm in developed county cities is 20 percent or more, and similar proportions are found in such high-density centers as Hong Kong and Singapore.

Thus, by any reasonable measure of scope involved, the urban economic transformation under way will require policymakers within China to focus serious attention on urban land management issues. China justly prides itself as one of the few developing countries that has largely avoided "disorderly" development, characterized by the proliferation of unplanned and unanticipated slums and squatter settlements. To maintain that enviable record will become much more difficult during this decade and beyond because the emergence of the market economy is loosening the control exercised by urban and economic planners over the timing and location of real estate development. Those planners are having to learn to live with an unpredictable world, where citywide and, more particularly, small area (district and subdistrict) population and economic activity cannot be anticipated as easily as in the past. This is particularly the case now, as cities like Shanghai and Beijing have formally granted lower-level authorities the right to approve project proposals, feasibility reports, and project contracts independently—up to a certain threshold—without clearance from the municipal governments themselves. Efficient and equitable urban development, following environmentally sound practices, will call for new skills, new policies, and new institutions. And China's urban planners will have to learn to live with the challenge of reinventing the Chinese city not merely to effectively compete within and across provinces, but also to gain an increasing share of direct foreign investment and world trade in goods and services. Success is thus like a two-edged sword. Having committed themselves to developing a world-class urban economy, closely interconnected with the international market, China's policymakers cannot rest on their laurels. What from the vantage point of 1984 looked like thoroughgoing reform is but a first step.

The Urban and Peri-Urban Environmental Challenge

Industrial redevelopment problems are enormous and pose serious challenges to planners. The most pressing problem is undoubtedly the old age and dilapidated conditions common to many industrial factories.[12] Land reform, providing factories with incentives to move from inappropriate, high-value CBD locations, can help improve environmental conditions while allowing technological renovation or the development of new product lines to take place. Other land users, more capable of using high-access locations, can then occupy the old sites and accelerate the transformation of Chinese cities, allowing land uses and production patterns to more closely resemble that of an internationally competitive city.

---

[12] In the *core area* of Shanghai, defined as containing 3,000 hectares, there are 5,603 factories occupying approximately 20,000 sites. These sites average 2,145 m^2, and total 429 hectares. Other analysts paint a picture which is equally startling by adding in the area occupied by warehouses: "It is estimated that over 30 percent of the built-up area of the central city is occupied by factories and warehouses. In the urban district of Nanshi, factories [and warehouses] occupy 61.6 percent of the total area of 4,175 hectares. Further, because of the shortage of storage space, many workshops use the neighborhood streets for storage ...." (Fung, Yang, and Ning, "Shanghai: China's World City," op. cit.).

The physical plant of Shanghai's industries is, on average, uncompetitive by international standards; nearly 50 percent of the physical plant and equipment of factories was built before 1949. Across Shanghai, manufacturing facilities have expanded incrementally into residential neighborhoods, and as a result, they are highly inefficient. Many of the inner city factories reveal a pattern: a series of houses or commercial shops have been linked together as businesses expanded output. In some cases, clusters of buildings in a residential district have been converted to industrial uses and raw materials and products at various stages of processing and fabrication are shuttled back and forth between these buildings. In more extreme cases, materials are literally hauled and backhauled across cities like Shanghai simply because industries have no access to contiguous sites for their operations. Such practices severely penalize manufacturing productivity.

Another serious and related problem posed by the inadequate manufacturing facilities found in most central cities is the fact that cramped quarters frequently makes it difficult for factories to update their equipment. Despite the fact that new machines might double or triple process efficiency, low ceilings, small elevators and small or awkward floor-space configurations make upgrading impossible.[13]

Overall, in terms of potential industrial productivity gains, industrial redevelopment is of critical importance in China's large urban areas. But there is another pressing reason for industrial redevelopment—*urban environmental pollution*. Although there have been few systematic surveys of industrial pollution, officials in every city visited expressed considerable concern over dangerous conditions—houses next to polluting factories, chemical spills, noise pollution, vibrations, dust, congested alleys and lanes.[14]

Therefore, one aspect of environmental policy involves moving polluting enterprises away from dense urban areas into rural areas. Except for the Ministry of Light Industry, industry ministries and the State Planing Commission appear to support this policy. Rural areas clamor for such firms to augment the local tax base.[15] For a variety of reasons, firms that move tend to be small and fairly profitable. This leaves the large firms (polluting or not), and the small unprofitable firms, in the cities. The latter are likely to pose severe environmental problems since they are likely also to be scrimping on pollution control. The firms that move may also be presumed to be highly polluting. Whether moving them makes sense depends, in part, on the economic costs of such a move and the net environmental benefits. In a market economy, profit maximizing firms take the price of land, labor, and

---

13/   Shanghai is merely a representative case. In Guangzhou, most buildings are no more than two or three stories high and, as of 1984, half were built before 1949. Within this low-density environment, extensive industrial use of former domestic structures, and a lack of separation of residential and factory structures is the norm (S. Li, "A Comparative Study of the Urban Land Use Patterns in Guangzhou and Hong Kong," op. cit.).

14/   Guangzhou's Construction Commission made particular note of this issue.

15/   World Bank, *China: Environmental Strategy Paper*, Report No. 9669-CHA (Washington, DC: 1992), Annex 1, p. 9.

capital into account (as well as any benefits from being located in a city or outside a city) in their location and output decisions. In this case, it may be presumed that forcing a relocation will reduce profits and social welfare. When pollution of the firm is taken into account, this presumption cannot be made, as environmental damages from the firm's activities may be far larger if located in some locations than others, but such damages are not considered in the firm's location decisions. In a planned economy with tight restrictions on firm and labor mobility, it is difficult, if not impossible, to make inferences about whether economic benefits would be reduced after relocation. The presumption is that health impacts would fall after the move because population exposures to the firm's emissions would be lower when the firm is in a rural area, even if emissions were the same. However, as the relocated firms are expected to meet the restrictions in the environmental impact assessment process, total emissions should to be far lower than they were in the central city. Nevertheless, if the firm locates near fragile ecosystems or irrigated areas and has high levels of pollution,16/ serious damages could result and could conceivably exceed those avoided in the urban area.

In rural areas, where implicit and explicit land values are low, the density development would be expected to be low as well, and evidence of "market-driven" trends is limited to measuring the extent to which land use has switched from agricultural to nonagricultural purposes. Though the evidence is spotty, the impact on urbanization is undeniable (Tables 1.4 and 1.5). *Ironically, the key issue is whether there is too little planning in such areas and thus how best to introduce appropriate planning practices, consistent with market forces, into these areas* (Box 1.7). The worst-case scenario has it that in peri-urban

Table 1.4: SHANGHAI: CHANGE IN CULTIVATED LAND
IN PERI-URBAN TOWNSHIPS, 1980-88

County (no. of townships)	Cultivated land change (ha)			% Change
	1980	1988	Reduced land	
Baoshan (5)	2,226.67	1,746.67	480.00	-21.56
Jiading (3)	3,046.67	2,593.33	453.34	-14.88
Shanghai (7)	7,420.00	6,586.67	833.33	-11.23
Chuansha (10)	7,666.67	7,106.67	560.00	-7.30
Total (25)	20,360.01	18,033.34	2,326.67	-11.43

Source: State Land Administration.

16/   The law places very fragile areas off-limits to industrial location. Enterprises are not permitted to be sited on the windward side of a city or in protected (including water resource) areas. A related policy prohibits certain types of TVE production activities from even being established (such as sulfur production, tanning, and dyestuff manufacturing). The study team was not able to ascertain the degree to which these laws and policies are implemented.

Table 1.5: SHANGHAI: DISTRIBUTION OF REDUCED CULTIVATED LAND,
1980-88
(ha)

County (no. of townships)	Productive/a	Nonproductive/b	Fish-pond	River	Road	Total	Share
Baoshan (5)	374.00	82.67	16.00	3.33	2.00	478.00	20.5%
% share	78.2%	17.3%	3.3%	0.7%	0.4%	100.0%	
Jiading (3)	295.33	46.67	60.00	8.67	41.33	452.00	19.4%
% share	65.3%	10.3%	13.3%	1.9%	9.1%	100.0%	
Shanghai (7)	583.33	179.33	38.00	0.00	38.67	839.33	36.0%
% share	69.5%	21.4%	4.5%	0.0%	4.6%	100.0%	
Chuansha (10)	397.33	107.33	45.33	3.33	6.00	559.32	24.0%
% share	71.0%	19.2%	8.1%	0.6%	1.1%	100.0%	
Total (25)	1,652.12	416.49	159.54	15.36	88.14	2,331.65	100.0%
% share	70.9%	17.9%	6.8%	0.7%	3.8%	100.0%	

/a Productive: industrial and storage land uses.
/b Nonproductive: housing and other nonfarm land uses.

Source: State Land Administration.

Box 1.7: THE ROLE OF SUBURBAN COUNTY AUTONOMY IN HINDERING
METROPOLITAN GUIDED LAND DEVELOPMENT STRATEGIES

In Fuzhou, the urban districts do not contain any farmland. They are, in general, smaller than the actual urban built-up area spilling out beyond its boundaries. As a result, those built-up areas outside the urban districts, located in suburban districts, are very difficult to monitor. Although the urban district will expand to reflect new urban development, such expansion lags far behind reality, and not all new development is covered. One reason for this is that the suburban district governments, who control all surrounding rural townships, do not want to give up these areas, since they are the most productive "revenue cows" within the suburban district. As a result, nobody, even local planners, have any comprehensive data regarding urban built-up area and population.

---

areas, agricultural land is unnecessarily squandered by the proliferation of unconnected urbanized sites, scattered across the farming landscape. In addition, concerns exist that limited infrastructure and neglect of the environment is allowing polluting factories to dump untreated effluents and contaminate adjacent agricultural land and the water sources that nourish it. *In most instances, land management reform in China's cities implies greater deregulation; in peri-*

urban areas, more regulation may be necessary (Box 1.8), covering an area which is growing in scale as fast as or faster than that of China's cities.17/

Box 1.8: PERI-URBAN DEVELOPMENT REGULATION IN HONG KONG: A NEW STRATEGY

For historical reasons, the Town Planning Ordinance only covered the existing and potential urban areas which basically included the main urban areas and the new towns in the New Territories. Areas outside these areas were not covered by the ordinance. There was little problem in the pre-war period (1939) because most of the population and development was mainly concentrated in the main urban areas of Kowloon and Hong Kong Island. However, with the development of new towns in the New Territories, many developments have spilled over to places outside the new towns. Much agricultural land has been converted to open storage uses, for use as car dumps, open-air workshops, container storage and vehicle car parks. They have been carried out in a haphazard and disorderly manner, creating incompatible land use, and environmental and traffic problems. To stop the environment from further rapid deterioration, the government proposed to amend the Town Planning Ordinance in July 1990, while a more comprehensive review of the ordinance was still under way. The Town Planning (Amendment) Bill 1990 was passed in January 1991. It extended the jurisdiction of the Ordinance to cover the whole of Hong Kong, with new types of zonings covering country parks, greenbelts, village-type development and open storage uses. Interim planning control through the use of development permission area plans was used to guide developments in the New Territories while the Outline Zoning Plans, which are statutory plans for development control, are under preparation. The Town Planning Board may designate areas which require immediate planning control as Development Permission Areas (DPAs). The DPA plans have to be exhibited and publicly consulted, the same as the statutory Outline Zone Plans, and will be effective for three years. All developers in DPAs have to obtain planning permission from the Town Planning Board. To give the Town Planning Ordinance enforcement power to control unauthorized development in the DPAs, enforcement notices, reinstatement notices and stop notices, similar to those used in Britain, were introduced. Enforcement notices may be served to the landowner/occupier/responsible person to reinstate the land to authorized development if planning permission has not been obtained upon expiry of the period of the enforcement notice. If the unauthorized development seriously constitutes a health or safety hazard, adversely affects the environment or makes it impractical or uneconomic to reinstate the land within a reasonable time period, a stop notice will be served to discontinue the unauthorized development immediately. Any person who fails to comply with the enforcement notice, stop notice, or reinstatement notice is liable to a fine and imprisonment. An Appeals Board will be set up to deal with appeals related to objections and refusals of planning permissions of the DPAs.

Source: A. Yeh, "Land Leasing and Urban Planning in Hong Kong," Hong Kong: University of Hong Kong, November 1991, processed.

Recent field work and the results of large-scale surveys undertaken by the Nanjing Research Institute for Environmental Studies suggest that peri-urban pollution is a matter for at least selective concern, particularly in the case of such contaminants as hexavalent

---

17/   The built-up area of China's cities is expanding at a rate of about 40,000-50,000 hectares per year. Nationwide, rural land converted to nonagricultural construction (industry and related urban uses) is estimated to average 100,000 hectares per year, with the presumption that most of this is peri-urban in nature. Most rural industries, for example, are located within 25 kilometers of cities or along transport arteries fanning out from those cities.

chromium, lead, and waste gas emissions (particularly dust emissions). The chief offenders are older enterprises, established before the widespread introduction of environment contract responsibility systems for enterprises built during and after the Seventh Five-Year Plan Period (1986-90). New enterprises are increasingly subject to environment impact statements, incorporated into project feasibility studies, and scrutinized at various critical project development stages, including applications for loans from the China Investment Bank and the Agricultural Bank of China. It is too early to assess the degree to which these requirements are being implemented, and whether supervision is adequate. Both bear monitoring.

The Nanjing Institute survey estimates that about 70 percent of the output of TVEs is derived from TVIEs, employing 57 million workers and concentrated in the periphery of large coastal cities.18/ Rural industrial pollution is caused largely by 600,000 enterprises, or 8 percent of all TVEs. Heavily polluting enterprises total 366,000 in number, and are responsible for 75 percent of measured discharges. As is typical of the industrial structure of Chinese cities, TVIEs are involved in all of China's 40 designated industrial sectors. The main polluting industries include pulp and paper making, dyeing, electroplating, chemical production, food and alcohol processing, smelting, asbestos, refining, coking and building material production (cement, bricks and tiles). Production efficiency and pollution control are serious problems for these industries in the face of strong market competition. While rural industry in the aggregate may be less polluting than its urban counterpart, either in absolute terms or in terms of total output of pollutants per unit of production value, this in large part reflects differences in output composition. Individual TVIEs' waste discharges can be quite serious in relative and absolute terms. For example, in 1991, TVIEs as a whole discharged only 10.7 percent of the industrial wastewater in China, while accounting for 28 percent of production output value. More revealing, however, is that the TVIE pulp and paper industries alone accounted for 44 percent of the TVIE wastewater discharge. Many such plants do not comply with effluent standards and cause serious local damage. The concentration levels are due to low process efficiency and poor waste treatment in the factories concerned, despite fines and sanctions.

The situation with regard to air quality and solid wastes is similar. In 1991, TVIEs produced about 9.4 percent of total waste gas emissions and 11 percent of solid wastes, again levels well below their share of output. Treatment levels for waste gas are about 20 percent of urban levels, themselves often inadequate. The chief hazards are fluorine and sulfur dioxide. The cement industry accounts for the bulk of the dust emissions.

The sector study team did not have the resources to investigate this topic thoroughly. Other sources, including those from Shanghai's Municipal Bureau of Environmental Protection, confirm progress, while emphasizing hazards yet to be tackled. On the one hand, sewerage treatment facilities have improved dramatically in selected suburban counties, including Chuansha and Shanghai. Yet the Bureau's Agro-Ecological and Macro-Natural Protection Division claims that its suburban counties contain 3,211 rural enterprises (out of a total of

---

18/   By way of contrast, the entire urban labor force with permanent residency status is only about 140 million in number, and the total TVE labor force amounts to 92 million.

16,000) with pollution problems requiring remedial action. Some relocated state-owned factories were also identified as polluters. The full scope of the problems involved remain beyond the scope of this report. The issue does, however, merit close monitoring, as peri-urban development gradually merges into the "field" of a greater metropolis, and can no longer be considered in isolation from urban land use issues, broadly defined.

The Issue of Industrial Redevelopment

Urban planners in China's largest cities are starting to focus their attention on industrial relocation and redevelopment. Most planning strategies call for the relocation of factories to outlying areas, often located in new towns and smaller villages, which have been targeted for industrial development. In some cities, these efforts are potentially enormous. In Shanghai, for example, plans to develop Pudong call for the construction of millions of square meters of industrial facilities. In virtually every case, efforts to relocate industrial facilities have been, until very recently, administratively driven and constrained by a lack of resources. While this difficulty is to be expected given the scale of potential redevelopment, the lack of a transparent land market prevents the relocating factory from capturing the income associated with the sale and/or redevelopment of its relinquished site to a more productive use. Financing its modernization at a new, more suitable site is thus made more difficult. Very recently, some coastal cities, like Shanghai, have begun to allow existing occupants to retain most of the income derived from the transfer of land-use rights.

Chinese planners and industrial developers and factory operators confirm the similarity of the present pattern of industrial relocation and redevelopment across most cities (although activities in Guangzhou are the exception). The usual process uncovered during the sector study preparation mission was as follows. First, based on some rudimentary surveys of industrial conditions and urban environmental pollution, factories were targeted for relocation. Those factories targeted for relocation were normally compensated for the value of vacated buildings, and equipment and ancillary facilities that could not be relocated. In some cases, the party carrying out the redevelopment would also pay for lost wages resulting from the idling of workers. *Compensation provided for relinquished land was the exception*, though estimates of the depreciated value of vacated structures may have been inflated to allow for some implicit compensation for land rights relinquished.19/

In some cases, the new user of the relinquished site would pay the actual costs of acquiring a new site. In other cases, government grants and loans were provided to cover the costs of land acquisition. In all cases surveyed, the industries paid for the actual

---

19/ The State Land Administration has monitored several forms of spontaneous transactions involving the transformation of *administratively* allocated land into an active commodity with market prices. It also reports these are taking place on a large scale. First and foremost, buildings and land are "sold" together, and the land price is included in the total building price. Second, buildings are leased, along with the associated land use rights. (Zou Yuchuan, "Speeding Up the Regularization of Land Market Transactions and Strengthening the Management of Administratively Allocated Land Use Rights According to the Law," Beijing, State Land Administration, December 20, 1991, processed.)

construction costs of new facilities themselves, and in most cases, the factories invested heavily in new equipment and accessory investments.

The limitation of capital markets for industrial debt and the failure of factories to receive adequate compensation for relinquished land together made the financing of industrial relocation difficult. As a result, the pace of industrial relocation so far has been very slow, as the following sections describe.

Industrial Relocation in Shanghai

Shanghai has been hampered in implementing industrial relocation, inter alia, by limited resources. Overall, in the city proper, between 1985 and 1990 (the Seventh Five-Year Plan), 103 factories were relocated from old areas, accounting for less than 0.02 percent of all industrial facilities in the municipality. These factories had a total constructed area of 810,000 m^2. The land area of these sites totaled 820,000 m^2. In the new areas, these 103 factories were given land totaling 1,270,000 m^2. The new constructed area was 760,000 m^2. The industries usually require less space because the old space was used in an extremely inefficient manner.

Even though inner city land could be extremely valuable if converted to commercial shops, office buildings or commodity housing; during the Seventh Five-Year Plan (1986-90), only limited attempts were made to capture the differential value associated with relocating inner city factories to suburban locations. Instead, the government stitched together a variety of programs to partially fund industrial relocation. Funding for industrial relocation came from five principal sources: soft (i.e., concessional loans from the Environmental Bureau (20 percent); the Economic Commission for Industrial Restructuring (20 percent); general revenues from the municipal budget (12 percent); factory payments (14 percent); and bank loans (42 percent).

During the Seventh Five-Year Plan, total relocation costs were Y 1.4 billion. Table 1.6 illustrates the breakdown of the costs for industrial relocation in Shanghai. The total Seventh Five-Year Plan costs work out to an average of approximately Y 1,700/m^2 of relocated old factory land. Of the total, about 39 percent went to pay for land requisition and infrastructure provision—Y 550 million. This works out to Y 433/m^2 or Y 289,000/mu, for the 1,270,000 m^2 of land acquired for the relocating factories.

Clearly, a more ambitious industrial relocation program will require substantial resources. While there are no surveys of industrial conditions in the inner-city area, a rough estimate of the potential costs of industrial relocation for Shanghai can be made. If one conservatively estimates that 25 percent of the city's core area factories require relocation, then about 5,000 sites need redevelopment. The land area covered by this redevelopment activity would approach 1,100 hectares. Using cost figures from the Seventh Five-Year Plan, the total cost of such an industrial redevelopment effort is likely to exceed Y 18 billion. Based on estimates of the actual relocation cost during the Seventh Five-Year Plan, the cost of acquiring and servicing new suburban land was about 40 percent of the total relocation cost. Using this

Table 1.6: SEVENTH FIVE-YEAR PLAN INDUSTRIAL
RELOCATION COSTS, SHANGHAI

	Total cost (Y mln)	Per m^2 of relocated factory (Y)
Land and infrastructure	550	671
Building construction	750	915
Moving costs	20	24
Other costs	80	98
Total Costs	1,400	1,708

proportion, the total land acquisition and infrastructure cost of relocating these 5,000 establishments would be approximately Y 7.2 billion.

Since, under the approach followed until 1992, factories did not receive explicit compensation for the land that they left behind, and since the new users did not finance the acquisition and improvement of new industrial estates, either the old factories or the government were required to come up with the funds for relocation. While this may have been easy for profitable firms, many firms do not have sufficient cash flow to cover the cost of relocation. Thus, the government has more often than not been called upon to provide subsidies. During the Seventh Five-Year Plan Period, enterprises provided only 54 percent of the costs of relocation (12 percent in cash and 42 percent in loans).

The Eighth Five-Year Plan (1991-95) calls for the relocation of 131 factories from the city center. The projected cost of these relocation efforts is estimated at Y 2.5 billion, about Y 19 million per factory. This estimate is approximately 40 percent greater than the per-factory cost incurred during the Seventh Five-Year Plan, and reflects the fact that the next round of relocation projects will focus on more problematic cases; there will be more difficulties in relocating such factories. Other problems will emerge as well—good suburban industrial estate sites will become more expensive and factories will be forced to move out to more remote locations. Operating at these distant sites will make relocation more costly in terms of worker relocation, if commuting is excluded as an alternative. One possible way around these problems is to capture the differential land value associated with the industrial relocation; this policy is now gaining acceptance in Shanghai.

Industrial Relocation in Hangzhou

In 1984, the city conducted a detailed survey of the land uses in the West Lake area, identifying 86 factories and work units which needed to be relocated. Of the total, 52 enterprises were targeted for relocation because of pollution problems. The remaining 34 factories and shops were identified for relocation because of other redevelopment requirements, such as the expansion of infrastructure and the upgrading of old urban areas. The combined constructed area of these 86 businesses totaled 694,000 m². The new industrial areas will have a FAR of 1:0.87, a level more consistent with modern standards. This will require the requisitioning of 800,000 m² of land for new industrial estates.

By 1990, 59 factories had been moved. All of the polluting factories had been removed from the West Lake area and all temples previously converted to other uses had been returned to religious organizations. With the relocation, factories have had their industrial production facilities revitalized. Beyond improving environmental quality in and around Hangzhou, relocation has greatly enhanced factory productivity. Most of the old factory sites have been recycled to uses consistent with the Comprehensive Plan. In the West Lake area, all industrial sites vacated will be transformed to open space or tourist-oriented uses.

Like Shanghai's, Hangzhou's industrial relocation program is expensive. A total of 376,000 m² of new industrial space has been built at a total cost of approximately Y 380 million—an average cost of approximately Y 1,010/m². Costs of relocation are higher than projected, and the city expects the actual costs to approach Y 550 million, about 20 percent higher than planned. Another problem which compounds the high costs is the fact that some of the factories needing relocation are not profitable. Of the 86 firms targeted for relocation, 17 do not generate retained earnings which could be used for relocation. The government creatively assembled a variety of funding sources. Of the 59 factories which were relocated up to 1990, the funding sources break down as follows:

	Y million	Percent
Grants from state and province	17.6	4.6
People's Construction Bank loans	54.5	14.3
Local grants (municipal)	47.9	12.6
Enterprises	260.0	68.5
Total	380.0	100.0

Despite the relatively high costs of industrial relocation in Hangzhou, and the problem of low profitability of targeted industrial enterprises, industries paid a higher share of the relocation costs (69 percent) than in Shanghai (54 percent). Many enterprises in Hangzhou have received substantial compensation for their old buildings since they were then occupied by other users. Vacated industrial buildings in Hangzhou can be recycled and, as a result, relocating factories receive significant compensation for the structures left behind.

Industrial Relocation in Fuzhou

Like Hangzhou and Guangzhou (see below), Fuzhou has conducted an environmental and land use assessment of its industrial uses located in its inner urban area. As a result, a number of old factories have been targeted for relocation. Over the past seven years, 22 factories have been moved out of the city center. To date, the government has invested Y 50 million to underwrite relocation and the total cost of the industrial relocation to date is estimated at Y 200 million—about Y 9 million per factory. Most of the vacated industrial land has been recycled to accommodate residential uses and commercial activities.

The process of industrial relocation starts with the factory agreeing to relinquish its site. When it does, the local SLA Bureau obtains the use right. The new user pays the factory compensation for the old buildings, fixed investments, and lost wages and production and moving costs, but not for land. Instead, compensation is paid for requisitioning a new piece of land for the factory in one of Fuzhou's new suburban industrial estates. At present, differential land values are not used to determine the level of compensation paid to the old factory. Monies paid are based on the actual costs of finding a new site, compensation for old facilities and equipment and payments to idled workers. Brokers operate in Fuzhou, and negotiate with factories to identify redevelopment possibilities. New users typically pay these brokers commissions of 1 percent of the total level of compensation costs. In some cases, where the site was used by heavy industry, the city will itself identify new users, and clean up any pollution.

The costs associated with acquiring new industrial sites in suburban areas have been rising over the past three to four years. In 1988, the cost to requisition unimproved land in the suburbs averaged between Y 150 and Y 190/m^2. In addition, the relocating factories must pay infrastructure fees (Y 150/m^2), other fees totaling Y 15 to Y 30/m^2, and costs for the construction of new buildings (averaging between Y 400 and Y 600/m^2). Given a FAR in the new industrial areas of 1:1.0, the typical costs for new facilities on a 10,000 m^2 site with a 10,000 m^2 building would range from Y 7.9 million to Y 10.8 million.

In Fuzhou, the net cost to factories for relocation should be the difference between the cost of construction for the new building and the compensation received for old buildings. By paying this difference, the factory gets a new and much more efficient physical plant. The typical relocation compensation received by factories in 1991 exceeded 50 percent of the total relocation costs, and in some rare cases, where more than one new users competed for the old site, the relocation compensation was even higher.

Nevertheless, despite the generous compensation received by factories for relocation, planners and brokers claim that it is difficult to persuade factories to relocate. The process of industrial relocation is long and complex, and most real estate development companies (REDCs) 20/ prefer to engage in greenfield development or in residential redevelopment projects. Despite these difficulties, the city has targeted seven major polluters for relocation from the city center: Fuzhou Barrage Factory; Fuzhou Tire Recapping Factory; Fuzhou Forged Steel Factory; Fuzhou Sewing Machine Factory; Fuzhou Roofing Materials Factory; Fuzhou Motor Factory; and Fuzhou Dyeing Factory.

The present system of financing industrial relocation in Fuzhou (and to a lesser extent in Hangzhou) whereby land requisitioning costs are borne by the new user of the original site, goes a long way towards covering the costs of industrial redevelopment. However, it still

---

20/   These for-profit companies were first authorized in 1984, and are discussed in Chapter III.

leaves the relocating enterprise with the problem of covering 30 to 50 percent of the costs of relocation. Guangzhou's market-driven approach, discussed below, serves as an alternative worth considering.

Industrial Relocation in Guangzhou

Guangzhou, like other cities, has conducted environmental assessments of its inner-city factories and identified 14 polluting factories for relocation in 1985-90 and 28 for relocation in 1991-95. Factories targeted for relocation are provided with replacement sites and are compensated for their buildings and immovable facilities. Vacated sites are put up for tender or otherwise allocated and the proceeds are used to finance industrial relocation.

Enterprises targeted for relocation normally receive financial assistance from the state investment plan. There are four sources of funds to pay for relocation: (i) state funds; (ii) retained earnings; (iii) the relevant manufacturing or industrial bureau of the municipality; and (iv) bank loans. These channels are similar to those outlined above for Shanghai and Hangzhou.

As is typical in southern China, industrial redevelopment is, to a relatively large degree, market-driven. In Guangzhou, some industrial users in the inner city area have decided to move to suburban areas to acquire more space for expansion. Enterprises may approach the municipality's Construction Commission and request relocation assistance or they may decide to sign cooperative agreements with one of Guangzhou's numerous REDCs. When industries link up with REDCs, the REDC typically acquires and develops a new site for the industrial enterprise, usually in a suburban district. In exchange for agreeing to relocate, the industry receives a percentage of the profits (usually 50 percent) associated with the redevelopment of the original site, less the costs of the new suburban facility.

This arrangement is legal only if the factory reports the business arrangement, obtains government approval, and pays a transfer fee to the municipal government. The fee averages about 20 percent of the profit of the project. This fee was imposed two years ago. Through early 1992, it had been levied on 30 to 40 industrial redevelopment projects. Such an approach has considerable merit and has the obvious benefit of being able to finance redevelopment without the use of massive government subventions.

<u>Residential Redevelopment Issues</u>

In market economies, redevelopment (residential or otherwise) occurs only when the revenues generated by building and selling or leasing new space exceeds the cost of site acquisition, clearance and new construction. Where there is government intervention, the government assists in assembling land for redevelopment and provides infrastructure to support and service residences and businesses operating in redeveloped areas. Regardless of the extent of government intervention, current users of the land and property to be redeveloped are compensated for the loss of their property. This compensation is almost always paid in the form of cash compensation, although in some countries, such as Japan and Korea, compensation can be paid in the form of plots of land in the project after the site has been cleared and equipped with new infrastructure services. Rarely is compensation made in terms of in-kind transfers—flats for flats, or shops for shops.

In China, since the land is owned by the state, it has rarely been transferred for financial consideration, except when long-term leases were made to foreign investors. In such cases, the local government cleared sites and incurred the cost of relocating and resettling former users, with the proceeds from the leases used to cover these costs.

The situation when inner-city urban land is redeveloped for domestic users has been different. The first and foremost difference is that relocation laws revolve around the principle of in-kind compensation—if a household or business must give up its accommodation, the redeveloper must replace the space in kind. This concept leads to a very high incidence of on-site resettlement of households and businesses. Most cities seem to strive to provide as much on-site relocation as possible; examples abound of virtual 100 percent on-site relocation in Guangzhou, Tianjin, Hangzhou and Shanghai. Other cities, including Beijing, recognize the high costs of in-kind, on-site replacement of housing and have started to develop alternatives aimed at reducing on-site resettlement and increasing the percentage of households willing to move to lower-cost suburban projects.

While reducing the incidence of on-site resettlement works to increase the financial feasibility of redevelopment projects, other government policies also impose financial costs on these projects. In virtually all cities, REDCs charged with carrying out inner-city redevelopment projects have often been required to make significant improvements to the base of community facilities provided in old areas (unless the site involved is very small), and to do so without receiving compensation from the district governments to which these facilities are transferred. Such requirements have imposed considerable financial burdens, making it difficult for REDCs to build feasible redevelopment projects.

Another burden most redevelopment projects must shoulder is the payment of fees, taxes and charges. A myriad of exactions is levied on real estate development projects. In Guangzhou, most inner-city real estate developers assume that taxes, fees and charges will comprise at least 20-25 percent of total project costs.21/

The high incidence of in-kind and on-site resettlement, entitlements, heavy requirements for the provision of community facilities at no cost to local district governments, and the payment of numerous fees, taxes and charges, makes it difficult for REDCs to undertake redevelopment projects. Unless they are permitted to redevelop cleared sites at substantially higher densities, projects are financially feasible only if the price of commodity housing or commercial space can be aggressively marked up to provide enough revenue to carry the cost of project development, including the provision of replacement housing. In some instances, the associated high markups might not be feasible and the purchasers of commodity housing units

---

21/   This topic is reviewed further in Chapter III.

pursue other alternatives. *To the extent that these "clawbacks" are due to the fact that the REDCs receive their land outside the market economy, paying little or nothing for acquiring rights, the issue is best dealt with by forcing them to switch to leasehold agreements; transparency and fairness is the issue, not the payment of fees based on the possession of land.*

An Overview of Redevelopment Projects

This part of the report reviews policies and practices in use in a range of Chinese cities and assesses alternative policy options for improving the financial feasibility urban residential redevelopment. The survey is based on case studies prepared on redevelopment projects in Fuzhou, Guangzhou, Hangzhou, Shanghai and Tianjin. Annex 2 provides detailed information on these projects, which, in spatial terms, have tended to avoid the oldest and densest core areas of the city, except in the case of Fuzhou.

Over the past several years, missions have gone to Beijing, Fuzhou, Guangzhou, Hangzhou, Shanghai and Tianjin to assess housing and land development practices and issues. As a result, 11 detailed cases of redevelopment projects have been assembled. These are listed in Table 1.7. Most projects were started between 1985 and 1987 and were completed within the past two to three years. The projects range in size from 0.5 to 29 hectares, and after completion, range in size up to 737,000 m² of constructed space. There is considerable variation in terms of the percentage of former residents which were resettled on the site, ranging from 0 to 100 percent.

Table 1.7: PROFILE OF REDEVELOPMENT CASE STUDIES

Project name	City	Date started	Site area (ha)	Built area Old (m²)	New (m²)	% On-site resettled
An Deng	Fuzhou	1987	0.5	6,213	0	0
Jin Hua	Guangzhou	1986	29.0	335,000	737,000	90
Xiao Fuqing	Hangzhou	1985	0.7	6,000	15,417	100
Hu Lang Garden	Shanghai	1985	1.7	12,589	84,000	100
Hui Yi Garden	Shanghai	1984	1.3	8,630	8,250	0
Jian Guo	Shanghai	1985	1.9	26,221	88,400	0
Ordinary Citizen	Shanghai	1985	16.5	116,040	325,000	90
Tian He	Shanghai	-	0.5	13,880	17,200	45
Ying Xiang	Shanghai	1985	5.5	33,000	190,000	86
Pingshan Road	Tianjin	1985	1.4	8,756	33,967	100
Wujiayao	Tianjin	1985	3.4	15,715	61,319	100

Source: Redevelopment project surveys, 1991, 1992.

Table 1.8 illustrates the project densities before and after redevelopment. In all but two cases (An Deng, where the site was converted to a park, and Hui Yi Garden, where a high-income project was developed), redevelopment took place at considerably higher densities. On average, the FAR of the projects increased by an average of 151 percent. The greatest increases took place in Shanghai, where the density of development increased by 567 percent for Hu Lang Garden and 477 percent for Ying Xiang. These project statistics illustrate that developers have been successful in overcoming urban planning policies aimed at reducing inner-city development densities. The higher densities have enabled REDCs to construct and sell commodity housing to finance their projects. Before turning to the actual financial performance of these projects, we need to consider the process and approach of redevelopment.

Table 1.8: PRE- AND POST-REDEVELOPMENT FLOOR AREA RATIOS

Project	City	FAR before	FAR after	Percent increase
An Deng	Fuzhou	1:1.24	1:0.00	-
Jin Hua	Guangzhou	1:1.15	1:2.54	120.9
Xiao Fuqing	Hangzhou	1:0.81	1:2.08	156.8
Hu Lang Garden	Shanghai	1:0.74	1:4.94	567.6
Hui Yi Garden	Shanghai	1:0.66	1:0.63	-4.5
Jian Guo	Shanghai	1:1.38	1:4.65	237.0
Ordinary Citizen	Shanghai	1:0.70	1:1.97	181.4
Tian He	Shanghai	1:2.78	1:3.44	123.7
Ying Xiang	Shanghai	1:0.60	1:3.46	476.7
Pingshan Rd.	Tianjin	1:0.63	1:2.43	285.7
Wujiayao	Tianjin	1:0.46	1:1.80	291.3
Average		1:1.01	1:2.54	151.5
Average excluding An Deng		1:1.11	1:2.79	151.4

Source: Redevelopment project surveys, 1991, 1992.

An Overview of Compensation and Relocation Policies

The most critical determinant of the financial feasibility of redevelopment projects is how the owners and tenants of demolished housing are compensated. The exact nature of this compensation, in terms of the size and quality of the replacement housing, where such housing is sited and what kinds of temporary accommodation are provided, largely determines the costs of redevelopment projects. This section outlines relocation policies followed in a variety of Chinese cities through early 1992 (see Annex 3).

In most instances, but with some exceptions (Box 1.9), the redevelopment of any site begins with a careful and protracted negotiated assessment of property compensation.

Box 1.9: THE FUZHOU REDEVELOPMENT MODEL OF RESIDENTIAL NEIGHBORHOODS

Fuzhou has tried to overcome some of the hurdles created by conventional housing redevelopment projects, which account for 40-50 percent of total land redeveloped, and thus has increased the proportion of land redeveloped (as a percent of all new land development) to a relatively high yearly average of over 40 percent. Elsewhere, 25-30 percent is the norm. One option adopted in Fuzhou is to encourage the redevelopment of sites leased to foreign joint ventures. These areas now account for 30-40 percent of all land redevelopment. In addition, *in situ* "self-help" redevelopment by enterprises or by neighborhood block is promoted, with commercial use of ground space permitted as an added incentive. Ten to 20 percent of all redeveloped land now follows this pattern. The conventional system is thus curtailed, as are the onerous compensation arrangements associated with such planning strategies.

Source: Fuzhou State Land Administration Bureau.

While practices vary from city to city, the principles generally are similar, and are dictated by municipal and provincial statute. The resulting compensation depends on the ownership of the structure to be demolished. In the case of municipally owned properties, the typical pattern is for the developer to provide replacement housing. Sometimes the units are located on the site, and in other cases, they are located in a new project area.

The actual negotiations take place between the REDC and building owners. In the case of private owners, the REDCs negotiate directly with them and payments go to each and every individual owner. Compensation proceeds can be used to purchase a new unit or owners can forgo compensation and, instead, exchange their property ownership right for the right of occupancy in municipally owned rental housing. In the case of units owned by enterprises, negotiations are with the enterprise, not the tenant, and the payments or exchanges take place between the enterprise and the REDC. After resettlement, the enterprises are free to set new rents. In most instances, new rents increase to partially reflect the higher costs of the units. In cases where the municipality owns the units, the housing authority negotiates with the developer over the level of compensation. Rental rates for the tenants usually remain at the same level on a per m² basis.

Looking Back: The Government's Rationale for Urban Land Management Reform During the Transition to a Regulated Market Economy

As in most sectors, the Government's agencies charged with land and real estate management have had no unified vision of issues and options.22/ Particularly at the national level, there is no urban development ministry or systems reform commission overseen by a vice-premier that can encourage all relevant actors to agree on what needs to be done and by whom. The problem at the local level is less severe, because "urban construction" is under the supervision of one vice-mayor and because metropolitan areas are administered as single

---

22/ Chapter VI suggests that this situation is now changing.

jurisdictions, without competing central cities and independent suburbs. Even so, no vice-mayor has the authority to oversee land management, if that rubric is broadly defined to include *all* the issues and actions required for thoroughgoing systems reform.

This fragmentation results in a set of partial reform agendas, often working at cross-purposes with one another, and uninformed by the need to overhaul the land management system in a comprehensive manner. What should that agenda consist of, if the overarching objective is to maximize the contribution of the real estate sector to the effort to create an internationally competitive network of cities and towns working within a regulated market economy?

China's overall reform agenda needs to focus on five major objectives. First, a framework that encourages rapid, noninflationary growth is needed, along with strong central macroeconomic management institutions to implement it. Second, sectoral policies are required to guide the provision of local and regional infrastructure, so as to lessen the constraints on economic activity, while promoting the wider use of beneficiary financing. Third, an adequate "safety net," financed by the broadest possible revenue base, must be provided for the unemployed, the sick, the disabled, the retired, and the poor. Fourth, economic transactions should be shaped, to the greatest extent possible, by market signals generated in competitive markets free of barriers to trade. Finally, economic development must take place in a manner consistent with environmental protection.

These objectives all have implications for urban land management. Macroeconomic considerations require enterprise reforms that force businesses, particularly state-owned enterprises, to operate within hard-budget constraints, forgoing subsidies such as tax relief and nonpayment of debts. Enterprises must be able to change product lines, the mix of inputs, and locations so as to respond to market demand. Such flexibility would allow existing businesses to relocate from inappropriate locations, in part assisted by the proceeds from the resource value of the older, more valuable sites relinquished. *This would, in turn, allow existing and new personal and producer services greater opportunity to expand in the downtown core of China's cities, where such activities are seriously underdeveloped.*

The goal of progressively removing infrastructure constraints, while devising ways to increase beneficiary contributions to finance the required investments, also has implications for urban land management. The development of urban areas is dependent, in part, on the provision of adequate serviced land and of related trunk infrastructure. The urban planning and budgeting practices followed at the local level have serious implications for economic efficiency as well as consumer welfare. Practices developed for a simpler "command" economy, where local and central government functions were not sharply differentiated, are increasingly out of step with the emerging demand-driven economic system, where local governments are largely self-financed.

The introduction of "safety net" programs that provide worker housing and social security benefits independent of any given place of employment is a prerequisite for the better use of enterprise assets and the revenues derived from the use of those assets. This, in turn, will allow urban land use rights to business users to be priced and traded like any other commodity, and for "affordability" concerns involved to be set aside as irrelevant. Social protection of family incomes will also enable housing demands to be duly reflected through market signals, rather than treated as a near-free good. With the emergence of explicit market prices for land users, achieving the fourth goal—competitive markets driven by deregulated prices—will be facilitated.

Environmental considerations require a set of interrelated actions in the field of urban land management. It is important to expedite the relocation of polluting factories from residential areas, protect ecologically sensitive locations, selectively upgrade neighborhoods slated for preservation on historical or cultural grounds, and ensure that peri-urban development does not create land use patterns that threaten unnecessarily the agricultural sector or make the provision of infrastructure excessively costly.

Overall, as explicit land prices emerge, land users' willingness to pay will depend, in part, on interrelated government decisions on rules affecting property rights, planning restrictions, infrastructure availability, tax laws and regulations, and the availability of up-to-date cadastral information.

By this standard, the priorities of key government agencies to date have been inadequate. The principal actors in urban land management are SLA, MoC, and the Ministry of Finance (MOF), along with their subordinate agencies at the local level. Clearly involved, as well, are those agencies that supervise state-owned and collectively owned enterprises in the industrial and services sector, as well as nonprofit institutions (Annex 4).

MoC, at the central level, and the Construction Commissions, at the local level, has placed highest priority on developing and overseeing the implementation of metropolitan "master plans" that set out the general outline of future trunk infrastructure, provide for the pattern of permissible (large-area) land uses, and set limits on the overall expansion of the built-up area. Within this framework, district and subdistrict plans often provide for more exacting use and density controls. The REDCs, as discussed in Chapter III, fall under the jurisdiction of the Commissions, as does the registration of buildings and the enforcement of building codes. Operating in a system within which land is largely allocated administratively, the Construction Commissions and their supervising Ministry view the actual requisition of a land plot for an activity as only the last step in a process otherwise controlled by them (once SPC and other economic control agencies have approved a given investment). Their top priority, in the reform, has been to continue to do what they have done, but to do so more "scientifically" and to exercise, on occasion, more control than in the past. For example, compiling and updating a cadaster of building registrations is identified by these agencies as a reform objective, as is the introduction of GIS to facilitate project preparation, and the eventual provision of zoning or quasi-zoning plans for each part of the city. However, enabling market-led development by redirecting infrastructure investments, providing land users with the right to choose where to locate, letting prices regulate and control land use densities, and facilitating the recycling of land (and limiting pressure on greenfield development) through the creation of redevelopment strategies, are perceived to have lower priority. In sum, these agencies have acted as if conventional land transactions, as found in market economies, are likely to emerge only on an exceptional basis, at least for the foreseeable future. As documented in Chapter VI, though, this "framework" may change dramatically as a result of policy work currently under way.

SLA, created in 1986 after "exceptionally large" areas of cultivated land were converted to other uses, is the result of a merger of personnel previously working for construction and agricultural commissions. Their key responsibilities are to monitor and strictly control land consumption at the project and macro area level, while implementing land requisition procedures within the administratively allocated system. They are also charged with developing and updating *land* cadasters in urban and rural areas.

Reflecting the agency's original mandate to control the conversion of rural to urban land, and hence preserve cultivable land; and reflecting, as well, the fact that the staff was recruited largely from specialists in agricultural land use, the Administration places high priority on control of "wasteful" land use in rural areas, and the preservation and reclamation of cultivable land, at the project and citywide level, through administratively determined norms and quotas, enforced and monitored at different levels of government (depending on the amount of land requisition involved). Various fees and charges have been introduced to finance land reclamation and deter "excessive" requisition demands. This approach has little "market" content, however, and reflects the concerns of planners in the late 1950s, who viewed "wasteful" land requisition as an administratively created problem, requiring administrative solutions. Until 1992, the Administration measured successful performance principally by the extent to which the enforcement of rules minimized the loss of cultivable land.

SLA also monitors and attempts to control urban *land*-use conversions, though these usually involve a change of *building* use or ownership, rather than vacant land (thus placing SLA bureaus in conflict with their Construction Commission counterparts). While acknowledging the need to supervise the nascent market in the leasing of land use rights, they have focused more on technical changes (how to prepare lease documents, and how to develop the valuation procedures needed to determine "reservation" prices for leases) than on developing strategies that would promote the rapid emergence of land markets with explicit prices and clear property rights (including the trading of land use rights among existing occupants of administratively allocated land). This too is changing. By 1992, a commitment to promote land leasing as a *major* component of reform became clear both at the central level and in selected cities.

MOF has had two "reform" objectives: to minimize the loss of tax revenues that may result from the introduction of explicit land prices, as these create exemptions that impinge on business enterprise taxable income; and, where land revenues do become explicit, to ensure that these are monitored and, wherever possible, shared with the central government. The emergence of land markets, per se, has not been viewed as a high priority except to the extent that reforms enlarge the state's revenue sources.

As subsequent chapters make clear, in the past these agencies supported a number of "reforms" in cities across China that were disarticulated and did little to advance systems reform as defined in this report. More often than not, "reform" in practice meant greater control over land-use activities, and the refinement of mechanistic tools and techniques, with the hope of improving the operation of the administrative allocation system inherited from the past. A significant reevaluation of objectives and policies is now taking place, for reasons to be discussed further.[23]

Why does the "vision" of central agencies really matter? Within the present system, the Center passes general laws or executive regulations that often impose conditions affecting reform. Cities must prepare Master Plans and have these approved by the State Council; they are required to follow land use tax schemes that ignore local conditions and bar experimentation; land requisition and even investment projects are often subject to central approval; and, until recently, trading of land use rights was forbidden and could not, therefore, allow for the emergence of land markets. Norms and guidelines issued by central urban planners have intimidated local authorities, who have often treated these as legally binding. The fact that local authorities actually prepare the detailed implementation regulations, and the fact that these localities have often found creative ways to undermine central supervision, means that some inappropriate practices mandated or suggested by the Center have been modified to fit local "realities." But these local adaptations are often illegal and may subject local authorities to disciplinary action. This is hardly a healthy state of affairs.

What should the Center's role be? Simply put, to promote regulated autonomy. Issues such as who really holds title to the state land, and how the roles of MoC and SLA are to be defined, require central direction. The fiscal framework in place must be clarified, as must regulations involving the environment. Beyond that, the Center should remove obstacles to market reform and deregulate urban planning on a selective basis (e.g., eliminate the requirement that cities produce static Master Plans subject to State Council approval; concentrate on disseminating best practices gathered from domestic and international experience, with a competitive local economy as a key objective; while strengthening township planning regulations in peri-urban areas, now subject to limited supervision).

Subsequent chapters first review the theory and international experience on the functioning of urban land markets. They then discuss in more detail what has been accomplished to date under the broad rubric of urban land management reform, what reassessments the Chinese authorities have themselves begun to make, and what remains to be done. The range of reforms involved is large and interrelated. Prices and property rights must be redefined, laws must be clarified, planning regulations must be reviewed, and the whole process of urban land use planning and legal and planning institutions must be extensively reformed.

---

[23]   SLA has produced an internal report (dated October 1991) identifying the need to administer the urban land management process in a holistic fashion. The State Council (Cabinet) Policy Research Office has also produced a new report on land reform, whose contents are confidential. MoC expects to produce a similar type of report by June 1992, under the leadership of the Center for Policy Research. Other key players, including MOF, have so far failed to take active policy research initiatives.

II. URBAN LAND PRICE BEHAVIOR IN A MARKET ECONOMY: AN INTRODUCTION

Economic Model of Land Price Behavior

This section outlines a relatively simple economic "model" of how land prices in different locations are determined by market forces—a model on which general consensus among economists would exist. This model would be applicable to a regulated market economy in China. The second section of the chapter reviews available evidence on the actual behavior of land prices in a range of economies around the world.

In simple terms, the market price of any productive assets—including land—will be determined by the expected future flow of income, or returns, to be yielded by the asset. The technique of discounting, using an appropriate interest rate, is applied to convert the future revenue stream into the "present value" of the asset.[1]

Postponing, for the moment, the issue of the spatial pattern of land prices, many factors affect the price of land. Whoever invests in land does so with alternative investment opportunities in mind. This means that land prices respond to the paucity or abundance of attractive alternative investments, the tax treatment of all such investment opportunities, and expectations about the yields of such alternatives over a long period of time. If land supplies available for urban development are severely restricted, relative to expected demand, or if financial assets yield relatively unattractive rates of return, then the expected annual yields from land may be relatively enormous and prices will be commensurately large. If, on the other hand, developable land supplies are viewed as relatively abundant and if alternate investment, after taxes, are viewed as competitive, then prices and their rate of increase will be more moderate in scope.

Tokyo and Seoul provide excellent examples of urban land price trends influenced by factors involving a number of apparently unrelated decisions. Yukio Nogushi compared the price of inner-city sites in London and Tokyo and found that, per m², Tokyo's

---

[1] The price of land, then, is the sum of actual or unrealized earnings from that land, per time period, discounted in each case by an appropriate discount factor that translates these into "present worth or value." Expressed as a formula,

$$(1) Po = \sum_{t=0}^{\infty} \frac{Rt}{(1+i)^t}$$

where Po = present price,
    Rt   =   earnings in any given year,
    t   =   the number of years involved (here expressed as o = the present and ∞ = infinity)
    i   =   discount or interest rate considered appropriate.

prices were 40 times higher than London's.2/ To a lesser extent, the same proved true for commercial properties. However, annual per m² *rents* differed by only a factor of two. What appeared to be at work was a pattern of annual rental increases that rose in step with the (differential) growth of the two economies, while land prices in Tokyo seemed very susceptible to "speculative bubbles" that allowed the ratio of prices to rents (i.e., the flow of expected future rents and the expected level of interest rates utilized to discount such rents into "present values") to deviate dramatically between the two cities, particularly during the period 1986-89, when Japan's interest rates fell sharply. Japanese bank practices, willingness to lend heavily against land used as collateral valued at ever-rising levels, added fuel to the speculative frenzy. This exacerbated the impact of other local constraints operating in Tokyo, including the relatively large amount of land within the city subject to explicit (planning regulations) or implicit (tax regulations involving land) penalties discouraging rural-urban conversion. Land prices grew at unprecedented rates. Land price trends in Seoul reflect the complementary impact of local planning practices, restricting serviced land development described above, and financial sector policies that provided relatively low after-tax rates of return for those holding financial assets, thus inducing investors to readjust their wealth portfolio toward real estate acquisition.3/ As a result, Seoul's average annual land price increases far exceeded such predictors as the growth rate of nominal GDP in the municipality.

Certain underlying facts cannot be denied, however. Land price increases are a normal and expected feature of urban development. Using data from land markets in developed economies, where constraints are relatively small and alternative investment opportunities are relatively ample, one can confidently assert that land values will grow, in nominal terms, at least as fast as economic development pressures dictate. If an urban economy expands at 10 percent per year, then urban land prices will almost inevitably respond to that by growing by at least that rate. By contrast, in a stagnant economy, expanding at only 1 or 2 percent per year, or experiencing a recession where output is actually declining, then, all other things being equal, land prices will mimic the underlying economic development "fundamentals" and increase more slowly.

Similarly, if an economy undergoes a fundamental set of "shocks," including a massive increase in remittances from abroad, a drastic change in the rate of return on financial instruments, or a sudden change in the "rules of the game" under which land is made available for development, then investors will react rapidly, creating land "booms or busts" that would only surprise urban policymakers ignorant of the interconnected nature of the urban economy. *The worst possible response to such a "crisis" is to view the evaluation of land prices as an isolated "land management" issue, when, in fact, a far wider agenda is at stake.*

2/   Yukio Nogushi, "Land Problems in Japan," *Hitotsubashi Journal of Economics*, Vol. 31, No. 2, December 1990, pp. 73-86.

3/   B. Renaud, *Compounding Financial Repression with Rigid Urban Regulations: Lessons of the Korea Housing Market*, World Bank, Report No. INU21, June 1988.

For the sake of simplicity, land prices can be viewed as having two basic components: current use value and potential reuse value (capital gains). Owners of a nonproductive resource, such as vacant land, must be compensated for not developing (or transferring for development) land in the present period. That compensation comes in the form of as-yet-unrealized "capital gains" that emerge in monetary form when the land is sold. Developed land yields explicit or implicit use rents. In between, land can appreciate because realizable rents *and* future appreciation through resale will enter into value calculations.

From a spatial perspective, capital gains drive land prices at the urban periphery, while the stream of rents is the key determinant of land in developed areas. This leads one directly to the need to differentiate between the land values across space as well as the value *changes* at different distances from the CBD.

Implicit in the discussion that follows is the assumption that, unlike sectors such as agriculture, urban development follows fairly standard spatial patterns. Cities around the world are basically alike, under market-type incentive structures. The reason for this phenomenon has never been fully explained, but one plausible hypothesis can be labeled as the "Ingram paradigm."[4] The first assumption is that the prices of tradeable goods produced in any city reflect world prices, and that the wages paid workers producing such goods are a function of both those uniform prices and of the technology employed, which can vary greatly. Second, the wages of workers producing nontradeable goods are a function of prevailing wages in the tradeable goods sector; the higher the latter, the higher the former. Third, the prices of nontraded goods and services is a function of the wages of workers of nontraded goods and services, with very little leeway provided in terms of technology used, which thus becomes a minor explanatory variable. Fourth, urban infrastructure technology (particularly for large, densely populated cities) has the characteristics of nontraded goods, and is similar across cities around the world. Where real estate and urban infrastructure are involved, the ratio of output prices, input prices and incomes are roughly the same around the world, and vary only in absolute levels. Thus, the behavioral responses expected of producers and consumers are roughly the same around the world, since *relative* price signals and incomes are similar. Chinese cities look very much like American cities, while American farms and Chinese farms have spatial and technology characteristics that are polar opposites. One can thus generalize about cities and label certain types of outcomes as policy-distorted much more easily when discussing city structures than when reviewing other types of spatial behavior.

The easiest way to illustrate this phenomenon is to assume that, within cities, land values and activity densities are radially symmetrical around the city core. Simply put, this allows the analyst to collapse a three-dimensional story into a two-dimensional graph that features prices on the vertical axis and distance from the CBD on the horizontal axis. Experience suggests that the best mathematical expression of land price behavior, under those assumptions, is a negative exponential function; which assumes a constant percentage decline in price per unit of distance from the CBD center:

---

[4] Though never published, Gregory Ingram developed a hypothesis several years ago, and graciously shared his assumptions with the sector study team.

$$(2) V_x = Vo \ e^{-bx}$$

where V_x =   level of activity or price at distance "x" from the CBD,
        Vo =   level at the city center,
        b   =   gradient value representing the proportional change in V for every one-unit change in "x".

Using this formula, one can demonstrate a number of empirical facts:

(a)   The gradient can typically be described as a concave curve peaking at the CBD.

(b)   The gradient flattens out over time, even if the overall absolute average value of prices is increasing.

(c)   That flattening process reflects both the expansion of the city and the relatively more rapid appreciation of land prices in the periphery versus the CBD.

(d)   The gradient declines more slowly in big cities than in smaller ones, implying that the "urban field" of a smaller city ends more abruptly, while that of a metropolitan area obviously covers a larger radius.

(e)   The gradient of "activity" (population, employment) is closely linked to the land price gradient, though land value gradients are consistently *less steep* than "activity" gradients, implying that the user response to price increases (in terms of land use density) is less than 1:1. In other words, the "elasticity of substitution between land and structures is less than unitary."[5]

(f)   Further empirical work suggests that "activity" response to land price gradients is *not* instantaneous, and that the lags in adjustment are large enough (data from the United States and Japan suggest that only about 10 percent of any disequilibrium in the population gradient is corrected each year)[6] that one can expect investment behavior, resulting in job and residential locations/

---

[5]   Estimates of such elasticity of substitution have been calculated for various cities. In Seoul, within the housing sector, the elasticities range from 0.5 to 0.8 (L. Hannah, K. Kim, and E. Mills, "Land Use Controls and Housing Prices in Korea," World Bank, February 1991, processed). For Bogotá, a similar rate, around 0.7, was documented in D. Dowall and T. Treffeisen, "Spatial Transformation in Cities in the Developing World: Multinucleation and Land-Capital Substitution in Bogotá, Colombia," Regional Science and Urban Economics, Vol. 21, 1991. In the United States, values of 0.8 are commonly cited as appropriate "stylized facts."

[6]   E. Mills and K. Ohta, "Urbanization and Urban Problems," in H. Thomas and H. Rosavsky, eds., *Asia's New Giant—How the Japanese Economy Works*, Washington, DC: Brookings Institution, 1976. The adjustment rate in China, given existing policy and institutional constraints, is probably much slower.

relocations, with use density consequences, to continue for several years, *regardless of any other changes in underlying economic or policy variables.* Population and employment locations and densities are always "catching up" with a "moving target" equilibrium land price gradient that leads the way. The rate of adjustment can be accelerated or delayed by policy decisions, often made by decisionmakers in the public sector who have little understanding or interest in real estate development.

Work on a number of large cities across Asia and elsewhere found the difference in land prices between average prime commercial land in the CBD core and exurban land not yet been considered ready for urban development to be roughly 100:1, though CBD prices show enough dispersion that the sample chosen to calculate "the" prime average price will influence the ratio.7/ In cases where impediments to land development are relatively few, exurban land not yet deemed for inclusion into the urban development stream can be assigned an index number of 10. The same land, once considered developable for urban purposes, would have an index number of 30; and, once zoned for officially sanctioned development, the number can reach 60 to 70, while the provision of services will double or triple the figure to an index number of 150-200. By contrast, the average value of prime commercial space would hover around an index number of 800 to 1,000.

By implication, the average annual increase in land prices reflects vastly different growth patterns in the rate of realized or unrealized land values at different distances from CBD (as well as dispersion in increases at any given radius from the CBD). Much of policymakers' concern about urban land prices typically lies less in what is occurring in and around the CBD than in what is occurring in the suburban areas undergoing the transition from rural to low- and medium-level density development. Failure to understand the fundamentals behind land price increases can lead to misguided land price control interventions (Box 2.1).

Land Price Behavior Across Socialist and Market Economies: Evidence from Large Cities

Where dramatic deviations from the above stylized facts are observed, they can generally be linked very closely to the impact of massive planner-led distortions on land markets. For example, de facto public control over recent land development,8/ and the simultaneous imposition of a strictly controlled wide greenbelt around Seoul have raised developable suburban land prices to levels not dissimilar from those in core areas. The price density gradient is,

---

7/   The actual ratios cited are based on field work by David Dowall and colleagues in various Asian countries. However, in cities like Tokyo, subject to a mass of disincentives to services land development, the ratio between land around Shinjuku Station and land 50 to 60 kilometers away is 350:1. (G. Tolley, "Urban Land Prices and Land Use in Market Economies," 1992 processed.)

8/   Renaud reports that in 1989 only 22 percent of residential development in Seoul is controlled by the private sector (B. Renaud, "Confronting a Distorted Housing Market: Can Korean Policies Break With the Past," op. cit.).

Box 2.1: THE RELATIVE ADVANTAGES OF CBD AND SUBURBAN LOCATIONS

The CBD has one enduring advantage, traced back to the time when urban areas emerged as major centers of economic power. Central locations appeal to economic activities that need face-to-face communications with customers or suppliers, given the state of communications and transport technology in place. In developed countries, these centralized activities are now generally restricted to executive functions, dealing with nonroutine decisions that often require rapid updating of information based on instant access to external expert professional advice. These are largely service sector activities and include certain functions related to government, law, accounting, insurance, banking, trading, advertising, special-interest associations, consultancy, and related support services (hotels, restaurants, entertainment). Some specialized types of manufacturing activity can also benefit from core locations because of the need to have access to "external economies" that are reaped by proximity to other types of nearby firms. These include firms producing unstandardized goods, continually changing products, using little space, and able to avoid significant commitments to fixed capital investments. These enterprises share an overriding characteristic: instability and uncertainty associated with swiftly changing product lines, driven by highly unpredictable demand. High-fashion clothing and publishing are but two examples. In each case, these activities must be able to tap a wide pool of nearby skills and facilities on very short notice, and do so in locations where sufficient demand exists to make such ancillary suppliers available at relatively low cost. Given swiftly changing product lines, such businesses cannot afford to invest in self-contained, large plants filled with extensive equipment. They do not require large amounts of inexpensive land. Instead, these management-intensive operations rely heavily on outside suppliers for goods or services, supplies that typically demand face-to-face communication to specify the exact nature of the specified inputs required. Letters, telexes, facsimiles, or telephone calls alone cannot, in these cases, adequately satisfy the requirements involved in these buyer-seller relationships. Physical proximity, or clustering, is an economic necessity.

Why then does decentralization proceed across the world's cities? Because, for many activities, the elements of uncertainty and the need for frequent and speedy communication, as defined above, have declined or have simply become inapplicable. The revolution in infrastructure technology and the massive investments that have accompanied it, primarily in transportation and communications, have rendered CBD locations less relevant, releasing its land for the new uses created by the growing producer services sector.

Suburban locations, in most instances, are vastly less expensive places to locate industrial plants and residences, along with many personal service activities. In most developed countries, even exurban locations in metropolitan areas or relatively isolated regional centers (Omaha, Nebraska in the field of telemarketing, credit card processing, and hotel reservations) can depend on the nation's accumulated stock of regional trunk infrastructure investments to facilitate rapid development. In such suburban, exurban and regionally isolated environments, the population's choices concerning preferred residential locations coincides with that of employers. Suburban and exurban locations allow consumers access to relatively inexpensive residential amenities, including housing space, yards, and recreational opportunities that cannot be matched by close-in locations. The population that remains clustered in and around the CBD has become increasingly idiosyncratic: "footloose" households that place great emphasis on the core-area man-made recreational opportunities and the ethnic diversity available in and around the CBD, along with others who weigh the spatial implications of policy distortions (rent control in central areas; planner restrictions on low-income, single-family or apartment dwellings in the suburbs) and decide that suburbanization is not a viable option.

---

essentially, flat and thus incentives to redevelop the CBD, any other factors aside, are dramatically diminished by the inability of original occupants to acquire the rights to consume more land, per unit of expenditure, in the periphery (Figures A1.4 and A1.5).

The juxtaposition, in turn, of the population density gradients of Paris, four Chinese cities and Moscow, measured from the CBD, reveals that Paris' pattern is very much in accord with the stylized facts (Figures A1.6 and A1.7). St. Petersburg and Moscow, by contrast, have *positive* (and counterintuitive) density gradients which reflect a land development policy that has ignored inherent land values in determining the location of activity over several decades (Figures A1.8-A1.11). In particular, note should be taken that St. Petersburg, Moscow, and Warsaw deliberately reserved large amounts of prime land, close to the CBD, for low-value nonresidential uses (primarily industrial and warehouse), invested enormous amounts of money in trunk infrastructure linking the core to the distant suburbs, and then drove large numbers of core-area residents to peripheral locations, where combinations of walk-up apartments and high-rise structures were erected in configurations exactly like those found in close-in residential neighborhoods outside the historic core. The consequences of this were not merely aesthetic. This deliberate disregard for consumer preferences, and for the necessary trade-offs between loss of accessibility and improved amenities, including greater residential space at distant locations, meant that the "market value" of the more distant communities probably does not cover their investment costs. *Neglect of elementary economics has created a potentially large stock of properties yielding negative value added*! Box 2.2 suggests that even some Western economies suffer from excessive regulation and uninformed urban planning.

Box 2.2: STOCKHOLM'S HOUSING RENTAL PRICE GRADIENT

Stockholm operates largely within a municipally controlled land lease system. Land for residential development is leased largely to nonprofit municipal corporations at nominal rates, who build rental units. *The Municipality can force housing development to occur in areas which would be rejected as undesirable if "market" rules applied and developers had a greater choice of sites.* Construction and rental or homebuyer mortgage finance is heavily subsidized. *However, the building materials industry is organized along oligopolistic lines and is unregulated, charging "market" prices for its products.* Rents are set yearly so that the average rent per m² for the *pooled* stock of any one development company covers its costs and the company gains no "profit." Clearly, different companies have housing stocks of different vintage. Newer companies, whose stock is relatively new and, almost always, built in outlying areas, have much higher average costs than older companies, whose stock is largely concentrated in the core of the city. The rent-setting rules, set on a company-by-company basis, yields a perverse result: apartments that are nearly identical in characteristics, except location, carry very different rents. A unit in central Stockholm is cheaper than one built (more recently) in the suburban areas. The price gradient thus behaves in a perverse way, contradicting the presumptions of accepted land use models created with market economies in mind. As in the Post-Socialist economies, deregulation of prices would vastly increase the value of older, core-centered housing and yield many suburban development unmarketable except at deep discounts that might not even recover investment costs.

Perhaps surprisingly, Figure A1.6 also illustrates the fact that some Chinese cities, in spite of their exposure to 40 years of "Socialist" urban construction policies, resemble market-economy outcomes in some respects, and have not merely reproduced the anomalous patterns found in the Russian Federation or Poland. The reasons for these divergences are explored further in Chapters III and IV.

Interestingly enough, during the last five years, researchers in command economies undergoing the transition to a regulated market have been able to mimic the stylized facts referred to above by the use of "scientific" formulas that give varying weights to accessibility, amenities, and infrastructure availability. They began by noticing that urban land price gradients in Chinese cities, around 1950, corresponded exactly with the predictions of the simple model discussed earlier. In Beijing, for example, land prices per m^2 in 1950, averaged across 18 land classes, varying from most desirable and accessible to those outside the area of immediate urbanization pressure, yielded a predictable land gradient and a ratio of 100:1. Data from Guangzhou and Tianjin provided roughly similar orders of magnitude.9/

In China, SLA published "Procedures for Land Classification in Cities and Towns" (1989), to direct the classification of land values across China's urban areas. Each land parcel is classified by aggregating a large set of land-value-determining elements, weighted through a variety of methods ranging from the intuitive to the "scientific," using regression analysis. The key elements included various obvious factors such as transport conditions, infrastructure services, environmental conditions, commercial development, and population density. As summarized by the urban land management report prepared by the Chinese Academy of Social Sciences, results from cities like Shanghai, Beijing, Tianjin, Nanjing, and Ningbo all exhibit the negative land price gradient pattern predicted by the theoretical discussion and market signals summarized above.10/ St. Petersburg also performed a similar exercise in 1992 and, again, the synthetic land price gradient is consistent with outcomes found in market economies, though few would agree that the implicit extremely high absolute values would be "validated" by market transactions negotiated freely among individuals and/or enterprises facing current hard budget constraints.11/

Unfortunately, these exercises, while useful introductions to the subject, are misguided *if they assume that planners can estimate absolute land prices, parcel-by-parcel, by the use of formulas* and if these exercises are not constantly updated to take into account real transaction data (Box 2.3). Land prices, regulatory and policy impediments aside, can only emerge spontaneously within market economy frameworks, as individual sellers and buyers bargain with one another in much the same way that other commodity markets operate. Policymakers in post-command economies are spending an inordinate amount of time trying to outguess market outcomes. Instead, as Chapter III suggests, they should be focusing their attention on facilitating the spontaneous emergence of market prices, and enabling existing users of property to release plots, where potential gains to existing users coincide with the expected gains to new occupants. This conclusion appears to be gaining acceptance in China's coastal cities, after the rapid increase in land-lease activity proved the limited utility of standard land

---

9/   State Land Administration.

10/   Institute of Finance and Trade Economics, Chinese Academy of Social Sciences, Urban Land Use and Management in China, draft final report (processed), Beijing, June 1991.

11/   Alan Bertaud, personal communication.

prices as a predictor of "real world" outcomes. The top priority of systemic reform in urban land markets lies in price and property rights reform. There are no shortcuts.

Box 2.3: STANDARD LAND PRICES IN CHINESE CITIES

In the case of China, the so-called standard land prices are set across five to eight zones, any within each zone, prices are set at different levels depending on current use. A commercial enterprise set next door to a residential user may carry a differential theoretical price burden which is in the neighborhood of 25:1. Unless these "prices" are used as very rough guidelines, sensitive to the fact that land prices (in a market economy) can drop precipitously from a high-access road to a more isolated land site one block away, "zone" considerations aside, they will add little information and provide planners and regulators with bogus specificity with respect to land transactions. These exercises are acceptable as academic experiments. They may even alert urban planners that in high-access zones and locations there are many users whose relocation would be desirable.

III. FIRST THINGS FIRST: PRICES AND PROPERTY RIGHTS

Do Urban Land Prices Exist in China?

The prevailing model of land allocation in urban China evolved during the 1950s, following the establishment of the People's Republic in 1949. The most simplistic descriptions of the process of land allocation have implied that urban land became a free good, and that this fact is still true today, complicating any move from a command economy to a regulated market economy, within which land would become a tradeable commodity like any other. The truth is that, while the process followed prior to the introduction of urban economic reform in 1984 may be interpreted as confirming such a hypothesis, the reality today is different and land in urban areas increasingly has a "value" ranging from plots with prices revealed by "black market" property transactions; to those that have prices that are more clearly sanctioned (land lease contracts); and those that can be described as quasi-market prices in nature (land requisition from rural communities; compensation paid to those land users involved in reuse and redevelopment projects; and the value of land assets transferred by bankrupt enterprises in the process of merger with profitable enterprises). Today, real estate market researchers can draw rough actual land value maps for any city in China, on the basis of the indicators listed above. At the margin, market forces are emerging, even if the scope of the market is limited to particular cities or areas of cities, and especially if stringent definitions of "market prices" (one-on-one deregulated transactions) are used as the standard of evaluation.

Furthermore, along with these price signals, there is a real estate market constituency in place, ready to promote change. In China's cities, there is an active real estate development market emerging, with a small but increasing proportion of property developed on a for-profit basis by domestic and foreign-funded business enterprises; and a growing number of occupants ready to acquire that property on commercial terms. *The key issue, then, is not how to invent prices for a free good but how to introduce mechanisms that expand the scope of explicit market prices, and provide for the property rights that must accompany them, allowing these to emerge as expeditiously as possible.*

The Abolition of Urban Land Prices and Property Rights: A Retrospective Look

The 1982 Constitution, written prior to the liberalization of the urban economy, nationalized all urban land, leaving rural land in the hands of the local "collectives" that emerged in the aftermath of the collapse of the "commune" system. In fact, private urban property rights, except for those over pre-1949 individually owned housing stock, ceased after 1953, in the political upheaval that coincided with the Korean War. At that stage, private land was first converted into a joint state-private ownership system and then nationalized by the end of 1956.

Private ownership of rural land, including that in the periphery of the preexisting built-up areas of the cities, was also terminated after 1949. In 1950 the Chinese Agrarian (Land) Reform Law formally confiscated land held by "the landlord class" and vested property in the hands of the cultivating farmers, who were promised title deeds and the right to manage, buy, sell or even rent out land freely, subject only to Government's right to requisition land for urban uses. These rights were reaffirmed in the 1954 Constitution. However, subsequent campaigns led progressively to the "cooperative" movement, when private rural ownership rights were restricted to small plots surrounding farmer housing. This was followed, in 1957, by the creation of People's Communes, which effectively eliminated private property in the countryside, including rights over housing and the surrounding small private plots.

The state continued to claim formal title only to urban and industrial land, but developed procedures for expropriating rural land, as needed for urban development, with compensation paid to former occupants. These procedures, issued by the central Government Administrative Council in 1953 and 1954, were confined to basic guidelines that called for state construction units 1/ to acquire land only as needed, and to avoid encroaching on land suitable for agricultural purposes unless necessary. Other than requiring nominal compensation for land taken, the new users were relieved of the obligation to pay fees for using the newly acquired land. And even the funds used to pay for expropriation were covered out of the state budget, freeing beneficiaries of the constraints imposed by "hard budgets." Actual implementation of these procedures was divided between local authorities and the central industrial ministries, acting individually under the weak supervision of the Government Administrative Council and the People's Committees (governments) at the local level.

Following Soviet practice, the relevant supervising economic planning authorities first approved the investment plans of subordinate enterprises and institutions, and then authorized local land administrative bureaus to acquire land, turning it over to the user free of charge and for perpetuity, but with no rights to exercise the unauthorized transfer of such land to third parties.

Examples quickly proliferated of waste and inefficiency, as users demanded and frequently received far more land than justified by their investment plans. In addition, driven by the desire to create more attractive and "modern socialist cities," local authorities set aside large areas of land for open space, recreational facilities, and large public buildings, and did so

---

1/   In effect, this covered most urban expansion, since private development was quickly limited in scope, and ultimately eliminated.

well ahead of any conceivable mid-term implementation plan.2/ The problems were first evident among the so-called 18 key cities 3/ designated for intensive industrial development during the First Five-Year Plan (1952-57). Many of these were cities with little prior industrial development history. Their built-up areas expanded at often enormous rates, with Zhengzhou, for example, increasing in size ninefold between 1949 and 1957. By the mid-1950s, the central government decided to utilize more fully the existing industrial capacity of older industrial cities, and suburban land acquisition sprees spread to cities like Guangzhou and even Shanghai. Table 3.1 illustrates selective instances of built-up area expansion during this period.

Table 3.1: CHANGE IN THE SIZE OF BUILT-UP AREAS
IN SELECTED CITIES: 1949-57
(km²)

	1949	1957	% growth
Beijing	109	221	103
Xi'an	13	65	392
Zhengzhou	5	52	900
Hefei	5	57	1,007
Wuhan	34 (1953)	130 (1959)	382
Jinan	23	37	61
Shanghai	80	116	45
Tianjin	61	97	59
Nanjing	42	54	29
Fuzhou	11	19 (1960)	73

Source: State Land Administration.

2/ "During the First Five-Year Plan, model plans of large Soviet cities were universally adopted for the planning of all Chinese cities, despite wide variations between Russian and Chinese urban centers with regard to size, type, geographical location, terrain characteristics and cultural attributes. Thus, even the plan for a small workers' town of less than 20,000 inhabitants would include all the urban features and amenities of a large city. These included large municipal public squares with wide central boulevards, east-west axis roads, civic centers for municipal government buildings, district parks, and several sports stadiums. Also, public squares, a typical feature in Soviet cities, became a basic land use characteristic in many plans for Chinese cities. These included municipal squares, district central squares, traffic squares and other squares of special types. All of them occupied large amounts of land. For example, the area of the municipal central squares in the urban plans of Lanchow, Loyang and Harbin exceeded the 9 hectare Tiananmen Square in Beijing. In some cities, the district central squares were planned to be larger than Red Square in Moscow!" (Source: K. Fung, "The Spatial Development of Shanghai," in C. Howe, ed., *Shanghai: Revolution and Development in An Asian Metropolis*, New York: Cambridge University Press, 1982.)

3/ Beijing, Chengdu, Luoyang, Zhengzhou, Wuhan, Xi'an, Zuzhou, Shenyang, Anshan, Datong, Shijiazhuang, Qiqihar, Harbin, Jilin, Changchun, Lanzhou, Taiyuan, and Baotou.

At the microlevel, enterprises and institutions often squandered land, driven by a desire to build up future reserves; guided by Soviet norms and standards that promoted low floor/land area ratios (FAR); encouraged to establish buffer zones between factories and other uses; allowed to set up "security zones" around their plants; and permitted to build self-contained communities that ignored the potential offered by existing nearby city public and commercial facilities.

The distortions permitted and encouraged by this approach soon began to receive widespread publicity. Typically, these individual case studies reported that only 20 percent or less of the land area requisitioned was actually occupied by structures. A 1956 central government assessment of land requisition in selected cities, including Beijing, Changsha, Hangzhou, and Chengdu, reported that 40 percent of the requisitioned areas were taken without justification, even by the nonmarket standards of that date. Central authorities responded in 1958 with new legislation amending earlier land administration regulations, increasing administrative controls over expropriations and individual project requirements. Among the changes introduced, the most significant were the following: (a) the enterprises' request for land (size, location) had to be approved by the same institution responsible for evaluating and approving the investment projects; (b) local governments were given greater discretion in both controlling land allocation and supervising the use of land after expropriation; and (c) the amount of land that any given level of government could allocate to a project was restricted by physical quotas, so that large land allocations would need central government approval.

Over the next two decades, particularly through 1975, the expansion of cities built along Soviet lines slowed dramatically, a factor that should be kept in mind when comparing the characteristic features of Socialist cities across countries (outside China, massive expansion continued). Tables 3.2 and 3.3 provide data for one so-called key city, Beijing, and one traditional coastal center, Guangzhou. Land expropriation in Beijing, which had totaled 205 km^2 from 1952 to 1962, fell to only 35 km^2 between 1962 and 1980. In Guangzhou, land requisition between 1951 and 1960 totaled 8,119 ha, but between 1961 and 1974, dropped to 2,343 ha. Lack of systematic data from other cities prevents generalization, but anecdotal evidence suggests that trend was national in scope. Recently available data provided by SLA summarize the best estimates of cultivable land losses since 1957, and include not only strictly urban activities, but also all other sources of demand, including the growth of the built-up areas of rural communities, the requirements of stand-alone mining districts, and the land taken for interregional infrastructure investments. The data are accompanied by no systematic explanation. They support the hypotheses of the report, however: (a) relatively unfettered, land-consuming development during the first decade of Socialist transformation; (b) a systematic antidevelopmental strategy during the 1960s and 1970s; (c) a return to unfettered growth in the late 1970s and early 1980s; and (d) expansion more mindful of the implicit and explicit cost of

Table 3.2: FARMLAND EXPROPRIATION IN BEIJING: 1949-85

	Expropriated farmland in suburbs (km^2)	Increased urban built-up /a area (km^2)	Ratio of developed land versus acquired land (%)
1949-52	42.11	17.60	41.9
1952-57	106.52	53.80	50.5
1958-62	98.47	64.90	65.9
1962-65	5.35	9.60	178.9
1966-70	8.78	16.60	188.7
1971-75	10.56	17.60	167.0
1976-80	10.03	18.80	187.3
1981-85	23.30	24.60	105.7
Total	305.10	223.50	73.3

/a Developed.

Sources: Beijing Academy of Social Sciences, Urban Institute, "A Study on the Urbanization Process in Beijing Near Suburbs," 1989; and Yu Xuewen, 1986, "Analysis of Urban Construction Land Development in Beijing by Applying Remote-Sensing Technique," *City Planning Review*, 1986-3: 9-14.

Table 3.3: URBAN LAND REQUISITION IN GUANGZHOU (1951-90)

Year	Total land area (ha)	Of which: arable land (ha)	Percent of arable land (%)
1951-55	2,240.12	642.30	28.67
1956-60	5,879.05	3,652.79	62.13
1061-65	832.21	413.57	49.69
1966-70	860.20	234.40	27.24
1971-75	1,054.33	379.59	36.00
1976-80	1,752.90	950.59	754.22
1981-85	2,937.27	953.97	32.47
1986-90	2,645.39	1,808.81	68.37
Total	18,201.48	9,036.02	49.60

Source: Guangzhou Real Estate Bureau.

land in the period after 1984, driven by rising costs, profit-maximizing behavior, and the reimposition of more effective administrative controls.4/

To some degree, the decline in land requisition after 1960 can undoubtedly be ascribed to the refinement of bureaucratic procedures; however, the wholesale relocation of urban land use planning personnel to farms and factories during the Cultural Revolution period (1966-76) makes this unlikely as a primary cause.5/ Instead, the trends are best explained by the drastic decline in "capital construction" during the period in question, combined with an assignment of roughly half those fixed asset investments to the development of "Third Line" factory centers in very remote regions of China, meant to preserve core industrial capacity in case of a nuclear attack aimed at the preexisting industrial centers.6/

The impact created by the period of Soviet-style planning methods was evident beyond greenfield areas. In the name of renewal, some cities, particularly Beijing, were stripped of significant portions of their inherited architectural heritage (though most cities were spared, more through neglect or lack of resources than by conscious intent, this force-fed redevelopment). Tiziano Terzani reports that almost half of the surface of 1949 Beijing was transformed, as traditional *pialos* (arches in marble and painted wood built across streets) and the inner and outer great city walls were systematically destroyed during the 1950s and 1960s.7/ The princely palaces (wang fu) were demolished or drastically altered to fit the requirements of new occupants. Temples became factories or were simply demolished to make way for roads, stadiums, and new structures. During the Great Leap Forward period alone (1958-60), 1,400 factories were opened in the city center. Only the inherited stock of vernacular architecture—courtyard houses, lined up along narrow residential lanes (*hutongs*)—was left. Today, individual "monuments" deemed worth preserving number only 100-200, though *hutong*

4/   According to SLA sources, net loss after reclamation fell from 15.1 million mu in 1985 to 1.0 million mu in 1990. Whereas between 1979 and 1985, 234 million mu of arable land (after reclamation) were taken out of production, only 34.8 million mu suffered the same fate in the period 1985-90. One mu corresponds to 667 m^2.

5/   Hong Kong analysts, in a recent comprehensive report on urban land management practices suggest that during the period covering 1966-76, "... urban land planning and land management organs were rescinded and the urban planners and property managers were either transferred to a lower level or compelled to do manual labor in the countryside or in a factory. Laws and regulations ... [concerning] urban planning and management were criticized as being creatures of the bourgeoisie" (J. Ratcliffe, S. Tsui, and L. Yu, *Land Management in the People's Republic of China: A Research Report on the Present System of Land Management in China*, Hong Kong: Hong Kong Polytechnic, April 1990).

6/   Other assessments of the extent of Third Line investments are even more dramatic. One recent report suggests that from 1960 to the mid-1970s, 73 percent of state investment in capital construction went to these remote locations, resulting in the establishment of 29,000 state enterprises employing one third of the state-owned workers once the program was terminated (Chreod Development Consultants, *Towards Land Management Reform in Shanghai: A Case Study of the Central Core*, Shanghai: Shanghai Urban Planning and Design Institute, March 1991, processed draft).

7/   T. Terzani, *The Forbidden Door*, Hong Kong: Asia 2000 Ltd., 1985.

housing rehabilitation is now being pursued vigorously. What remains of the old city is the Forbidden City, the *hutongs*, and a few temples. Undoubtedly, as previous Bank reports on urban development have acknowledged, Beijing is an "orderly" city, but it has lost much of its distinctive character. There is a cautionary lesson here for cities like Shanghai, which earlier lacked the resources or the opportunity to carry out similarly drastic "renewal." Urban land management reforms need not merely create the new; conservation also has its place, and may well contribute to the economic revitalization of a city center, by providing amenities that, directly or indirectly, enhance the competitiveness of the city as a center of diversified economic activity. It does so by attracting scarce international and national physical and human capital that values the overall urban fabric as a key "amenity" that supplements monetary compensation.

Urban development increased in scale after 1975, but the accelerated economic transformation of the urban sector dates back only to 1984. This point is critical to understanding why China's cities and towns, today, are better placed than their post-Socialist counterparts in adapting urban market management techniques and producing land use outcomes more compatible with a market economy. A core hypothesis of this report, difficult to prove on the basis of the rapid assessment techniques used in preparing sector reports, is that *China's land use planners have had relatively limited opportunities to replicate the practices of the 1950s and that, within the time span of only one decade, they were soon face to face with an embryonic market economy that forced them, however imperfectly, to refocus their efforts and adopt new policies and tools. In addition, the imperative to save arable land reasserted itself.* All this had to be done by the remnants of the original core of urban planners predating the Cultural Revolution and their young apprentices.

Furthermore, and even harder to document, it appears that, striking exceptions aside, *Chinese planners, prior to the internalization of market signals, did not have the investment resources to invest in the regional transport networks necessary to allow the low-density "Socialist" city to expand as originally planned. The bicycle and the bicycle-bus commuting requirements of the working population acted as a land value proxy, forcing suburban development to be more compact than in other Socialist economies, where extensive highways and metropolitan subway systems allowed distant Socialist suburbs to emerge. Furthermore, because the cities examined in this report were systematically denied the resources to fund massive industrial investments in and around old cities, the Soviet syndrome, where valuable land close to the CBD was heavily preempted for new industrial estates, was never fully implemented.* Finally, zones 5-10 km² from the city center, containing lower-density "old-city" developments and later developed as "Socialist" suburbs (with a mix of industrial uses and low-density walk-up apartments) are now targets of redevelopment, densification, and land use change. Though the rate of change is relatively slow, and city-specific in its pace, this will bring the population density profile that radiates out from the CBD of Chinese cities more in line with what is expected in market economies.

At first, instead of promoting land market reform, the central authorities reaffirmed their hostility to land pricing and individual property rights, in favor of administrative solutions. Article 10 of the 1982 Constitution, which banned the sale, lease, or "unlawful" transfer of urban land, was followed by a 1983 State Council (Cabinet) Circular on Preventing the Sale, Buying, and Leasing of Land. The 1986 State Land Administration Law's opening paragraph was emphatic in placing the Government monitoring and control of land use ahead of any other objective. It was only in 1988 that the Constitution and the Land Administration Law formally recognized the right to transfer state-owned land to users who would pay for the rights to use such land, becoming leaseholders. However, one major benefit that emerged from the political disorder that characterized the decades of the 1960s and 1970s was that China's leaders effectively devolved administrative decision-making power over urban development to local authorities. With the endorsement of the 1978 Third Plenum of the Twelfth Party Central Committee, local experimentation with unorthodox reforms became possible, even in the absence of a national set of laws and regulations covering the practices involved. It proved instrumental in accelerating the pace of policy and institutional reform in the urban sector, particularly after urban reforms were explicitly endorsed in and after 1984.[8] This one clear and positive outcome of two decades of intermittent decentralization meant that local autonomy became finally embedded in the Chinese political system.

Local authorities, particularly among the more developed and outward-looking coastal centers, took advantage of this leeway, and experiments in urban land revenue generation and enhanced property rights began to take place. Having no comprehensive framework within which to develop a market-oriented strategy, however, these experiments proved, in retrospect, to be largely fragmentary. That comprehensive framework, along with enabling legislation and regulation, is one of the functions the Center could have performed, but chose not to exercise. The conclusion, then, is that the momentum for reform is building, but that, by the criteria used in this report, much remains to be done.

China's recent urban land management reform has been shaped by factors absent until now in command economies in transition. First, as noted, the massive urban investments led by Soviet-style planning in China's cities were both spatially and temporally contained and were not able to transform most cities as rapidly as was the case in other Socialist states. Moreover, during the last decade, foreign and overseas Chinese investors became important actors in the real estate scene, both downtown and in the suburbs and exurbs. They brought with them a new perspective: that "capitalist" tools could be put to work in reforming a command economy without necessarily threatening the prevailing political order. Greenfield development became more expensive, as land requisition from rural "collectives" was often transformed into a set of negotiable transactions among increasingly equal parties. The key ingredients of market-led enterprise behavior began to emerge from a variety of sources. One quarter of all industrial production is now produced by the township and village enterprises operating largely within the urban field, having no access to preferential policies in the acquisition of inputs, and selling output in a relatively competitive environment that allows for bankruptcy when economic conditions justify such outcomes. Collective and private enterprises have grown in scope, facing largely similar market-determined constraints. The state-owned enterprises, which raise the stiffest challenge to the introduction of market forces, now control

[8] These reforms are documented in *China: Country Economic Memorandum: Planning and Reform in the 1990s*, op. cit.

barely over one half of industrial production, and even they are progressively being exposed to market discipline. China's urban economy was the first among the economies in transition where market prices became dominant and a buyer's market emerged, so that producers could no longer ignore the consequences of neglecting consumer demand. Today, for example, only one third of agricultural output is purchased at fixed prices. Nearly 70 percent of all consumer goods have been deregulated and price controls have been removed from 58 percent of industrial raw materials and producer goods. Producers and managers now have full authority over about two thirds of the country's price decisions. In some provinces (Guangdong, Fujian) and cities (the Special Economic Zones and Wenzhou), inputs and outputs are traded almost entirely within a market system.

Furthermore, central authorities overseeing the unified state budget have been quick to identify price subsidies, forgone tax income and otherwise unnecessary infusions into loss-making enterprises;9/ measure the inventory of unsold goods lying in warehouses, victims of bad marketing decisions;10/ track the enormous amount of unpaid interenterprise debts that have accumulated to date;11/ and realize that the banking sector's likely unrecoverable loans threatened the viability of the country's financial intermediaries. The year 1992 may mark the time when state-owned enterprises, many of which are overstaffed and poorly managed, will be forced to take restructuring seriously. The mechanisms used—mergers between firms with differing levels of profitability; managerial demotions and dismissals; de facto layoffs of redundant workers (who are sent home, receiving only one third of expected monetary compensation); and the creation of subsidiary service enterprises to absorb unneeded manufacturing labor—may not be "first best" solutions from the viewpoint of market-system economists. Given Chinese conditions, however, these events, if not reversed, mean *the "rules of the game" are changing dramatically, reinforcing trends anticipated over the last several years*.

Managers and the supervisory governmental bodies that act as proxy "boards of directors" have now no choice but to behave increasingly as hard-nosed businessmen whose investment decisions—including those involving location and relocation—must respond, more and more, to the same incentives that drive their counterparts in market economies. Urban planners cannot but adapt to this environment. And, from the real estate market's perspective, this situation was immeasurably assisted by the 1984 State Council decision to issue "Temporary Regulations Involving Systemic Reform of the Administration of the Construction Industry," which directed that "urban real estate development companies (REDCs) should be formed to carry out the comprehensive development of urban land and housing" and that these companies

---

9/ Twenty percent of the 1991 unified central-local budget, or Y 88 billion, was devoted to loss-making enterprises, excluding unrecorded tax exemptions and portions of budgetary expenditures under the rubric of "enterprise development funds" that were used to bail out loss-making enterprises.

10/ By June 1991, Y 136 billion worth of goods were stockpiled by state-owned enterprises, adding to commercial inventories equal to three times that amount.

11/ Intercorporate arrears totaled approximately Y 200 billion at the end of 1991.

could transfer serviced land, housing and related facilities on a for-profit basis, acting as business enterprises largely responsible for their profits and losses, even if their initial equity was "public" and thus "ownership" rights were vested in municipal, or other governmental units.

Chapter IV will document the fact that Chinese urban planners are clearly (if selectively) responding to market demand, even if this means radical departures from past practices. That being the case, the first priority is to expand the scope of market forces in the land allocation process, and expect that urban planners will play "catch up" and do so at an increasingly rapid rate. Once convinced, Chinese policymakers have few rivals in the implementation of new approaches. Technical assistance needs aside, the key problem facing urban economic development is enhancing the underlying incentives being set in place. Nevertheless, one should not underestimate the difficulty facing Chinese planners. If, as this report declares, the redevelopment of densely populated areas and the associated massive relocation of factories and warehouses is the key priority in urban land management, then the task will not be achieved in the short or medium term.

The Search for a Third Way: Evaluating Price and Property Reforms to Date 12/

The concept of land as a commodity resurfaced, oddly enough, as early as 1980, at a National Conference on City Planning Work, which proposed the collection of locally retained land use fees as a source of revenue for urban infrastructure development. In 1980, the State Council endorsed the collection of land use fees from foreign-funded ventures. Urban land markets began to be reinvented.

Experiments to date have been modest in scope if one uses a simple and absolute indicator of systemic reform, such as the amount of land use rights that have been sold off as fixed-term leaseholds that give property owners the right to mortgage and transfer their lots. Little of this was leased on the basis of competitive bidding, and most "prices" were merely meant to recover serviced land development costs. Typically in the cities examined, land leased through competitive bids equaled an area only two to five times the size of Beijing's Tiananmen Square. As of August 1991, a total area of only 2,500 hectares of state-owned land had been leased, covering 1,071 tracts, and acquired for Y 2.47 billion (1988-August 1991). This amounts to approximately 3 percent of all annual built-up land expansion in urban areas. MOF received only Y 20 million of this amount. Through the end of 1991, 645 hectares had been leased in Shenzhen, yet *all but 3.5 percent of the land area involved was made available through private treaty or negotiation at nominal average prices, or exempted from payment altogether.* Land actually sold by bidding and auction amounted to 15 hectares between 1987 and 1989, while an additional 11 hectares were subject to bidding in 1990; and 9 hectares were let through bids in 1991. Auctions were discontinued after 1988, out of a declared fear that participants in auctions might bid "irresponsibly" and "distort" market values to the extent that they operated under soft budget constraints. Some sense of the revenue gained from land lease

---

12/   Selective updates, reflecting developments after the preparation missions, are reported in Chapter VI.

sales can be gained from an examination of Table 3.4, while Table 3.5 provides evidence of current market prices and their range (from Y 620/m² to Y 3,012/m²) around the average of Y 1,213/m² or $220/m².

Table 3.4: LAND USE RIGHTS TRANSFER IN SHENZHEN: 1987-91

	1979-87	1987	1988	1989	1990	1991	Total 1987-91
Number of lots		5	110	83	123	324	645
Total land (ha)	8,125.0/a	15.73	225.84	199.78	204.00	308.60	953.95
Of which: Negotiated		10.24	221.87	194.57	193.37	300.00	920.05
		65.1%	98.2%	97.4%	94.8%	97.2%	96.4%
Bidding		4.64	3.08	5.21	10.67	8.60	32.19
		29.5%	1.4%	2.6%	5.2%	2.8%	3.4%
Auction		0.86	0.89	0.00	0.00	0.00	1.75
		5.5%	0.4%	0.0%	0.0%	0.0%	0.2%
Total revenue (Y mln)		31.15	218.27	187.85	-	-	437.26
Of which: Negotiated		12.84	97.21	130.27	-	-	240.32
		41.2%	44.5%	69.3%			55.0%
Bidding		17.06	82.06	57.58	-	-	156.70
		54.8%	37.6%	30.7%			35.8%
Auction		5.25	39.00	0.00	-	-	44.25
		16.9%	17.9%	0.0%			10.1%
Unit price (Y/m²)		198.01	96.65	94.03			
Of which: Negotiated		125.39	43.81	66.95			
Bidding		367.65	2,666.16	1,106.12			
Auction		610.47	4,366.32				

/a By administrative allocation.

Sources: (1) Between 1980 and 1989: Chen Rueirong, 1990, "Views on Land Lease and Real Estate Market in Shenzhen," *China and Foreign Real Estate Times*, 1990, No. 3, p. 12.
  (2) For 1990: *Shenzhen Real Estate Yearbook*, 1991, p. 27.
  (3) For 1991: *China Real Estate Information*, 1992, No. 2, p. 2.

Shenzhen's record in land leasing has often been exaggerated; however, local authorities have introduced one transition measure worth replicating across China: while annual ground rents for leaseholders are symbolic and thus very low in value terms, *holders of administrative land must pay annual rents equivalent to the expected annual return on the value of the land, had it been leased.* The strategy is meant to encourage users operating under the old system to switch to leasehold arrangements, benefiting from the rights that accrue to such "ownership." Tables 3.6 and 3.7 illustrate the significant penalties involved in continuing to hold land under the administratively allocated procedures, and suggest potential incentives involved in encouraging all land users to enter into a "market economy" system.

Shanghai is also one of the cities experimenting with land leasing, though so far it has confined itself to foreign-investor deals. By mid-1992, 16 parcels had been leased, for a total area of 24 hectares, sold for $106 million equivalent, or an average price of $448/m²

Table 3.5: LAND LEASE SALES IN SHENZHEN BY BIDDING: 1991

ID	Location	Land (m²)	Total floor space (m²)	Total revenue (Y mln)	Land unit price (Y/m²)	FAR
1	B108-9	13,176	18,200	8.17	620.10	1.4
2	B119-13	5,146	28,000	15.50	3,012.30	5.4
3	B119-14	7,274	12,600	19.00	2,612.04	1.7
4	H312-17	5,000	10,000	15.00	3,000.00	2.0
5	B207-5	9,337	14,600	26.70	2,859.68	1.6
6	B119-24	3,580	14,800	18.00	5,028.49	4.1
7	B207-4	11,042	15,800	28.00	2,535.70	1.4
8	B119-25	3,580	14,800	18.00	5,028.49	4.1
9	B119-23	3,976	14,800	20.00	5,030.43	3.7
10	B119-26	3,976	14,800	20.00	5,030.43	3.7
11	B207-6	11,859	35,600	38.45	3,242.51	3.0
12	B207-9	7,694	9,235	19.63	2,551.24	1.2
Total		85,639	203,235	246.45	1,212.65	2.4

Source: Chen Guangyan, 1992, "1991 Land and Real Estate Market in Shenzhen," *China and Foreign Real Estate Times*, 1992, No. 2.

Table 3.6: LAND CHARGES COLLECTED FROM USERS WHO LEASE LAND

Types of land use	Y/m²/year
Various commercial	3.0
Residential (excluding villas)	2.0
Industrial	1.0
Others	0.5

Source: Shenzhen Land Bureau.

(Table 3.8). The land area involved is but a fraction of the land requisitioned during roughly the same period (1988-91), and equivalent to only 2.5 percent of the total land requisition completed within the city proper, or 675 hectares.

In Fuzhou, 17 hectares have been leased to date, with 10 hectares leased in 1991 alone. The sales have been made almost entirely to foreign-funded ventures (90 percent). Like Shanghai, they involve primarily (91 percent) negotiated "private treaty" contracts, rather than auctions or tendering; however, unlike Shanghai, where leased tracts tend to be 7 km or

Table 3.7: LAND CHARGE COLLECTED FROM USERS OF
ADMINISTRATIVELY ALLOCATED LAND
(m²/year)

Land grade	Land use pattern				
	Commercial	Residential	Industrial	Public square	Others
1	32.0	12.0	10.0	2.6	2.0
2	22.0	10.0	8.0	1.5	1.4
3	15.0	7.0	5.0	1.0	0.7
4	10.0	5.0	4.0	0.5	0.5
5	8.0	3.0	3.0	0.3	0.3

Source: Shenzhen Land Bureau.

Table 3.8: SHANGHAI LAND LEASES: 1988 - June 1992

ID	Location	Date	Use	FAR	Method	Length (year)	Land (m²)	Total revenue ($ mln)	Unit price ($/m²)	Price per floor space ($/m²)	Distance to center (km)
1	HQ-26	08-08-88	COM	5.0	Bidding	50	12,973	28.05	2,162.18	432.44	7.1
2	HQ-28-3c	01-19-89	COM	7.2	Bidding	50	3,614	8.28	2,291.09	318.21	7.0
3	CHJ-b7-10	03-28-90	IND	2.7	Negotiation	50	42,724	10.88	254.66	94.32	9.2
4	Taopu /a	10-23-90	RES	0.5	Negotiation	70	16,140	0.89	55.00	110.00	14.5
5	HQ-245T	10-30-90	HOT	0.45	Conversion /b	50	21,992	13.81	627.92	1,395.39	7.0
6	Gubei-24	07-14-91	RES	1.4	Bidding	70	55,400	15.00	270.76	193.40	7.5
7	Pudong-1	11-04-91	IND	2.5	Negotiation	50	5,270	0.53	100.00	40.00	5.4
8	Pudong-2	11-07-91	COM	6.5	Negotiation	50	8,116	7.30	900.00	138.46	7.5
9	Gubei-22	11-07-91	COM		Negotiation	50	6,003	4.79	797.93	-	4.6
10	Dapu-Xie	01-25-92	RES	4.2	Negotiation	70	19,790	1.00	50.53	12.03	3.3
11	Pd-136	03-09-92	COM	6.0	Negotiation	50	3,555	0.98	275.11	45.85	4.6
12	Liyang	03-10-92	RES	3.9	Negotiation	70	2,025	0.71	352.00	90.26	3.5
13	Huashan	03-23-92	RES	1.9	Negotiation	70	8,524	1.15	134.91	72.93	3.8
14	Beiji-71	04-11-92	COM	5.0	Negotiation	50	23,800	4.60	193.28	38.66	3.8
15	Changle	04-21-92	RES	2.1	Negotiation	70	3,228	0.65	201.36	95.89	3.5
16	Jingming		COM		Conversion /b		3,699	7.50	2,027.58		
	Total						236,853	106.12	448.04		
								(Y mln)	(Y/m²)		
17	Pudong-1j /c	06-22-91			Negotiation	70	1,510,000	670.00	443.71		5.4
18	Pudong-jg /c	06-22-91			Negotiation	70	4,000,000	240.00	60.00		12.1
19	Pudong-wgq /c	06-22-91			Negotiation	70	4,000,000	240.00	60.00		14.6
	Total						9,510,000	1,150.00	120.93		

/a Unserviced land.
/b These negotiated leases involved the conversion of existing joint-venture agreements, where the Chinese partners had originally contributed land as equity.
/c Parcels 10-15 all require resettlement and related expenditures.
/d This land was assigned to real estate development companies and the lease price can best be viewed as government equity investment.

Source: Shanghai Land Bureau.

more from the CBD, the land involved in Fuzhou is almost all within the "old city" (85 percent). Prices differ according to use. For example, in 1991 the eight cases of leases for commercial use were sold for an average of Y 829/m², while the nine residential tracts sold for only Y 436/m².

In other cities visited by the mission, there was little evidence of leasing activity. Chengdu had none to report; Hangzhou had leased two tracts in the city proper to domestic investors, covering 0.66 ha and sold for Y 3,080/m^2 in one case and Y 2,600/m^2 in the other.13/ Even Guangzhou has followed a fairly cautious policy in leasing land. Between 1988 and 1991, 20 sites, covering 14 ha, were leased, primarily to foreigners, in the autonomous Economic and Technological District, 25 km from the city center. Land lease sales in the rest of the city began officially in 1990, and totaled 26 ha, with an additional 6 ha leased since then (Table 3.9). Prior to 1990, a few housing development sites were leased to domestic REDCs. The key transaction involved Huadiwan, and covered 107 ha. It sold for Y 304/m^2, reflecting its proposed use and the lack of infrastructure for servicing the site. Little other activity took place prior to 1990.

Table 3.9: LAND LEASE TRANSFER IN GUANGZHOU: 1990/91

	Number of leases	Total land area (ha)	Total revenue (Y'000)	Unit price (Y/m^2)	Land area per lease (ha)
Total	71	121.97	211,010	173	1.72
Of which:					
For foreign	6	5.88	170,029	2,896	0.98
For 1990	24	86.87	22,860	26	3.62
For 1991	47	35.10	188,160	536	0.75

Note: Sales made within the semiautonomous Economic and Technological District are excluded. Unit price calculations omit the value of any in-kind payments, such as donations of completed floor space. As noted in Table 3.22, total revenue figures differ from the aggregate data provided by the Finance Bureau, and appear to underrepresent the actual level of activity.

Source: Guangzhou Construction Commission.

The process of change, providing building blocks for the comprehensive reform process prescribed in this report, can best be described as involving the introduction, recognition and eventual legalization of a variety of land pricing mechanisms that had been largely dormant between the mid-1950s and the early 1980s. These mechanisms include the following: (a) the emergence of de facto land market transactions in the urban periphery, both in the requisition of rural land, and the creation of suburban township and village enterprises, operating within a

---

13/ Given the fast-paced environment of 1992, the "shelf life" of all aggregate data and conclusions has been shortened. Hangzhou transferred 200 ha to a Hong Kong concern in May 1992, at a location 4 km from the West Lake, for 50 years, at a total cost of $111.5 million.

market system; (b) the realization, on the part of local governments in particular, that urban land development can generate resources for financing urban infrastructure development, in the form of fees, taxes, rents, and leases; (c) the recognition that unregulated transactions in central (core) area land have become a significant element in shaping land use changes, followed by a decision to regularize such exchanges rather than merely trying to suppress them; and (d) the acceptance of the fact that redevelopment of older city centers, to accommodate the surging demand of the producer services sector and of consumers willing to buy or rent housing at commercial prices, provides a unique opportunity to reap benefits from land with exceptional access characteristics. In this process, the REDCs, authorized in 1984, began to introduce and popularize the concept of commercial transactions in real estate, particularly in the form of "commodity" housing sold on a for-profit basis to both enterprises, nonprofit institutions, and individuals. Today, in the case study cities and nationwide, 40-80 percent of all new housing units completed are sold under "regulated" market conditions by REDCs. Such "commodity housing" has, in varying degrees, become a permanent feature of the urban economy (Table 3.10). *And, because commodity housing carries an implicit land price linked to location, such housing developments have had a far greater impact in introducing market prices that the more publicized land leases.*[14]

Land requisition fees, as noted, are paid to farmers and their communities, with additional fees accruing to governmental authorities, by those urban land users who encroach on legally defined agricultural land. Prior to the reform period, taking 1958 as a point of reference, these fees were nominal in nature and covered only four categories of compensation: land loss; crop loss; residential displacement allowances; and payment for "improvements" already existing on site. By the 1990s, each of these had been inflated in value, as villagers grew more adept as negotiators, and as market forces increased the value of each of the various categories involved. In addition, new items appeared on the compensation list. Three of these reflected Government's desire to conserve agricultural land: a loss of cultivated land fee, a fee to recreate lost cultivated land elsewhere, and a fee to replace vegetable plots nearby. Other fees reflected the fact that the "farm environment" had evolved and new rights and entitlements had emerged: displaced rural industrial facilities had to be compensated; additional fees were required to cover the subsidies implicit in turning the legally defined agricultural residents into urban residents (grain price subsidy fees, public housing fees, and, often, new urban employment); and fees were required to cover farm-related "installations" that were more broadly defined than under the prior set of regulations (Annex 5).

Data collected by the Chinese Academy of Social Sciences [15] as well as mission estimates, indicate that between 1985 and 1990 suburban land requisition prices for

---

14/   Nationally, 32 percent of all commodity housing space is sold to individuals. In Guangzhou, the level has reached 44 percent, while in Shenzhen the level totals 38 percent. In other large cities, having made less progress in introducing regulated market practices, the level typically falls to 10-15 percent. Among such cities are Shanghai, Tianjin, and Chengdu. (Source: *Guangzhou Real Estate*, 1990, No. 8, p. 17; *China Real Estate*, 1991, No. 2, p. 72.)

15/   *Urban Land Use and Management in China*, op. cit.

Table 3.10: COMMODITY HOUSING SALE IN SELECTED CHINESE CITIES: 1989

	Total new housing ('000 m²)	Commodity housing completed		Amount sold		Sold to individuals	
		'000 m²	%	'000 m²	%	'000 m²	%
Beijing	5,541.0	2,434.0	43.9	1,173.0	48.2	15.0	1.3
Shanghai	3,710.0	750.0	20.2	462.0	61.6	58.0	12.6
Tianjin	3,093.0	750.1	24.3	506.6	67.5	56.0	11.1
Guangzhou	2,990.0	1,931.0	64.6	927.7	48.0	409.1	44.1
Shenzhen	1,700.0	1,091.1	64.2	532.3	48.8	203.7	38.3
Hangzhou	624.7	410.6	65.7	174.2	42.4	n.a.	n.a.
Chengdu	744.0	301.3	40.5	232.8	77.3	25.2	10.8
National /a	109,557.6	37,840.3	34.5	24,913.8	65.8	8,054.9	32.3

/a The level of market-led development is markedly higher in the smaller cities of China, where the concept of state-supplied housing, linked to a massive "state-owned"-dominated local employment, was never implemented.

Sources: *Guangzhou Real Estate*, 1980, No. 8, p. 17; *China Real Estate*, 1991, No. 2, p. 72.

comparable land doubled, and now averages from Y 100/m² to Y 200/m² for a range of large coastal cities 16/ (Box 3.1). By way of comparison, the average costs of buildings alone averaged Y 413/m² in 1990, for state-owned investments. In China, urban building costs do not vary dramatically on a city-by-city basis; a ±25 percent adjustment to the national average should suffice to cover differences among most cities. Thus, land requisition costs have become significant, since the floor/land area ratio in suburban locations is unlikely to exceed 1.0. By comparison, at the beginning of the reform process in 1979, suburban requisition costs were relatively minor, amounting to Y 10-15/m² in the suburbs of a metropolitan area, while construction costs already amounted to an average of Y 125/m². Furthermore, as noted, the former price was treated as a free good by the user, covered by budgetary funds. Today, the user is most likely to use its own resources (retained earnings and repayable bank loans) to finance the same transaction.

The original requisition fees left little for the government; even today, the fees that go to the public sector—25-35 percent—are earmarked for agricultural land reclamation. Urban authorities, therefore, have sought other avenues to extract revenue from land, thereby creating a set of "prices" and "rents" which may or may not bear much linkage to market prices, but do validate the notion of land as a commodity.

16/ Shenzhen expropriated all the land needed for its foreseeable future (say, 15± years) by 1980 and set compensation terms at that time. Requisition prices for prime land are only one tenth of those cited for other cities.

Box 3.1: GUANGZHOU: A CASE STUDY IN RISING LAND REQUISITION COSTS

The Jiangnan Housing Estate, located in Haizhu district, has, during different phases of housing development, faced very different land requisition costs:

1979: Y 30,000 per mu, or Y 44 per m²
1983: Y 37,500 per mu, or Y 56 per m²
1985: Y 55,000 per mu, or Y 82 per m²
1987: Y 105,000 per mu, or Y 158 per m²
1991: Y 300,000 per mu, or Y 450 per m²

Within 10 years, land requisition costs for this project have increased tenfold; this is typical of general trends in Guangzhou. One reason behind such rapid increases of land requisition costs is the rising expectations of farmers. Since Guangzhou did not adopt a unified land requisition approach until July 1992, most land requisitions were carried out between individual development companies or land users and local farmers. According to the City Real Estate Bureau, as much as 80 percent of land requisition prior to mid-1992 was done without the involvement of city authorities.

Source: Guangzhou City Construction Development Corporation.

As noted, the above-cited 1980 National Conference inspired various cities to launch land fee collection experiments. These fees were meant to proxy land rents, appropriately adjusted to reflect political pressures from users complaining about "affordability." Fees came into effect in Shenzhen (Special Economic Zone) in 1982, in Guangzhou in 1984, and 100 cities thereafter. Fees for domestic concerns were set uniformly at much lower rates than those applied where foreign capital was involved. Table 3.11 illustrates the range of fees for foreign-funded and domestic firms in Guangzhou, and is broadly representative of the orders-of-magnitude involved. The fees applicable to new local users were lower, in nominal terms, than rent levels prevailing in the mid-1950s, before pricing was abolished. They acted, more than anything else, to reassert the public ownership rights over urban land, and had little to do with systemic urban land management reform.

The next step in making land values explicit, or, alternatively, generating revenues form land, came in the form of land development exactions in greenfield and redevelopment locations. The former exactions were made possible by the emergence of real estate development companies, described earlier, often competing for business to remain profitable. The latter exactions, involving massive entitlement payments to existing occupants of redevelopment projects, greatly exceeded the former (Annex 6). Furthermore, from a market economy's perspective, the redevelopment exactions were directed at compensating occupants; greenfield fees were more clearly meant to finance off-site infrastructure through nontax mechanisms that would not be subject to revenue-sharing arrangements with higher-level governmental authorities. All collected revenues would be retained and spent locally. *This theme, whereby land revenue generation and the emergence of market prices is obstructed or made opaque by disputes over distributional (i.e., tax) objectives and by intergovernmental revenue-sharing requirements, recurs throughout all of the subsequent discussions of related*

Table 3.11: 1984 GUANGZHOU LAND USE FEES
(Y/m²/year)

A. Applicable to New Land Allocations for Domestic Enterprises

	Land grade						
	I	II	III	IV	V	VI	VII
Fee	4.0	3.5	3.0	2.5	2.0	1.0	0.5

B. Applicable to All Foreign-Funded Ventures

	Land grade			
	I	II	III	IV
Commercial	36-56	28-44	12-28	8-20
Residential	18-25	14-18	10-14	5-10
Industrial	8-12	6-10	4-8	2-6
Other	28-40	20-28	9.6-16	4.8-9.6

C. Applicable to Special Economic Development District

Commercial and storage	12
Housing	8
Industry and transport	2
Science-related	1
Other	9

Source: Guangzhou State Land Administration Bureau.

prices, taxes and fees. This can only impede the emergence of explicit land prices, and transparent land markets, which this report takes as the key objective of any substantive systemic reform. The emergence of explicit land prices is too important to the Chinese urban modernization effort to be stalled by disputes involving the distribution of taxation receipts.

In greenfield locations, one would expect development projects to cover land, building and on-site infrastructure, with some debate remaining over responsibility to freely provide "public facilities," particularly when these would normally be a private responsibility in a regulated market economy (e.g., retail space operated by local authorities). Greater controversy surrounds the degree to which off-site infrastructure (including those labeled as citywide in scope) should be paid for by the investors of a particular estate or subdivision. North American and Western European practice, for example, provides precedents for some of these exactions (Box 3.2). Unfortunately, not all such practices are automatically fair or efficient, merely because they have emerged in developed market economies. Retrospective assessments of "Western" practices are often critical, and demonstrate that they should be examined on a case-by-case basis. Precedents do not provide practitioners with "best practices," particularly when those tools are utilized in countries wealthy enough to afford to make mistakes. China's urban planners, operating in a low-income environment, have less leeway than that available to urban land management planners elsewhere.

Box 3.2: THE FRENCH EXPERIENCE WITH LAND FEES AND EXACTIONS

France has, over the last two decades, experienced a process of administrative and municipal finance decentralization that led to the experimentation with various means to recover off-site infrastructure costs. Vincent Renard has concisely summarized the process of searching for an equitable and transparent solution:

"In France, after two decades of wavering between a systematic fiscal device (a local development tax calculated as a percentage of a preset lump-sum price of the to-be-built floor area) and case-by-case negotiated agreements between developers and municipalities, such as it is practiced in comprehensive development areas, a new tool between them has been introduced in 1985 as 'special exaction areas'....

The municipal council delineates the geographical area within which developers ... will have to pay all or part of the costs of the public infrastructure required by present and future residents.... The amount ... is not preset; the statute only says that the amount cannot exceed 100 percent of the real cost of infrastructure. The municipality must establish the nature of these public facilities ..., their cost, time schedule for building; as well as the developer's share (per m^2 of floor area to be built) of the total cost and how it will be apportioned among the various building types. The exactions can be in-kind or monetary."

Renard concludes that this experiment is too recent to evaluate, but that it may provide an incentive to force private landowners to lower their "offer price." In China, private landowners do not exist and it is not clear if the rural land occupants will respond to this device, reducing their "reservation price" for land in negotiations with the local land bureau in the same manner. Renard also offers evidence that local municipalities are adopting in-kind "linkage" payments, requiring developers to provide some low-cost housing, that was also introduced in San Francisco and Boston, in the United States, and Guangzhou, in China.

Source: V. Renard, "Affecting Land Prices Through Taxation: Perspective From the French Experience," Cambridge, Massachusetts, *International Conference on Property Taxation and Its Interaction with Land Policy*, Lincoln Institute, 1991.

The merits of the debate set aside, what are China's municipal authorities collecting in terms of off-site infrastructure "exactions," largely from REDCs, be they in terms of money or in-kind contributions? In cities like Guangzhou, such exactions were reported to have reached the equivalent of Y 250-300/m^2 as early as 1985, when sites were opened to "competitive bids." Today, exactions average Y 200-500/m^2, measured in terms of square meters of "commercial" building area constructed. These exactions are often provided as "in-kind" benefits (i.e., physical facilities), but overall begin to resemble prices paid for leases, though without the property rights that accompany them.17/ Between 1984 and 1988, approximately half of total urban infrastructure investment was financed through these "off-off-budget" sources, paid largely by REDCs, according to city officials. Thereafter, the majority of such expenditures were covered by "off-off-budget" fees.

In Shenzhen, practices are even more dramatic. Following national policy guidelines to develop "standard land prices" as a basis for negotiating land leases or determining the likely accuracy of property exchange prices which may yield capital gains or other such transfer fees, Shenzhen established a scheme that divided the city into five zones (or classes) within which different land uses are subject to presumed lease values that vary dramatically depending on intended use (Table 3.12). Here, as elsewhere, one must question why land values

Table 3.12: STANDARD LAND PRICE FOR NEGOTIATED LAND
IN SHENZHEN, 1991
(Y/m^2)

	Land use				
Land class	1	2	3	4	5
Class I	1,200	300	180	130	50
Class II	700	280	160	110	40
Class III	400	220	140	90	30
Class IV	250	180	120	70	20
Class V	190	160	100	60	10

Note: Five types of land uses are:
(1) commercial, retail, financial, office land use;
(2) all types of housing except villas;
(3) various industrial, storage and transport facilities;
(4) construction sites and other open production sites;
(5) planting, and other types of open fields.

Source: *China Real Estate Information*, 1992, No. 14, p. 3.

in prime locations (Class I) should be assumed to vary by a factor of 24:1. As noted elsewhere, however, the citywide ratio of highest values (Zone 1, commercial) to lowest values (Zone 5, agricultural) is plausible, and is set at 120:1. All in all, this is an example of anachronistic changes that do little to advance the emergence of a regulated market economy. More significant, however, was Shenzhen's simultaneous decision to require all new land users to pay high off-site infrastructure charges even if the user received the land as a free good. Though

---

17/ As of early 1992, Guangzhou has only one reported major local lease (107 hectares in Huadiwan), which was awarded to the highest bidder, the Guangzhou Credit and Trust Company, for Y 304/m², excluding land requisition costs.

the exactions are only significant in some cases (notably land use types 1 and 2 in zones I through III), Shenzhen has at least taken an important step in the direction of reform by monetizing the off-site exactions and making the standards to be used transparent and not negotiable (Table 3.13).

Table 3.13: OFF-SITE INFRASTRUCTURE FEE SCHEDULE IN SHENZHEN, 1991
(Y/m^2)

Land class	Land use				
	1	2	3	4	5
Class I	1,800	460	270	160	100
Class II	1,050	380	240	150	80
Class III	510	340	210	140	70
Class IV	330	290	180	130	60
Class V	230	220	150	120	50

Source: *China Real Estate Information*, 1992, No. 14, p. 3.

If one combines the guidelines suggested by the standard land prices and the requirements of the off-site charges, the resultant "price" of land in certain areas of Shenzhen, particularly in zones I and II, and land use categories 1 and 2, begin to resemble outcomes expected from the leasing of land through competitive bidding or tendering (Table 3.14). Though this process is administratively driven, it obviously reflects "feedback" from market transactions and, in an imperfect way, promotes systemic reform of urban land management.

Table 3.14: COMBINED LAND PRICE AND OFF-SITE FEE: SHENZHEN, 1991
(Y/m^2)

Land class	Land use				
	1	2	3	4	5
Class I	3,000	760	450	290	150
Class II	1,750	660	400	260	120
Class III	910	560	350	230	100
Class IV	580	470	300	200	80
Class V	420	320	250	180	60

Source: *China Real Estate Information*, 1992, No. 14, p. 3.

Elsewhere in China, the evidence is that more moderate exactions are the norm, if local official estimates are deemed reliable. Officials in 14 cities,[18] during discussions with a Bank mission reviewing housing reform proposals potentially eligible for Bank financing, revealed the existence of exactions for off-site investments ranging from Y 100/m^2 to Y 500/m^2, where greenfield development was involved. These exactions are calculated on the basis of per square meter of "commodity" housing, and their recalculation, in terms of contributions per square meter of land depends on the average floor area to land area ratio. Casual empiricism suggests that a 1:1 ratio can be used for purposes of this discussion.

It is instructive that no outsider, not even the central authorities, can say with certainty how much any one city spends on infrastructure development and maintenance. As noted earlier, the sources of funds involved prove particularly difficult to unravel. One recent Bank report estimated Shanghai's urban infrastructure expenditures average 3-4 percent of local GDP; information supplied separately to the Bank by Shanghai's Finance Bureau director suggests levels on the order of 9-10 percent of local GDP, a total which equals or exceeds the locally retained revenues of the municipality, which one would normally label as "the budget."[19]

It is also clear that, city by city, practices have varied greatly, including the degree to which land-related exactions contribute to the de facto infrastructure budget. In some cities, including Guangzhou, Wenzhou, and Shenzhen, budget revenue financing of infrastructure is being phased out in favor of off-budget earmarked sources. In others, like Hangzhou, the official budget (including the so-called official extrabudgetary public utility surcharges) may still finance half of all infrastructure investments (even here, however, as in other cities visited, detailed information on the infrastructure budget was not made available to the sector study team). Finally, there are cities, like Chengdu, which claim to frown upon the use of "off-off-budget" financing to any extensive degree. The full story is thus complex and not likely to be clarified any time soon.

Compensation paid to occupants of sites redeveloped in recent years in cities like Beijing and Shanghai averaged Y 1,000/m^2 to Y 2,000/m^2 for centrally located projects. In addition, projects in those areas are saddled with additional infrastructure fees and charges similar to those reported earlier for greenfield sites *if the scale of a redevelopment is large*. This encourages REDCs engaged in redevelopment to confine the scale of projects to small sites, where off-site infrastructure fees are relatively low.[20]

The very year (1988) that land leases were authorized, MOF conceived of a land market "reform" strategy that could be extended across all of China's cities, under the assumption that leasing was not likely to evolve as a major force in the spatial restructuring of

---

18/   Including "outliers," particularly Guangzhou.

19/   *China: Industrial Restructuring: A Tale of Three Cities*, op. cit.

20/   In Shanghai, Y 95/m^2 of all newly constructed space; in Fuzhou, Y 43/m^2 of newly built structures.

cities during the foreseeable future. The strategy chosen was to use one tool, and to introduce land use taxes, with very low maximum and minimum rates mandated from the center, dependent on city size, and with revenues to be shared on a 50-50 percent basis between the collectors and the center. The taxes were meant to accomplish a variety of rather ambitious objectives. They were supposed to raise revenues from land, giving land official recognition as a semicommodity whose use required the payment of a "rent." They were intended to provide users with incentives to return underutilized land to city authorities without any compensation, and encourage spatial restructuring, as enterprises which found themselves in "high-rent" districts would voluntarily, and without any assumed additional compensation, relocate to "low-rent" districts.

The land tax has proven to be a failure in achieving its ambitious objectives, mostly because central authorities had little understanding of the implicit value of land and failed to realize that, given international experience, land taxes were unlikely to ever reach levels required to match the impact of explicit prices. They lacked any coordinated intergovernmental strategy to create real land markets based on explicit prices.[21] They also gravely underestimated the reluctance of local governments to undertake reforms that resulted in substantial revenue transfers to central authorities, and reduced local autonomy by abolishing the original land use fee experiments except for isolated cases involving foreign-funded land users. And the mounting evidence from city-specific studies, begun as early as 1985 in Shanghai, and mandated by the State Land Administration for all cities in 1989, that were meant to reveal implicit land values, together with less systematic studies of regulated and unregulated land use rights transfers negotiated between individual users, was ignored and never internalized.

Though land taxes were actually implemented nationwide, the absolute value of the taxes and the range of permissible values across any one city proved very low if the taxes were meant to act as quasi-land rents. The highest annual tax allowable, at the center of China's largest cities, was set as Y 10/m^2/year. Given the revenue-sharing requirements attached to the tax, cities, in issuing implementing regulations, restricted the range and the spatial scope of the tax to levels well below those anticipated by MOF. Total revenues for 1990 and 1991 equaled Y 6.2 billion nationwide, with MOF receiving Y 3.1 billion.

The tax proved to have little impact as a revenue mobilization device and certainly did not affect the location decisions of present or future land users, caused land to be returned to the local authorities or provided incentives to relocation. The tax was rightly viewed locally as a nuisance tax whose only (albeit very important) contribution to reform was to accelerate the work in creating fiscal cadasters that would provide a rough mapping of occupant land area boundaries. From the viewpoint of this report, with its focus on comprehensive systemic reform, the tax initiative proved that "reform" measures can often be labeled as merely "changes" whose reform content is minimal. Now that this deficiency has been illustrated with this one case study, the central authorities, including MOF, may realize that urban land management reform cannot be successfully ordered by the center in isolation of local market

---

[21] For a brief description of related international experience, see the section on *Land Revenues*, below.

forces; that revenue-sharing objectives can obstruct land reform; and that systemic reform requirements involve tapping into the vast reservoir of knowledge on land market behavior, available at the local level and overseas and documented throughout the report.22/

       While the land tax initiative demonstrates how "reform" measures can be ineffective, more recent initiatives, driven by SLA and by agencies promoting serious enterprise reform, show promise of greater progress in the future. The Government has committed itself to regularizing (and perhaps facilitating) selective unregulated real estate transactions, accelerating not only the emergence of land markets, but also accommodating the restructuring of local economies, viewed by outside observers as chronically short of consumer and producer services, particularly in central area locations.

       Evidence of unregulated transactions is fragmentary, but suggestive. Hangzhou's SLA bureau officials suggest that the transfer of ground-level housing space to commercial users varies from Y 2,000/m²/year in prime locations (Jiefang Road), to Y 600-800/m²/year for slightly "off-center" locations, Y 300-400/m²/year around the city railroad station, falling off to Y 100/m² or less a year in periphery areas with few locational advantages for commercial activity. The same authorities estimate that there are a minimum of 10,000 such cases in the city at present. Chengdu, which has allegedly not entered the process of market reform until recently, reports at least 7,000 similar cases of black market activity. Among the more desirable locations (Sichuan Hualong Department Store), annual rents of Y 2,300/m² were reported; while in less central sites (Galaxy Department Store), rents reached Y 470/m²/year.

       SLA bureau representatives in Fuzhou were also able to draw land value maps based on unregulated rents. Peripheral locations rent for Y 15-30/m²/month, while prime locations, including those around the intersection of Dongda and Baiqi Roads, rent for over Y 200/m²/month. These, again, reflect the conversion of ground-floor housing space to commercial uses, and appear comparable in magnitude to those described for Hangzhou.

       Extensive studies of unregulated transactions were also conducted by the Chinese Academy of Social Sciences.23/ Based on end-of-1988 data, the study team reported data for two districts in Beijing, the Da-She Lan (DSL) district near Quiamen, a busy commercial center; and the Zhong-Guan-Chun (ZGC) district, an emerging high-technology center. In each case, rents as high as Y 300/m²/month were reported, with averages of around Y 70/m²/month in the first district and approximately Y 80/m²/month in the second. These numbers reflect largely the subletting of enterprise structures to other enterprises, exclusive of "joint venture" arrangement, where profit sharing is also involved. In the small number of cases where enterprise land use rights were rented, with no structure transferred, rents often proved

---

22/   These contentions are amply documented in R. Bahl and J. Zhang, *Taxing Urban Land in China*, World Bank, Report No. INU39, March 1989.

23/   *Urban Land Use and Management in China*, op. cit.

to be higher than those reported above, with average rents of Y 426/m²/month in the ZGC, based on deals negotiated in 1985/86.

For reasons that are not entirely clear, but that may reflect the relatively vigorous anti-"black market" activity of the Beijing Construction Commission, backed by MoC, public housing "black market" rents in the DSL district proved distinctly lower than those reported above, averaging Y 20/m²/month, though these should be compared to allowable rents of roughly 10 fen/m²/month.

Other measures could potentially help reveal land values. Enterprise reform efforts at central and local levels have approached bankruptcy options with great trepidation. The prospect of significant numbers of workers rendered unemployed in large cities is viewed as sensitive and a potential source of social instability. Mergers of loss-making enterprises with profitable enterprises offer a possibility of advancing both enterprise reform and urban land management reform *if* the loss-making enterprises' assets, including land occupied, can be converted to new uses more conducive to market demand, and *if* the dominant partner is highly motivated to maximize profits after the merger.

The cumulative land assets of loss-making enterprises can provide significant resources to promote reform and the redundant labor can be transferred to higher-value uses if three assumptions hold true: (a) that significant numbers of potentially redundant urban workers can be retrained and shifted to service sector activities; (b) that urban labor supplies will grow more slowly during the next decade, in response to the effects of past birth-control initiatives and continued restraints on migration; and (c) that China's cities will be restructured while experiencing rapid economic growth.

Once again, such partial information is no substitute for in-depth local research. This report cannot assess the magnitude of potential gains to urban land reform made possible by enterprise reform mergers. Anecdotal evidence, clearly weighted to emphasize success stories, suggests that the potential is great. If mechanisms promoting the relocation of viable industrial enterprises away from inappropriate central locations are actively encouraged, the outcome, in terms of urban land market reform, is likely to be even brighter.

Implementing Comprehensive Reforms in Urban Land Price and Property Rights Reforms

A Suggested Strategy

Reform to date has been piecemeal, with incremental changes too often masquerading as "systems reform." Piecemeal changes obviously promote the ultimate objective, i.e., the emergence of land traded as a commodity, subject to regulatory, legal and fiscal constraints. They should not be belittled. The point is that postponing broad-based reform handicaps China's cities seeking to be internationally competitive centers within this decade. A broader strategy is needed, one that is bold in scope and introduced rapidly enough to give China's land markets the opportunity to contribute fully to efficient, equitable, and environmentally sensitive economic development by the year 2000. The report cannot flesh out the details of the transition to a regulated market economy; only the general outlines of such a transition can be described and justified.

International experience provides essentially two avenues to land price and ownership reform: the freehold system and the leasehold system. Most countries adhere to the first approach, but significant exceptions exist worldwide, including places such as Hong Kong, Singapore, Amsterdam, Stockholm, the inner city of London, and Honolulu, among others. China has chosen to preserve state ownership of urban land, while permitting user rights to be leased out, giving leaseholders most of the significant rights of freehold ownership. *Reviewing evidence from other cities, one can argue that the leasehold method is not an obstacle to market-led reform, and that there is no need to reopen the debate and present freehold strategies as a serious option* (Box 3.3).

Leasehold arrangements are not without possible drawbacks. They presuppose a government bureaucracy competent and honest enough to manage the conveyance of land to individual lessees in a manner consistent with the overall objectives of urban land management systems reform. They assume that the length of the leasehold, and the arrangements surrounding leasehold renewal, are handled with regard to possible detrimental effects, particularly shortsighted behavior on the part of users as the end of a leasehold approaches. They take for granted that the conflict between changing urban land management objectives, including those that affect plot-specific profitability, can be accommodated by leasehold documents that may contain use rights and conditions covering 50 to 99 years. And they downplay the possible detrimental effects of a rent-seeking strategy open to a local monopolist who has effective control over a key urban resource, and is thus open to the temptation to use mechanisms that restrict land supplies for development or redevelopment in order to achieve short-term revenue-maximizing objectives.

None of these potential barriers proves to be sufficiently serious to avoid endorsing a leasehold strategy. Each potential problem has a remedial antidote. This report recommends that lease terms and renewal conditions be drawn up to minimize shortsighted user behavior; that the process of awarding leases be subject to maximum public scrutiny, and follow transparent and elementary rules maximizing fairness; that lease documents permit the planning regulations incorporated into them be subject to changes after a certain time period, a period long enough not to disrupt the assumed profitability of the original development planned, yet short enough to allow the "rules of the game" to be altered when and if longer-term redevelopment and conversion to alternate uses is at issue (Box 3.4). Finally, local authorities must be held accountable for balancing all objectives of an urban land management strategy, forgoing the temptation to maximize land revenues when the costs of shortchanging other

---

Box 3.3: WHAT DO LEASES ENTAIL?

A lease involves an agreement between a landowner, in which the owner agrees to permit the lessee to use the land. A sublease is an agreement by which a lessee permits a third party to exercise the land-use rights granted to the lessee by the landowner. Leases contain numerous provisions, and form the basis for the agreements reached on prices paid, whether by negotiation, competitive tender, or auction. Leases typically stipulate:

- length of lease;

- land uses permitted;

- building restrictions;

- design, arrangement, and height of structures;

- provision for private streets, roads, and lanes, along with vehicular access privileges;

- green space requirements;

- anti-nuisance clauses, and other "performance" indicators;

- lease modification provisions, including associated premiums to be paid and new restrictions imposed;

- lessor rights to repossess property for noncompliance reasons;

- Government rights to expropriate land for public purposes;

- timing limits for construction of all or part of the investment to be made by the lessee;

- rights and terms associated with mortgaging, transferring, or granting the leased land to a third party;

- terms and premiums associated with the renewal of a lease at or prior to the formal end of the lease; and

- dispute resolution procedures.

---

objectives is self-evident and well-documented.24/ Individual Chinese cities which chose to follow an unduly restrictive policy on land supply would suffer, over time, in efforts to compete

---

24/ In Seoul, based on project-specific data, serviced land development yields internal rates of return for parcels sold on the market in excess of 70 percent, even though the Government's borrowing costs at the time equaled 10 percent. Internal rates of return simply allow benefits and costs to be "discounted" back to the time of land acquisition, even though cost and sales streams occur over various years. Costs and revenues are thus expressed in "comparable" terms, excluding the element of time. (Hannah, Kim, Mills, "Land Use Controls and Housing Prices in Korea," op. cit.)

with other localities. There is always potential for "government failure" as well as "market failure," but there are mechanisms for minimizing both that are well-tested by international experience.

Box 3.4: HONG KONG EXPERIENCE WITH LEASEHOLD REGULATION

Hong Kong's experiences, past and present, provide the bases for these recommendations. For example, nominally nonrenewable leases not required by the government for other purposes are renewed, at a premium representing the market value of the land. Land lessees can apply for a renewal of the lease within the last 20 years of the lease, thus providing land users with incentives to continue to invest and redevelop the property. If the lease is due to expire in 10 years, a new lease can be negotiated covering that period plus the normal time span of a new lease (75 years), or a total of 85 years.

Under the recommendations provided in the "Report of the Special Committee on Compensation and Betterment" (March 1992), leases previously written to contain very specific planning conditions would now be subject to a time limit, long enough to allow development "conditions" to remain in place for a specified period of time that would allow the original development to take place as planned. Thereafter, however, new development controls and conditions, including those that would restrict the redevelopment potential of the sites, would be automatic, as overall city zoning regulations changed, without the need to compensate the lessee for otherwise unexpected losses due to "down-zoning." The issue of compensation for "breach of contract" is thus mitigated.

What then is the recommended implementation strategy? It takes as its model the previously issued urban housing sector reform report, which suggested two guiding principles: (i) that new investments enter the new system, to the maximum extent possible, thus diminishing the impact of past practices in spatial terms; and (ii) that the transformation of the prevailing, nonmarket system be comprehensive in nature, announced at one time, and provided with an implementation time schedule that is both responsive to the disruptive effects of instant change and yet forces all users operating under the traditional system to begin making transition plans to allow users to enter the market economy within a certain period, preferably within five years.

The previous Bank report on property markets focused on housing, issued clear warnings that thoroughgoing reform would affect an interconnected set of issues and interests, including the monetizing of "in-kind" benefits now made available to urban workers, the inability of many loss-making enterprises to survive the reform, and the fiscal implications of any set of fundamental changes. Land reform will raise similar issues. The maxim stated in the earlier report remains true in this case: it is far easier to abolish markets and market signals than to reestablish them. Reform must, nevertheless, proceed.

One of the most difficult issues to be resolved concerns the mechanisms and institutional responsibilities for requisitioning suburban land to be converted into urban land. Two possible models can be identified: one in which a single agency, at the local level, would undertake this responsibility on a comprehensive basis for all the new land required by a particular city; the second under which individual purchasers would directly deal with potential suppliers of land. On the face of it, the latter approach appears more consistent with typical practice in market economies. The report concludes, however, that in current Chinese circumstances, it faces two very serious obstacles. First, at this stage, many potential buyers still operate under soft budget constraints, and may well offer prices that "overshoot" likely market values. Second, rural sellers as yet pay virtually no taxes on any "windfall gains" that accompany the conversion of agricultural land to zoned and serviced subdivisions. They are thus in a position to hold out for a high percentage of such "windfall gains" that far exceed compensation for land and structures as presently zoned (i.e., for rural use). As such, a uniform public land acquisition approach, implemented under appropriate controls, may be considered as a short-term "second-best" substitute for a market where hard budget constraints prevail for end-users and for an explicit tax system to mitigate distributional concerns. Over time, as hard budget constraints take hold and rural communities must share any part of the "windfall gains" with the government, this second model of land can become the norm.

The report therefore recommends that, for the immediate future, local branches of SLA should be responsible for the requisition of all suburban land to be converted to urban use, following a plan that allows for market-led urban demand in terms of locations requisitioned and hectares acquired during the year. Given the well-known fact that anticipated urbanization greatly increases the implicit price of rural land, requisition should take place somewhat ahead of anticipated use; occupants could continue to use the land until actual urban development became necessary. Compensation rules should be reviewed for transparency and equity, with the aim of reducing the degree of leeway available for bargaining, and reducing all compensation to cash terms. There should be no explicit or implicit obligation for the state to provide "welfare" public housing, guarantee "urban" jobs for the displaced population, or provide for price subsidies covering the "newly urbanized" displaced population, involved in the process of land requisition. Government might instead explicitly set aside a portion of the land area requisitioned, giving former users the right to "first refusal," exercising the option to lease that land before it becomes available for leasing to outsiders. Government would then lease the remaining land, through auction, tender, private treaty (negotiation), or grant, to urban users; *land development companies could service the land and then either develop the sites for sale (land lease included) or transfer the serviced plots directly to new leaseholders, including smaller REDCs.*

All greenfield development would thus enter the reform system immediately, and all new users would hold leases. As far as possible, sites would be leased in a well-publicized and competitive manner, to both state and nonstate-owned enterprises, including those belonging to other cities or provinces. This would allow market prices, and property valuation data, to emerge spontaneously. Auctions of land should be encouraged, unless the particular priorities associated with a site require local authorities to reserve the right to choose a "preferred use plan," as defined in relevant tender documents, even if it is not accompanied by the highest bid. Leaseholds, other than those awarded through auctions, should always be assigned following a competitive process based on the issuance of tender documents easily accessible to any interested potential investor. The evaluation of bids should be conducted in an open and transparent manner. "Private treaty" leases based on negotiations with only one party should be discouraged, because these provide no obvious benefits to the landowner, while opening up too many opportunities for the exploitation of *guanxi*, influence gained through the possession of good "insider connections."

Institutional users who are nonprofit in nature should only receive land grant leases where little if any money is paid out, after a well-publicized, high-level local government review, to ensure that the opportunity cost of the relinquished site is justified by the benefits involved, and that alternative, lower-value sites have been considered and found to be unacceptable. This goal may not be achieved in the short run, yet it is imperative to press forward with its implementation. In addition, all users favored by such grants should be subject to strict minimum floor/land area ratios, so that the density of development reflects the implicit, shadow price of the land areas. Any transfer of grant land to profit-making users should be subject to close scrutiny and taxation.

Occupants of existing, developed sites should be given the option to lease or rent land, with rent levels set high enough to provide a competitive rate of return on the implicit price (lease value) of the property. All redevelopment sites would be transferred to the leasehold system outlined earlier for greenfield sites, and auctioned off or subjected to competitive and well-publicized tenders, except where land grants are deemed to be absolutely necessary.

Redevelopment has proceeded at a relatively slow pace in China's cities. Within Shanghai's old city (9,000 ha), actual and planned redevelopment covers 50-100 ha per annum (1985-95). This should not be blamed simply on urban planning and regulatory practices. The *scale* of potential redevelopment involved is enormous, and the density of old core areas, where residential and nonresidential uses are intermingled without regard for underlying land values or environmental considerations, makes the task very difficult, even if those planners had at their disposal all the tools, policies, and institutions recommended in this report. Successful redevelopment requires, inter alia, a citywide (but core-oriented) strategy that provides for swift land acquisition; transparent compensation terms for existing occupants; and a set of planning regulations that balance minimal restrictions meant to ensure public policy objectives while maximizing the returns on invested capital; along with an "accommodating" infrastructure-upgrading strategy. In summary, redevelopment strategies should evolve from a dialogue between physical planners, existing occupants, and promoters of a more competitive economy. Once targeted, following widely publicized hearings that provide for individual and enterprise inputs, land should be expropriated unless local occupants present plans that are consistent with citywide objectives and can be implemented in a voluntary but swift manner. The comparative experience of Singapore and Hong Kong provide polar opposite approaches to large-scale redevelopment; the first being more compulsory in nature; the second resulting in such limited outcomes that the head of the local redevelopment authority himself declared the model inoperative (Annex 7).

Compensation arrangements should be defined in cash terms alone, avoiding the plethora of in-kind or itemized benefits that bedevil land requisition in China's residential suburbs. As previously recommended in the Bank's housing report, existing occupants should be free to "buy into" the properties built in redeveloped sites; they would not possess significant entitlement rights, particularly while housing reform plans are still so modest in scope that prime locations could be held hostage to prior residents demanding reoccupancy rights for real estate on nonmarket terms, with housing treated as a near-free good. Issues raised by compensation arrangements are discussed further below.

The formula recommended for nonresidential land transfers, where the original occupants received land through administrative allocation mechanisms (assumed to involve little "price discipline" in terms of a profit-maximizing model), could apply here. Unless the local community could provide a viable alternative, the redevelopment project would be placed on the market for bids, based on tender documents. The original occupants would then receive the bulk of the proceeds, distributed according to space previously occupied, with the Government retaining the residual. The locational choices of the displaced occupants would thereafter be driven by budget-constrained preferences. All this assumes that the planning norms and regulations governing redevelopment would be "developer-friendly" in nature, allowing a range of residential and nonresidential "solutions" including, in the extreme, the right of new occupants to lease relatively small amounts of prime space, while benefiting from the exceptional amenities provided by close access to the CBD.

Redevelopment aside, rents and lease values for occupants of existing sites, who generally received their occupancy rights as a free good, must be established. The process could begin in locations and corridors that are self-evidently choice sites, either from a commercial point of view or from an assessment of their attractiveness as high-value residential sites. But, in short order, all the built-up area should enter the new system.

Based on emerging valuation data, present occupants of commercial and nonresidential space, generally, would face several choices. They could sign time-bound rental agreements that would subject them to "market-level" rents within, say, 3-5 years, but would be initially set at lower levels, particularly for noncommercial users. At that point, the occupants could opt to sign new rental agreements, based on annually adjusted market rents; participate in a competitive lease process, with the right to limited preferential treatment (e.g., only 75-80 percent of the bid would have to be paid in cash); or relocate to new sites, in return for a significant share of any revenue generated from the (automatic) market leasing of the abandoned site.25/

Alternatively, existing occupants could lease the site immediately, if they were willing to allow that site first to be placed on the market, and offered to alternate users, again in a well-publicized and competitive manner. As above, the winning bid, if it involved the existing occupant, would require that only a portion of the bid price be paid in cash. If the lease was awarded to a new occupant, then the original occupant would relocate and lease a new site. Here, as elsewhere, it bears reemphasizing that government revenue generation from land,

---

25/   Bank recommendations on a rent and price reform in the housing market are covered in great detail in the previously released report, *China: Implementation Options for Urban Housing Reform*, op. cit. It recommends rents be increased, gradually, to cover full costs, using formulas to calculate such costs, and implemented by fiat. The deregulation of existing public housing stock rents is thus seen as an issue involving a different process and time frame than that recommended for nonresidential users.

though one objective of urban land management reform, should not be allowed to obstruct the emergence of explicit land prices. Thus, local authorities should err, if anything, on the side of generosity, giving the bulk of the lease revenue generated through relocation to prior occupants.26/ Central or provincial authorities should, for exactly the same reasons, avoid injecting intergovernmental revenue-sharing considerations that would simply delay the reform process or drive it "underground" (Box 3.5).

This reform plan is audacious but also realistic. To begin with, actual or proposed experiments along these lines are emerging in 1992. In Guangzhou, all new urban land is now leased or granted on a fixed-term basis. In experimental cities, like Jingzhou (Liaoning Province), all existing users will be allowed to pay a conversion tax that depends on the existing land use category involved;27/ thereafter the user becomes a leaseholder free to trade rights, mortgage property, etc. For all new urban land, land requisition will be "unified" and performed by the city, which will service the land and then lease the land at a price that covers: (a) land requisition costs; (b) infrastructure development costs; and (c) a cost-plus markup ranging from zero percent for nonprofit institutions to 10-20 percent for industrial users, 20-30 percent for residential users, and 30-40 percent for commercial users. *One disappointing feature of the model is that it precludes competitive bidding and views leasing as a mere "cost-recovery" mechanism driven by arbitrary cost plus formulas, rather than as a means to arrive at explicit market prices. This view obviously has widespread approval among local and central policymakers, since most leases are understood as noncompetitive "negotiated" deals, where establishing market prices is obviously not facilitated.*

Shanghai, as part of its Pudong development plan, is considering a series of initiatives, which would subsequently be introduced into Puxi, within a "suitable" period of time. All new land developed for commercial use would be leased. All commodity housing, direct foreign or joint venture investment, would be built on leased land or land requiring quasi-market "land use charges" bearing a relationship to likely leasehold values. New domestic users of industrial land would, however, be exempt from the reform, and would continue to pay only nominal land use taxes, while existing users of land on both sides of the river would find themselves obliged to pay a special "land use charge" which may or may not approach the levels required of *new* land users. The proposal would be accompanied by other, complementary

---

26/   The transformation of land use rights involved has few if any precedents. The sector team cannot confidently cite what the capital gains or transfer tax should be. On the one hand, Government should share in the proceeds of the transactions; on the other hand, "confiscatory" taxes could simply halt the acceleration of legal transactions, which is seen in this report as a key element of reform. The obvious answer is to utilize the Chinese genius for experimentation. Cities should be given latitude to set the share captured by the Government, on a temporary, experimental basis. It would quickly become obvious, summing up the experience from a large number of cities, what tax rates are appropriate, i.e., rates that reserve a "fair share" of the proceeds for the government while promoting market-validated land transfers. Obviously, very high taxes, say 50 percent or above, will stymie the process. But the fine-tuning will have to be done by the Chinese, without the benefit of "best practices" drawn from international experience.

27/   Would a moderate transfer tax make more sense based on the time transactions occur?

Box 3.5: CAN INDUSTRIAL REDEVELOPMENT BE FINANCED THROUGH DIFFERENTIAL RENT?

One question to ask is whether the differential in land value is sufficiently large to finance industrial relocation. If one draws on economic principles, then in cases which do not involve large "externalities" (e.g., pollution amelioration), it could be concluded that—if the transaction does *not* result in a financial surplus—the overall economic benefit from the move must be suspect (in market economies, a firm will only move if it anticipates net savings). To look at empirical evidence, consider Fuzhou and Shanghai. In Fuzhou, the current cost of land acquisition in suburban industrial estates runs between Y 225 and Y 300/m². Total land costs, including infrastructure improvements and taxes, currently range from Y 390 to Y 480/m². If we add to this Y 400 to Y 600/m² for building construction costs, then the total costs of new facilities is between Y 790 and Y 1,080/m² (assuming a FAR of 1:1).

In the inner city of Fuzhou, where there is great development potential and where planning controls permit the construction of buildings with FARs between 1:1.8 and 1:2.5, the Fuzhou Construction Commission has recently tendered four sites to REDCs for the construction of commodity housing and commercial projects. Tender prices for these sites range from Y 1,950 to Y 2,850/m². Thus, the differential land values between the city center and the suburban industrial areas are considerable, with the ratio of serviced inner city to suburban industrial land ranging from 4.1:1.0 to 7.5:1.0. If enterprises located in the central area of Fuzhou were permitted to sell their parcels or enter into cooperative agreements with REDCs, they could easily finance their industrial relocation.

In fact, the Fuzhou Municipality could levy a tax on an enterprise's land sales profit and still leave enough after-tax profit to fully fund a typical industrial relocation project. Thus, it is possible to permit and tax land transfers and still provide the resources to funding industrial relocation and redevelopment. Another added benefit of permitting such market transfers is that it introduces market discipline to inner city redevelopment. The REDCs would be forced to more carefully consider market demand for redevelopment before purchasing land for projects.

In Shanghai, the potential benefits of permitting factories to sell their land to REDCs could be substantial. As outlined above, under the Seventh Five-Year Plan, the typical industrial relocation project cost Y 1,700/m² of vacated land area (in terms of the site relinquished by the enterprise). It is thus the actual break-even price that an enterprise would need to receive in order to pay for the relocation. Recent sales prices of parcels sold to overseas developers for industrial and commercial activities in the city center exceed Y 2,000/m². In fact, the Shanghai Municipal Government's recent proposal to the World Bank for the financing of nine pilot redevelopment projects in the city center estimates that the cleared sites could be leased for Y 10,000/m². Thus, while the actual market value for specific industrial sites in the inner area of Shanghai will vary according to location, size, and configuration and development potential, many sites in the city center can command prices that exceed relocation costs.

Limited evidence from Fuzhou and Shanghai suggests that inner city industrial redevelopment could be fully financed if industrial factories were permitted to sell their plots to REDCs through competitive bidding or tender procedures. Government could tax a portion of the proceeds and still leave enough revenues for the enterprises to fully finance their relocation. Given the enormous requirements of industrial relocation and modernization, this proposal warrants serious consideration.

---

reforms. It assumes *all* corporate income taxes will fall from 55 percent to 33 percent within 2-3 years, beginning immediately. The Shanghai Housing Development Company, which now builds the bulk of noncommodity housing, would set up a land acquisition and land development subsidiary which would sell serviced land to the Government, and recover all costs incurred. This land would then be leased.

If implemented, these experiments will represent major new initiatives. They require concurrent reforms in planning, regulations, laws, and institutions, *and* they require the accelerated development of a *central* consensus. For example, will MOF, which explicitly abolished locally set land use fees in 1988, agree to the quasi-rent land charges proposed by Shanghai? This is not the time to keep key agencies isolated from the cutting edge of reform studies and proposals.

There are other reasons to believe the time is ripe for reform. After a decade of rapid increases in real household income, and in the wake of a rent reform program offset by compensating wage adjustments, it is not unreasonable to ask owners of residential structures to pay land rents or acquire land leases (particularly since reforms would begin with the limited pool of new housing occupants, who would rent or buy the annual increments to the urban housing stock, which average about 5 percent of the existing stock). By the year 2000, the World Bank Housing Report recommended that occupants of the existing (pre-1992) stock be expected to shoulder cost-recovery rents, fulfilling an objective essentially in line with current Government goals. Since these rents would be phased in gradually; since urban households can be expected to continue to experience rapid increases in real income;28/ and since massive housing construction in suburban locations is the norm; affordable alternatives should be available for those unwilling, for example, to pay for the right to occupy sites with high amenity values (like the CBD). Hardship cases could be dealt with through "safety net" programs that subsidize the incomes of the certifiably needy. Government and other workers associated with nonprofit institutions could be included in these "safety net" programs or, better still, be allowed to earn annual incomes in line with their skills and responsibilities.

The thornier issue is what *entitlement rights* should be due to existing residents and users, as explicit or implicit land values rise (even if the areas involved are protected from the pressures of redevelopment, through historic preservation legislation). The best approach might be that resident entitlements, even in conservation areas, be limited and subject to market-value tests. No household or business would have the right to live or operate in a particular location at the expense of the community at large. The systematic preservation of a neighborhood can be defended, for reasons that transcend economics (even though market forces often validate these choices, after the fact). "Grandfather" clauses could allow long-term residents to live out their lives in such areas, under rules and conditions unapplicable to others, and revocable if they agree to "buy out" agreements that provide relocation incentives. But all other residents should be subject to market rules, including relocation. Market economies, at the local level, provide many examples of the inequities involved in trying to repress market transactions in neighborhoods slated for redevelopment or preservation. The public sector gains

---

28/   Almost uniformly, the 14 cities that submitted proposals for consideration in recent discussions on a proposed World Bank Group Housing and Social Security Reform Project assumed household income, in real terms, will grow at 8-9 percent per annum during the 1990s.

little from obstructing market forces in this context. And residents with no claims to entitlement rights should be encouraged to relocate to areas that their budgets dictate as feasible.29/

Options for Improving the Feasibility of Residential Redevelopment Projects

In many redevelopment projects across urban China, new commodity housing and commercial space is priced at two to four times its economic cost because redevelopment policies require this new space to fully cover the costs of all replacement housing. This cost differential is inefficient and imposes severe price distortions on the housing market. This section considers several alternative methods for reducing the break-even price of commodity housing in redevelopment projects. There are essentially three options for reducing redevelopment costs and lowering break-even commodity prices. One approach maintains the existing allocation system and tries to lower the "shadow costs" of the allocations; the other two monetize the transactions between the existing residents and the redeveloper. The options can be stated as follows:

(a)   To the extent possible, increase the density of new development; limit the ratio of replacement to existing housing provided to existing occupants; limit the provision of public facility space to only what is required to service the project population, taking into account the capacity of adjacent facilities and services; and increase the off-site replacement of housing when off-site construction costs are low and replacement standards are generous.

(b)   Provide cash compensation for the (depreciated) value of the housing of redevelopment area residents; all housing constructed on-site is sold as commodity housing and priced accordingly.

(c)   Modify (b) to include cash compensation for land as well as structures.

The various figures presented in Annex 8 describe the logic of option (a). To assess option (b) on monetizing redevelopment compensation, Table 3.15 illustrates various break-even commodity housing prices, assuming existing households in redevelopment projects are paid cash compensation for the loss of their units instead of in-kind compensation. Under such circumstances, all new constructed space (less any public facilities) would be available for sale on the commodity market. As Table 3.15 reveals, even if substantial cash compensation were offered for old units, break-even prices would still be lower than in comparable cases providing in-kind compensation.

However, if low rates of cash compensation were paid, existing owners of housing would need to find substantial sums to be able to buy new units built in the

---

29/   Annex 6 documents resettlement regulations emerging since 1991. These new rules have reduced entitlement rights.

Table 3.15: CASH COMPENSATION AND ON-SITE, NEAR-SUBURBAN AND
FAR-SUBURBAN COMMODITY HOUSING PRICES
(Yuan)

Cash compensation per building (m²)	Total compensation per unit	Commodity price of replacement housing		
		On-site per unit	Near suburban per unit	Far suburban per unit
100	3,500	60,200	50,000	32,500
200	7,000	62,300	50,000	32,500
300	10,500	64,350	50,000	32,500
400	14,000	66,400	50,000	32,500
500	17,500	68,500	50,000	32,500
600	21,000	70,550	50,000	32,500
700	24,500	72,650	50,000	32,500

Note: On-site prices are based on simulations of break-even prices. Near-suburban prices are estimated at Y 1,000/m². Far-suburban prices are estimated at Y 650/m². Cash compensation ranges reflect the depreciated value of the building, with no compensation for lost land use rights.

Source: Redevelopment Project Survey, 1991, 1992.

redevelopment project area.30/ Depending on the amount of compensation offered to existing residents, the commodity purchase price of new, on-site units would range from Y 60,200 to Y 72,650 (assuming that replacement units are 50 m²). In the case of very low cash compensation, existing households would receive only Y 3,500, less than 6 percent of the price of new on-site units. If existing residents received Y 700/m² in compensation, they would have Y 24,500, about one third of the purchase price of a new on-site unit.

If households were willing to relocate to other sites, they could purchase new flats at lower costs. By relocating to "near" suburban areas, typical flats could be purchased at about Y 1,000/m², or Y 50,000. The lowest level of cash compensation would provide 7 percent of the purchase price. At the highest level, it would provide 49 percent. If the household was willing to relocate to "far" suburban projects, it would typically pay Y 650/m² or Y 32,500 per unit. In such cases, the lowest level of cash compensation would provide 11 percent of the commodity purchase price; the highest level of compensation would cover 75 percent of the purchase of a new unit. A substantial shortfall would still exist.

30/ The use of a compensation standard linked to the ability to buy does not presuppose displaced tenants would be *forced* to buy. They could well rent commercial housing, priced to cover all costs. However, compensation arrangements presuppose that sitting tenants have quasi-ownership rights and, as such, must be compensated at levels appropriate to holders of such rights.

Without a functioning housing finance system, households or owners (enterprises and government units) would be forced to pay cash for new units. If, however, there was long-term mortgage finance available, households or owners could borrow money on a mortgage basis. Table 3.16 illustrates hypothetical mortgage loans and per m² monthly repayments for the repurchase of on-site, near-suburban, and far-suburban housing, assuming that loans are based on the purchase price less cash compensation, and they are for 20 years at an annual interest rate of 10 percent. Two important results are reflected in Table 3.16. First, purchasing on-site replacement housing is expensive, regardless of the level of compensation received. Second, if households moved to far-suburban locations and received Y 500-700/m², they could actually afford to purchase units and service mortgage debt.

Table 3.16: PURCHASE /a AND FINANCING /b OF ON-SITE, NEAR-SUBURBAN AND FAR-SUBURBAN REPLACEMENT HOUSING FOR VARIOUS LEVELS OF CASH COMPENSATION
(Yuan)

Cash compen-sation per building (m²)	On-site replacement		Near-suburban		Far-suburban	
	Loan amount	Payment/ month/m²	Loan amount	Payment/ month/m²	Loan amount	Payment/ month/m²
100	56,700	10.94	46,500	8.98	29,000	5.60
200	55,300	10.67	43,000	8.30	25,500	4.92
300	53,850	10.39	39,500	7.62	22,000	4.25
400	52,400	10.11	36,000	6.95	18,500	3.57
500	51,000	9.84	32,500	6.27	15,000	2.89
600	49,550	9.56	29,000	5.60	11,500	2.22
700	48,150	9.29	25,500	4.92	8,000	1.54

/a   Assumes that loan amount is the commodity purchase price less total cash compensation paid for old dwelling. Replacement units are 50 m²; original units are 35 m².

/b   Assumes a 20-year fully amortizing mortgage at an annual interest rate of 10 percent.

Source: Mission estimates.

The payment of cash compensation for the loss of a dwelling unit, excluding compensation for lost land use rights, would even in the best of circumstances still leave the household or owner with a substantial gap. As Table 3.16 reveals, the differential between the cash compensation and the purchase price of replacement housing ranges from Y 48,150 to Y 56,700 for on-site replacement, from Y 25,500 to Y 46,500 for near-suburban replacement, and from Y 8,000 to Y 29,000 for far-suburban replacement housing. The gap reflects the fact that it is current practice in Chinese cities not to pay compensation for land, since it is assumed that urban land is under state ownership. If redevelopment compensation was paid for land as well as buildings, following option (c), the gap between cash compensation and the commodity price of replacement housing could be closed.

If all redevelopment housing was sold on the commodity market, and if the pricing of such commodity housing was based on demand as well as supply factors, the prices of commodity housing would be based on location, access to services and the quality of construction, not merely on the cost of the project. In such cases, developers would purchase sites or carry out redevelopment projects predicated on the potential revenues generated from the redevelopment, construction and sales of commodity housing or commercial space on a site. When commercial developers in market economies bid for sites, they typically use a technique called the "backdoor approach." This method is based on projecting the total sales revenues from building and selling commodity space in the potential project, subtracting all costs of construction and development (including fees, charges, interest, materials, provision of public facilities), developer overhead, and profit. The remaining amount, the "residual," is the amount the developer could pay for the land and still maintain his target profit level.

To illustrate this approach, Table 3.17 presents estimated residual land values, assuming various commodity housing prices. The estimates are based on the baseline case presented above, and assume that all existing residents receive cash compensation of Y 400/m^2 of constructed area for the loss of their old dwelling unit. As the table illustrates, the land residual value can be substantial, particularly with greater FAR and higher commodity housing prices.

Table 3.17: RESIDUAL LAND VALUES FOR VARIOUS
COMMODITY HOUSING PRICES, BY FAR

Commodity housing price (Yuan)	Yuan land value per m^2 of site area		
	FAR 1.5	FAR 2.0	FAR 2.5
1,400	22	136	250
1,600	307	516	725
1,800	592	896	1,200
2,000	877	1,276	1,675
2,200	1,162	1,656	2,150
2,400	1,447	2,036	2,625
2,600	1,732	2,416	3,100

Source: Simulation of base-case redevelopment project, 1992.

If existing residents and owners were fully compensated for their units, including land value, they would receive substantial sums. If households elect to relocate to suburban projects, they would receive most, if not all, of the funds needed to purchase replacement units. As Table 3.18 shows, compensation for land can be more significant than for the structure and provide substantial resources for the purchase new units on the commodity market.

Table 3.18: ESTIMATES OF POTENTIAL LAND AND BUILDING COMPENSATION
(Yuan)

Commodity housing price	Building compensation per unit	Land compensation per unit	Total compensation per unit
1,400	14,000	5,953	19,953
1,600	14,000	22,578	36,578
1,800	14,000	39,203	53,202
2,000	14,000	55,828	69,828
2,200	14,000	72,452	86,452
2,400	14,000	89,078	103,078
2,600	14,000	105,703	119,703

Source: Simulation of base-case redevelopment project, 1992.

If cash compensation were paid for land and buildings, redevelopment projects could be implemented through competitive bidding for redevelopment project sites; REDCs wanting to redevelop areas would bid for the purchase of the site. The bid-purchases would reflect the REDCs' estimates of the construction costs, sales revenues and compensation for demolished buildings and land. The highest bidders would gain redevelopment rights. Existing owners of buildings on the site would receive compensation for the depreciated value of their structure and a pro-rata share of the land value of the site. The pro-rata share should be based on the land value bid, divided by the original constructed area of the site. Occupants of the site would receive a payment based on their preredevelopment ownership of constructed space.

Local government could tax away some of the land-related compensation. The tax rate should be set to ensure that existing owners were left with enough proceeds to purchase comparable replacement housing. This would be set by limiting total compensation to the lesser of the cash compensation for the structure and the pro-rata value of the land or the prevailing commodity housing price (per square meter times the amount of space to be purchased) for comparably located commodity housing.

Cash compensation for buildings and land given up for redevelopment would greatly enhance the efficiency and transparency of redevelopment financing. By broadening compensation payments to include land, affected households and owners would receive substantial funds to apply toward the purchase of replacement housing on the commodity market. Note, however, should be taken that land reform and housing reform are inseparable. Commodity housing options (location, unit size) available to *individuals* are still limited in many cities. Mere improvement in compensation rules, without greater choice of alternative commodity housing, might render the strategy unsustainable.31/

Is the Proposed Strategy Affordable?

The reasons why urban residents should be able to afford the proposed price changes were outlined earlier. But will business enterprises find this price and property rights reform affordable? Here, one should differentiate between enterprises that do (or should) already face hard-budget constraints and others (largely state-owned industrial enterprises), and then only temporarily. If the Bank's interpretation of Government's reform objectives is correct, standard corporate income tax rates will drop from 55 percent to 33 percent, all enterprises will be responsible for their profits and losses by the year 2000, and face bankruptcy or merger as the only real options to overcome poor performance. Enterprises subject to price controls would, by then, be a vestige of the past. Most prices would be set by the market, and even regulated utilities within monopoly markets would charge regulated prices yielding cost-recovery rates, including an "adequate" rate of return on investment.

Even now, commercial enterprises have no reason to operate under a protective "state-owned" umbrella. The political imperative to keep the "commanding heights" of the industrial sector under state ownership and management no longer covers the urban services sector. There is little reason why commercial activity should be run by other than leaseholders with anything but profit maximization in mind. Certain enterprises, including large department stores, operating outside the market economy, should be transferred to the market system, using the various mechanisms already employed to effectively privatize their smaller-scale counterparts. The "problem" industrial enterprises owned by the state and today viewed as not viable will, in time, be stripped of nonmarket constraints that prevent profit maximization, and be forced to "sink or swim." These enterprises will either cease to exist or be able to shoulder the burdens of operating within a market-driven, competitive economy.

Beyond this, and anticipating the discussion of the net increases in government revenues that can be expected once the new system is fully in place, note should be taken of the implications of the tax code on affordability. Depending on the assumptions made about the annual tax liabilities of a given enterprise, which, in China, can vary dramatically—for reasons dealt with in other Bank studies—at most one third of any land rent will represent net additional revenue, the rest being offset in the process of estimating taxable income because these will be treated as pretaxable deductible costs. Similarly, land lease costs would not simply become an added burden to the enterprise, or net income to the Government that first conveys the land; these costs will be treated as assets subject to depreciation allowances that reduce taxable income. Under current rules, allowing loan repayments as well as interest to be treated as tax-deductible, under most circumstances. Enterprise tax liabilities could be further decreased to

---

31/   For regulations in other Asian cities, see Annex 7.

the extent that land leases are financed by bank loans.32/ At the same time, of course, the net revenue gains to the Government would be correspondingly reduced.

Particularly for industrial enterprises located in suburban locations, the new arrangements will have their greatest impact in making land prices explicit, and *not* in greatly affecting prices, enterprise retained earnings or generating massive net increases in Government revenue.

Obviously, there are many factories that are inappropriately located. The work by Bahl and Zhang,33/ regressing profits against location, controlling for other variables in two cities; and less sophisticated studies correlating gross profits per m² of land use at different locations (e.g., Shanghai's 1985 study);34/ document the fact that "centrality" adds little to most industrial activities and that, by implication, the emergence of explicit land prices could force relocation. This is precisely one of the intents of urban land reform, one which can be achieved in a gradual manner by phasing in the full impact of market prices, and one which can bring residual benefits to the relocating firms, which would share in the monetized value-added created by the old site's occupancy by a new user paying market prices. This reform is likely to take place in an environment of rapid economic growth and low rates of inflation, with enormous demands for additions to the urban services sector. Both offer favorable opportunities for restructuring in urban areas that are currently denied to virtually all other economies in transition to a regulated market economy, where high inflation and negative growth rates are the norm.

Land Revenues: Will They Prove Significant in Financing City Expenditures?

Cities and towns will require substantial investments in serviced land development and in infrastructure to recycle land uses in the existing core areas and accommodate greenfield expansion. Because redeveloped land currently provides for only one quarter of that required for new construction, the built-up area of cities and town is expanding at a rate of 6 percent a year, enough to double the developed urban area every 15 years. The true burden of associated infrastructure investments is not easy to calculate because cities resort to elaborate "off-off-budget" mechanisms to finance infrastructure construction. This practice is due partly to a reasonable desire to make direct beneficiaries shoulder a greater share of the costs than in the past, and partly to the fact that China's taxation system allows cities and towns to retain all such revenues locally, while having to share the proceeds of most conventional revenues with provincial and central government authorities. This creates enormous incentives to shift expenditure sources away from those subject to intergovernmental revenue-sharing (Box

---

32/   The tax deductibility of loan principal is currently being phased out, as the above-cited tax reform is introduced.

33/   R. Bahl and J. Zhang, *Taxing Urban Land in China*, op. cit.

34/   Ibid.

3.6). Mission estimates suggest that the actual average expenditure on urban infrastructure and maintenance is close to 5-6 percent of urban GDP, and may well be higher than that.

<u>Box 3.6</u>: URBAN CONSTRUCTION FINANCING IN SHANGHAI

Before 1980, urban construction was financed by city budget allocations as part of the fixed capital investment program. Most of the completed urban infrastructure and services were provided free of charge. Certain public utilities utilized user charges, but there were large gaps between revenues and costs.

During the 1980s, demand for additional urban infrastructure and services increased dramatically. In order to finance such increases, there was a shift from local budget allocations and greater reliance on drawing upon the resources of enterprises and "society." There are now basically three arrangements for obtaining additional urban construction funds:

(a)   to tie nonprofit urban construction projects to profit-oriented industrial projects, and implement them at the same time. Once the projects are completed, the profits from the industrial projects are used to pay back loans used for urban construction projects. Such loans are treated as tax-deductible items. For example, the Nanpu Bridge, Shanghai's No. 1 Subway Line, and the Shanghai Sewage Project are all financed through this mechanism;

(b)   to have enterprises include in their costs items that cover urban infrastructure investments in industrial districts or development zones. Such costs are tax deductible. The Taopu industrial district and Caohejin development zone have been financed through this mechanism. The urban infrastructure of the Hongqiao and Minghang development zones have been financed through government interest-free loans. They will be paid back by enterprises within the zones over the next few years;

(c)   to collect various user charges or fees, including off-site infrastructure fees, bridge and tunnel tolls, sewerage fees, land use fees, excess water consumption fees, and more conventional utility charges.

In April 1988, to reinforce the management of the urban infrastructure financial resources, a "Shanghai Urban Construction Fund" (SUCF) was set up. Its main responsibility was to collect, use and manage those funds.

In 1992, the City Construction Investment Corporation (CCIC) was established; the assets and liabilities of the SUCF were taken over by the new entity. CCIC is an extrabudgetary trust account, administered by the Construction Commission. Revenues will be generated by appropriating part of the municipal share of land transactions; as well as from various fees and charges, profits from subordinate real estate development companies, dividends from assigned equity shares in various joint-stock companies, budget appropriations, bond issues, and foreign or domestic loans. CCIC will make loans for infrastructure development, repayable from income generated by or budget allocations to the municipal service agencies and public utilities that borrow from CCIC.

Source: Shanghai Construction Commission.

The issue of municipal finance clearly goes beyond one of merely accounting for the ever-widening sources of infrastructure financing. Cities need to consider increased user charges for municipal services, the monetization of land values, and greater reliance on long-term financing from capital markets and banks. They must also, however, pay far more attention to expenditure planning and budget programming, as well as financial management and accounting. This means, inter alia: (a) preparing medium-term consolidated revenue and expenditure forecasts for the purposes of evaluating the feasibility of development options; (b) developing "rolling" three-year investment programs, including operations and maintenance (O&M) implications, based on transparent criteria for determining preferred capital and recurrent expenditures; (c) reviewing fiscal subsidies, their objectives, and their incidence, knowing that every yuan in subsidies means one yuan less to promote municipal development; (d) reviewing possible borrowing and debt options and management strategies, and develop relevant debt service risk analysis tools; and (e) exploring ways of strengthening tax and fee administration, while reexamining the incidence, efficiency, equity, and transparency of such taxes and fees.

A cross-section of land-revenue time series suggests that such income could become an important source of urban construction financing (Tables 3.19-3.24). At present, however, much of the revenue is earmarked for expanding the supply of land available for cultivable uses, or is subject to intergovernmental revenue-sharing rules. Furthermore, any judgment depends on the rate at which land lease sales expand and what proportion of that money is held back by local governments. Land leasing is clearly growing in scope, but potential revenues have been kept down because local authorities fear the impact of market prices for land on new occupants. In addition, the incentives required to attract *present* land occupants into the market dictate that the latter be allowed to retain a significant share of lease revenues for the foreseeable future. Given that the central government is also entitled to roughly one third of gross revenues, it is unlikely that local governments can count on land revenues as a providential source of money with which to expand infrastructure construction and maintenance budgets in the short or medium term.

Today, local governments are trying to finance serviced land development and major infrastructure projects by adding a plethora of fees and charges to budget and nationally sanctioned off-budget sources. While a move to greater beneficiary financing is necessary and defensible on both efficiency and equity grounds, the proliferation of fees and charges appears to be a hit-and-miss affair. This topic should be studied carefully, to determine both the best sources and the likely size of local government land revenues. International experience already suggests, however, that expectations should be held in check. Hong Kong is often cited as a case where land revenues, driven by the sale of leasehold rights, can substantially alter the budget constraints experienced at the local level. One or two years excepted, this is simply not borne out by the data (Table 3.25). Worldwide, land lease revenues aside, the experience with *land tax instruments* has proved uniformly disappointing. In *some* market economies, it is possible to collect the equivalent of 1-2 percent of real estate market value in the form of property taxes. This is the case in the United States. If land is considered to equal an average of 20-25 percent of the property, then the *land* portion of the tax typically contributes 2-7 percent of all local revenues in cities like Boston, New York, Philadelphia, Atlanta, Baltimore, and Los Angeles. More likely, China will learn more from the experience of developing countries, where the property tax yield is only one tenth to one fifth of that level, and is even less of a major revenue generator.

Table 3.19: LAND REVENUE IN SHANGHAI: 1987-91
(Y million)

	1987	1988	1989	1990	1991	Total
Cultivated land tax /a	37	89	57	39	88	310
Vegetable land fund	103	106	65	25	40	339
Land use fee for joint ventures	6	11	9	11	17	54
Land lease sale /b	-	104	31	134	149	418
Urban land use tax /c	-	-	236	206	230	672
Total /d	146	310	398	415	523	1,793

/a The cultivated land tax ranges from Y 3 to Y 10/m², based on different per capita land use and economic conditions in each township. The revenue is shared with central government, which receives 30 percent of the proceeds. The tax rate is cut in half for farmer housing. For land taken for rural highway use, the rate is Y 2/m². Total charged land area for each year is as follows: (hectares)

1987	1988	1989	1990	1991	Total
23.67	20.53	12.13	11.67	n.a.	68.00

/b The "state" (MOF) shares 32 percent of the gross revenue.

/c The tax is shared 50/50 with the state. In 1990, however, unpaid taxes by the Baoshan Steel Company (Y 24 million) and Shanghai No. 1 and No. 5 Factories (Y 6 million) were not included.

/c By comparison, Shanghai collects approximately Y 500 million each year through its urban maintenance and construction tax.

Source: Shanghai Municipal Government.

Table 3.20: LAND REVENUE RETAINED BY SHANGHAI: 1987-90
(Y million)

	1987	1988	1989	1990	Total
Cultivated land tax	26	62	40	27	155
Vegetable land fund	103	106	65	25	299
Land use fee for joint ventures	6	11	9	11	37
Land lease sale	-	71	21	91	183
Urban land use tax	-	-	118	103	221
Total	135	250	253	257	895

Source: Shanghai Municipal Government.

<u>Table 3.21</u>: LAND REVENUE IN FUZHOU: 1986-91
(Y million)

	1986	1987	1988	1989	1990	1991	Total
Cultivated land tax /a	-	-	-	2.33	1.62	1.97	5.93
Vegetable fund	1.80	2.21	0.42	2.15	2.67	4.70	13.95
Fishpond fund	0.51	0.16	0.02	0.57	0.93	1.15	3.39
Off-site fee /b	1.06	9.70	11.00	6.75	4.90	11.46	44.87
Education fee /c	-	-	-	-	8.11	10.50	18.61
Location price /d	-	-	-	1.62	-	-	1.62
Land value-added fee /e	-	-	-	6.45	9.10	1.60	17.15
Land use tax /f	-	-	0.16	6.63	10.36	13.55	30.70
Lease sale /g	-	-	-	-	10.88	4.64	15.52
Total /h	3.37	12.07	11.60	26.50	48.62	49.58	151.73

/a   The tax rate ranges from Y 2 to Y 10/m², based on different per-capita land area and different economic conditions in each county.

Per capita arable land	Tax rate	
	Paddy field	Arable land
Less than 0.5 mu (33.5 m²)	Y 10/m²	Y 8/m²
0.5-1.0 mu (33.5-66.7 m²)	Y 8/m²	Y 6/m²
1.0-1.5 mu (66.7-100 m²)	Y 6/m²	Y 4/m²
More than 1.5 mu (100 m²)	Y 4/m²	Y 2/m²

/b   The off-site infrastructure fee was implemented in 1985. Based on different classes (hot spring protection zone and three land classes) and different land uses, the fee ranges from Y 45/m² to Y 7.5/m².

/c   The urban education construction fee, implemented in 1990, is designed to improve school conditions for Fuzhou. The rate is Y 12/m² of floor space in the city proper, Y 10/m² for county towns, and Y 8/m² for designated towns. All commercial real estate projects have to pay Y 15/m².

/d   The location price differential fee is collected from all commodity housing development that is not on leased land. About Y 100/m² of floor space is collected.

/e   The land value appreciation fee is based on the percent of sale price as the comprehensive building cost. If the sale price is below 100 percent of building cost, 15 percent of value appreciation fee will be collected. For the portion between 100 percent to 200 percent of building cost, 30 percent value appreciation will be collected. For the portion between 200 percent to 300 percent, 40 percent value appreciation fee will be collected. For the portion above 300 percent, 50 percent value appreciation fee will be collected.

/f   The land use tax was implemented in 1988. Unlike many other large cities, where land use taxes are shared between the central government and municipal government, the land use tax in Fuzhou is shared between Fujian Province and the central government.

/g   The land lease revenue is shared with the central government. Land lease sale revenue figures only include the amount retained by the city, not total number.

/h   By comparison, Fuzhou collected approximately Y 28.71 million each year through its urban maintenance and construction tax (1989 figure).

Source: Fuzhou Municipal Government.

Table 3.22: LAND REVENUE IN GUANGZHOU: 1984-91
(Y million)

	1984	1985	1986	1987	1988	1989	1990	1991	Total
Cultivated land tax	-	-	-	20.7	36.6	25.2	10.9	n.a.	93.4
Vegetable land fund /a	-	-	-	n.a.	n.a.	n.a.	n.a.	n.a.	n.a.
Land use fees /b	1.5	13.5	14.5	20.0	20.2	4.5	5.0	5.4	84.6
(1)	1.5	12.0	12.3	17.0	17.8	-	-	-	60.6
(2)	-	1.5	2.2	3.0	2.4	4.5	5.0	5.4	24.0
Land lease sale /c	-	-	-	-	280.0	109.7	129.7	205.5	724.9
Land use tax /d	-	-	-	-	-	69.1	66.2	63.9	199.2
Total /e	1.5	13.5	14.5	40.7	336.8	208.5	211.8	274.8	1,102.1

/a No data are available.

/b (1) Fees were collected from domestic and foreign land users from 1984 to 1988.
(2) Fees are still collected from joint ventures.

/c The state shares 32 percent of gross revenue. In-kind payments, particularly donations of completed floor space, are excluded. According to city officials, total revenues included over Y 300 million (120.76 ha), plus HK$155 million, as well as donations of 60,000 m^2 housing during the period of 1986 to 1990. The Guangzhou Construction Commission reports different results for 1989, 1990, and 1991, which appear to underrepresent the level of activity (see Table 3.9).

/d It is shared 50/50 with the state. The potential taxable area is 58 km^2, and the area actually covered by the tax, after "exemptions," totaled 30 km^2. A tax revenue of Y 63 million is an estimate.

/e By way of comparison, Guangzhou collects about Y 200 million a year through its urban maintenance and construction tax.

Source: Guangzhou Municipal Government.

Table 3.23: LAND REVENUE IN CHENGDU: 1987-91
(Y million)

	1987	1988	1989	1990	1991	Total
Cultivated land tax (04/87) /a	82.63	25.05	21.24	30.48	30.00	189.40
Vegetable land fund /b	n.a.	n.a.	n.a.	n.a.	n.a.	n.a.
Urban land use tax (11/88) /c	-	-	18.42	20.50	18.00	56.92
Land use fee for joint ventures (1991) /d	-	-	-	-	-	-
Land lease revenues /e	-	-	-	-	-	-
Total /f	82.63	25.05	39.66	50.98	48.00	246.32

/a The cultivated land tax ranges from Y 1 to Y 10/m^2, based on different per-capita land area and different economic conditions in each township. The revenue is shared among four levels of governments:

Central government	30%
Provincial government	10%
City government	10%
County/district government	50%

The amount of cultivated land involved are as follow:

	1987	1988	1989	1990	1991	Total
Average area (ha)	533.13	335.87	496.73	341.07	n.a.	1,706.80
Average price (Y/m^2)	15.50	7.46	4.28	8.94	n.a.	9.34

/b The rate for the vegetable fund is set at Y 10,000 per mu, or at Y 15/m^2. No data are available on this item.

/c The tax is shared 50/50 with the state.

/d The land use fee is set at Y 0.5-19/m^2. It started in 1991. Estimated annual collections would total about Y 1.87 million per year. So far, Y 0.31 million have been collected, because widespread "exemptions" have been granted.

/e No land lease sales have been made in Chengdu.

/f By way of comparison, Chengdu collects approximately Y 100 million through its urban maintenance and construction tax.

Source: Chengdu Municipal Government.

Table 3.24: LAND-RELATED REVENUE IN HANGZHOU: 1988-90
(Y million)

	1988	1989	1990	Total
Land reclamation fee /a	3.10	2.71	1.84	7.65
Vegetable land fund /b	2.50	3.17	1.61	7.28
Land use tax /c	-	18.93	21.20	40.13
Cultivated land tax /d	5.39	5.39	3.55	14.33
Total	10.99	30.20	28.20	69.39

/a The land reclamation fee was implemented in 1982. The rate was Y 5,000 per mu. Only cultivated land was charged this fee. Since 1987, with adoption of the cultivated land conversion tax, the rate was cut by half, to Y 2,500 per mu.

/b The vegetable land fund was implemented in 1986. The rate is Y 7,000 per mu. On vegetable land, no land reclamation fee is collected.

/c The land use tax was implemented in 1989. The rate in Hangzhou ranges from Y 3 per m^2 to Y 0.5 per m^2.

/d The cultivated land tax was implemented in 1987. The average rate is Y 6,000 per mu, or Y 7-10 per m^2.

Source: Hangzhou Municipal Government.

Table 3.25: REVENUE FROM LAND IN HONG KONG
(HK$ million)

	Total land premium	Crown rent	Property rates	Property income tax	Total land revenue	Total government revenue	Land revenues as % of total revenue
1974	318.6	34.7	368.9	141.1	863.3	5,305.8	16.3
1975	287.4	40.8	407.9	148.0	884.1	5,973.1	14.8
1976	345.9	68.2	534.4	147.7	1,096.2	6,724.6	16.3
1977	557.3	60.5	618.7	252.7	1,489.2	7,575.8	19.7
1978	1,831.3	89.4	722.9	243.2	2,886.8	10,232.6	28.2
1979	2,007.8	92.5	806.9	238.5	3,145.7	12,557.0	25.5
1980	2,845.2	136.0	889.3	297.8	4,168.3	16,796.1	24.8
1981	10,769.8	158.4	986.1	330.9	12,245.2	30,290.3	40.4
1982	9,676.5	238.5	1,050.9	766.2	11,732.1	34,312.9	34.2
1983	5,048.2	180.2	696.9	779.5	6,704.8	31,097.6	21.6
1984	2,267.1	231.1	1,155.5	601.9	4,255.6	30,399.7	14.0
1985	4,267.2	235.3	1,222.2	850.8	6,575.5	36,342.5	18.1
1986	3,895.0	272.4	1,770.0	701.5	6,638.9	43,695.0	15.2
1987	756.0	342.6	1,188.0	902.7	3,189.3	48,602.0	6.6
1988	461.0	491.3	1,373.0	895.1	3,220.4	60,875.0	5.2
1989	365.0	632.1	1,517.0	869.5	3,383.6	72,658.0	4.7
1990	212.0	767.8	1,663.0	953.1	3,595.9	82,429.0	4.3

Sources: Director of Accounting Services, *Annual Departmental Report*, 1974-90; Commissioner for Inland Revenue, *Annual Departmental Report*, 1974-90; and Hong Kong Government, *Hong Kong Yearbook*, 1974-91.

Recent World Bank work on property taxes, moreover, carries a set of cautionary warnings, which, by extension, can apply to any land tax instruments:35/

- Property taxes can be extremely unpopular as they often represent one of the few instances where a large percentage of households confront a tax bill. In developing countries, revenues from households are usually derived from indirect taxes, whose incidence is largely hidden in the form of higher prices. Where payroll and income taxes exist, their coverage is often limited (and evasion is minimized through withholding at the source).

- Too much time has often been spent on the "upstream" stages of property taxation—discovery and valuation, important, but also costly—to the neglect of collection.36/

- Property tax policies—on the rate structure and method of periodic *revaluation*—have generally led to decisions to impose low nominal tax rates,

35/ W. Dillinger, *Urban Property Tax Reform: Guidelines and Recommendations*, World Bank, April 1991; R. Bahl and J. Zhang, *Taxing Urban Land in China*, World Bank, Report No. INU-39, March 1989.

36/ See footnote (c), Table 3.19 for a cautionary tale involving China.

often in response to *political pressures* from those assessed, which have proved uniformly heavy around the world.

- The costs of administering the tax are not negligible and, if low tax rates are adopted, the program may generate little *net* revenue, once such costs are deducted.

- The imposition of a tax will require not only the completion of a plot-by-plot cadaster but also a computerized system linking the industrial and commercial bureaus, the state land acquisition authorities, the building administrations, and the tax authorities to update the cadaster.

- Property valuation is a major roadblock and procedures should be simplified, by omitting or charging a flat licensing fee for most small properties. The bulk of revenues are likely to be concentrated among major land users and CBD users such as hotels, department stores, and office buildings (and, therefore, valuation efforts should also be focused on this small group).

- Authorities should avoid giving tax concessions to users who are self-evidently located on land too valuable to justify current use. However, the efficiency benefit of property taxation in encouraging the relocation of such occupiers should not be exaggerated.

The Legal Underpinnings of Price and Property Rights Reforms

Properly functioning property markets presuppose a legal framework in place, broadly defined to cover ownership, instruments, institutions, and resolution-dispute mechanisms comparable to those found in market economies. As leasehold systems are adopted more widely, China's authorities will face challenges in each of these areas.

Currently, who actually represents the state as the titleholder is uncertain. China should assign that role to either a national or local institution. The issue may appear academic; it is not. Particularly for foreign investors, it contributes to a perception of opaqueness and lack of sophistication. As always, those investors have many options across the Pacific Rim; these concerns should not be taken lightly. The report recommends that the local State Land Administration, which is already the key *management* agent in land-related issues, be clearly designated as the agency to act on behalf of the state with respect to urban land and conversions to urban land.

Market-driven property transactions, including land use rights transfers between enterprises and institutions, require: (a) easy access to a systematic body of information, including land title documents that summarize all present rights, obligations, and encumbrances (mortgages, etc.); land use master plans and zoning or equivalent site-specific use restrictions; (b) dispute-resolution systems by an independent judiciary with a credible mandate to render judgments against Chinese nationals and Government itself; and (c) property markets that allow leaseholders to sell their use rights, and mortgagors who hold property gained by default to dispose of these with relatively little interference from the public sector. And, quite obviously, lease documents, and the tender documents that will precede them, must follow a format and level of detail consistent with international best practices.

Chapters IV and V deal with the information requirements of urban land management reform. Anticipating those discussions, one can simply assert that fragmentation of authority in record-keeping (leading to relevant documents being assembled and filed by different agencies, reporting different sets of rights and obligations); the lack of mechanisms to rapidly access data (which often cannot be retrieved using modern data-processing techniques); and the perception that information is, in general, proprietary in nature and not available on demand; all these hinder the emergence of markets. The Bank study team was often forced to work with tourist city maps that omitted scale measures, and was sometimes denied access to large-scale master plans. If similar information in competing cities of Asia can be obtained as a matter of right, and with a minimum of Governmental interference, then China's cities will have to do a far better job of acknowledging consumer rights in this field. Secrecy and land market development are simply incompatible.37/

Anecdotal evidence, gathered from foreign-funded enterprises which has not yet been complemented by any systematic study, suggests that property dispute-resolution procedures are unsatisfactory, relying primarily on administrative arbitration methods and then, as a last resort, on a court system that has a reputation for limited independence, when confronted with litigants linked, directly or indirectly, to Government. The presumption exists that arbitration and judiciary procedures, when put to the test, will rule against the plaintiffs, be they foreign or domestic. Again, this judgment is subject to verification possible only after an extensive review of experience to date. Until such a time, one can only record that prevailing anecdotal evidence presents a negative verdict, with arbitrators and judges often viewed as acting on behalf of the interests of local authorities. That this will have a chilling effect on urban land management reform hardly needs underlining.

The accumulation of huge interenterprise unpaid debts, documented earlier, and the almost total absence of successful default judgments resulting in lenders acquiring real estate collateral, suggests not only that the judicial system is weak but also, upon further investigation, that the disposal of collateral property returned to the lender is not without problems. The transfer of property from one "owner" to another requires the fulfillment of onerous reviews and permissions, and renders the option often so problematic that overseas mortgage holders simply fail to foreclose on a property that would otherwise be taken and disposed of in a market economy. The Bank's previous report on housing reform stressed the pivotal role of financial intermediaries in the development of a commercial real estate market. This report can only reaffirm those conclusions. If foreign and domestic financial intermediaries feel existing procedures discriminate against them in property-related lending—making default judgments

---

37/ As noted, this penchant for secrecy extends to otherwise routine documents like municipal budgets. Foreigners also complain that procedures for issuing permits and permissions that accompany investments in China are often unpublished and unavailable for scrutiny.

difficult and property disposal subject to heavy public sector interference—then the reform effort will be stalled by what might appear, superficially, to be a mere technicality.

Legal rights and obligations, properly recorded, open to public inspection, and easily enforceable, may seem peripheral to the overall reform of real estate markets. Nothing could be further from the truth. A building incorporating one fundamental structural flaw may be rendered unusable though all other elements are in order. However difficult it may be to move in a coordinated fashion across all aspects of urban land management reform, an effort must be made to meet this goal as expeditiously as possible.

IV. REINVENTING THE CHINESE CITY: PLANNING WITH PROPERTY MARKETS IN MIND

Introduction

How have urban planners responded to the emergence of market and quasi-market pressures? And what remains to be done in the reform of urban planning? Those are the key issues to be addressed in this chapter.1/ The key messages can be summarized from the start: (a) actual development and its accompanying small-area infrastructure investment requirements are not synchronized, due to the rigidities imposed by rarely revised Master Plans; and (b) monitoring of actual small-area development is critical to any systemic reform which accommodates actual development with supportive infrastructure investments. However, at the margin, particularly at the district level of coastal cities, planners are beginning to accommodate developer-driven demands for more flexible norms and regulations that allow new developments and redevelopment in old core-city areas to achieve rates of return that are roughly comparable with other investment opportunities, and certainly higher than returns from "passive" investments in bonds or long-term savings accounts. In addition, criticism of local planning practices, catalogued below, does not imply that local urban planners are themselves blind to the inadequacies of the resultant "outputs." Planners in China operate within a bureaucratic environment that often precludes "first best" solutions because coordinated responses to the issues cited are not easy as long as decision-making authority is fragmented between and within layers of government.

The Orderly City: Local Urban Development Planning in China

In most countries self-described as "unitary" in character, and with a strong ideological commitment to administer the structure and spatial distribution of economic activity, one would expect local development planning, sensitive to market demand, to be of secondary importance. Detailed plans, laws, and regulations would be prepared by powerful central ministries, and central budget allocations would help implement the key infrastructure, economic and social projects that would shape the urban landscape. The outside observers would therefore look first to the central bureaucrats for an understanding of what is happening and why. In China, with some exceptions, one should direct one's attention to the local level instead. The central authorities continue to produce laws, regulations, norms and guidelines, many of which influence local planning, and these Beijing-based planners have the power to approve or deny many local practices. They do so within a traditional land use management framework that does not have thoroughgoing market-driven reform at its core. But de facto they exercise such power

---

1/ As background, the Bank has produced two reports bearing directly on this topic. One, on urbanization in Zhejiang Province, was based on field work carried out in five cities in 1986, and was issued in 1987. The other, focused on housing, drew upon preparation missions undertaken in 1990, was issued in June 1991; it was based primarily on a study of the provincial municipality of Tianjin (World Bank, *China: Zhejiang: Challenges of Rapid Urbanization*, Report No. 6612-CHA, August 3, 1987; *China: Implementation Options for Housing Reform*, op. cit).

very selectively. Particularly today, the power that comes with the ability to allocate significant budgetary resources to implement centrally conceived "visions" has been replaced by a decentralized model, characterized by self-reliant cities, enterprises and households.2/ A central *policy "vacuum,"* viewed from the perspective of the requirements for developing a regulated market economy, is detrimental to overall systemic reform, even if local development can be viewed, quite properly, as an area that should be largely managed at the local level.

To understand how cities are built in China, one must first review the role of the local Planning Commission, Construction Commission, Finance Bureau, and Land Administration Bureau. Within the Construction Commission, the City Planning and Real Estate Management Administration Bureaus are also key second-tier institutions. Land allocation follows a set pattern. Investments proposed by licensed enterprises and nonprofit institutions are vetted by the local Planning Commission and, once approved, are passed on to the City Planning Bureau for decisions on a site consistent with the overall or "macro" Master Plan that governs the future spatial development of the city, as well as any detailed control plans that may exist at the local (district, subdistrict) level. The Bureau works with the enterprise not only in identifying the exact location, but also on all land use and associated facilities' plans. These plans, once finalized, are reviewed by other city and subcity agencies, who are given an opportunity to register objections. Thereafter the site plan is followed by the issuance of various permits and by the acquisition of the site, as necessary, by the local bureau of SLA, in line with land requisition quota guidelines. Very large projects require additional provincial or central government approvals, complicating the above process (Box 4.1). The 1990 Urban Planning Law codifies this procedure as follows:

> "A construction project in the urban planned area that needs
> to apply for urban land shall apply to the urban planning
> department by presenting the relevant documents indicating
> the state approval of the project. The urban planning
> department shall approve the location and boundary of the
> site to be used by the project, provide conditions for
> designing and planning, and approve and issue the planning
> license for construction land. The unit or individual
> undertaking the project may apply to the land administration
> department at or above county level for use of land only after
> receiving the planning license for construction land. After
> the application has been examined and approved by people's
> government at or above county level, the land administration
> department will then allocate the land to the unit or
> individual undertaking the project."

2/ The sample of cities used to document this study is biased in favor of cities with provincial status or with powers to report directly to the central government. The roles of provinces may be understated. (For greater details, see Annex 4.)

Box 4.1: LAND REQUISITION REGULATIONS IN CHINA

Where a project requires less than 3 mu (2,000 m^2) of cultivated land or less than 10 mu (6,700 m^2) of uncultivated land, local governments at the local (county) level can make the appropriate authorizations. Projects requiring up to 1,000 mu of cultivated land or 2,000 mu of uncultivated land require provincial government authority, except for local authorities who have special autonomy, including many of the large metropolitan coastal cities (Guangzhou included). If land requisition for a project requires more than 1,000 mu of cultivated land or 2,000 mu of uncultivated land, then the State Council (Cabinet) itself must grant the necessary approvals. *Local authorities and representatives of the SLA in Beijing suggest that the practice of subdividing a project into phases, each small enough to avoid approvals from higher-level authorities, is rare for very small projects. Projects requiring provincial or State Council approval, however, are frequently divided into discrete segments with the precise intent of avoiding scrutiny.* The degree to which such practices are followed are unfathomable to foreign analysts, and apparently poorly monitored by the SLA. Physical quota controls on land use requests, though intuitively attractive as a transitional device during periods when enterprises can avoid "hard budget constraints," are no substitutes for land prices that have a direct bearing on enterprise after-tax profits. Quotas are but one of many devices cited in this report as "changes" that are labeled "reforms" without advancing the ultimate objective of introducing a regulated market economy.

The quota system is not only a second-best "market" proxy tool, it is misdirected because it assumes implicitly that the loss of cultivated land is driven by urban (city and town) construction requirements. In fact, *a careful review of recent evidence suggests that the loss of cultivated land has very little to do with urbanization requirements* (Table 1). This is consistent with the well-established fact that urban development requires very little land, in terms of cultivated land conversion. Meat-cleaver tactics, though labeled as reform, are both inadequate and inappropriate. Too much administrative control is being devoted to what is a minor problem. Once again, prices, not bureaucratic quotas, is the simple and only reasonable method to deal with the competing claims of agriculture and high "value-added" expansion of urban areas.

Table 1: STRUCTURE OF LOST CULTIVATED LAND IN CHINA: 1988 AND 1989

	1988		1989	
	'000 ha	Percent	'000 ha	Percent
Total Cultivated Land Loss	676.3	100.00	417.3	100.00
State Construction	71.2	10.52	51.2	12.27
City	9.2	1.36	6.0	1.44
Designated towns	9.0	1.32	5.3	1.27
Independent factories	14.9	2.20	10.9	2.62
Railway	3.5	0.52	3.7	0.89
Highway	16.3	2.41	8.4	2.02
Hydroelectric projects	13.0	1.93	11.7	2.80
Other	5.2	0.77	5.1	1.23
Collective Construction	29.0	4.29	22.7	5.44
Roads	7.6	1.12	4.9	1.17
Irrigation	9.1	1.35	13.2	3.17
TVEs	7.7	1.14	2.9	0.69
Farmer housing	22.0	3.25	15.3	3.68
Other	4.6	0.68	1.7	0.41
Agricultural Restructuring	394.8	58.37	231.1	55.38
For fruit trees	119.4	17.65	69.2	16.57
For forest	155.3	22.97	93.4	22.39
For grassland	99.5	14.71	60.0	14.37
For fishponds	20.6	3.04	8.5	2.04
Natural Disaster Related	159.4	23.56	97.0	23.24

Source: State Land Administration Bureau.

In theory, almost all decisions regarding urban land development, including the uses, location, density, timing, and size of the real estate development are controlled by city agencies responsible for the close monitoring of the "city planning area," which is that part of the city proper subject to strict urban growth management.*3/* This state of affairs needs to be modified to deal with an emerging regulated market economy. *The current system is not effectively organized to deal with an alternative demand-driven model, whereby individual developers or investors would prepare investment proposals, seek out appropriate sites for physical development, and request permits to be processed by agencies interested primarily in ensuring that certain performance indicators are met.* Such performance indicators could, for example, deal with health, safety, and environmental concerns; or they could involve assessments as to the ability of the existing infrastructure network to accommodate the proposed investments, requiring remedial steps. As noted below, in Section C, this formal structure of planning controls has begun to change at the margin, particularly among southern coastal cities and in the Special Economic Development Zones, which are given broad autonomy and encouraged to experiment with market-driven planning tools. This was not clearly apparent to international observers until 1991/92.

For example, according to the Bank's earlier Zhejiang and Housing reports, even the emergence of the REDCs, building commercial estates with properties for sale to a number of buyers, did not appear to fundamentally affect the physical planning system. In market economies, such multioccupant subdivisions originate with developers, who draw on various independent agents, including architects, brokers, contractors, and bankers, to satisfy perceived demand. Given assumptions about market trends, developers decide what to build, how much to build and when, where to locate the development, and how to price the resulting product. They assume a financial risk and are thus rewarded or penalized, depending on the astuteness of their judgment.

The REDCs, instead, appeared to be builder-centers, with land, project financing and subcontractors as the only elements outside a self-contained system. Land continued to be allocated in a noncompetitive manner, and producers were encouraged by public policy (and rewarded by an absence of competing alternative delivery systems) to focus on gross output measures, with little regard for variety in unit size or type of units marketed. A set of norms and regulations left little latitude, in any case, encouraging the construction of similarly configured walk-up apartments containing four to seven floors; with the associated production of obligatory, comprehensive "support facilities and infrastructure"; utilizing land rather

---

3/   Between theory and practice, good connections and practical political considerations play an undocumented role.

indifferently, so that developments seemed to differ little in intensity regardless of the implicit value of the land.4/

With residential greenfield developments largely in mind, those earlier Bank reports concentrated on the housing delivery system's ability to produce enormous amounts of floor space, while issuing a series of warnings:

(a)   In complete disregard for underlying land values, gross population densities (i.e., the ratio between population and the total built-up area) across "Socialist" suburbs were converging over time, due to the fact that land use standards in housing estates tended to be uniform from suburb to suburb, independent of the city or city location involved.

(b)   Master Plans, governing the location of various types of land uses and the location of trunk infrastructure and citywide social amenities in China, were rarely revised, static products that ignored alternative-growth scenarios, neglected the cost implications of the plans, and, over time, promoted implementation of major investments within a time frame and in dimensions that ignored actual demand. In addition, Master Plans were criticized for encouraging an unnecessary separation of land uses and promoting self-standing satellite zones costly to service with connective infrastructure; and discouraging the more compact, continuous expansion of cities.

(c)   Both the Master Plans, in advocating "city beautiful" models, and associated regulations involving compensation arrangements to existing occupants, conspired to promote a policy of dedensification of inner cities, with an accompanying neglect of the package of infrastructure investments needed for redevelopment, and a failure to recycle downtown property through a change to more profitable uses. That same strategy, in neglecting the value of land (and governed by less burdensome compensation rules for the displaced), was held responsible for the excessive demolition of structures to improve cross-city transportation facilities, even when these were otherwise justified, and for the neglect of historic neighborhoods.

4/   Even so, by contrast with their Soviet counterparts, the Chinese companies have had the advantage of being able to acquire building materials through the market, and the good fortune to adopt "appropriate" building technologies that have avoided the use of large, prefabricated panels requiring factory construction and installation using cranes. They are also largely driven by the type of constrained profit maximization model described in Chapter III.

(d)   At the project level, in greenfield sites, the very low gross residential floor to land area ratios,5/ averaging less than 1:1, were criticized as wasteful, and the relative absence of high-density redevelopment projects was noted, again with disapproval.

Yet some countertrends, viewed favorably in the cited Bank reports, were identified, but labeled exceptional in scale, both within any one city and in terms of all cities involved. By 1990, efforts at making redevelopment projects more profitable emerged in places like Beijing, with the promotion of mixed-use development (including office and commercial space) and the creation of new financial incentives to deter former residents from automatically returning to a redevelopment area at little or no cost. Similarly, note was taken of the changing land allocation process in Guangzhou, where real estate development companies were entering into a more competitive system of site selection, and where land allocation was no longer viewed as a free good (requisition of land from farmers excepted), but one for which the city should receive compensation in cash or in kind. It is now clear that such changes, at the margin, are more significant than anticipated by the earlier cited Bank reports.

Chinese Planning Practices in Response to Emerging Land Markets:
A Reassessment

The Bank's current reassessment, based on a review of continuing and accelerating experiments across many cities and benefiting from greater exposure to the vanguard cities of the South, reconfirms the validity of many key earlier conclusions, while modifying others. *The reliance on "macro" Master Plans has remained unchanged, even though most were prepared in the late 1970s or early 1980s, predating the emergence of the reforms catalogued above, and based on outdated assumptions concerning population and employment growth, at the municipal and small-area level.* New or amended Master Plans (Shenzhen; Shanghai) prove only that the Design Institutes in charge, reporting to the local Urban Planning Bureaus, continue to be dominated by architect-planners with little access to "feedback" based on systematic monitoring of relevant small-area demographic and economic indicators, and that these agencies still show little apparent concern about the economic costs or consequences of the actions outlined in the Plan. These same static planning exercises, still concerned with an immutable final product, are being replicated as new plans are developed. Mere updating of plans using inappropriate assumptions and tools does not represent systemic reform.

A distillation of international best practices (Annex 9) suggest that China's urban planners charged with developing macrospatial, metropolitan plans should develop Structure Plans, which:

5/   The gross residential floor to land area ratio is the ratio between the total floor area, excluding community facilities, and the total land area of the estate, including green space and that occupied by all mandated community facilities, whose existence, location and layout reflects norms, not land values. In contrast, gross building floor to land area ratios incorporate all building stock in the numerator, and automatically yield higher floor to land area ratios.

(a)   begin with an examination of the global configuration of *the existing city*, including detailed (small area) information on present land use, land prices, and population and employment densities. This exercise, which should be updated at frequent intervals (at least every two to three years) can benefit from tools not available to the original group of Chinese master planners, including satellite imagery and the computer-assisted digitization of local maps upon which one can superimpose both the present and emerging trends in location behavior, and the existing and projected network of trunk infrastructure;

(b)   develop *alternative scenarios* of expected expansion and redevelopment, with the associated basic infrastructure networks and other facilities needed to support related urban configuration of the city, clearly spelled out, and backed up in each case by enough data to allow the cost consequences of each scenario to be estimated;

(c)   subject each scenario to *widespread review* both by all the affected public authorities, and *by the ultimate "beneficiaries" or consumers* of urban land. In no way should this process be viewed as an exclusionary or elitist exercise driven by the preferences of the few;

(d)   judge scenarios by *multiple criteria*, including the infrastructure costs of producing additional developable land in each case and the degree to which the proposed macrospatial plan conforms with evidence of consumer preferences regarding desirable densities, locations, and land use patterns. These preferences should be disregarded only if the consequences of endorsing them, in any one instance, create serious problems which cannot be mitigated by complementary public policies and investments. *The Structure Plan, then, would not be "owned" by the planners, but emerge, instead, as a "living" document subject to extensive public review.*

The Structure Plan, with its vision of the future spatial configuration of the city, would become a reference framework used to coordinate the demand-driven, phased introduction of infrastructure investments, and to develop and apply complementary regulatory instruments (performance indicators in developed areas, subdivision regulations affecting the urban development of "raw" land, environmental controls, and historic preservation of selected neighborhoods). Unlike Master Plans, these Structure Plans would be prepared relatively quickly, and periodically reviewed and updated to accommodate unexpected changes in user preferences that are not self-evidently damaging in their consequences, with the ultimate goal—to establish an internationally competitive city—borne in mind (Box 4.2).

Structure Plans should form the basis for infrastructure development and financing plans, drawing on a variety of cost-recovery mechanisms that allow the overall scheme to be implemented in an efficient manner. Clearly, as noted earlier, *this Structure Plan approach presupposes that what matters is process, not static outcomes, and that sensitivity to*

Box 4.2: SHANGHAI: AN ALTERNATIVE APPROACH TO THE MASTER PLAN?

An excellent case study of an alternative approach was produced in 1989 using Shanghai as a model, by a combined team from the Shanghai City Planning and Design Institute and French consultants. The conceptual approach of the report consisted of a comparison between the objectives of the Master Plan and the urbanization trends of the city, followed by the formulation of alternative spatial development scenarios which took into account the inconsistencies noted between objectives and trends. These scenarios differed in that one forcibly reoriented trends, another guided trend development, while yet another simply accommodated emerging trends. The costs and benefits of each was then examined, with priority placed on the best way to encourage potential investment promoting a more competitive city.

The trends, countering Master Plan assumptions, and often identified using satellite imagery included: (a) the fact that the agglomeration already greatly surpassed the limits set by the Plan, particularly in the West, led by extension of the city and the densification of the peri-urban areas and supported by extensive interregional transport investments, as well as various economic development zones; (b) the failure of a city center dedensification strategy, due to relocation financing problems, the relative attractiveness exercised by the core in terms of amenities and employment, and the growing impact of previously neglected "temporary residents"; (c) the failure of the east shore of the Huangpu River to develop as desired, given the delay in installing cross-river investments, the presence of existing storage and industrial uses incompatible with the amenities required to turn Pudong into a high-quality tertiary center; and the degree of commuting imposed on newly located Pudong residents.

Design Institute managers, interviewed during the current sector study, claimed that a new plan, using newer tools and analyses, would be prepared by 1993, and be more accommodating of actual growth trends. A review of work done through August 1992 suggests that traditional practices prevailed and that the 1989 exercise was never internalized.

---

monitoring indicators and user preferences is critical to planning. It also presupposes that these are *local* exercises guided by very broad central guidelines and not otherwise subject to central approval, including submission to the State Council (Cabinet). *It is unlikely that central bodies have any comparative advantage in vetting urban planning exercises, particularly if the emerging model of a regulated market economy is to have any meaning.* Requiring a "stamp of approval" from the State Council virtually guarantees that cities will continue to produce static plans subject to minimal change over time.

This suggested reform approach contrasts sharply with China's existing macrourban spatial planning, which still responds to central guidelines, partly because most such plans are at least a decade old and are legally binding documents approved by the State Council (Cabinet). The existing system neglects present land use and densities, and has no mechanism to monitor them at the municipal level and, where possible, adapt to them, by modifying policies, regulations and infrastructure development phasing. Consumer preferences are conspicuously ignored, even though a regulated market economy has been endorsed as the overall key objective of reform. Instead, the Master Plan resembles the architectural design plans for an office building or an apartment complex, proprietary in nature, "cast in concrete," and nothing less than a "product" meant to be built as is.

China's existing urban plans, which carry the unusual disadvantage of being implemented in a rapid and single-minded manner, have imbedded within them several specific abstract and outdated ideas which previous Bank reports did not fully explore and subject to critical scrutiny. Six items are particularly striking:

(a)   the building of trunk infrastructure without regard to "rate of return" calculations, particularly in terms of timing, scale and design, given self-evident demand; and in terms of foregone options, involving alternative subsector infrastructure investments during a five- to ten-year horizon;

(b)   the failure to tackle the challenge (and value-added opportunities) of redevelopment and historic preservation in a systematic manner, covering a whole pre-1949 city core;

(c)   the related failure to assess the negative consequences of a central area strategy undergirded by assumptions that dedensification is an undisputable "good";

(d)   the adoption of administrative control mechanisms as a means to preserve valuable, urbanizable land for the inherently lower-value cultivation of food supplies intended to guarantee each city a means of "self-sufficiency" in a very narrow geographic sense;

(e)   the creation of discrete satellite towns and economic development districts, far from the CBD, as greenfield islands intended to offset pressure on the existing built-up areas, but with total disregard of the costs of the local and connective infrastructure investments involved; and

(f)   the related adoption of a segregated land use strategy that, in its extreme form, designates such towns and districts as single- or limited-purpose activity centers, devoted to electronics here, transport equipment there, or (Pudong, Shanghai) the creation of a central business district built *de novo*. Concomitantly, there is a tendency to funnel foreign-funded industrial activities to particular zones, as if they could not otherwise be accommodated by the existing urban fabric. Worse still, where sector team members were able to interview local officials, there was little evidence that comprehensive feasibility studies, with potential market demand in mind, have ever been conducted to validate these decisions to promote special-purpose, segregated development islands. *In areas like Pudong, Shanghai, and the various special economic zones established in Guangzhou or Hangzhou, the investors are expected to be primarily or significantly offshore in nature. They are free to ignore the presumptions of local planners, who still think in terms of assigning sites to enterprises patiently waiting in a queue.* Given the magnitude of infrastructure investments involved, and the danger that these may drain resources away from other locations with high-priority infrastructure investment requirements, this is a very serious flaw that demonstrates all too graphically how the planners that shape each city have failed to grasp the "new rules of the game" that accompany a demand-driven economy.

In this report, only five examples will be used to illustrate the harmful effects of abstract Master Plan efforts devoid of economic content that were documented during the course of the sector study: (a) Pudong, Shanghai; (b) Fuzhou; (c) Shenzhen; (d) Hangzhou; and (e) Guangzhou.

Pudong, on the east side of Shanghai's Huangpu River, appears to be a physical planner's dream: a deceptive "blank slate." Centered across from the famed Bund, the heart of the west-side CBD, and paralleling the heavily urbanized old city, both north and south; it seems to be an obvious choice for introducing the land use changes required to create a restructured Shanghai, ready to face the international competition as a Pacific Rim center, yet free of the messy requirements imposed by redevelopment constraints.

Pudong, as currently envisioned, will expand from a built-up area of 38 km^2 in 1990 to more than 100 km^2 in the year 2000. The urban population is expected to double from 600,000 to 1.2 million. Currently a center of more than 2,000 industrial sites (400,000 workers), several dormitory suburbs, and many rural communities, Pudong is to be administratively transformed into spatially and use-segregated "islands," whose (1990-2000) infrastructure costs (including cross-river connections) will total Y 60 billion or $10 billion. In addition, significant if undocumented costs will be incurred for relocation of existing users, replacement of market gardens and food production, and cleaning up hitherto unpublicized polluted sites. There will be five self-contained districts, each separated by a greenbelt 2-3 km in width:

- *Liujiazui*, located across from the Shanghai Bund, is to be the "golden triangle" of Pudong, and, covering 28 km^2, will become a center for commercial services;

- *Wai Gaoqiao*, encompassing 75 km^2, and located 20 km from the center of Shanghai, on the Yangtze River, will be developed as a state-of-the-art port, capable of accommodating 10,000-ton class ships. Within the area, a 10-km^2 free-trade zone will be created to accommodate export processing, storage, and entrepôt trade;

- *Qingningshi-Jingqiao* and *Zhoujiadu-Liuli* (21 km^2 and 34 km^2, respectively) will be set aside for high-technology, nonpolluting enterprises;

- *Beicai-Zhangjiang* will be the fifth and final area, covering 17 km^2, and designed by the physical planners as a science, research and educational center.

It has proved difficult for the sector study team to determine how the size, locations, and uses of the users could be so confidently determined by planners lacking information about real estate development as a market-driven economic activity. The Pudong scheme is extremely ambitious, costly, and driven by physical planning parameters, uninformed by marketing feasibility studies. Only the plans regarding the planned new CBD, at Liujiazui, have been reviewed carefully by the Bank, and the remarks that follow do not necessarily reflect a more generalized skepticism concerning other component parts of the Pudong scheme. The Liujiazui plan is driven by a "city beautiful" model that attempts to address the perceived lack of green space on the west side of the river (Puxi) by prescribing extravagant uses of "CBD" land: fully 30 percent of the district will be devoted to open space, including the very valuable riverfront area facing the Bund. Floor to area ratios are planned with limited regard to relative land prices: the choicest sites, facing the west bank, and having greatest access to the existing center, will be set aside for low-rise developments; densities will increase toward the periphery, while implicit land values would dictate the exact opposite.6/

More generally, key transport nodes, created by the Nanpu and Ningpu bridges, the extension of the subway into Pudong, the reconstruction of Yanggao Road (Pudong's spine),7/ and the completion of the citywide inner-ring road, seem to have limited bearing on land use plans, with the potential real estate development impact of key "nodes" severely underestimated. And finally, all statements to the contrary, it is not clear that Pudong's development strategy will necessarily contribute in an optimal manner to the self-evident objectives of modernizing Puxi. Particularly with major cross-river investments in place, Pudong would appear to be ideally suited to relocate low-value Puxi land users to the east bank. If Shanghai's objective is to be at the cutting edge of a foreign-financed technological transformation of industry, backed by the requisite commercial and personal services, then existing sites in Puxi (including the development zones of Hongqiao, Caohejing, and Minghang) and other redevelopable plots on the west side seem *prima facie* potentially more efficient ways to achieve that objective. These alternatives do not seem to have been seriously studied. Perhaps the most important lesson, overall, is that past practices of ignoring trade-offs, and

---

6/ This "vision" is graphically described in a recent official document, *Shanghai Property 1991*: "The center ... together with parts of the Nanjing Road-Bund form the Shanghai CBD.... [T]he riverside area will be mainly arranged with open grounds as well as low-density buildings with public open space, amusement parks, recreation centers, exhibition hall, etc. ..., while the central part will be composed of high-density and high-standard modern comprehensive developments for finance, trade, office, and hotel services. In order to leave a clear field of vision from the skyscrapers in the center of Liujiazhui Finance and Trade Zone to the Water Front, the building heights will be designed to fall gradually from the central part of the riverside area." (Source: Office of the Shanghai Municipal Committee for Land Use Reform and Shanghai Municipal Statistical Bureau in conjunction with Jones, Long Wooten, Hong Kong, *Shanghai Property 1991*, Hong Kong, 1992.)

7/ The reconstruction of Yanggao Road provides another example of planning where costs and benefits appear to have been ignored. Now barely more than a local road carrying little traffic, local planners initially proposed a 35 m wide highway plan, with land reserved for a 50 m wide road when demand justified this. The plan has since been revised by central authorities and a 50 m wide road will be built in one stage. The step was taken without the benefit of economic analysis, according to Shanghai Construction Commission sources.

market research, in making infrastructure investments or assessing the feasibility of the plans for land development, apparently continue to prevail.8/

Fuzhou's new Master Plan, still under preparation and not made available to the sector study team, covers 30 years (1990-2020). It envisions the creation of a 3 km² park along the most important commercial street (May First Road), where two proposed light rail lines will intersect. The city's growth will promote dedensification of the center city, prevent incremental suburbanization, and focus growth in five self-sufficient satellite cities, amply separated from one another and the existing city by greenbelts, acting as buffer zones. Light rail systems will be built to connect each satellite with the city center. There appears to have been little analysis of alternatives undertaken, to compare benefits and costs, measured in terms of developable land made available per unit of investment required (on- and off-site). The scheme was developed with the assistance of Singapore consultants, and provides an example of the fact that foreign expertise, in and of itself, may not be appropriate; in fact, it may "validate" concepts that will harm the economic competitiveness of the city in the future.

Shenzhen, often viewed as in the vanguard of real estate reform, produced a second comprehensive Master Plan, approved by the State Council in 1989. Given a variety of geographic constraints, and the saturation of the existing CBD, the new Plan calls for a new urban downtown, in Fujian district, to the west of the existing core, covering 44.5 km². If intended to extend the CBD, whose functions are primarily tertiary in nature, the plan is quite inadequate. The new district is zoned primarily for residential uses, though considerable space will be devoted to governmental institutions. This area will be built using relatively low floor to land area ratios, and dominated by green space and recreational activity centers. As a result, per capita land consumption (124 m²) will resemble levels found in towns and townships rather than large city centers. Ironically, this plan was developed at the same time the city was planning to carry out expensive land reclamation projects along its coastline.

Hangzhou Municipality, as part of work financed under the preparation of the Zhejiang Multicities Project, engaged foreign consultants to evaluate its 1983 Master Plan, given trends since then.9/ The Master Plan was developed around at least two premises: (a) that the interregional transport investments (roads, railroads) would be spatially dispersed, and thus have limited district-level impacts; and (b) that urban expansion could proceed in several directions from the city center, promoting, for example, the development of "virgin" agricultural land in the southeast quadrant of the city (300 ha), while accommodating the infrastructure requirements of already urbanized or urbanizing areas, particularly the northeast quadrant. In fact, the interregional infrastructure investments that actually took place during the decade created a strategic node of highways, railways, canals, and airports in the "northeastern

---

8/   Even in 1992, the Shanghai Government proposed World Bank financing of a cross-river link between Pudong and Chongming Island, involving 20 km of tunnels (4 tunnel lanes) and 18 km of surface roads (8 lanes wide). The total cost of the project (1992 values) will total Y 8 billion for the tunnels alone. No land use marketing feasibility study or physical plan accompanied the proposed scheme.

9/   Groupe Huit, *Zhejiang Multi-Cities Project: Final Report*, November 1991.

extension," a development unforeseen by planners. Yet the Master Plan dictated a fixed development plan for that northeastern corridor, provided it with the trunk infrastructure linked to those assumptions and then, ignoring the benefits of ongoing monitoring of actual economic activity location, did little more. Recent initiatives to build spatially segregated economic development zones, to the south, and far from the city center, graphically illustrate a failure on the part of municipal planners to set demand-driven priorities with budget constraints in mind.

The consultants pointed out specific deficiencies in the planning process, zeroing in on the problems of the "Northern Extension" (Box 4.3). Local planners maintained that trunk infrastructure investments had accommodated (in the main) developments that actually took place in different suburban extensions of the city. They agreed, however, that district-level control plans, with accompanying secondary and tertiary investments, were inadequate and had underestimated the cumulative impact of plot-by-plot locational choices that took place during the decade. Blame was placed on individual locational decisions that took place immediately after the Cultural Revolution (1966-76) and thus, by implication, unlikely to have continued since then. The foreign consultants, aided by modern monitoring tools such as those afforded by satellite imagery, suggested a different unfolding set of events. The end result, however, is one and the same. In summary, major infrastructure investments are being scattered across the municipal landscape, while major quadrants of the city develop in a disorderly fashion, with planners failing to redirect public investments to rectify problems created by past (and present) development trends subject to inadequate monitoring.

Box 4.3: HANGZHOU: THE URBAN PLANNING PROBLEMS OF THE NORTHERN EXTENSION

Overall, substantial outlays have been granted for facilities and organization of the road system within the city, over the last 10 years, and are programmed for the next five years; however, outside a few main axes, little effort has been expended on or is programmed for the outlying areas, in particular to the north of the city, where a huge zone of unanticipated and poorly monitored housing and industry has been allowed to emerge (i.e., premises built at random according to the land requisition possibilities available; factories lining the roadsides, leaving huge gaps of cultivated areas and producing noncontrollable discharges of liquids and gases).

The ad-hoc way in which industrial companies have set up in the northern zone is resulting in environmental problems and excessive use of land, in difficulties in services being provided by the road system and other infrastructure networks, and in operating infrastructure service costs which are higher because of the low densities involved. A redevelopment plan for the industrial fabric is required: it will have to rationalize land occupancy, while absorbing new demand, including that from units being displaced from the old city.

Source: Hangzhou City Planning Bureau; mission assessments.

An assessment can also be made of infrastructure planning in Guangzhou, whose reputation for being in the vanguard of reform is often confused (and enhanced) by the achievements of its Pearl River Delta neighbors. Figures A1.12 and A1.13 illustrate the existing *land* uses and the requirements imposed by the Master Plan in terms of trunk infrastructure requirements that partly shape those land use patterns. A quantitative analysis of the Plan reveals that 72 percent of the new areas to be developed under the Plan are located at between 10 and 42 km from the city center, while most of the economic, physical, and demographic growth is actually taking place within a 10 km radius of the city center. The Plan does not block small area development, which is facilitated by the district plans developed by lower-level authorities and described below, but it directs long-term investment in trunk infrastructure away from the areas with the greatest, self-evident potential for market-driven growth.10/ Finally, Box 4.4 on Tianjin's decision to build its Third Ring Road ahead of demand, while crowding out necessary infrastructure investments in core areas, merely reinforces the contention that the problem of misdirected Master Plan exercises is not confined to a few cities.

Box 4.4: TIANJIN'S THIRD RING ROAD: WHEN PLANNERS AND MARKET FORCES COLLIDE

Tianjin's urban population is largely contained within 9 or 10 km from the CBD, with approximately 80 percent living within 7 km of the city center. Most of this area has been historically poorly serviced with infrastructure; funding for secondary and tertiary sewer connections, for example, is still a problem to this day. Nevertheless, driven by the Master Plan, prepared before 1980, the local government decided to build a 100 km long Third Ring Road, 11 to 12 km from the city center, in an area largely reserved for greenfield uses. The expressway has three lanes in each direction, and, for a distance of approximately 25 km, is paralleled by a provincial expressway, with two lanes in each direction, linking Beijing and the Tianjin port area of Taegu. World Bank funds were used in the latter case. The Ring Road was costly to build, is expensive to maintain, and is grossly underutilized, though exact figures on the latter were not provided to the sector team.

In contrast to this rather bleak reassessment of macrospatial planning and associated trunk infrastructure investment locational priorities, the sector study team found significant if selective modifications at the district and subdistrict level, favoring market forces and the more efficient use of land.

At the district level, when actual real estate projects are being designed or vetted, "realism" sets in, and the local planners find it necessary to take economic feasibility and "local realities" into account. The result is ad-hoc but generally sensible planning. The key problem lies in the fact that the two exercises—Master Plan and district-level plan—are sequential and that no mechanism exists to allow for "feedback" that recasts the Master Plan's priorities, including the nature, location, and phasing of infrastructure investments. If local planners could follow Hong Kong and Singapore's example in developing more flexible macro

---

10/   Notwithstanding the fact that most of the newly setup factories are located in peripheral areas, some 55.7 percent of industrial establishments, 58.1 percent of the workforce, and 53.1 percent of the total industrial output were, in 1984, found in the inner core (S. Li, "A Comparative Study of the Urban Land Use Patterns in Guangzhou and Hong Kong," Hong Kong: Department of Economics, University of Hong Kong, Discussion Paper No. 79, December 1986, processed).

Structure Plans that allow for such feedback, the problem whereby infrastructure investments and actual spatial development diverge would be largely solved.

The undermining of the macrospatial "command economy" model at the localized level can best be understood by examining metropolitan trends in a spatially segmented manner. Land use systemic reform has to be seen as a phenomenon proceeding at a different pace, with different results, in four spatially distinct areas: the "old" (1949/50) city center; the suburban "Socialist" districts developed thereafter; the satellite towns, largely outside the city proper, assumed to bear the burden of accommodating much of the displacement required by the planned "dedensification" of the old city; and the peri-urban areas, variously defined to include the zones of the city proper that are not closely supervised by city planners (who focus on a more spatially compact "city planning area" and the even smaller "built-up area") and the suburban counties operating under the control of county authorities, who act largely in their own interest, except for the few satellite towns developed in their territory by municipal authorities. The aggregate outcome of this spatially segregated battle of plan versus market will not become clear for some time.

Typically, within the "old city," in the municipalities studied by the sector study team, and the near suburbs, redevelopment has emerged as a mechanism that is, *on a site-by-site basis*, raising floor to land area ratios from very low levels (0.3-0.6) to much higher ones (2.5-10.0), while transforming land uses. *Unfortunately, the scope of such redevelopment is still limited.* Table 4.1 provides a typical example of land use transformation at the city block level in areas in or near the old city. Notably, land devoted to industrial uses declines, as does land (but not necessarily building space) dedicated to residential uses. Other uses show dramatic increases. This varies city by city (Tables 4.2-4.4). Population densities, however, have not changed very much, because redevelopment has led to much higher consumption of floor space per capita. Using Shanghai as an example, on a district-by-district basis, a decade of redevelopment has led to either insignificant alterations in densities or to decreases that rarely exceed 9-10 percent of those recorded earlier. Redevelopment is accompanied by selective upgrading of local infrastructure; street widening projects are now often the catalyst for this intensification of land use, though other infrastructure upgrading typically lags behind and hinders redevelopment. As an example, Shanghai Municipality has requested Bank assistance in redeveloping nine parcels in the city, covering only 34 hectares, and characterized as having very great "value-added" potential. Of the nine, however, only one (covering 3.5 hectares) is rated as currently well-equipped for redevelopment.

Redevelopment, broadly defined, requires a change in land uses. China's "old city" areas have typically devoted too little land to the services sector, too much space to factories and warehouses, and, arguably, excessive land to accommodate residential uses. Change has taken place in various ways. Physical redevelopment is one mechanism, but, in the absence of redevelopment strategies endorsed at the municipal level, the scope of land use change induced by this tool is still limited. Alternatively, land use is altered as residential structures are converted to commercial uses, with or without official permission. And many factories and institutional land users, with land to spare, have established joint-venture arrangements with partners eager to accommodate market demand. Occasionally the original

Table 4.1: TYPICAL LAND USE CONVERSION IN CITY CENTERS

	Before redevelopment %		After redevelopment %	
Land Area				
Street	8.0		18.0	
Residential	55.0		30.0	
Office	20.0		25.0	
Commercial	12.0		27.0	
Industrial	5.0		0.0	
Total	100.0		100.0	
	%	FAR	%	FAR
Floor Area				
Residential	49.7	0.6	24.3	2.5
Office	24.1	0.8	36.4	4.5
Commercial	21.7	1.2	39.3	4.5
Industrial	4.5	0.6	0.0	0.0
Total	100.0	0.7	100.0	3.1
	m^2		m^2	% Increase
Floor Area per Hectare				
Residential	3,300		7,500	127.3
Office	1,600		11,250	603.1
Commercial	1,440		12,150	743.8
Industrial	300		0	-100.0
Total	6,640		30,900	365.4

Note: It must be noted that while the residential area generally decreases, the residential floor space increases due to a much higher floor area ratio. The population density increases only slightly due to increases in floor consumption per household.

occupant has been forced (by mergers or other mechanisms) to simply relocate to suburban locations or to remain *in situ* but switch to other economic activities. A note of caution is necessary on this point. The original occupant always reports to, and is "owned" or supervised by a local industrial bureau; that bureau may insist that the property be reused for activities over which it can continue to claim "ownership" or supervisory rights. This intervening agent can thus block the emergence of appropriate reuse, from the perspective of citywide comparative economic advantage. Evidence that this may be happening is suggested by items such as are shown in Table 4.5, particularly within the old-city districts. Local authorities confirm this hypothesis is correct and constitutes a major barrier to developing a citywide industrial relocation strategy.

Table 4.2: SHANGHAI CITY: 23 REDEVELOPMENT PROJECTS

District	No. of blocks	Land area (ha)	Approved building area (m^2)	Of which: Public use (m^2)	Housing	Gross FAR
Yangpu	10	24.03	563,452	50,111	513,341	2.34
Yangpu	8	8.89	216,870	13,797	203,073	2.44
Hongkou	65	32.40	523,624	98,689	424,935	1.62
Hongkou	14	25.04	322,464	3,100	319,364	1.29
Zabei	16	18.04	624,265	220,361	403,904	3.46
Zabei	15	21.73	528,040	51,827	476,213	2.43
Putuo	26	30.14	746,886	25,758	721,128	2.48
Putuo	15	12.18	330,837	45,364	285,473	2.72
Jin'an	9	7.05	211,935	30,602	181,333	3.01
Jin'an	6	4.82	159,200	13,800	145,400	3.30
Jin'an	9	10.27	364,800	46,900	317,900	3.55
Changning	12	14.51	269,861	52,465	217,396	1.86
Changning	10	48.06	349,380	32,620	316,760	0.73
Xuhuei	26	66.40	1,767,800	213,500	1,554,300	2.66
Xuhuei	-	-	-	-	-	-
Luwan	12	8.56	448,182	13,420	434,762	5.24
Luwan	4	3.56	206,462	-	206,462	5.80
Nanshi	4	23.89	811,848	72,304	739,544	3.40
Nanshi	9	-	-	-	-	-
Nanshi	8	-	-	-	-	-
Huangpu	8	4.96	303,420	184,579	118,841	6.12
Huangpu	6	7.51	490,610	325,446	165,164	6.53
Huangpu	1	5.51	137,596	8,224	129,372	2.50
Total	293	377.55	9,377,532	1,502,867	7,874,665	2.48

Source: Shang Rongling and Zhong Yongjun (eds.), 1991, *One Apartment for Each Family—The Objective of Housing for the Year 2000*, pp. 131-132.

In the post-1949 "Socialist" suburban belt of development, comparisons of early and recent project-level development show evidence of improved land use, but the trends are far less dramatic. Floor to land area ratios that were once uniformly below 1:1 are now often above that, but the absolute improvement in land use efficiency is typically low (Tables 4.6-4.8). The driving force behind any change is probably the rising cost of land requisition, and the increased proportion of suburban land development carried out by profit-motivated real estate development companies.

Furthermore, and unlike evidence gathered in earlier Bank assessments, it is now clear that newer housing and commercial projects, *particularly in southern provinces*, typically devote *less* land to "public facilities" that are donated to the local neighborhood

Table 4.3: REDEVELOPMENT PROJECTS IN FUZHOU

Name of projects	Land (ha)	Building (10,000 m²)	FAR	Use type
1 Donghu	1.70	5.00	2.94	Housing
2 Jianhai	2.14	18.60	8.69	Mixed
3 Taohuashan	0.63	1.15	1.81	Housing
4 Qixinjing	5.00	11.00	2.20	Housing
5 Zhujing	4.00	9.56	2.39	Housing
6 Mingdong	0.37	3.00	8.11	Mixed
7 Yuanhong	1.40	11.70	8.36	Mixed
8 International	0.39	3.60	9.26	Mixed
9 Xianshi	0.80	2.56	3.20	Retail
10 Twin Towers	0.59	2.08	3.52	Office
11 Hua Lian	0.22	2.20	10.00	Mixed
Total	17.24	70.45	4.09	

Source: Fuzhou Land Administration Bureau.

Table 4.4: HOUSING REDEVELOPMENT IN HANGZHOU

Name of projects	Land (ha)	Building (10,000 m²)	FAR	Year of construction
1 Chenghuan	14.10	15.55	1.10	1981
2 Jiangchen	23.00	23.30	1.01	n.a.
3 Dongyuan	37.40	41.92	1.12	1988
4 Changqing	11.70	14.37	1.23	n.a.
5 Huazhang	13.75	20.79	1.51	n.a.
Total	99.95	115.93	1.16	

Source: Selected Works of Hangzhou Housing Plan, 1990.

authorities, but—at the same time—provide *greater* attention to landscaping and other factors meant to respond to consumer demand. Clearly these regionally segmented developments are market-driven. In areas, particularly in southern China, where *individuals* are buying houses, and relatively high incomes generate high demand for retail space, the "new look" project is more likely to emerge, simply because market forces are forcing developers and planners to change their practices more rapidly than elsewhere in China. For example, free-standing retail space located within the inner confines of a project, and implicitly disconnected from the larger community of potential customers, is giving way to ground-level shops that are incorporated

Table 4.5: SHANGHAI: CHANGING INDUSTRIAL FLOOR SPACE (1987-90)

	Land area (km²)	Building stock		Industrial building		Change (%)
		1987	1990	1987	1990	
		-- (10,000 m²) --		- (10,000 m²) -		
City proper	748.71	152.30	172.56	44.90	48.22	7.4
Huangpu /a	20.46	12.34	13.39	1.63	1.76	7.7
Nanshi /a	27.92	12.28	14.23	3.20	3.18	-0.6
Luwan /a	8.05	7.64	8.29	2.03	2.14	5.6
Xuhuei	46.64	16.99	18.81	4.32	4.61	6.8
Changning	28.82	11.69	13.88	3.07	3.20	4.3
Jingan /a	7.62	8.27	9.08	1.98	2.04	3.1
Putuo	29.88	14.50	16.73	4.13	4.50	8.9
Zabei	27.95	13.32	14.04	4.02	4.20	4.4
Hongkou	23.48	14.47	16.19	3.58	3.78	5.6
Yangpu	59.63	24.72	27.72	9.62	10.46	8.7
Minghang	43.08	6.17	7.51	2.93	3.38	15.6
Baoshan	425.18	9.90	12.69	4.39	4.97	13.1

/a These four districts lie entirely within the old "1949" city.

Source: *Shanghai Statistical Yearbook 1989*, p. 433.

directly into residential structures, particularly those adjacent to streets with heavy pedestrian traffic or otherwise considered comparatively accessible. Since these projects are closely supervised and regulated developments, such changes can be assumed to be "validated" by urban planners and their supervisory authorities (Box 4.5).

Less apparent is the degree to which approvals may have been obtained for the spontaneous conversion of ground-floor dwellings built in earlier periods for residential use and now devoted to commercial uses. Some of this "retrofitting" can hardly be characterized as unregulated, however. Many older estates were built with deep setbacks from the street. Often one finds that this open space is now occupied by recently built and *highly visible* low-rise commercial facilities that block easy pedestrian access to the residential structures behind them.

The satellite towns and economic development districts found in China's cities are, by contrast, creatures of the command system promoting a supply-driven, norm-restricted pattern of real estate development, unresponsive to market forces.11/ In fact, during the

---

11/ As noted, urban planners should not be held fully responsible for this, particularly when heavy industry projects authorized by the Planning Commission force planners to find suburban locations that protect residential land users from the environmental effects of massive heavy industry investments.

Table 4.6: NEW HOUSING PROJECTS IN SHANGHAI (1980-90)

No.	Project	District	Land area (ha)	Building floor area (10,000 m²)	Of which: Housing	Nonresidential	% of high-rise	% of nonresidential	FAR
1	Shiguang	Yangpu	45.33	49.79	43.18	6.61	23.06	13.28	1.10
2	Changbai	Yangpu	34.20	51.44	45.46	5.98	-	11.62	1.50
3	Gongnong	Yangpu	65.87	68.75	59.68	9.07	7.00	13.19	1.04
4	Mingxing	Yangpu	26.22	27.59	23.86	3.73	45.48	13.52	1.05
5	Quyang	Hongkou	78.37	107.32	87.58	19.74	38.00	18.40	1.37
6	Fengzheng	Hongkou	17.80	15.59	12.86	2.73	34.90	17.53	0.88
7	Yunguang	Hongkou	23.33	24.44	20.84	3.60	29.50	14.75	1.05
8	Pengpu 456	Zabei	56.31	51.10	46.00	5.10	-	9.98	0.91
9	Guangnong	Putuo	28.41	31.53	27.16	4.37	22.78	13.87	1.11
10	Hutai	Putuo	74.20	71.52	59.11	12.41	20.76	17.35	0.96
11	Changfeng	Putuo	45.50	47.80	43.25	4.65	-	9.73	1.05
12	Xianxia	Changning	74.40	82.85	73.62	9.23	40.63	11.14	1.11
13	Tianling	Xuhuei	97.10	116.30	105.60	10.70	51.50	9.20	1.20
14	Kangjian	Xuhuei	94.25	74.30	66.10	8.20	-	11.04	0.79
15	Dezhou	Nanshi	120.00	110.58	99.32	11.26	18.00	10.18	0.92
16	Shangnan	Nanshi	119.40	125.03	111.23	15.84	-	12.67	1.05
17	Shanggang	Nanshi	72.00	82.00	74.00	8.00	5.00	9.76	1.14
18	Xueye	Nanshi	28.44	28.50	26.66	2.84	26.00	9.96	1.00
19	Weifang	Huangpu	58.70	75.90	66.10	9.80	-	12.91	1.29
20	Zhuyuan	Huangpu	37.35	44.85	40.03	4.82	-	10.75	1.20

Source: See Table 4.2.

Table 4.7: NEW HOUSING DEVELOPMENT IN HANGZHOU

	Name of projects	Land (ha)	Building (10,000 m²)	FAR	Year of construction
1	Hemu	15.82	15.96	1.01	1980
2	Caohui	74.24	61.15	0.82	1979
3	Caohui-5	10.02	10.80	1.08	1982
4	Yujia-Lin	21.49	26.81	1.25	n.a.
5	Cuiyuan-1	10.98	15.22	1.39	1985
6	Cuiyuan-2	8.71	11.14	1.28	1986
7	Cuiyuan-3	11.59	12.16	1.05	1987
8	Cuiyuan-4	11.65	13.82	1.19	1988
9	Caihe-2	21.23	23.02	1.08	1984
10	Desheng	19.54	20.57	1.05	n.a.
11	Pujia	18.00	20.23	1.12	n.a.
12	Shibang-3	4.50	3.68	0.82	n.a.
13	Gudang	33.30	36.40	1.09	1988
14	Hangyang	18.90	21.93	1.16	n.a.
	Total	279.97	292.87	1.05	

Source: Selected Works of Hangzhou Housing Plan, 1990.

Table 4.8: NEW HOUSING DEVELOPMENT IN FUZHOU

Name of projects	Land (ha)	Building (10,000 m²)	FAR	Year of construction
1 Wangdian	53.90	61.50	1.14	1982
2 Shanchajie	16.41	22.28	1.36	1982
3 Puxia	7.86	11.63	1.48	1980
4 Yangqiao	8.81	11.82	1.34	1985
5 Yangxia	25.29	19.96	0.79	1979
6 Shanghai	14.30	19.14	1.34	n.a.
7 Liming	9.93	13.26	1.34	1986
8 Fenghuang	7.30	8.54	1.17	n.a.
9 Wufeng	2.87	4.23	1.47	n.a.
10 Pingdong	2.98	4.96	1.66	1981
11 Pingxi	11.47	13.10	1.14	1983
12 Station	7.00	21.00	3.00	1979
13 Xiaolu	2.49	4.20	1.69	1985
Total	170.61	215.62	1.26	

Source: Fuzhou Land Administration Bureau.

1980s many satellite areas were simply relabeled as economic development zones, requiring internal and connective infrastructure to attract joint-venture investors. The Master Plan of each city, developed on the basis of other criteria, somehow seemed to dovetail, at the local level, with spatial strategies to attract investors. Some might suggest that this spatial coincidence was driven by the lack of financial resources to fully implement the proposed satellite towns. Among the cities visited, the following examples of expedient conversion from satellite town to development magnet can be documented, though many more exist:

Guangzhou: Huangpu Economic Zone (25 km from city center)
Hangzhou: Xiasha Economic Development Zone (19.5 km from city center)
Fuzhou: Mawei Economic Development Zone (20 km from city center)
Chengdu: Longquanyi Industrial District (19 km from city center)
Shanghai: Minghang (30 km from city center) and Wujing (20 km from city center)

These are few in number, within any one metropolis, but they are typically disconnected from the built-up area, sited 20 to 40 kilometers away from the city center, and make relatively extravagant use of land, whether measured on a per-capita or a per-employee basis. They have been built at enormous cost, represented by such indicators as developable land per yuan of local and connective infrastructure invested, and have proved to be insignificant appendages to the urban network to which they belong. In both absolute or relative terms, few people work there, and most of these workers have to commute from their "old city" or suburban estates. Many forcibly relocated factory managers complain that their freight-related costs have grown dramatically; in addition, if meant to be self-contained communities, *and if intended to conserve*

Box 4.5: GUANGZHOU: INCREASING DENSITY IN NEW DEVELOPMENT

Like many other Chinese cities, land use density of new urban development in previous decades was not very high, particularly among industrial and institutional projects. According to a comprehensive urban land survey in Guangzhou in 1982, the general floor area ratio within the city built-up area was 0.33, with an average building height of 1.89 stories . Although there are no comparable data for more recent years, available information on individual projects indicates that much higher FARs are the norm. For example, among 50 new urban housing projects in Guangzhou completed in the past 10 years, the average floor area ratio is more than 2.0 with 2.53 for four central urban districts, and 1.91 for four suburban districts. Compared with many other cities in China, land value is clearly understood by both developers and planners. Here, we do not see large setbacks along major streets. We do not see significant amounts of unused land within housing districts. In order to save or intensively use land, many new building types have been created, and various innovative design and planning efforts have been made. Most apartment buildings along main streets are designed as mixed-used structures with leased retail space on the ground floor, leased offices on the second and third, and a landscaped terrace and housing on the fourth and above floors. The area between buildings is either used for additional retail space, or for well-maintained playground spaces. This contrasts with many old-type projects which leave vacant land in between structures.

Urban land use patterns consist of both different types of buildings and the way they are being arranged in space. In the past 30 years, new urban areas were developed in the form of identical apartment buildings placed in very similar arrangements across the country. Such land use patterns are now undergoing a series of changes in Guangzhou. One of these changes allows farmers to build preferred housing types within planned urban development areas. Farmers' houses, such as those in Tianhe and Shiqiao, reflect their preferences: 2-4 stories, with a small yard on the ground floor, and several balconies on upper levels. Each family is given a standard plot. They choose to use as much as they can, which results in very high floor area ratios—from 1.5 to 2.5. They provide an alternative housing type for urban dwellers. In some new housing projects, like Five Ram Village, a townhouse type of building was added to attract additional consumers. These new building types, and distinctive treatments along the main streets, have begun to create a different streetscape within the new projects.

Another new development in Guangzhou is that, unlike the past, farmers' interests are being carefully considered, and farmers' villages are being preserved during the process of urban expansion. In China, even though the Constitution states that rural land is collectively owned, rural property rights have not been well-protected. Whenever there is state land expropriation, only minimal compensation has been required. Both the economic interests and physical structures are sacrificed. Such practice has met increasing resistance from farmers. Instead of imposing government terms on farmers, in recent years Guangzhou has been experimenting with a "land readjustment" process, which has been widely practiced in Japan, Korea and Taiwan (China). In the Tianhe Railway Station area, besides the normal minimal land compensation for crops and structures, a parcel of prime land along the main street will be reconveyed to farmers for commercial development. And their village will also be maintained in the new area plan. This approach will reduce unnecessary delays during the land requisition process, and also protect farmers' interests. It also creates a more diverse urban environment. Many designers and planners would agree that most farmers' houses are more interesting, architecturally, than many modern apartment buildings. Unfortunately, most urban planners pay no attention to integrating such structures into new development. For example, in Minghang, Shanghai, the sector team was told that well-built village houses would be sacrificed for future urban expansion.

Source: Zhang Guixia, 1990, "Review of Urban Housing Development in Guangzhou," in Xu Shaoji (ed.), *Development of Guangzhou Real Estate Sector*.

---

land, the satellite cities have failed. Unfortunately, but most revealing of local monitoring practices, up-to-date information on "planned" versus "actual" outcomes is hard to find (Table

4.9), at the municipal level.12/ Again, such islands of development emerged as visions of planners, without the benefit of the sobering impact of comprehensive feasibility studies that incorporated marketability into their development equation. Perhaps state-owned enterprises could be *directed* to locate there, but, as locational flexibility becomes the norm, and foreign-funded ventures fill the void, this neglect of potential customer interest could prove to be an expensive experiment.

Table 4.9: SHANGHAI: BASIC SITUATION IN MINGHANG AND WUJING: 1980-90

Satellite town	Total town residents (10,000)	Built-up area (ha)	Land area per person (m²/p)	Number of workers (10,000)	Industrial	
					Land area (ha)	Land area per worker (m²/p)
Minghang						
1980	6.02	770	127.91	5.83	495	84.90
1990	12.52	1,818	145.21	n.a.	1,124	n.a.
Wujing						
1980	1.18	300	254.24	2.34	239	102.14
1990	2.88	381	132.34	n.a.	n.a.	n.a.
City proper						
1980	584.00	14,100	24.14	176.97	3,579	20.22
1990	706.01	21,600	30.59	n.a.	n.a.	n.a.

Source: Shanghai Institute of Urban Planning and Design, 1986, "Impacts of Satellite Town Development on Expansion and Redevelopment of Shanghai," Urban Redevelopment Plan, p. 154; Minghang District Planning Office, 1991.

Even in Guangzhou, where the costs of such a strategy have become obvious, the local Design Institute is busy planning more such satellite towns! Yeung, Deng, and Chen 13/ note that the Huangpu Economic and Technical Development Zone, 25 km from the Guangzhou city center, lacks a sound economic development rationale (from a marketing

12/ It is interesting to note that the most recent assessments (1992) made by specialists outside the Bank have encountered similar problems in documenting the same conclusions, have to cite data published in 1985 or 1986. They conclude that "in 1983 the total population of the satellite towns reached 580,000 or only 8.7 percent of Shanghai's total urban population. About half of the 430,000 industrial workers in these towns still have their household registration ... in Shanghai [city proper], and a substantial number of workers commute to work from the central city." K. Fung, Z. Yan, and Y. Ning, "Shanghai: China's World City," op. cit.

13/ Y. Yeung, Y. Deng, and H. Chen, "Guangzhou: The Southern Metropolis in Transformation," in Y. Yeung and X. Hu, eds., *China's Coastal Cities*, op. cit.

perspective) and has required large infrastructure investments, ignoring the relative benefits of investing in the city core and its near suburbs. As they rightly stress, "... as much as one third of the investment has been consumed in infrastructure ... [while] the overall objective of using the zone to revitalize technology in Guangzhou might be jeopardized by the ... [fact] that many of the enterprises set up so far were not large consumers of land,14/ public services, or environmentally polluting and could be located, in fact, in more central parts of the city." These authors then report (uncritically) on Guangzhou's plan to develop satellite towns within a framework stressing the need to locate these 20 to 80 km from the city centers, populated with 200,000 to 500,000 residents, too distant to ever be absorbed by the emerging metropolis. The lesson here is all too simple: Master Plan practices adapt reluctantly to the requirements of a market economy.

In spite of the trends over the last decade, most cities' Master Plans do not anticipate "exurban sprawl," and planners are yielding only slowly to such market economy signals. On the contrary, economic growth is expected to be confined to selective "old city" redevelopment, carefully regulated suburban development, and isolated exurban towns and zones. Satellite imagery confirms that a vast amount of peri-urban development has emerged in the last decade, often equal in scale to the officially requisitioned land meant to follow, however imperfectly, the Master Plan guidelines governing the growth of the officially sanctioned city. If China has a developing country equivalent of an "informal" land and real estate market ("black market" transactions aside), then one finds it at the margin, emerging, for example, in the suburban counties and even within the strips of land belonging to the city proper but outside the planning area closely supervised by municipal planners. It bears repeating that, from the vantage point of the year 2000, the de facto urbanized area of China's cities will far exceed anything found in the color-coded planning maps. Add to that the fact that, in selected areas of China (the Pearl River Delta of Guangdong Province; and the conurbation radiating from Shanghai into Jiangsu and Zhejiang Provinces, along particular transport corridors), cross-jurisdictional megapolitan areas are emerging. This unforeseen pattern of urban development dramatically illustrates the challenge faced by the conventionally trained Chinese planners focused on relatively limited portions of overall urban development, defined in purely spatial terms.15/

Peri-urban development is poorly understood, since few local or outside researchers have invested much time in studying the phenomenon. Nevertheless, even if one confines attention to any one metropolitan area, and ignores the development and implications

---

14/   Bank estimates suggest most leases fall below 1 ha in size.

15/   This report did not have the mandate or resources to explore the implications for urban planning and regulatory practices created by the emergence of cross-county or even cross-provincial conurbations.

of an interconnected set of cities creating an unprecedented "urban field," the fact remains that peri-urban development is the fastest growing part of China's urban economy.16/

It is ironic that, after all the arguments about the benefits of agglomeration economies have been documented, and given that, across countries, cities have always been labeled as the engines of modern economic growth, in China the market economy operates with fewest constraints away from the supervision of the city planners and their related agents of "control." Here, in the far suburbs, an unfettered market economy is emerging and a vibrant real estate market along with it.17/ The flexibility offered by this peri-urban economy has become self-evident not only to the local communities, but to "outside" investors as well. Casual empiricism, buttressed by satellite imagery of the cities studied in this report, suggests that ringing every city proper is a new economy whose development is supported by outsiders—seeking subcontracts or investing directly in land for factories, housing, warehouses, and solid waste disposal sites. A massive "leapfrogging" effort by otherwise constrained "urban" investors is complementing and often underwriting relatively unregulated, locally financed urbanization. Some municipalities have simply tried to accommodate these trends (Box 4.6), while providing elements of land use management regulation in rural areas. In most cases, county and township administrators have given little attention to peri-urban land use management.

On an experimental basis, whose scope is not possible to establish at this time, county land use planning (including industrial zoning) and centralized servicing of wastewater discharge is being introduced. During this decade, township planning regulations will have to become routine. Technical assistance, based on work funded or otherwise supported by multilateral and bilateral assistance, may be able to play an important role in this case. The balkanization of responsibilities, so often identified in sector studies as obstructing progress in reaching particular objectives, is here and in land management, generally, of great importance. Land development issues in and around cities require that institutions allow multidisciplinary teams to work together. The problems at hand cannot be resolved by independent initiatives led by those whose core responsibilities are labeled as "agriculture," "urban," "transport," "industry," "environment," or "finance."

16/ The Ministry of Agriculture and the State Council Development Research Center estimate that, by the year 2000, half of all industrial production will be accounted for by township and village industrial enterprises (TVIEs) (*China Daily*, June 2, 1992). Most of this is assumed to be peri-urban in nature.

17/ Vogel summarizes prevailing foreign perceptions in one paragraph: "'Compared to the counties of the Pearl River Delta,' observed one of Guangzhou's leading economic officials, 'Guangzhou is like a tired old man.' After reforms, the counties could establish new factories on former marshes or farmland without dislocating very many people or facilities. Guangzhou['s] ... large population was hard to move and its heavy industry plants ... expensive to replace.... Compared to the small, usually cohesive, group of county leaders who could act quickly, Guangzhou was slowed down by complex issues and four layers of bureaucracy above its enterprises.... [Given prevailing intergovernmental tax-sharing arrangements] ... counties or small cities that began with hardly any industry and grew rapidly had virtually a tax holiday for five years.... Guangzhou had no such advantage." (E. Vogel, *One Step Ahead in China: Guangdong Under Reform*, Cambridge, Massachusetts: Harvard University Press, 1989.)

Box 4.6: GUANGZHOU: SUBURBAN COUNTY URBAN LAND DEVELOPMENT POLICIES

Compared with other cities, such as Shanghai, the suburban counties in Guangzhou enjoy more autonomy. Guangzhou's city government has allowed counties and districts to set up their own export industrial zones to attract foreign and joint-venture investors. About 57 hectares of land have already been allocated for building industrial parks or residential quarters. Among 19 suburban towns, as many as 5 hectares of land were allocated for such purposes in *every* town. Even in villages, about 0.8-1.0 hectare of land area per village was devoted to attracting foreign investors. The county and district real estate companies have been encouraged to develop commercial real estate including residential, retail, and industrial buildings to attract consumers from the central city. According to city officials, many commodity housing units built in Panyu county, for example, were sold to residents from the central city, who obviously were attracted by the relatively low prices.

Such development has gradually integrated suburban counties, once separated by huge institutional barriers and income gaps, into a real metropolitan region. Much-improved transportation, such as several new bridges crossing the Pearl River, facilitates such development. In fact, most of this infrastructure was financed and built by the county governments. They certainly understood the importance of these transportation projects. This contrasts with some highway projects in Shanghai (connecting the city center with satellite towns) that followed the Master Plan, and whose utilization is very low.

V. INFORMATION AS INFRASTRUCTURE: ITS ROLE IN DEVELOPING AN INTERNATIONALLY COMPETITIVE CITY

Introduction

There is little "glamour" attached to promoting the systematic gathering, recording, accessing, and use of information. However, no fundamental reform of urban land management can succeed if this area is neglected. The systems involved can be divided into two component parts: legal and planning-related.

Note has been taken of the fact that legally binding documents, such as Master Plans, land use and building regulations, and the various laws, licensing requirements, and regulations governing property development are not always easily accessible in China. This section focuses on the systematic recording and easy retrieval of site-specific legal data that provides very basic information on the boundaries of each site, the "ownership" rights associated with each plot, the transparency of rules governing allowable uses, the "encumbrances" associated with that property (including mortgages), and the procedures and costs of transferring control from one party to another. It bears restating that *what is traded on the market is not land per se but a bundle of legally defined rights and obligations which provide control over particular parcels of property*, including stratified interests in buildings, land-use rights, mineral rights, and easements, each of which yields or constrains income-generation possibilities (Annex 10). And it is worth emphasizing that resolution-dispute mechanisms associated with this bundle of *recorded* rights and obligations are as important an element as the systematic recording of information.

The introduction of land cadasters in China offers an opportunity to provide not only an accurate land use register, and a necessary instrument for land use rights markets, but also a means by which to strengthen significantly the efficient management and financing of urban infrastructure programs. Modern digital technology, when applied to a cadastral database (or initially to a subdistrict database) offers a powerful means of storing sharing, and using land information to help planners to forecast the impact of planning and investment decisions, and the "timely adjustments" that are inevitably required by unpredictable market-led development (Annex 11).

Land Administration and Registration

Prior to 1949, a fairly complete land title cadaster was maintained in China, which recorded the current land description, title and encumbrances, as well as the historical records of ownership, transfer and subdivision or consolidation. In many cities today, the old cadasters exist intact in archives. Following 1949, they fell into disuse, given the abolition of private property rights and the effects of the Cultural Revolution. The need for a cadaster was seen as unnecessary since titles were now vested in only one owner, the state, and inalienable rights were allocated to users administratively (without charge and in perpetuity). Moreover, the trained cadastral surveyors were redeployed to other tasks such as engineering surveying. Registration recommenced, with limited resources, around 1982.

The Land Administration Law and the Constitution, duly amended in 1988, renewed the need for an operational cadaster, which became recognized, once again, as an important instrument of management. Local governments nationwide received a mandate to establish up-to-date cadasters over a five-year period. Following the enabling legislation, relevant central, provincial and municipal implementing regulations were also promulgated.

As noted earlier, in order to strengthen land administration and management, the 1986 Law established SLA. The staff of SLA are drawn from several existing agencies previously concerned with land administration in various ways, including the Ministries of Agriculture (MoA) and Construction (MoC) and the National Bureau of Surveying and Mapping (NBSM) and their respective line agencies at lower tiers of government. The new and traditional roles of these institutions with respect to land use regulation and information have not, however, been fully reconciled to date, delaying the issuance of implementing regulations and leading to some administrative confusion at central and, more particularly, at local levels. Particular anomalies lie in the separate registration required for *land* use rights and *building* rights, respectively, and in the terms of lease contracts which span both land use and building control conditions. Different local governments have chosen to try to resolve this issue with different administrative combinations and procedures,1/ but operations are clearly hampered by the plethora of maps, registers (and the separate staffs) being separately maintained.

In terms of land information, SLA is empowered to compile an inventory of different classes of land use in China (including urban land) and to maintain a register of user rights. In 1988, a national five-year program of land use classification, and land use rights (and building rights) registration began. Eight primary classes and 46 subclasses of rural land use, and 10 primary classes and 24 subclasses of urban land use are recognized by SLA's system.2/ Further class subdivisions, i.e., a third, and an even more detailed, fourth tier, can be

---

1/ Land use rights are the purview of SLA, while building rights are those of MoC. Both types of rights embody controls that would normally be part of "zoning" and subdivision control regulations. The organizational arrangements differ in the degree to which the respective administrative units concerned have been integrated. The units combined generally have different line reporting responsibilities (to SLA, MoC, MoA, NBSM, etc.), which naturally hampers unified management. In Shenzhen, the most advanced organization has been formed, with the creation of a completely integrated land administration system, combining land administration, urban planning, and surveying and mapping units under a unified structure. In Shanghai, a collaborative arrangement exists among the agencies concerned, under the leadership of a committee chaired by a Vice-Mayor. In Guangzhou, urban land and rural land are now administered jointly, and urban land and building administration personnel have been combined into one unit.

2/ SLA's rural land classification system conforms to the "Technical Regulations for Land Use Investigation" issued in 1984 by the National Agricultural Classification Commission. The urban classification system is defined by a separate regulation issued by SLA in 1989 entitled "Survey Regulations for Urban Land Cadaster," which applies to all urban, township and independent industrial and mining development areas.

recognized by local land bureaus. Another agency of government, MoC—through either its Urban Planning or Real Estate Management Departments—also exercises a close interest in urban land use classification through regulation ("zoning" and subdivision control) and building controls, and maintains detailed plans and records.3/

At the local level, it is clear that the land administration bureau must register land use rights and issue title certificates. However, the responsibility for compilation of the cadaster has not been clearly defined. Consequently, a conflict developed between NBSM, hitherto the surveyor of fundamental land information including boundaries, and SLA, as to the responsibility for surveying and mapping the boundaries of land parcels. This conflict has hindered the efficient allocation of resources to the topographical and cadastral mapping program now ongoing countrywide.

Cadaster Administration

Land Use Rights. The transition from free allocation of land use rights in perpetuity to the system of time-bound leaseholds for payment must pass through several phases before it will apply to all urban land. This will involve initial registrations and then reregistration as the rights are amended or transferred from time to time. Different local governments are following different timetables. In Guangzhou Municipality, for example, it has been decided that all new user rights should, beginning on July 1, 1992, be applicable for a fixed period. In general, those rights purchased by joint-venture, foreign, or domestic investors will be transferrable. In Shanghai, the decision to limit the period of all user rights has not been taken yet, but transferrable leases are already a feature of all foreign investments requiring land, as well as domestic commercial real estate ventures. User rights to most new land offered for development in the extensive Pudong Special Economic Zone (200 km^2) will be in the form of assignable leases or "market" rents reflecting a realistic rate of return on implicit land values.4/

Proof of title ownership is fundamental as a form of collateral security.5/ The cadastral registration system established does not appear to provide absolute clear proof of title, since it may be challenged in a Chinese court of law. Nevertheless, the registration system established is intended to establish reasonable proof of title ownership, and a meticulous process

---

3/   MoC, following from the provisions of the Land Administration Law as amended, has decreed that its line representatives at the local level should register building rights and issue corresponding title certificates. The conditions applying to the building rights often overlap with land use rights. Possibly adding to the confusion, an Urban Planning Act was passed in late 1989 in order to define and empower the urban planning function and to systematize the process of urban planning. The consistency between the two laws and the administrative implications have not yet been explored and resolved.

4/   For industrial land users, particularly for Shanghai-owned enterprises, this reform is likely to be relaxed.

5/   In Shanghai, a China Investment Bank loan derived from the proceeds of one of the Bank-supported industrial development credits could not be given to a proposed industrial borrower because of the lack of a valid land use certificate.

of examination and field investigation is followed to ensure the issue of a correct certificate (Box 5.1). Before recourse to legal adjudication, any title dispute is first adjudicated by SLA.

Box 5.1: TITLE ISSUANCE PROCEDURE IN GUANGZHOU

The process employed by Guangzhou's Real Estate Management Bureau (Land Management Division) is typical in many respects. The Land Management Division is organized into three units: a registration division (103 staff), a land survey division (105 staff), and an archives division (40 staff), and is responsible for registration of all parcels in the urban development area (approximately 600,000 cases). In other municipalities (e.g., Shanghai and Chengdu), this function has been devolved to District Offices (and County Land Administration Offices) in order to spread the workload. All legitimate land users are required to register their interests. The registration division publicly invites, accepts and records applications for land use rights certificates and carries out the examination of the application and supporting documentation, including field surveys to determine rightful ownership. Upon initial clearance, the parcel concerned is then identified in the field and the plot corners marked and sides surveyed in detail to produce a certified plot diagram indicating the plot location, dimensions, area and existing improvements (buildings, roads, etc.). With the confirmation of the physical aspects of the parcel, the intention to issue a certificate is publicly advertised. If no objections are received, a certificate is prepared, and registered. The original is filed in the Archives and a conformed copy is given to the applicant. (When district- or county-level offices are involved, a further copy is retained at the local level). Condominium or strata titles are registered through this same procedure. The Archives are well organized and generally well equipped for long-term storage and maintenance (including document restoration), and retrieval of the document files (the premises visited were generally housed in new buildings equipped with microfilming capabilities as well as climate-controlled air conditioning and fire protection). Processing of applications reportedly takes between 4 to 8 weeks, depending on the completeness and accuracy of the application. Fees related to the size and value of the parcel are charged for the registration and issue of the certificate (approximately Y 15/plot for households and Y 125/plot for enterprises). Fee income is not sufficient to cover administrative costs in the case of Guangzhou. Proposals are being made by SLA to increase investigation and registration survey fees substantially.

Building Rights. In two of three cities where the issue was carefully studied, progress of land use and building rights registration, which begin in 1988, was reported as well advanced.6/ Progress was greatest in the newer built-up areas of the city and the county areas (including reregistration, in some cases of redevelopment), but much less elsewhere. Registrations in such areas are being processed on an ad-hoc basis. Notable omissions were also found with respect to the land and buildings occupied by public agencies (administrations, schools, hospitals, etc.). Such gaps reduce the value of the information base and hamper analysis.

Delays in cadaster preparation (caused in part by inefficient surveying techniques) are quite serious in some instances and the resources allocated for the preparation of the cadaster may now be inadequate to complete the work in a timely fashion. Building

---

6/   The building registration process is also a meticulous discovery process which includes an examination of the structure to ascertain conformity with "zoning" and building controls. Illegal buildings must be rectified prior to the issuance of the building rights certificate.

registrations are, on the whole, generally more advanced than those for land use rights because of an earlier start promoted by MoC; however, each building is registered separately and there is no mechanism to determine the aggregate building rights, involving multiple properties, held by one property "owner." One issue which appears not to be a major barrier to cadastral work is emergence of "multiple claimants"; instances do obviously exist, but they cover fewer than 5 percent of all cases. In one example, in Shanghai, the issuance of a land use certificate was delayed because the original enterprise occupying the land had been restructured and it was unclear which of the resulting new entities had a claim to the assets of the original structure. Appeals procedures exist to cover such instances, beginning within the local land bureaus and moving on to the Provincial land bureaus; ultimately, cases could be turned over to the civil court system.

Information Access. The hard-copy cadaster information stored in the Archives is nominally open to public inspection, but in practice, only "authorized" persons (owners, attorneys acting for owners or purchasers, bona-fide potential developers, etc.) are allowed access. Nevertheless, the Guangzhou archives reported dealing with some 40,000 inquiries during 1990. A digital database has been initiated to improve retrieval and facilitate inquiries, but is far from complete. All new registrations are recorded in the database. Similar systems are being developed in other municipalities. In some cases, the cadastral mapping information is also being digitized for use in information systems for broad municipal planning and administration purposes. Too often, however, the statistical information is kept at the ward or district level. In the absence of automated aggregation of this information, *municipal authorities and potential investors have no way to access the information easily.*

Geographic Information Systems

The cadastral maps and their parent topographic base maps are a source of fundamental physical information. Other important urban information concerning thematic topics such as land use, land values, demography, ownership, social conditions, etc., or also physical data such as underground infrastructure, etc. is essential to efficient planning. Such information, when overlaid onto the fundamental database, provides a comprehensive GIS, invaluable to urban planners and administrators. Unfortunately, under current arrangements in China, such information is typically stored on separate maps or in tables or other forms of hard copy in inconsistent formats that are difficult to reproduce or manipulate and, therefore, often not consulted frequently. However, recent advances in planning technology have opened up the opportunity to store urban information in digital form suitable for convenient analysis and manipulation. The results could be readily presented and reproduced, thereby facilitating the use of current information in support of decision-making. Digital GIS and related applications (such as "zoning" analysis, public services demand modeling, infrastructure network analysis, etc.) are actively under development in China.7/ The desire to improve land management and urban management could benefit greatly (particularly in the face of the currently fragmented responsibilities for urban land use planning and regulation, as well as primary infrastructure planning) from the use of unified databases and the digital technology now available to conveniently acquire, manage, analyze and apply or present the information. This would obviously entail administrative reforms as well.

The advent of computer technologies and digitizing of data has made the acquisition and storage of information much simpler, and greatly facilitates its retrieval and manipulation. In addition, computer programs are able to present the maps and tables, perform the analyses, and generate the cartography automatically. All this is now possible with a relatively inexpensive, desktop personal computer (PC) system. Thus, the urban planner or administrator can have available a "live" database with which to work, as well as the tools to make projections and display results quickly. Hence, a more dynamic planning process is possible that can more accurately drive planned objectives and match expenditure proposals to reality. The information stored can include the location of people and their workplaces, the physical characteristics of the urban area, the level of services available and the location of physical infrastructure networks. This information can be used, for example, to forecast where people will live and work in the future, the problems they will face and the amount of services they will require. The information (and projections) can be updated easily and frequently, and used interactively with computerized models of supply and demand for transport and public utilities (such as water supply, power, sewerage and drainage) to optimize infrastructure networks and investment programs. It can be used to help select and appraise investment projects and can also be used to help manage the related O&M requirements of such infrastructure (Annex 12).

The advantages of an automated GIS have not escaped Chinese planners and engineers. Many GIS facilities have been established and an information engineering industry is beginning to emerge to support the potential demand. Many teething problems are apparent, as might be expected. For example, the technology is currently chiefly in the hands of information engineers, and means rather than ends dominate development. Moreover, the present urban planning system is rooted in the traditional static planning methodologies and regulations. Such traditions are not readily adaptable to the emerging dynamic planning methodologies. Exposure to dynamic planning methodologies is badly needed, as outlined in Chapter IV.

7/   Many national research institutes, university laboratories, provinces and municipalities are engaged in GIS development for municipal operations. Much of the research, although supported by external donors, is uncoordinated and may be duplicated. The Bank is supporting GIS development through the Key Studies Project (Report No. 2210-CHA) in three key state laboratories in the Wuhan Technical University for Surveying and Mapping, Tongji University in Shanghai, and Nanjing University. The project provides for collaboration and research exchange mechanisms which could be usefully applied in the case of GIS development. In addition, applications for GIS are under development in Bank-supported projects in the cities of Tianjin, Changzhou, Luoyang and Shashi, assisted by the National Laboratory of Resources and Environment Information Systems of the Chinese Academy of Science's Institute of Geography. For greater detail on implementing GIS, see Annex 12.

Not the least of the problems is the highly fragmented nature of the municipal administration and the data sources. The potential economies of scale and advantages of integrated planning are not yet been grasped because each agency embraces its particular area of responsibility and attempts, in the process, to develop its own independent GIS. Much duplication of software and experimentation is evident, and few usable results have so far been given into the hands of policymakers.

Issues and Constraints in Developing GIS

The development of GIS systems is a widespread activity in many municipalities and research institutes throughout China. Many are facing similar obstacles as well as local constraints. The major issues are:

(a) **Technology.** The GIS must draw upon many different data sources and support many different users. Each of these sources and users will likely have an existing information system in place or under development. Many subsystems have similar data needs and a common layer (or layers) of information such as topography, cadaster, population, etc. is called for. Unified, digital surveying and mapping technology, as well as systematic cooperation, should be used to facilitate topographic and cadastral survey work and the creation of a digitized, coordinated database. *The specialized information needs to be stored in a compatible form and referenced in a manner that can be understood by others. The data structure, its classification and coding should be standardized. Hardware and software interfaces are needed to allow exchanges of information.* Database programs should be relational and data acquisition and entry simplified. Software should be powerful, versatile, user friendly and inexpensive. Hardware should be as inexpensive and reliable as possible. An interagency central clearinghouse for technology development and evaluation would be a useful measure to avoid duplicate or redundant research.

(b) **Municipal Information Systems Policies.** Systematic policies on the management of (and access to) information are generally lacking, particularly in the area of data sharing and exchange, as well as updating and archiving. Local practices and security concerns affect this issue. Linkages among various commissions and bureaus information systems (Planning, Finance, Construction) are desirable in order to have the economic, financial and physical data necessary for integrated planning purposes. Guidelines on "best" practices in data sharing and exchange are needed. As mentioned above, data structure, classification and coding should be standardized to facilitate exchanges.

(c) **Applications.** Most effort to date has been applied to the information engineering aspects of GIS. Little effort has been spent on identifying applications for the data or integrating the use of the database into routine work such as macrospatial planning, sectoral planning, annual planning and budgeting, project analysis, O&M planning and management, or program and project evaluation. User requirements must be surveyed, and processes and procedures spelled out and their data needs and reports identified.

Strategic Information Systems

Chapter IV and section C of this chapter both acknowledge that comprehensive systems of information collection and processing, detailed enough to provide substantial inputs into the planning of infrastructure projects, must be preceded by less-detailed, land-use monitoring systems, or Strategic Information Systems (SIS).

The objective of such systems would be to identify *subdistrict-level development trends*, aggregating these in different forms and comparing them with expectations recorded in individual Master Plans. This, then, is not a parcel-by-parcel based system, and can thus be assembled quickly and inexpensively.

The number of subdistricts in any given city ranges from 60 to 300. In Shanghai's case, the 130 subdistricts were digitized into computer-manipulated maps in three days. For each subdistrict, the SIS would concentrate on a select set of data including: (a) population trends; (b) employment trends, by category; (c) land use trends, by category; (d) land use consumption trends, per capita or per employee; (e) land price trends, by land use category; and (f) building floor-space trends, by category and on a per-capita basis. Where necessary, such as in a path-breaking study on the link between infrastructure deficiencies and public health indicators, undertaken as part of the Tianjin Urban Development Project's preparation, other indicators, mapping death rates by category for each subdistrict, can be incorporated.[8]

The tools and end-results, which identify small-area trends in urban development, are a necessary part of a planning reform that allows Strategic Planning to replace static Master Plans. The key message drawn from Chapter IV is that producing immutable products is not what matters. With SIS, made operational even before GIS is in place, this transition can begin.

Figures A1.16 through A1.24, using Shanghai as a case study, provide evidence of various developments, and are drawn upon to document certain assertions in Chapter IV, many of which were identified by the earlier study undertaken in 1989 by the local Design Institute, with considerable foreign technical assistance. Among these one can highlight the following:

---

[8]   A. Bertaud and M. Young, "Geographical Pattern of Environmental Health in Tianjin, China," Washington, DC, Infrastructure and Urban Development Department, World Bank, February 1991.

(a)   Shanghai is expanding more rapidly that anticipated by the Master Plan, and now extends well beyond the planned area meant to contain urban growth (peri-urban included) (Figures A1.16 and A1.17).

(b)   Shanghai has benefited from the relatively little damage done to it by traditional Soviet planning practices, for reasons discussed earlier; the population density gradient is not unlike that found in a market economy, especially within a 4-5 km radius from the city center, and thus, very different from outcomes reported for Moscow, St. Petersburg and Warsaw (Figures A1.18-A1.21);

(c)   While local planning priorities appear to favor the development of Pudong (where the infrastructure cost of opening up serviced land for urban uses will be enormous), it is the Puxi districts which currently contain almost all population and housing in Shanghai (Figures A1.22 and A1.23);

(d)   As Shanghai restructures its land uses, the disproportionate land area devoted to industrial uses in central locations, inherited from past location practices, and subject to potential conversion to uses more consistent with implicit land values, is illustrated in Figure A1.24.

<u>Planning Without Facts: The Case of the</u>
<u>Temporary Population of Urban China</u> <u>9/</u>

Every graph and table in this report is in one sense incomplete and inaccurate: the resident population of cities and towns without permanent residency rights is missing from the data, because Chinese planners fail to draw systematically upon the temporary registration records kept by the local offices of the Public Security Bureau. Yet, as already noted, on any given day perhaps 66 million such individuals (defined as staying more than three days) fill the cities and towns, whose "permanent" population totals 301 million. Even if the in- and outflow restricts the average length of stay of such residents, with only 40 percent staying over one year, the fact remains that the stock of such residents present on any one day keeps growing, and yet local planners have no mechanism to track this group except through periodic surveys. These surveys do not yield small area data useful enough for planning public services and infrastructure investments.

The issue here involves both social and economic considerations. This population must be housed, and provided with services at home and at work, since approximately 70 percent are in the workforce. In Shenzhen, they represent 80 percent of the total workforce. Omitting them from consideration in information gathering, given that they will become a permanent feature of a regulated market economy, is pure folly.

9/   This section draws on Michael Rutkowski, "China's Floating Population and Labor Market Reforms," World Bank, December 1991, processed.

The maxim "last but not least" applies to information infrastructure in any effort to restructure urban land management in China's cities. Systemic reform involves an interconnected set of changes. Neglect any one of these and the reform will fail to achieve the objective of creating internationally competitive cities. And *this* goal is the only one that makes sense for China as it looks forward to the year 2000.

VI. **MOVING FORWARD**

In the transition to a post-command economy, China has no peers, either in urban or rural land management reform.[1/] As only one example, almost all of China's millions of farmers have effective ownership rights over their farms; in the Russian Federation, only 144,000 private farmers existed in mid-1992. Practices introduced into urban China over the last few years, involving land and building rights registration, land leasing, the development of profit-driven real estate development companies, are rare or nonexistent elsewhere in the post-Socialist world. Municipal governments, with identifiable budgets and local autonomy over real estate and infrastructure development, are still a "novelty item" in other post-command economies. The Chinese have moved gradually, but over several years, to set the legal, institutional and price framework needed for real estate reform. There has been no dramatic "big bang" reform, no effort to create a market economy in 500 days; instead, a very deliberate process has been at work, and the report provides evidence that China has accomplished a great deal, while generally maintaining the macroeconomic and political stability that is an undeniable prerequisite for urban real estate reform.

Within the last year the pace of land leasing activity has quickened in the approximately 30 cities where the reform process is most advanced. Thirty-five km^2 were leased from 1988 through 1991; 70 km^2 were leased during the first six months of 1992. However, in total this is equivalent to only 1 percent of the built-up area of China's cities. In individual cities like Shanghai, most leases involve for-profit redevelopment of previously occupied sites. And there is still a general reluctance to allow competitive bids for land to become an important tool, promoting the emergence of *market* (rather than *cost-recovery*) prices. The best that can be said is that land leasing no longer faces the political onus of being a reversible experiment. Authorities at the highest level have endorsed urban real estate market reforms as appropriate for China.

China's need to go through yet another readjustment in relative prices, now involving urban land, will be vastly eased by the experiences gathered over the last decade and by the fact that its inflation rates are low, its economy is growing rapidly, and the household propensity to save is unmatched in the world. China's links to its Overseas Chinese and compatriots in Hong Kong, Singapore, Taiwan Province, Malaysia, Thailand, the Philippines, and Indonesia, along with its growing links with investors from Japan, Korea, and Western countries, will also immeasurably ease the transition to market. More encouraging still, the Chinese at the central level are now taking the initiative in dealing with real estate reform in a comprehensive fashion and, in the last few months, to develop systemic reform plans that have required little prompting from outside advisors. The Bank's previous conclusions and

---

[1/]   The most detailed review of real estate reform in post-command economies is found in H. Matras and B. Renaud, "Housing Reforms in Transition Economies: A Survey Report on Country Reforms," World Bank, January 15, 1992, processed.

recommendations on urban reform, focused on Zhejiang Province and Housing, were frankly unanticipated and viewed as controversial and audacious; they were well ahead of contemplated local policy initiatives. Local research on these subjects was meager, at best. Policy analysis on urban land management reforms, however, is now well under way in China, and foreign expertise will clearly play a supplementary role in these efforts, adding useful "nuts and bolts" advice, and working at the margin. China is taking over the task of major policy reform analysis, as the following examples illustrate:

(a)   CASS, *Urban Land Management in China* (June 1991), op. cit.;

(b)   the Research Team on the Intensification of Land Resource Management, "Towards a Land Management System with Chinese Characteristics: A Study Report on the Intensification of Land Use Management," Beijing, State Land Administration, October 1991, processed; and

(c)   a comprehensive policy statement prepared by MoC, on the need to integrate land management into overall urban economic development.

In one report or another, most themes found in this report are now echoed:

(a)   CASS vigorously promotes a transition to a land market economy, the regularization of "black market" transactions, and the need to revamp the tax and fee treatment of REDCs, which are clearly recognized as the key players in the reform effort;

(b)   the SLA October 1991 report advocates the expansion of land market transactions. It recognizes that urban redevelopment is critical, and that land uses in urban areas need readjusting. It stresses the interconnected nature of urban land management reform, and calls for a Ministry of Land and Housing Administration, able to deal with the myriad issues involved that now cut across competing bureaucratic lines. It recognizes that the peri-urban economy is becoming part of the urban economy and announces various measures to introduce land use fees for urban uses of rural land (TVIEs, rural housing), with experiments already reported in 35 percent of China's counties. It advocates heavy reliance on monitoring of data and its use in making policy decisions. And it calls for greater involvement of financial institutions, including the use of land-based mortgages. Finally, it emphasizes the need to keep environmental issues "front and center" in all debates.

(c)   the MoC Policy Statement calls for specific action in the following fields:

•   urban planning should be restructured to make guidelines far more responsive to resource preservation in urban areas, allowing floor-to-land area ratios to rise, on average, and be more "developer-friendly";

- while advocating government monopoly over land requisition, land should then enter the market economy through such mechanisms as leasing, and be subject to only limited regulation thereafter;

- regulations should be set in place that facilitate the transfer of urban real estate according to market principles, and property rights reforms should receive particular attention;

- REDCs should be encouraged to expand the scope of their activities, and their profitability should not be endangered by "clawbacks" that could act as serious disincentives to their expansion;

- at the local level, the planning, regulation, legal, fiscal, and institutional arrangements should be "unified" to treat buildings and the land they occupy as one;

- urban and peri-urban planning should be "unified" and jurisdictional barriers inimical to that end should be eliminated;

- the financial sector and the household, as saver, should be encouraged to participate more fully in promoting the development of the real estate sector; and

- what governmental revenues accrue from the reform should be kept at the local level, to help promote infrastructure development.

What then can the Bank report add in a concluding statement? The key to success for reform is to recognize the need to balance the further unleashing of market reforms with the development of the necessary regulatory, legal, and fiscal framework. The key challenges faced by Chinese authorities include facilitating the redevelopment of densely populated core-city areas, while anticipating the incorporation of peri-urban areas into the year 2000 metropolis, and allowing for a more market-driven densification of the "Socialist" suburban belt.

This move to market calls for a holistic approach, with a role for both central and local authorities. The center's role begins with continuing to ensure that the reform takes place within a stable macroeconomic environment, with relatively low rates of inflation maintained even as relative price adjustments take place. Then, an overall policy environment is needed that: (a) promotes the emergence of competitive real estate markets; (b) provides for the legal framework that gives investors the confidence needed to make the buying and selling of land use rights to occur at a faster pace; (c) provides for further clarification of the fiscal regime relating to real estate, while insisting on the establishment of regulatory mechanisms to oversee the transition to markets; and (d) sets firm environmental policy guidelines.

The Center will have to follow up in specific instances, among which one can list as priorities:

- clarification of state titleholder responsibilities;

- guidelines governing leasehold terms and renewal conditions;

- introduction of a unified real estate registration and cadastral policy;

- creation of firm rules governing land use rights, vis-à-vis government authorities, including the guidelines governing expropriation and compensation;

- further insulation of the court system from political pressures, to ensure that perceptions of unfairness in real estate dispute resolution are lessened;

- development of unified guidelines involving real estate transaction taxes; and the rights of localities to set property taxes, utility rates, and other infrastructure fees, *in the context of a thorough overhaul of municipal finance and related intergovernmental arrangements*;

- strengthening (as necessary) of environmental protection legislation and regulatory mechanisms to see that factories comply with existing and future environmental regulations.

At the local level, initiatives are also needed, if only because no central policy, legal, fiscal or regulatory framework can work without follow-up, detailed enactment by provincial, municipal, and county authorities.

Among the key roles to be played locally, the following can be singled out:

- vigorously promote the expansion of urban land rented or leased on competitive terms, with reasonably unfettered rights over uses and transfers of title;

- unify and complete the real estate registration and cadastral programs under way;

- implement and publicize rules governing land expropriation, compensation, and appeals processes;

- monitor the performance of the local court system in dealing with real estate transaction disputes;

- within the limits set by central policy, review municipal finance arrangements, particularly policies regarding taxes and fees involving real estate transactions, to encourage transactions to take place (particularly core-area development), while ensuring that the government receives a "fair share" based on transparent rules;

- vigorously promote the monitoring and "information feedback" through the use of *coordinated* SIS and GIS systems, that can make it possible for Structure Plans to be developed and updated, and to redirect infrastructure investments as critical development and core-area redevelopment bottlenecks emerge;

- perform periodic regulatory audits with respect to land use development controls, to facilitate real estate transactions and to allow critical priorities like core-area redevelopment to proceed in a more "developer-friendly" manner, consistent with transparent "performance" criteria involving health, safety, and environment considerations;

- strengthen the capacity of local environmental protection authorities, and provide them with more staff and resources, in dealing with factory pollution among existing and new enterprises, including those located in township areas.

The report recommends the adoption of a comprehensive reform strategy, knowing that such an approach will not be easy to accomplish and that certain "strands" of reform will proceed ahead of others, for a variety of reasons, including political feasibility. The ideal model presented in the report is, in practice, probably unachievable in the short term. Not all measures will move forward in the simultaneous fashion that would bring urban land management into the market economy as expeditiously as possible. Nevertheless, while conceding the bottlenecks created by "practical realities," it bears restating that change is *not* necessarily systemic reform, and partial reform will not provide the potential benefits that thoroughgoing urban land management restructuring can contribute to the modernization and sustainable rapid growth of China's urban economy.

Finally, looking back with pride, and with satisfaction in comparing Chinese achievements with those of other post-command economies, local authorities must nevertheless watch out for the *real* competitors. Hong Kong, Korea, Singapore, Taiwan Province, Malaysia, Thailand, Indonesia, the Philippines, India and Viet Nam will be after the same investors and export markets as the Chinese seek. To a greater or lesser degree, as pointed out in this report (but requiring much more "fleshing out" through study tours and expert advice), many of these countries are ahead of China in resolving the relevant issues involved. Monitoring their institutions and practices, and adapting them *selectively* is the best advice the Bank can provide, detailed figures and tables aside. That selectivity will be guided by the need to keep the final target in mind: creating a regulated market economy that is internationally competitive.

ANNEXES

CONTENTS

ANNEX 3.   RESIDENTIAL RELOCATION POLICIES IN SELECTED CITIES .   192

ANNEX 1

SUPPORTING GRAPHICS

Figure A1.1: URBAN POPULATION DISTRIBUTION,
CUMULATIVE PROFILES

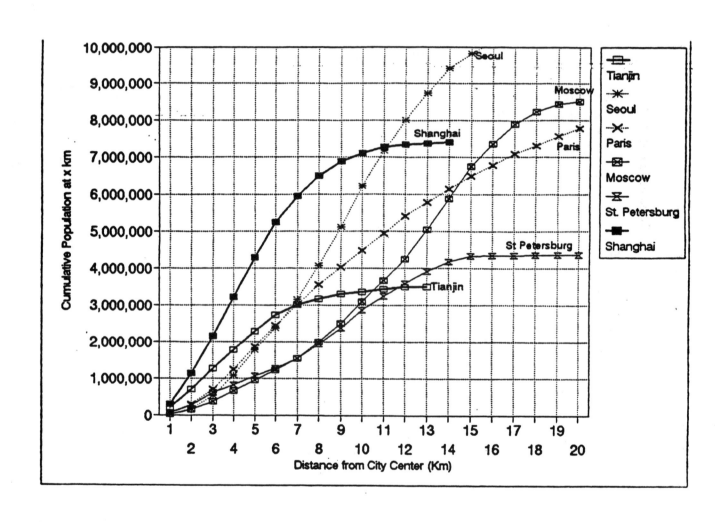

Figure A1.2: LAND USE PROFILE IN SEOUL IN 1988

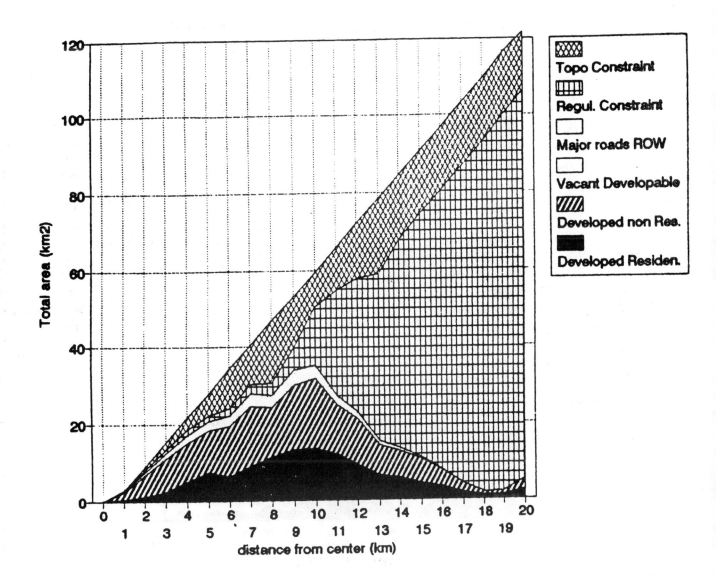

<u>Figure A1.3</u>: WARSAW - IMPACT OF LAND USE REGULATIONS ON LAND SUPPLY

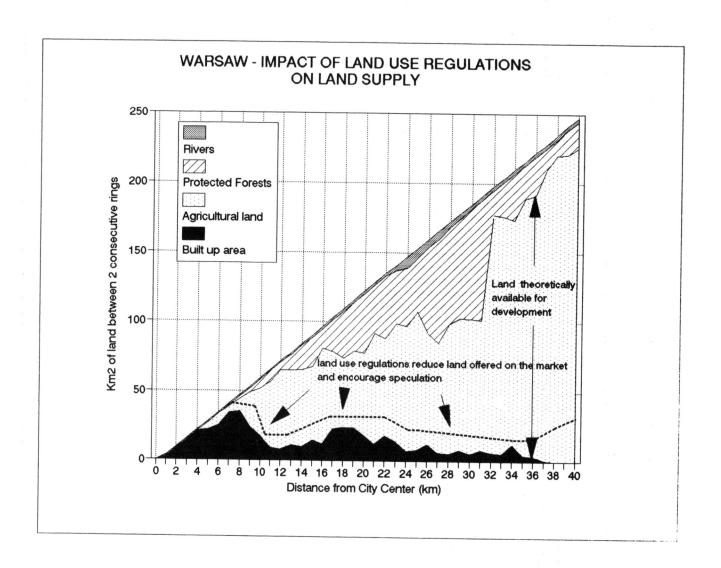

Figure A1.4: SAMPLE OF RESIDENTIAL LAND PRICES IN SEOUL IN 1989,
AVERAGE BY DISTANCE FROM CENTER

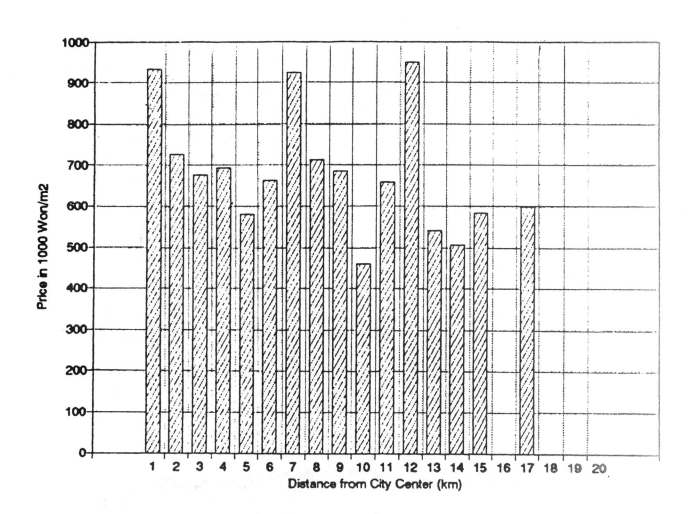

Figure A1.5: COMPARATIVE DENSITY PROFILE: SHANGHAI, PARIS, AND SEOUL

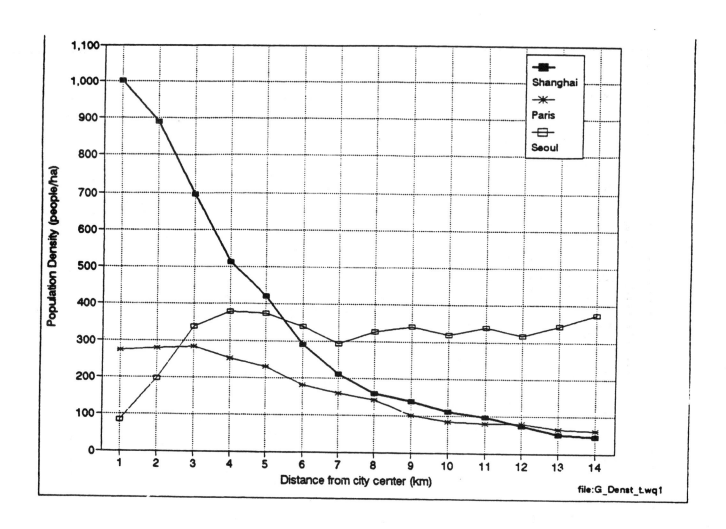

Figure A1.6: COMPARATIVE DENSITY GRADIENT IN THE BUILT-UP AREA OF FOUR CHINESE CITIES, PARIS, AND MOSCOW

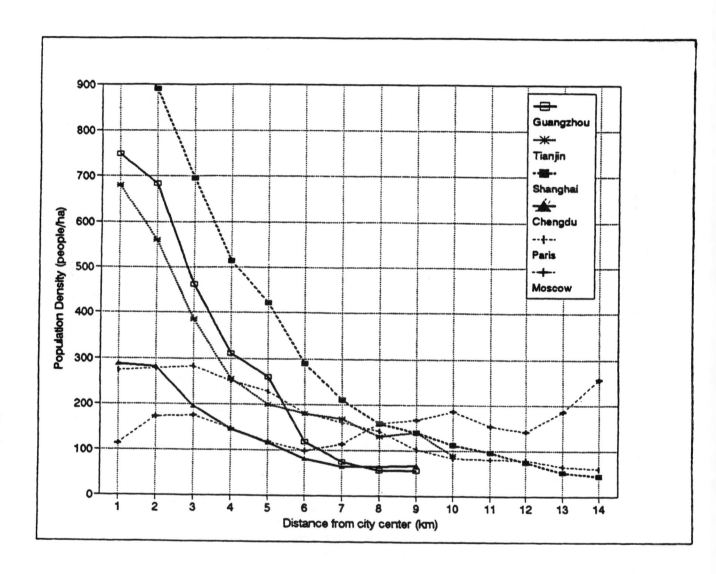

Figure A1.7: PARIS - LAND USE,
POPULATION DENSITY (1990)

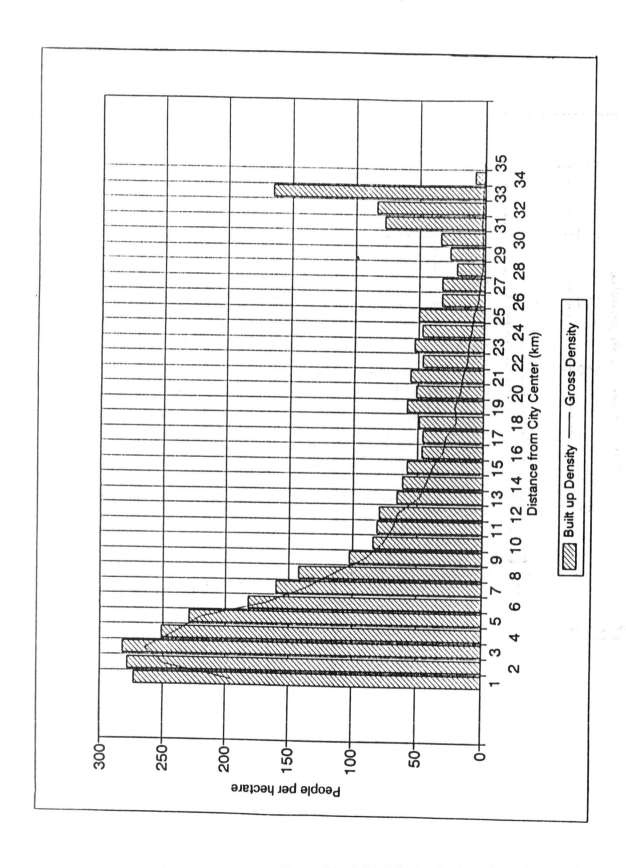

Figure A1.8: ST. PETERSBURG - LAND USE ANALYSIS
Gross Population Density Within the Built-up Area of 86 Districts

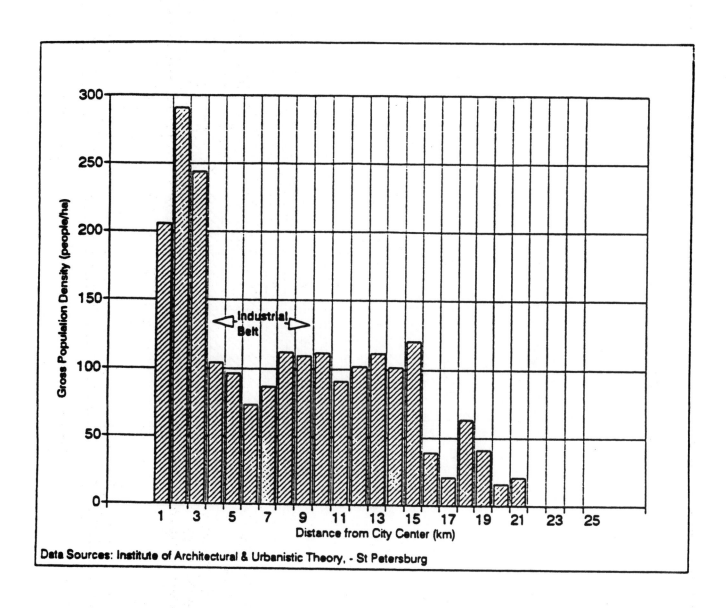

Data Sources: Institute of Architectural & Urbanistic Theory, - St Petersburg

Figure A1.9: MOSCOW - LAND USE ANALYSIS
Gross Population Density Within the Built-up Area of Municipality

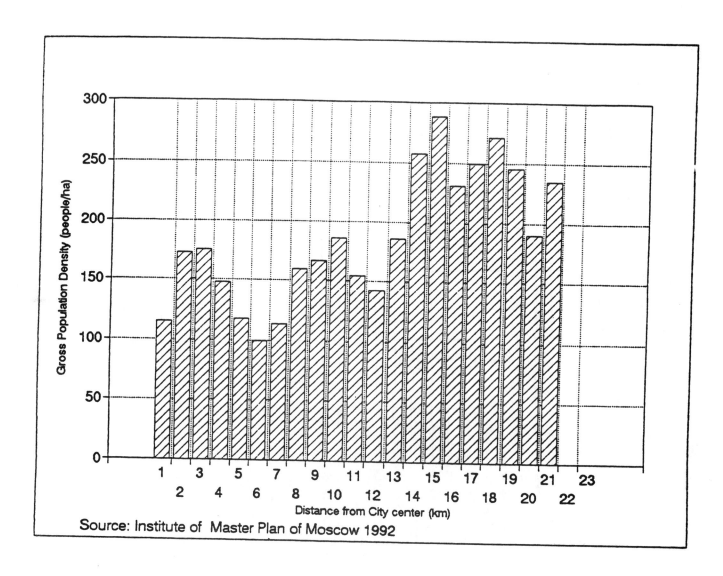

Source: Institute of Master Plan of Moscow 1992

Figure A1.10: ST. PETERSBURG - LAND USE ANALYSIS
Land Use in Concentric Rings from City Center

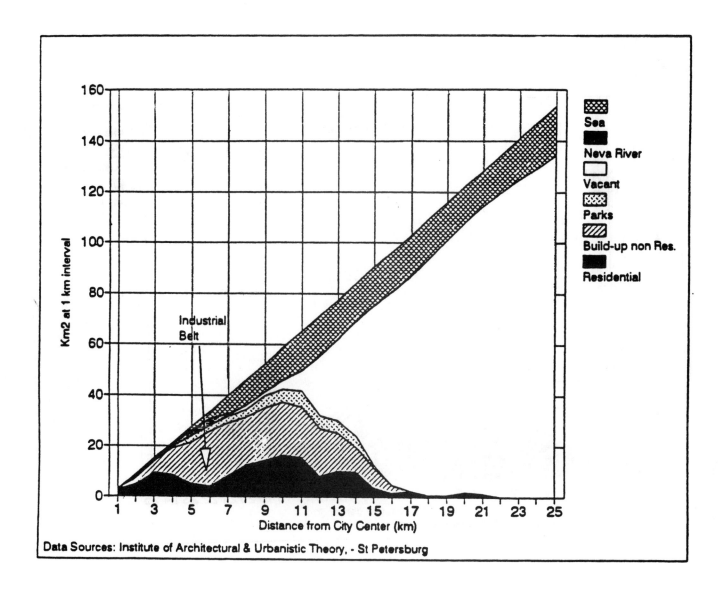

Data Sources: Institute of Architectural & Urbanistic Theory, - St Petersburg

Figure A1.11: MOSCOW - LAND USE ANALYSIS
Land Use in Concentric Rings

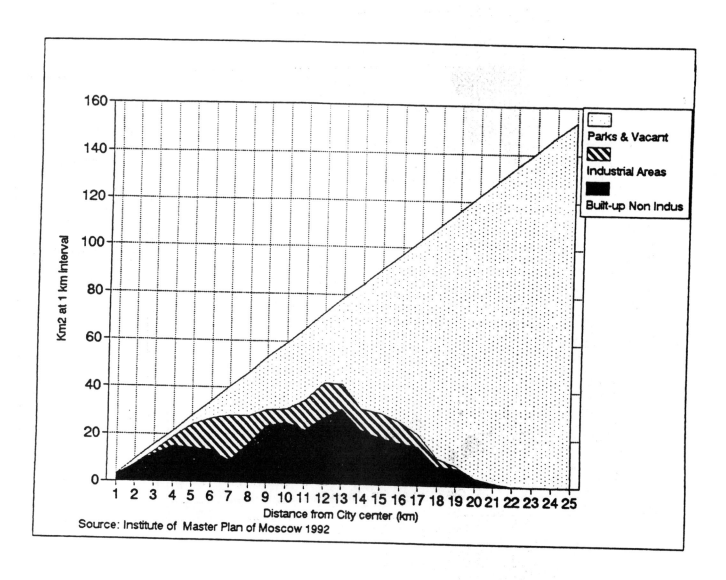

Source: Institute of Master Plan of Moscow 1992

Figure A1.12: GUANGZHOU MUNICIPALITY: LAND USE ANALYSIS

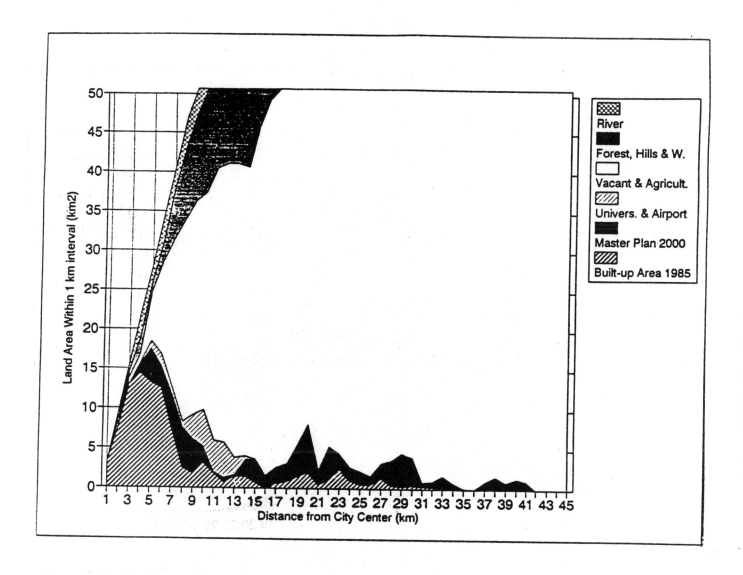

Figure A1.13: GUANGZHOU MASTER PLAN

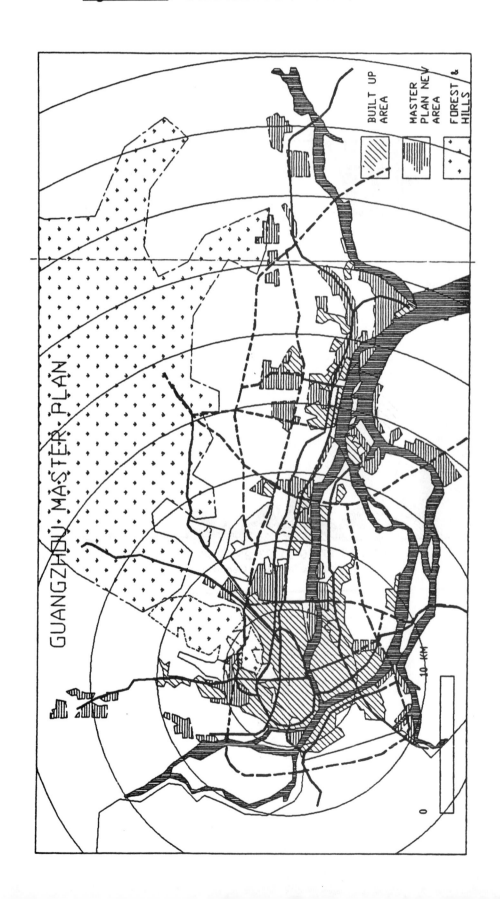

Figure A1.14: SHANGHAI - POPULATION CHANGES BETWEEN 1982 AND 1990

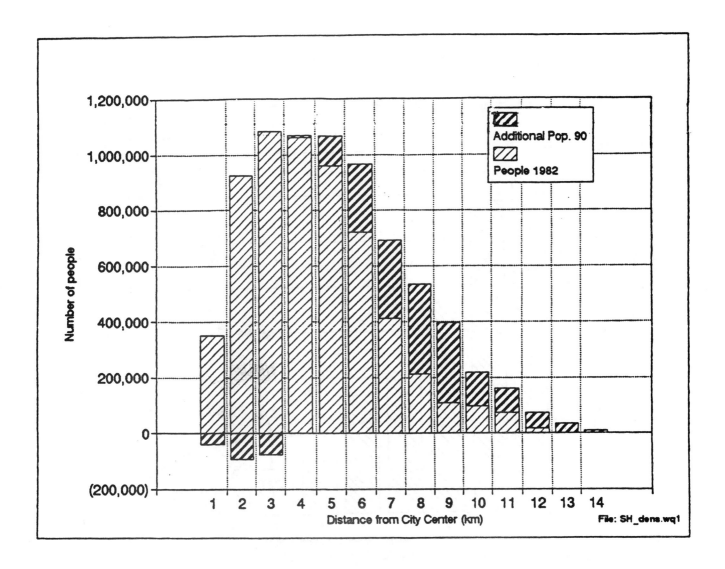

Figure A1.15: GUANGZHOU - DENSITY PROFILE IN FOUR CENTRAL DISTRICTS

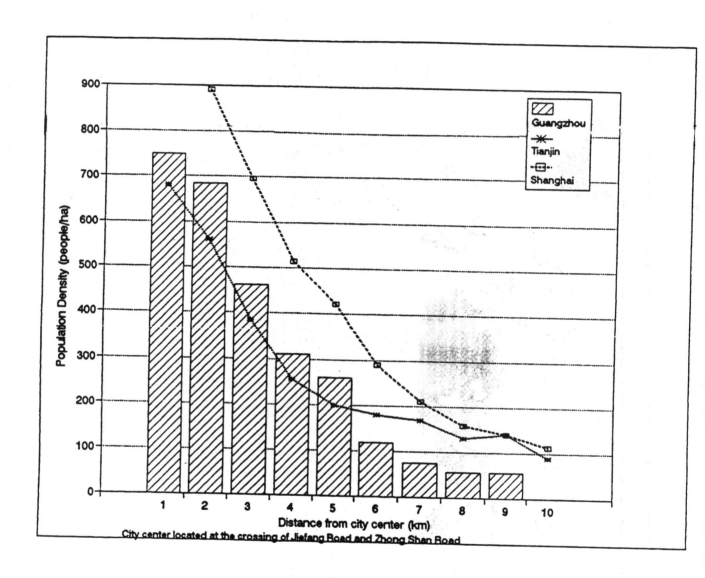

Figure A1.16: SHANGHAI: MASTER PLAN (YEAR 2000) VERSUS ACTUAL PLAN DEVELOPMENT (1990)

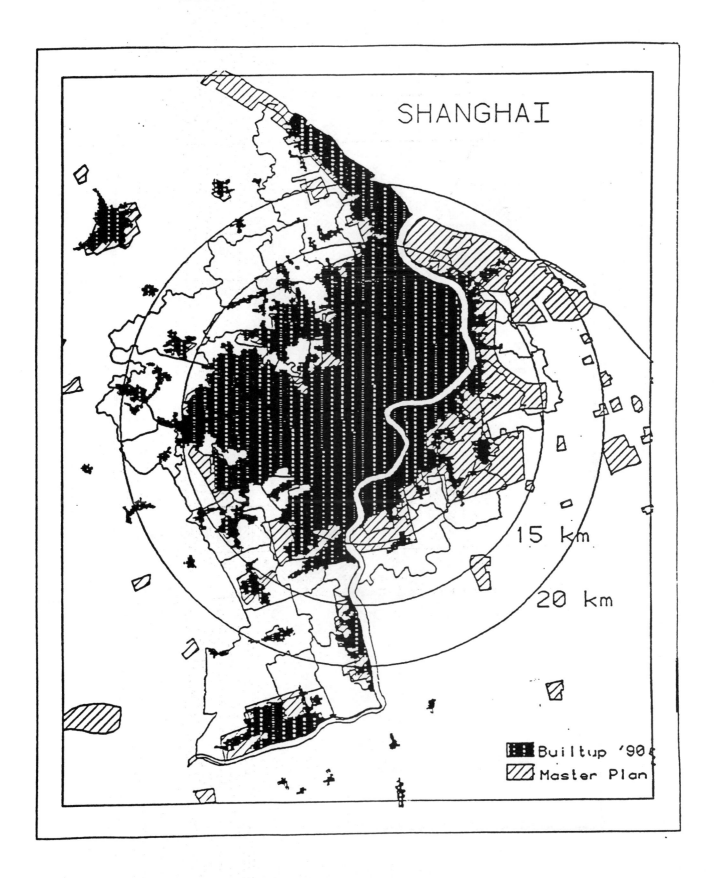

Figure A1.17: SHANGHAI: POPULATION DENSITIES 1982 AND 1990

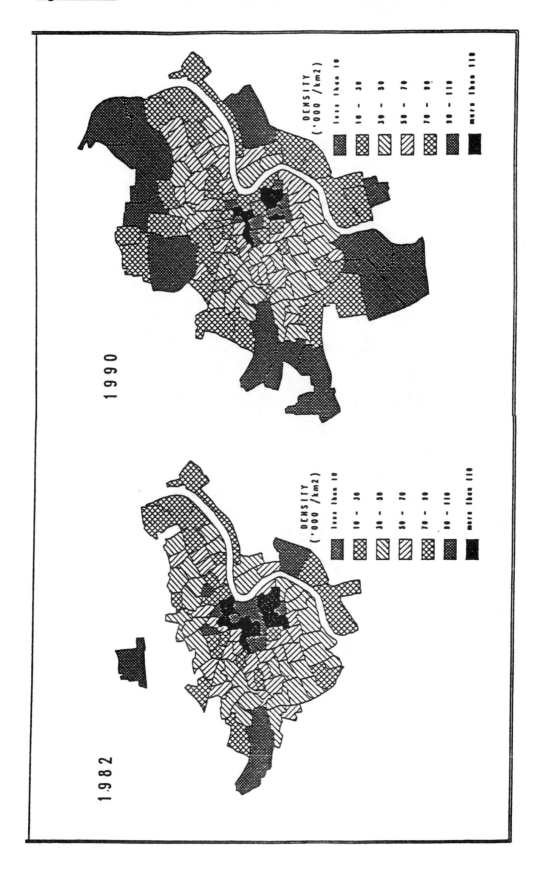

Figure A1.18: SHANGHAI: POPULATION DENSITIES, TRENDS
COMPARED WITH PARIS

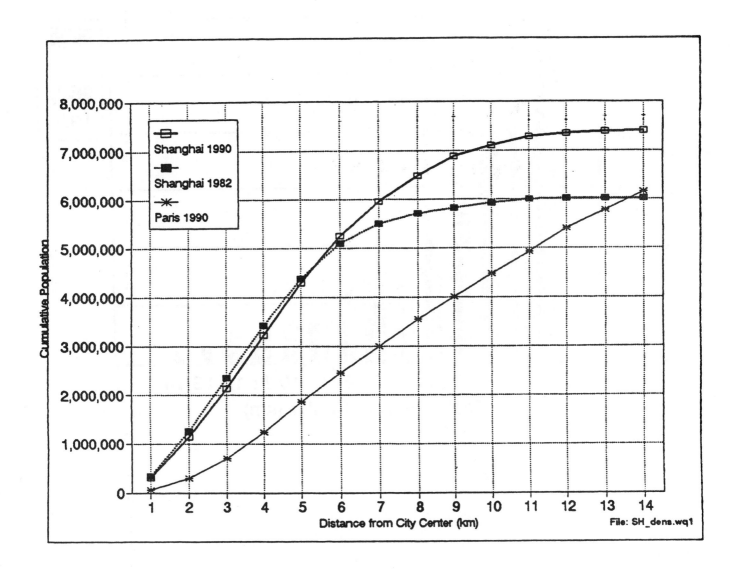

Figure A1.19: SHANGHAI: POPULATION DENSITY DISTRIBUTION

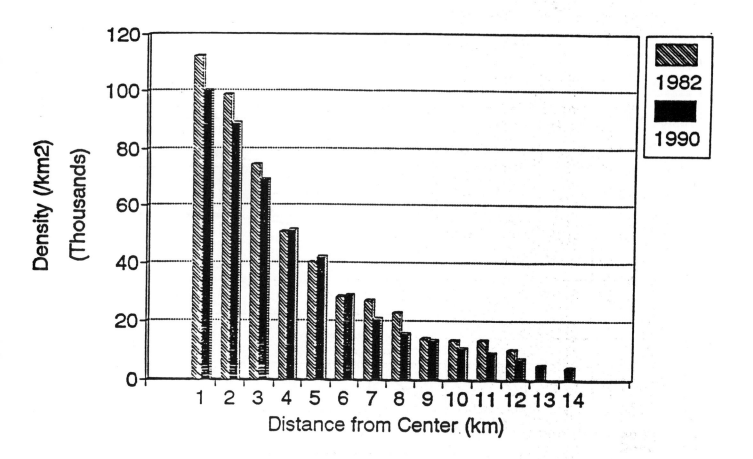

Figure A1.20: SHANGHAI: GROWTH IN BUILT-UP AREA

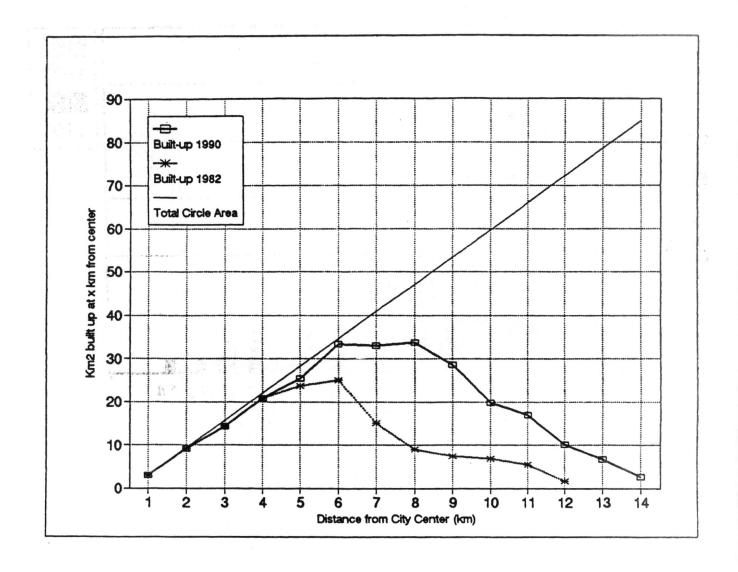

Figure A1.21: SHANGHAI: LAND USES, 1982 AND 1990

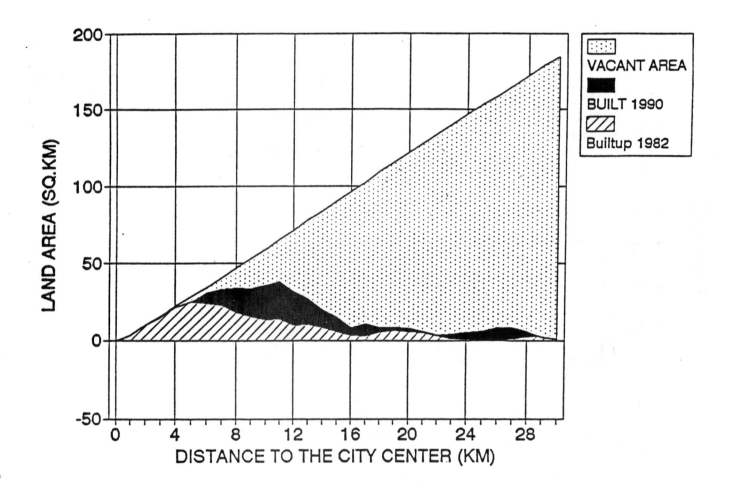

Figure A1.22: SHARE OF POPULATION, JOBS AND HOUSING
BETWEEN PUXI AND PUDONG

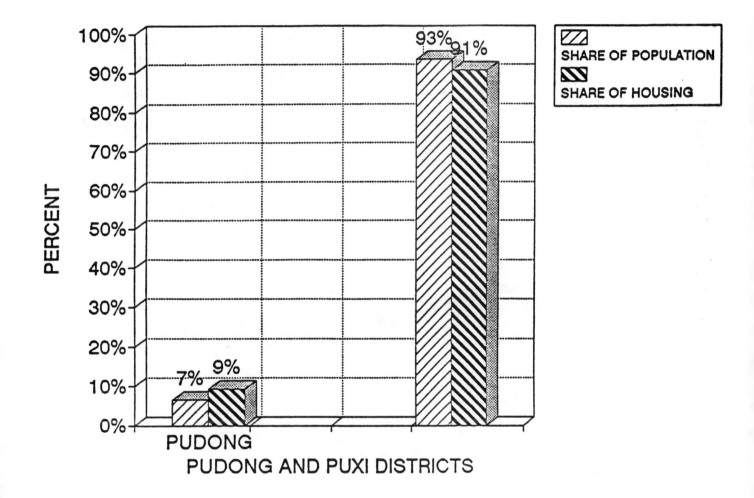

Figure A1.23: SHANGHAI: LAND USES: EXISTING AND EXPECTED
UNDER REVISED MASTER PLAN

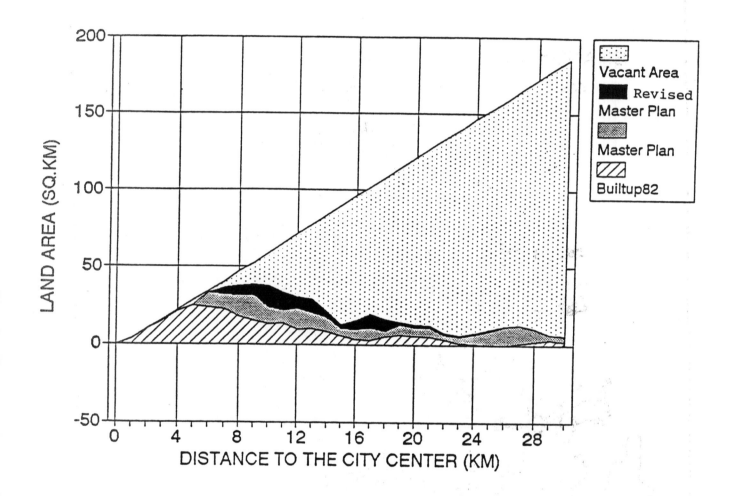

Figure A1.24: DISTRIBUTION OF SHANGHAI'S INDUSTRIAL LAND IN 1982

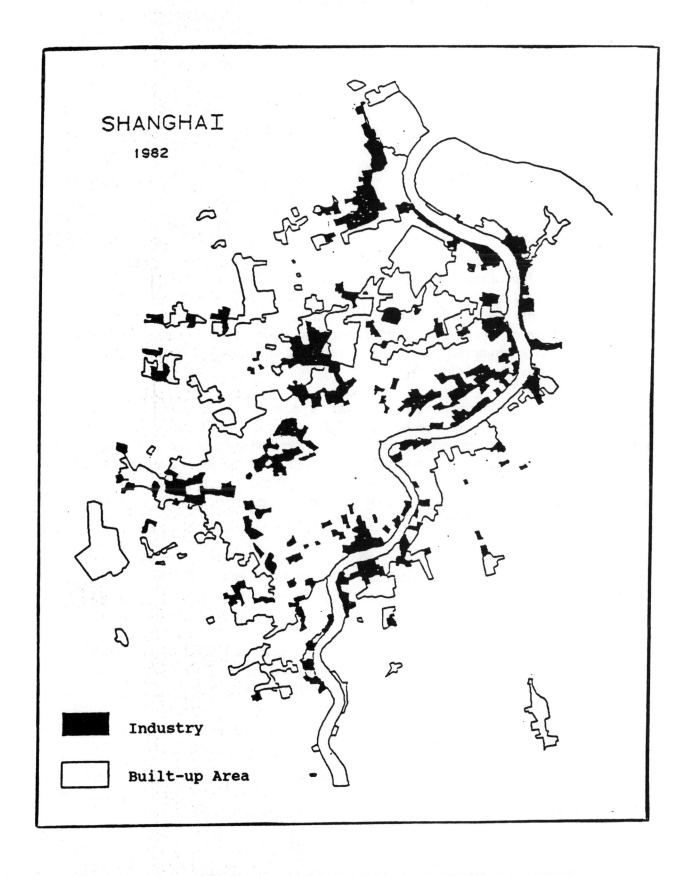

ANNEX 2

RESIDENTIAL REDEVELOPMENT PROJECT SURVEYS: ISSUES RAISED BY REAL ESTATE DEVELOPERS

In the course of conducting field surveys in Fuzhou, Guangzhou, Hangzhou, Shanghai and Tianjin, 11 redevelopment project case studies were developed. In most cases, financial information on project costs was obtained directly from REDCs. In some cases, the actual costs have been estimated, based on information gathered on other comparable projects.1/ This annex provides a brief description of the cases analyzed in Chapter V.

Fuzhou: An Deng Project

The An Deng project involved the clearance of a 5,536 m² site in central Fuzhou. The site was developed into an urban park, and all residents were relocated to a nearby suburban project. Before redevelopment, the site contained 108 households and 342 persons. The old constructed area was 6,213 m², an FAR of 1.12. Nearly all of the units (106) were privately owned, only two were held by the government. The typical owner-occupant had an average floor space of 60 m² of constructed space (in terms of living area, the space was 30-34 m²) before redevelopment. Afterwards, constructed area averaged 85 m² and living area averaged 36-44 m² per household.

To accommodate the relocation, a new project totaling 16,980 m² was constructed in suburban Fuzhou. The total cost of the new project is estimated at Y 8,060,000. A breakdown of the costs is provided in Table A2.1. The total construction cost works out to Y 475/m² of constructed area. In terms of marketable area, the break-even sales price is Y 811/m², assuming that resettled households pay a portion of the costs of their new units. If no funds were received from resettled households, the break-even price would be Y 881/m² of marketable area.

Resettled tenants, which originally held 6,213 m², received 7,833 m² of constructed space at concessionary prices and they purchased an additional 1,467 m² at the commercial price of Y 800/m². An additional 7,680 m² of housing was constructed and sold commercially at Y 814/m².

An Deng site residents received cash compensation for their demolished housing. Because the buildings were old and in poor condition, they got between Y 30 and Y 60/m² of constructed space. At the new project, which is located about 3 km from the old site, each household was permitted to purchase the same amount of space as they had before redevelopment at a net price of Y 62/m² of constructed space (Y 107 minus Y 45 in

---

1/ Local authorities charged with overseeing the REDCs cautioned that, in the absence of independent audits, project costs may not always be reported accurately by the developers. Those same authorities, however, provided no specific rebuttals to the case studies reported in this annex.

Table A2.1: FUZHOU: AN DENG PROJECT

Site area (m^2)	6,670
Total built area	16,980
Residential area	16,980
Marketable area	9,147

Construction costs	Cost (Yuan)	Cost/ site (m^2)	Cost/ TCA (m^2)	Cost/ RCA (m^2)	Cost/ MRA (m^2)
Preconstruction					
Relocation payments	385,000	57.72	22.67	22.67	42.09
Site preparation	75,000	11.24	4.42	4.42	8.20
Survey & design	50,000	7.50	2.94	2.94	5.47
On-site services	25,000	3.75	1.47	1.47	2.73
Fees & taxes	450,000	67.47	26.50	26.50	49.20
Subtotal	985,000	147.68	58.01	58.01	107.69
Construction					
Housing	4,400,000	659.67	259.13	259.13	481.03
Land	1,500,000	224.89	88.34	88.34	163.99
Management fees	100,000	14.99	5.89	5.89	10.93
Contingencies	200,000	29.99	11.78	11.78	21.87
Interest	250,000	37.48	14.72	14.72	27.33
Subtotal	6,450,000	967.02	379.86	379.86	705.15
Infrastructure					
Water	300,000	14.99	5.89	5.89	10.93
Sewer & drainage	75,000	11.24	4.42	4.42	0.00
Gas	50,000	7.50	2.94	2.94	5.47
Electric	100,000	14.99	5.89	5.89	10.93
Roads	100,000	14.99	5.89	5.89	10.93
Subtotal	625,000	93.70	36.81	36.81	68.33
Total Cost	8,060,000	1,208.40	474.68	474.68	881.16

TCA = Total Construction Area.
RCA = Residential Construction Area.
MRA = Marketable Residential Area.

Note: These estimated costs are for off-site new construction of replacement and commodity housing.

compensation). Each household could (and did) purchase an additional 15 m² of space at Y 145/m². If households wanted to, they could purchase additional space at the full commercial price of Y 811/m² of constructed space. The actual funds generated by this approach are as follows:

From resettled households:

Purchase of replacement space (6,213 m²) at Y 62/m²:	Y	385,206
Purchase of additional 15 m² (1,620 m²) at Y 145/m²:		234,900
Purchase of additional space (1,467 m²) at Y 814/m²:		1,194,138

From new commodity housing purchasers:

Purchase of commodity space (7,680 m²) at Y 814/m²:	6,251,520
Total Revenue (16,980 m²), average Y 475/m²:	8,065,764

In cases where the resettled occupants acquired no more than their initial space and the additional 15 m², households paid out Y 8,330 and received compensation of Y 2,589, a net outflow of Y 5,741. Virtually all households purchased the additional 15 m² of subsidized space, increasing their constructed area by 26 percent (57.5 to 72.5 m² per household). The additional increase of space through the purchase at commodity prices increased unit sizes by an additional 13.3 m². Together, the increase of 15 and 13.3 m² boosts unit sizes by nearly 50 percent over the 57.5 m² average. On average, each household purchased an additional 13.3 m², paying an additional Y 10,826.

By requiring resettled households to pay the difference between the depreciated value of their old unit, and the construction cost of the new space (Y 45 versus Y 107/m²) and by requiring them to pay higher prices for additional space, the financial burden of the redevelopment project is lessened for those purchasing commodity housing.

For example, if Fuzhou followed Tianjin's policies regarding redevelopment, the 108 households of the An Deng project would have received the 7,833 m² of space and would have paid no compensation. Instead, the sales price of the commodity housing would rise from Y 814 to Y 881/m², an increase of 8 percent. The strategy pursued in Fuzhou, where redevelopment project area residents are required to pay for the marginal cost of the new housing, is an appropriate policy option meriting further consideration.

Guangzhou: Jin Hua Project

In 1982 a real estate company specializing in redevelopment was established in Guangzhou. In 1986, it tackled a large redevelopment project in the city center—called Jin Hua. The project site covers 290,000 m². The site was home to 7,492 households and had a population of 25,198. The existing built-up area totaled 335,000 m²—reflecting an FAR of 1.16. The redevelopment plan calls for demolition of 277,000 m², and the construction of 220 new buildings, accounting for 737,000 m², an FAR of 2.54. One third of the project will be in the form of high-rise (24-story) buildings.

The overall redevelopment concept is to rebuild structures on the site, improve housing conditions of the 7,492 dwellings, provide additional community services and construct an additional 2,907 dwelling units. The total investment of the project is planned at Y 750,032,000. Estimates of the costs of the Jin Hua project are provided in Table A2.2. When completed, the project will comprise 10,400 units, with a total population of 41,000. *As of August 1991, only one fifth of the project had been completed, despite the fact that the project started in 1986.* Apparently, financial constraints have dogged the project.

There are numerous problems which make it difficult to implement redevelopment projects. The fundamental problem centers around the way in which project are financed. In virtually all cases in China, projects are financed through the sale of marketable commercial units. Existing residents have ironclad property rights guaranteeing the continuance of low rents. Despite the fact that the residential units of long-standing residents are vastly improved (most residents get toilets and kitchens) and which are frequently enlarged, most municipal regulations prohibit rent increases. As a result, redevelopment strategies center on methods for increasing the ratio of marketable commercial units to total constructed units.

In Guangzhou, laws on relocation of residents are strict and costly to follow. In the Jin Hua project, only small portions of the 29-hectare site can be developed at a time, because there are so few available relocation units. Another problem is the high costs of infrastructure required to support new redevelopment projects. Dedication requirements for schools, shops, clinic, security offices and so forth add considerable costs, because the facilities are transferred at no cost to the local government. The result of these costs is that the marketable units must shoulder an enormous burden and unless the commodity market is strong, commercial prices cannot be set high enough to recover these costs. Enterprises, the principal buyers of these new commercial units, do not want to pay the full fixed costs of the redevelopment project; they rightly expect to pay the direct cost of a unit plus some markup for profit and overhead.

For example, if all the nonresidential space was sold at cost (Y 1,018/m^2) to either the district government or to shopkeepers, Y 172 million in revenues would be generated. In this case, the break-even sales price of the commodity housing would be reduced from Y 2,622/m^2 to Y 2,021/m^2, a 23 percent price reduction.

Some developers of redevelopment projects have proposed a variety of reforms to reduce project costs. The typical proposals include: changes in tax and land fee policies of the government to exempt or reduce payments for redevelopment projects; subsidizes for infrastructure construction; faster, streamlined approval process for redevelopment projects; increase FAR from 2.8 to 3.0 for redevelopment projects in Guangzhou; and reduce facilities' construction costs by reducing requirements or by receiving government subsidies for community facilities.

Fees paid on development projects in Guangzhou are high. For example, 5 percent of total building costs are paid to government at the time building permit is issued, and another 2 percent is paid for air raid shelters. Other fees are levied for: fire services,

Table A2.2: GUANGZHOU: JIN HUA REDEVELOPMENT PROJECT

Site area (m^2)	290,000
Total built area	737,000
Residential area	568,000
Marketable area	286,000

Construction costs	Cost (Yuan)	Cost/ site (m^2)	Cost/ TCA (m^2)	Cost/ RCA (m^2)	Cost/ MRA (m^2)
Preconstruction					
Relocation payments	7,800,000	26.90	10.58	13.73	27.27
Temporary rentals	13,155,000	45.36	17.85	23.16	46.00
Site preparation	630,000	2.17	0.85	1.11	2.20
Survey & design	17,823,000	61.46	24.18	31.38	62.32
On-site services	670,000	2.31	0.91	1.18	2.34
Fees & taxes	115,988,000	399.96	157.38	204.20	405.55
Subtotal	156,066,000	538.16	211.76	274.76	545.69
Construction					
Housing	235,000,000	810.34	318.86	413.73	821.68
Public facilities	145,000,000	500.00	196.74	255.28	506.99
Management fee	37,500,000	129.31	50.88	66.02	131.12
Contingencies	20,000,000	68.97	27.14	35.21	69.93
Interest	29,000,000	100.00	39.35	51.06	101.40
Subtotal	466,500,000	1,608.62	632.97	821.30	1,631.12
Infrastructure					
Water	5,833,000	300.34	118.18	153.35	304.55
Sewer & drainage	5,833,000	20.11	7.91	10.27	20.40
Gas	18,700,000	64.48	25.37	32.92	65.38
Electric	87,100,000	300.34	118.18	153.35	304.55
Roads	10,000,000	34.48	13.57	17.61	34.97
Other	0	0.00	0.00	0.00	0.00
Subtotal	127,466,000	439.54	172.95	224.41	445.69
Total Cost	750,032,000	2,586.32	1,017.68	1,320.48	2,622.49

TCA = Total Construction Area.

RCA = Residential Construction Area.

MRA = Marketable Residential Area.

environmental protection, sewerage, real estate taxes (3 percent), land use fee (3 percent of requisition costs to acquire land), and property registration (1 percent). As a general rule of thumb, bankers and developers use the "one third rule"—total project costs normally divide into three equal parts: land and infrastructure, fees, and construction.

In the process of structuring the project, the REDC met with each and every household and negotiated with them a precise settlement in terms of temporary relocation, compensation, and the provision of a new unit. In the Jin Hua project, 6,712 households will return to the project, and each household will receive 13 m^2 of constructed area per person. In terms of living area, the standard is 8 m^2 per capita. Households electing not to return to the area receive Y 10,000 in compensation.

The most burdensome redevelopment occurs with the occupants of housing owned by overseas Chinese. These units need to be replaced twice—once to provide new housing for the tenant and once to provide the overseas Chinese with a replacement for their demolished unit. The requirement that overseas Chinese receive units has been a policy of Guangdong Province since 1987. It is intended to reassure the overseas Chinese that the province is a safe haven for investment. While this is a sensible policy, it places an enormous fiscal burden on redevelopment projects.

It is projected that the total project will cost Y 750 million. Of the 7,392 households occupying the site, 6,712 will be resettled on the site and will receive approximately 42 m^2 of space per household. Of the total project area of 737,000 m^2, 38.8 percent, 286,000 m^2 will be marketable, and 282,000 m^2 will be devoted to replacement housing. The remaining space, 169,000 m^2, is for public facilities such as clinics, schools, markets, etc.

Normal profit for developers would be on the order of 8 percent of total costs or, in the above case, Y 200/m^2 of constructed area. However, the project will not achieve that objective in its present form. As Table A2.2 illustrates, the current break-even price of commodity housing is estimated at Y 2,592/m^2. This figure is above the sales prices of other comparable commodity housing projects currently on the market in Guangzhou. As of August 1991, commodity housing prices have been running between Y 1,700 to Y 2,400/m^2, depending on whether the project is located in the city center or in the suburbs. Consequently, the REDC is having difficulties attracting buyers.

Guangzhou's Jin Hua project is a good example of how housing policies for existing residents and requirements for public facilities may make projects unattractive. Since the costs of the nonmarketable housing units (units returned to former residents) as well as community facilities must be paid for through the sale of commodity housing, financing redevelopment is difficult.

Hangzhou: Xiao Fuqing Lane Redevelopment Project

The project is located in the Xiachen District of Hangzhou City on a 7,350 m^2 site. The small site did not contain public facilities or commercial activities. It was settled with old, preliberation housing which was in poor condition and overcrowded. About 120 households lived on the site, and each had about 50 m² of constructed area—6,000 m². *The project was started in 1988 and was completed in 1990.* All area residents were resettled on the site and they received 9,530 m² of new residential constructed space, averaging about 80 m² per household. In addition, 4,485 m² of commodity housing was constructed on-site. Limited public facilities were constructed—1,420 m². The total cost of the project was Y 6,993,000, an average of Y 454/m² of constructed space. A complete breakdown of the costs is provided in Table A2.3. Relocation costs, including provision of new housing and temporary shelter, totaled Y 3,372,000. In terms of overall project costs, relocation and resettlement accounted for 48 percent of total costs.

All resettled residents were provided new housing and were required to make no payment for it, despite the fact that the quality of their new units was vastly improved and that households received additional space. As a consequence of these generous terms, purchasers of commodity housing pay Y 1,559/m², 3.44 times the actual cost of construction.

If Hangzhou followed a redevelopment strategy more in line with Fuzhou than Tianjin, it could reduce the cost burden it places on the purchasers of commodity housing. For example, if the 120 household were require to pay a modest Y 100/m² of original space returned (6,000 m²) and if additional space, allocated to each household to bring them up to citywide standards of 80 m² of constructed space per household, was sold to residents at 50 percent of the actual project cost, Y 227/m², the developer would receive Y 600,000 for the replacement of the original space, and Y 801,310 for the allocation of the 3,530 m² of space. After adjusting for these receipts, purchasers of commodity housing would pay Y 1,247/m², a 20 percent reduction. If the public facilities were sold at cost, the commodity housing price would fall even further, to Y 1,103/m².

Shanghai: Hu Lang Garden Project

The Shanghai Real Estate Corporation (SREC) was established in 1983, and works with the 12 Districts to manage and develop housing. It receives rental income of Y 1.04 billion per year, but this is not sufficient to cover management and operating costs. Consequently, the SREC receives an operating subsidy of Y 44 million per year from the Shanghai Municipal Government. Since 1987, it has annually constructed about 160,000 m² of housing. In 1991, it anticipates the completion of 170,000 m². So far, it has completed 10 redevelopment projects, one of which is the Hu Lang Garden (White Lily Garden). Hu Lang is located in southwest Shanghai near the second subway exit. The site area is 1.68 hectares. The total constructed area of the site before redevelopment is 12,589 m², reflecting an FAR of 1:0.75.

The project was approved by the Planning Bureau in 1985. Relocation was done in 1986, and construction commenced in 1987. The main structures of the high-rise buildings for the overseas market have been completed, and are expected to be finished by the end of 1991. The site was home to 553 households (population of 1,900), occupying 7,809 m² of constructed space—14 m² per household. Over 80 percent of the housing (6,520 m²) was

Table A2.3: HANGZHOU: XIAO FUQING LANE REDEVELOPMENT PROJECT

Site area (m²)	7,350
Total built area	15,417
Residential area	14,015
Marketable area	4,485

Construction costs	Cost (Yuan)	Cost/ site (m²)	Cost/ TCA (m²)	Cost/ RCA (m²)	Cost/ MRA (m²)
Preconstruction					
Temporary rentals	357,000	48.57	23.16	25.47	79.60
Site preparation	53,000	7.21	3.44	3.78	11.82
Survey & design	45,000	6.12	2.92	3.21	10.03
On-site services	56,000	7.62	3.63	4.00	12.49
Fees & taxes	1,214,000	165.17	78.75	86.62	270.68
Subtotal	1,725,000	234.69	111.89	123.08	384.62
Construction					
Housing	4,781,000	650.48	310.12	341.13	1,066.00
Public facilities	72,000	9.80	4.67	5.14	16.05
Management fees	81,000	11.02	5.25	5.78	18.06
Contingencies	0	0.00	0.00	0.00	0.00
Interest	85,000	11.56	5.51	6.06	18.95
Subtotal	5,019,000	682.86	325.56	358.12	1,119.06
Infrastructure					
Water	131,000	7.89	3.76	4.14	12.93
Sewer & drainage	25,000	3.40	1.62	1.78	0.00
Gas	0	0.00	0.00	0.00	0.00
Electric	58,000	7.89	3.76	4.14	12.93
Roads	35,000	4.76	2.27	2.50	7.80
Other	0	0.00	0.00	0.00	0.00
Subtotal	249,000	33.88	16.15	17.77	55.52
Total Cost	6,993,000	951.43	453.60	498.97	1,559.20

TCA = Total Construction Area.
RCA = Residential Construction Area.
MRA = Marketable Residential Area.

privately owned. The remainder was owned and managed by the municipality. There were seven enterprises occupying the site with a constructed area of 4,780 m².

The SREC borrowed a nearby piece of land on which to construct a temporary structures. They also utilized vacant houses owned by other Districts. Some of the site's residents managed to find their own temporary housing as well. One enterprise, the Wan Ti shirt factory was not relocated and the project was structured to allow it to maintain operations. The negotiations between the shirt factory and the REDC are interesting and pertinent. The shirt factory posed no problems for the surrounding neighborhoods; it was not polluting or noisy. The plan was to acquire some of the land from the factory and incorporate it into the scheme for housing development. Based on a series of negotiations, the factory agreed to vacate part of its buildings and give 1,130 m² of land. The REDC agreed to provide the factory with 1,695 m² of newly constructed space. A new four-story building of 1,251 m² was built. The new building cost Y 580,000. The factory paid Y 160,000 for improvements and finishes to upgrade the structure beyond what the regulations warrant. (These funds came from the factory's accumulated building repair account.) The SREC agrees to pay Y 420,000 towards the construction of the building. In addition, the factory is paid Y 20,000 for temporary relocation costs.

The redevelopment plan called for the construction of five high-rise buildings on the site. The total new building area after redevelopment is planned to reach 84,000 m², a dramatic increase in the density—an FAR of 1:5.0. The residential uses will total 76,500 m², of which 26,500 m² is for the original households (the households receive 3.39 m² for every one they originally held. The per-household average constructed area increased to nearly 50 m².

The remaining portion of the housing is to be sold as commodity housing to overseas Chinese—50,000 m². These units are contained in three of the five high-rise buildings and are provided with imported elevators and high-quality fittings. In addition to the residential buildings, SREC also provided a 3,000 m² market, a 500 m² kindergarten and nursery, a 2,600 m² civil defense shelter, and a 1,400 m² bicycle garage.

The total project cost including interest and profit is Y 186,332,000. This works out to an average cost of Y 2,218/m² of constructed area. In terms of marketable area, the cost is Y 3,727/m². A breakdown of the costs is provided in Table A2.4. The targeted sales prices for the commodity housing is $735/m² of constructed area, Y 3,896/m².

This example illustrates that redevelopment can be carried out if the commercial units are sold to overseas Chinese residents. On the other hand, if the units were targeted for the domestic market, it is not clear that they could sell for Y 3,800/m². It might be better for the REDC to relocate residents to suburban locations. For example, if SREC relocated tenants and incurred the same costs in the Jian Guo project (Y 950/m²), total relocation costs would have increased by Y 25,175,000 (26,500 m² times Y 950/m²), and the total project cost would have increased to Y 211,507,000. But since all of the residential space would now be marketable, the break-even price per marketable m² would decline to Y 2,765 from Y 3,727/m².

Table A2.4: SHANGHAI: HU LANG GARDEN REDEVELOPMENT PROJECT

Site area (m^2)	16,800
Total built area	84,000
Residential area	76,500
Marketable area	50,000

Construction costs	Cost (Yuan)	Cost/ site (m^2)	Cost/ TCA (m^2)	Cost/ RCA (m^2)	Cost/ MRA (m^2)
Preconstruction					
Relocation payments	2,100,000	125.00	25.00	27.45	42.00
Temporary rentals	0	0.00	0.00	0.00	0.00
Site preparation	3,200,000	190.48	38.10	41.83	64.00
Survey & design	950,000	56.55	11.31	12.42	19.00
On-site services	560,000	33.33	6.67	7.32	11.20
Fees & taxes	12,250,000	729.17	145.83	160.13	245.00
Subtotal	19,060,000	1,134.52	226.90	249.15	381.20
Construction					
Housing	88,060,000	5,241.67	1,048.33	1,151.11	1,761.20
Public facilities	18,440,000	1097.62	219.52	241.05	368.80
Management fees	2,460,000	146.43	29.29	32.16	49.20
Contingencies/profit	17,012,000	1,012.62	202.52	222.38	340.24
Interest	29,400,000	1,750.00	350.00	384.31	588.00
Subtotal	155,372,000	9,248.33	1,849.67	2,031.01	3,107.44
Infrastructure					
Water	3,500,000	0.00	0.00	0.00	0.00
Sewer & drainage	0	0.00	0.00	0.00	0.00
Gas	0	0.00	0.00	0.00	0.00
Electric	0	0.00	0.00	0.00	0.00
Roads	0	0.00	0.00	0.00	0.00
Other (off-site)	8,400,000				
Subtotal	11,900,000	708.33	141.67	155.56	238.00
Total Cost	186,332,000	11,091.19	2,218.24	2,435.71	3,726.64

TCA = Total Construction Area.

RCA = Residential Construction Area.

MRA = Marketable Residential Area.

Shanghai: Hui Yi Garden Project

Hui Yi Garden is located in Xu Hui District and was constructed by the General Urban Construction and Development Company of Xu Hui District. The company specializes in developing housing for overseas Chinese. Units are paid for in foreign currency. *The project was started in 1984.*

The total site area is 1.3 hectares. It was originally occupied by 264 households and 4 enterprises. The housing stock comprised 7,970 m², the four enterprises had 660 m². The total constructed area before redevelopment was 8,630 m², reflecting a low FAR of 1:0.66.

The new project, a housing estate, is targeted toward overseas Chinese, and consists of 33 commodity housing units totaling 8,250 m². Because of the upscale target market of the redevelopment project, all former tenants were relocated to other locations.

The total cost of the project was Y 46,292,000, averaging Y 5,611/m² of gross constructed area, reflecting the substantial relocation costs of Y 19,076,000, which averages out to Y 2,210/m² of relocated area. Table A2.5 provides a breakdown of construction costs. The basic construction cost of the new units is Y 1,300/m², and reflects the high-quality construction appropriate for the target market. The selling prices are set at $1,550/m² (Y 8,215), a premium of 46 percent over costs. Part of the increase reflects differential rent (set at 20 percent) and profit of 10 percent.

Marketing of the project started in December 1988. The project was sold out in September 1990, averaging about two sales per month. Ads for the units were placed only in Shanghai media—newspapers and local radio stations. Purchasers carried most of the financial burden. Upon signing a contract, 50 percent of the purchase price was paid. An additional 30 percent was paid at the completion of the shell, and the final 20 percent at move-in.

Like the Jian Guo project, Hui Yi Garden illustrates the financial feasibility of redevelopment projects which can relocate prior residents and build for higher-revenue-producing users. For example, the overseas Chinese pay over Y 8,000/gross m² for housing and relocated residents were rehoused elsewhere for Y 1,300/m² (the previous residents occupied 7,970 m² but were provided with 12,904 m² of replacement housing—1.62 new m² for each old one). In the Hui Yi case, the differential in prices is substantial and provides an opportunity to finance projects by exploiting the differences in the prices.

Shanghai: Jian Guo Redevelopment Project

The Jian Guo redevelopment project was constructed by the China State Housing and Real Estate Company *in 1985.* The 1.9 hectare site was occupied by very old two- and three-story buildings. Before redevelopment the site contained 1,394 dwelling units and 45 enterprises. The old residential dwellings were quite small, averaging approximately 15 m² for

Table A2.5: SHANGHAI: HUI YI GARDEN REDEVELOPMENT PROJECT

Site area (m^2)	13,000
Total built area	8,250
Residential area	8,250
Marketable area	8,250

Construction costs	Cost (Yuan)	Cost/ site (m^2)	Cost/ TCA (m^2)	Cost/ RCA (m^2)	Cost/ MRA (m^2)
Preconstruction					
Relocation payments	18,696,000	1,438.15	2,266.18	2,266.18	2,266.18
Temporary rentals	380,000	29.23	46.06	46.06	46.06
Site preparation	200,000	15.38	24.24	24.24	24.24
Survey & design	240,000	18.46	29.09	29.09	29.09
On-site services	280,000	21.54	33.94	33.94	33.94
Fees & taxes	4,575,000	351.92	554.55	554.55	554.55
Subtotal	24,371,000	1,874.69	2,954.06	2,954.06	2,954.06
Construction					
Housing	10,730,000	825.38	1,300.61	1,300.61	1,300.61
Public facilities	2,150,000	165.38	260.61	260.61	260.61
Management fees	728,000	56.00	88.24	88.24	88.24
Contingencies	1,823,000	140.23	220.97	220.97	220.97
Interest	3,670,000	282.31	444.85	444.85	444.85
Subtotal	19,101,000	1,469.31	2,315.27	2,315.27	2,315.27
Infrastructure					
Water	1,070,000	134.62	212.12	212.12	212.12
Sewer & drainage	0	0.00	0.00	0.00	0.00
Gas	0	0.00	0.00	0.00	0.00
Electric	1,750,000	134.62	212.12	212.12	212.12
Roads	0	0.00	0.00	0.00	0.00
Other	0	0.00	0.00	0.00	0.00
Subtotal	2,820,000	216.92	341.82	341.82	341.82
Total Cost	46,292,000	3,560.92	5,611.15	5,611.15	5,611.15

TCA = Total Construction Area.
RCA = Residential Construction Area.
MRA = Marketable Residential Area.

a total of 21,221 m². Forty-five enterprises occupied 5,000 m². It was estimated that it would cost approximately Y 22 million to rehabilitate the old housing units and the cost, at nearly Y 16,000/unit, would be difficult to recover from the existing tenants. The overall density of the project before redevelopment was moderate—an FAR of 1:1.38. Because of the high costs of rehabilitation and the site's important location in the center of Shanghai, all of the households and most enterprises were relocated to a suburban site.

Relocated households received 60 m² of living area. The estimated costs of the residential relocation is Y 79,458,000, Y 950/m², well below levels that would prevail if the households were rehoused on the site. Thirty of the 45 enterprise were relocated at a cost of Y 9,660,000, a average cost of Y 322,000 per enterprise.

The company built a 88,400 m² mixed-use project on the site. Residential uses comprise 42,900 m², retail and other commercial activities make up 41,200 m². Public facilities will account for 4,300 m². The completed project will has an FAR of 1:4.65.

The total cost of the project, including all charges for relocation is Y 266,903,000. In terms of total constructed area, the cost averages out to approximately Y 3,020/m². In terms of marketable area, the cost per m² is a little higher, Y 3,174. Table A2.6 presents a summary of the project's costs.

If all prior residential users had been resettled on the site, the total project cost would have been approximately Y 185 million. However, since these households would have been allocated 60 m² each, virtually all of the newly constructed space would not have been marketable. It would have been impossible to carry out the project unless the tenants were willing and able to pay for the improvements.

Based on the location of the project, the quality of construction and risk factors, the REDC initially set the prices of the high-rise commodity housing at Y 2,600/m² of constructed area and for the commercial buildings, prices were set at Y 3,200/m². Based on these prices, gross revenues were Y 243,380,000. Thus, this project will not break even, losing Y 23,523,000 (assuming that all fees and charges are levied). However, as of January 1992, the Shanghai Municipal Government permitted developers to set prices at cost (including interest expenses) plus 10 percent profit. Under this new pricing regime, China State Housing & Real Estate Company would be able to sell the space at an average price of Y 3,470/m². While this price is considerably higher, it is still below the market price for space in the area—Y 4,000 to Y 5,000/m².

This project provides a good example of how redevelopment projects can be structured more feasibly if tenants are relocated to suburban areas. In the current case, resettled households had their housing units increased from 15 m² to 60 m² and they did not have to pay any additional fees.

Table A2.6: SHANGHAI: JIAN GUO REDEVELOPMENT PROJECT

Site area (m²)	19,000
Total built area	88,400
Residential area	42,900
Commercial area	41,200
Marketable area	84,100

Construction costs	Cost (Yuan)	Cost/ site (m²)	Cost/ TCA (m²)	Cost/ RCA (m²)	Cost/ MRA (m²)
Preconstruction					
Relocation payments	89,118,000	4,690.42	1,008.12	2,077.34	1,059.67
Temporary rentals	140,000	7.37	1.58	3.26	1.66
Site preparation	1,060,000	55.79	11.99	24.71	12.60
Survey & design	1,410,000	74.21	15.95	32.87	16.77
On-site services	530,000	27.89	6.00	12.35	6.30
Fees & taxes	29,300,000	1,542.11	331.45	682.98	348.39
Subtotal	121,558,000	6,397.79	1,375.09	2,833.52	1,445.40
Construction					
Housing	42,830,000	2,254.21	484.50	998.37	509.27
Commercial buildings	49,800,000				
Public facilities	4,340,000	228.42	49.10	101.17	51.61
Management fees	6,690,000	352.11	75.68	155.94	79.55
Contingencies	9,670,000	508.95	109.39	225.41	114.98
Interest	30,321,000	1,595.84	343.00	706.78	360.54
Subtotal	143,651,000	7,560.58	1,625.01	3,348.51	1,708.10
Infrastructure					
Water	150,000	59.47	12.78	26.34	13.44
Sewer & drainage	220,000	11.58	2.49	5.13	2.62
Gas	130,000	6.84	1.47	3.03	1.55
Electric	1,130,000	59.47	12.78	26.34	13.44
Roads	64,000	3.37	0.72	1.49	0.76
Other	3,090,000				
Subtotal	1,694,000	89.16	19.16	39.49	20.14
Total Cost	266,903,000	14,047.53	3,019.26	6,221.52	3,173.64

TCA = Total Construction Area.
RCA = Residential Construction Area.
MRA = Marketable Residential Area.

Shanghai: Ordinary Citizen Project

This is a large redevelopment project located in the southwest corner of the inner city. The project was initiated in 1985 by the Xu Hui District's and involved the participation of several enterprises. They created a corporation called the United Construction Office. The site comprises 16.5 hectares and, before redevelopment, consisted of 3,620 simple houses and 62 small enterprises. It was one of 23 slum areas identified by the Shanghai Planning and Design Institute's 1985 survey. The residential area totaled 103,040 m^2 of constructed area, of which 21,055 m^2 was under municipal ownership and 81,985 was under private ownership. The houses were quite primitive and small (averaging 28 m^2 on average). There was no sewer system serving the area, and water was provided by standpipes. Residents of municipal housing received no compensation for losing their house. If they choose to relocate, their new rent will be Y 0.4/month/m^2 of constructed area. If they choose to remain on-site, they must pay Y 0.5/month/m^2 of constructed area. Nominal compensation was paid to private owners—Y 20/m^2. This amount was based on individual surveys of properties and regulations promulgated by the Shanghai Municipal Government.

The small businesses had 13,000 m^2 of space. Thus, before redevelopment, the site contained 116,040 m^2, reflecting an FAR of 1:0.7.

Despite the fact that the area was in dire need of redevelopment, the local district could not afford to fund the redevelopment or pay to upgrade existing housing structures. Instead, they decided to ask the participation of work units with shops or workers located in the site area. Of the 62 units, 43 agreed to provide financial assistance to carry out the project. A cumbersome management structure was designed to guide the project and, ultimately, the redevelopment project ran into serious problems. The project was undercapitalized and the 43 enterprises had problems coming up with money to meet periodic calls for capital pay-in. An REDC was brought into capitalize the project and help get it completed.

The developer brought in to save the project was the Xu Hui District General Company of the City Construction and Development Company. The company was chosen by the previous partnership because it was well-capitalized. Originally, the 43 enterprises were going to self-finance the project and then split the 111,000 m^2 of commodity housing according to their capital contribution. Instead, the REDC financed the completion of the project and will receive a share of the 111,000 m^2 of commodity housing, which it will sell off to repay its loan and take out its profit. The plan for selling the units is to price them at cost plus 10 percent (Y 3,968/m^2 of constructed area). The target market centers on Shanghai residents.

Even after reorganization, the management structure of the project is complex. The project is managed by a Representative Committee of 44 members (the original 43 enterprises and the REDC). There is a Directors Office comprised of four directors, chosen by the District Government. The individuals represent the interests of residents and enterprises. Under the Directors office are five Departments: planning, construction, materials, relocation and administration and finance. Most of these offices are staffed by REDC professionals.

In the reworked project, 400 households (out of 3,620) elected to relocate to other areas. The remaining 3,220 households will be allocated 178,000 m², between 45 and 55 m² of constructed area, almost double what they had initially. These households will be relocated into 37 walk-up flats and one 24-story high-rise building. The remaining 111,000 m² of housing will be sold as commodity housing, and is programmed into 10 high-rise buildings.

The total cost of the project is estimated to be Yuan 400,470,000—Y 1,232/m² of constructed area (see Table A2.7 for a breakdown of the project costs). The enterprises partially paid for the new units, by donating materials (estimated to be Y 91 million). They will also pay all taxes and interest charges accrued by the project. Enterprises provided temporary housing for their workers and assisted in their relocation.

Shanghai: Tian He Project

The Tian He project is located in the Lu Wan District. Its site area is 4,700 m². Before redevelopment, the site contained a constructed area of 13,880 m², reflecting an FAR of 1:2.95. The population density was extremely high, and the buildings were very old and deteriorated. To compound problems, the site was subject to persistent flooding problems. Before redevelopment, there were 204 households (12,200 m², an average of 60 m²/unit) and eight shops located on the site (1,680 m²).

After redevelopment, all shops were provided with new and larger space on the site (increased by 20 percent to 2,016 m²). Housing was both privately and municipally owned and about 45 percent of the households were resettled on-site. Upon completion, the new project contained approximately 17,200 m² of constructed space—an FAR of 1:3.66. The redevelopment plan called for relocating 112 households to Pudong, keeping 92 houses on the site. The remaining households will receive 7,600 m²—82.6 m² on average. The households being relocated to Pudong will be housed in two projects being built by CEC. The relocation negotiation and the management of the process was jointly administered by the CEC and the Lu Wan District. Those going to Pudong were self-selected, and the relocation regulations offer a strong incentive for opting to go to Pudong. In the initial stages, only 60 households wanted to relocate, but incentives (larger dwelling units) were offered to persuade more to go to Pudong. Those who stayed tend to be older, whose member households work close to home.

To help finance the project, 7,600 m² of commodity housing was developed. The total cost of the project was Y 16,607,000. The revenue from the sale of the 92 housing units is projected to reach Y 16 million and come close to break-even. Table A2.8 presents a cost breakdown of the project. This project, like Jian Guo and Hui Yi, illustrates the potential feasibility of carrying out redevelopment projects which are based on the relocation of all or a portion of the existing residents. In Shanghai, given the high inner-city population densities and the relatively cramped living conditions, it is extremely difficult to resettle all existing residents on-site. Instead, a variety of incentives can be offered to encourage tenants to opt for suburban housing locations.

Table A2.7: SHANGHAI: ORDINARY CITIZEN REDEVELOPMENT PROJECT

Site area (m²)	165,000
Total built area	325,000
Residential area	289,000
Marketable area	111,000

Construction costs	Cost (Yuan)	Cost/ site (m²)	Cost/ TCA (m²)	Cost/ RCA (m²)	Cost/ MRA (m²)
Preconstruction					
Relocation payments	1,900,000	11.52	5.85	6.57	17.12
Temporary rentals	1,000,000	6.06	3.08	3.46	9.01
Site preparation	2,000,000	12.12	6.15	6.92	18.02
Survey & design	1,300,000	7.88	4.00	4.50	11.71
On-site services	650,000	3.94	2.00	2.25	5.86
Fees & taxes	35,500,000	215.15	109.23	122.84	319.82
Subtotal	42,350,000	256.67	130.31	146.54	381.53
Construction					
Housing	293,000,000	1,775.76	901.54	1,013.84	2,639.64
Public facilities	18,540,000	112.36	57.05	64.15	167.03
Management fees	6,500,000	39.39	20.00	22.49	58.56
Contingencies	0	0.00	0.00	0.00	0.00
Interest	32,500,000	196.97	100.00	112.46	292.79
Subtotal	350,540,000	2,124.48	1,078.58	1,212.94	3,158.02
Infrastructure					
Water	1,625,000	9.09	4.62	5.19	13.51
Sewer & drainage	815,000	4.94	2.51	2.82	0.00
Gas	975,000	5.91	3.00	3.37	8.78
Electric	1,500,000	9.09	4.62	5.19	13.51
Roads	815,000	4.94	2.51	2.82	7.34
Other	1,850,000	11.21	5.69	6.40	16.67
Subtotal	7,580,000	45.94	23.32	26.23	68.29
Total Cost	400,470,000	2,427.09	1,232.22	1,385.71	3,607.84

TCA = Total Construction Area.

RCA = Residential Construction Area.

MRA = Marketable Residential Area.

Table A2.8: SHANGHAI: TIAN HE REDEVELOPMENT PROJECT

Site area (m^2)	4,700
Total built area	17,200
Commercial area	2,000
Residential area	15,200
Marketable area	7,600

Construction costs	Cost (Yuan)	Cost/ site (m^2)	Cost/ TCA (m^2)	Cost/ RCA (m^2)	Cost/ MRA (m^2)
Preconstruction					
Relocation payments	4,158,000	884.68	241.74	273.55	547.11
Temporary rentals	0	0.00	0.00	0.00	0.00
Site preparation	1,000,000	212.77	58.14	65.79	131.58
Survey & design	0	0.00	0.00	0.00	0.00
On-site services	0	0.00	0.00	0.00	0.00
Fees & taxes	2,090,000	444.68	121.51	137.50	275.00
Subtotal	7,248,000	1,542.13	421.40	476.84	953.68
Construction					
Housing	5,035,000	1,071.28	292.73	331.25	662.50
Commercial buildings	663,000	141.06	38.55	43.62	87.24
Public facilities	2,541,000	540.64	147.73	167.17	334.34
Management fees	107,000	22.77	6.22	7.04	14.08
Contingencies	462,000	98.30	26.86	30.39	60.79
Interest	320,000	68.09	18.60	21.05	42.11
Subtotal	9,128,000	1,942.13	530.70	600.53	1,201.05
Infrastructure					
Water	231,000	0.00	0.00	0.00	0.00
Sewer & drainage	0	0.00	0.00	0.00	0.00
Gas	0	0.00	0.00	0.00	0.00
Electric	0	0.00	0.00	0.00	0.00
Roads	0	0.00	0.00	0.00	0.00
Other	0	0.00	0.00	0.00	0.00
Subtotal	231,000	49.15	13.43	15.20	30.39
Total Cost	16,607,000	3,533.40	965.52	1,092.57	2,185.13

TCA = Total Construction Area.
RCA = Residential Construction Area.
MRA = Marketable Residential Area.

Shanghai: Ying Xiang Villas Project

Ying Xiang Villas is located in the Yang Pu District of Shanghai. The 5.5 hectare site is located in the northeast portion of the city center. *This redevelopment project was initiated by the China State Housing and Real Estate Development Corporation in March 1985.* Before redevelopment, the project contained approximately 33,000 m² of buildings—1,400 dwelling units and over 40 enterprises. The site had a population of 5,000. The area was of relatively low density—an FAR of 1:0.6. The relocation negotiations were handled by the Yang Pu District government. The site was then purchased and developed by the Chung Wah Real Estate Development Corporation. Both the District and Chung Wah Real Estate Development Corporation will share profits from the redevelopment.

Redevelopment of the site will result in a significant increase in the density of development. When completed, the project will contain 190,000 m², an FAR of 1:3.45. *The project is divided into three phases: phase 1 was completed in 1991 and phase 2 started in 1991.* About 86 percent of the original occupants will be rehoused in 85,000 m² of on-site replacement housing. Another 14,000 m² of replacement housing located nearby will also be used for rehousing. Thus, the redevelopment site occupants will receive about 3 m² of new housing space (constructed area) for each m² they occupied, and their new housing will have a constructed area of 71 m².

Considerable commodity housing will be constructed on-site—88,000 m². These units will be sold to enterprises and individuals. In addition. 17,000 m² of public facilities will be constructed as well.

The completed project cost is Y 153,458,000, an average of Y 808/m² of constructed space. As Table A2.9 illustrates, the break-even sales price per m² of marketable space is Y 1,744 and is well within the prices of comparable commodity housing projects offered for sale in Shanghai in the early 1990s. Ying Xiang Redevelopment Project reveals the easy feasibility of projects, which are developed on sites where densities and FARs can be substantially increased. In this particular case, the FAR increased nearly fivefold from 0.6 to 3.45. As a result, even after accommodating 86 percent of the residents and providing them with three times more space, the constructed area of the project could still be doubled to provide 88,000 m² of commodity housing space.

Tianjin: Pingshan Road Redevelopment Project

The Pingshan Road redevelopment project was developed by the Tianjin Real Estate Development Corporation (TREDC). *Started in 1985, the project took 1.1 years to complete.* The project has a site area of 1.35 hectares. Before redevelopment, the site contained 8,756 m² of buildings, all of which was demolished. Before development, the FAR was 0.65. There were 253 housing units consisting of one-story unreinforced brick structures, averaging less than 50 m²/unit before the redevelopment. The breakdown of existing units was as follows: 154 one-room; 89 two-room; and 10 three-room. The average living space was 20.2 m² per

Table A2.9: SHANGHAI: YING XIANG REDEVELOPMENT PROJECT
(Estimated)

Site area (m^2)	55,000
Total built area	190,000
Residential area	173,000
Marketable area	88,000

Construction costs	Cost (Yuan)	Cost/ site (m^2)	Cost/ TCA (m^2)	Cost/ RCA (m^2)	Cost/ MRA (m^2)
Preconstruction					
Relocation payments	43,080,000	783.27	226.74	249.02	489.55
Temporary rentals	0	0.00	0.00	0.00	0.00
Site preparation	250,000	4.55	1.32	1.45	2.84
Survey & design	725,000	13.18	3.82	4.19	8.24
On-site services	358,000	6.51	1.88	2.07	4.07
Fees & taxes	18,800,000	341.82	98.95	108.67	213.64
Subtotal	63,213,000	1,149.33	332.70	365.39	718.33
Construction					
Housing	59,400,000	1,080.00	312.63	343.35	675.00
Public facilities	5,830,000	106.00	30.68	33.70	66.25
Management fees	3,650,000	66.36	19.21	21.10	41.48
Contingencies	0	0.00	0.00	0.00	0.00
Interest	17,300,000	314.55	91.05	100.00	196.59
Subtotal	86,180,000	1,566.91	453.58	498.15	979.32
Infrastructure					
Water	1,200,000	12.73	3.68	4.05	7.95
Sewer & drainage	420,000	7.64	2.21	2.43	0.00
Gas	535,000	9.73	2.82	3.09	6.08
Electric	700,000	12.73	3.68	4.05	7.95
Roads	460,000	8.36	2.42	2.66	5.23
Other	750,000	13.64	3.95	4.34	8.52
Subtotal	4,065,000	73.91	21.39	23.50	46.19
Total Cost	153,458,000	2,790.15	807.67	887.04	1,743.84

TCA = Total Construction Area.
RCA = Residential Construction Area.
MRA = Marketable Residential Area.

household. The housing contained no toilets and had only simple kitchen facilities; there were no on-site facilities such as schools, shopping, or health care.

In the process of redevelopment, residents were granted relocation assistance. Most of those relocated lived with relatives or close friends. They received a payment of Y 10/month. Those that could not find shelter with relatives or friends went to dislocation buildings. They received a lump-sum payment of Y 150. In some cases, the households living in dislocation shelters had their enterprises pay the monthly rent. The rent in the dislocation shelters was Y 1/month/room. The actual relocation period ran 18 months.

At the completion of the project, all relocatees returned and continued paying the same monthly rent per m^2 as before, despite the fact that they now live in a vastly improved environment (they all now have kitchens and toilets and, in some cases, they get slightly more space). Rents paid per m^2 are set by the municipality, and currently stand at Y 0.2/m^2/month. This rent does not cover maintenance, let alone debt service. The return of units to these prior residents at very low rents generates no income to support redevelopment construction costs. Tenants of municipal units were not compensated for the loss of their unit, since they were given new housing. After completion of the project, the municipality was granted title to the new units.

In the case of privately owned units, owners received compensation of the loss of their houses. The actual amount of building compensation is set according to statute. In Tianjin, the statute sets prices according to four classes of buildings. In the case of Pingshan Road, building compensation payments were Y 36,822, about Y 4.21/m^2 of preredevelopment constructed area. After redevelopment, the private owners become tenants in municipally owned housing.

Redevelopment increased the constructed area of the Pingshan Road project from 8,756 to 33,967 m^2, an increase of over 3.5 times more space. The FAR rose to 2.37. The size of the dwelling units in the redevelopment projects is generous by Tianjin standards, averaging from 34 to 90 m^2 for one- to four-room units. In virtually all cases, preredevelopment households received housing units equal to or larger than their previous units. All of the new units have individual toilets and kitchens. On a per capita basis, the units are much larger, increasing the amount of constructed space from 6.6 m^2 per person to 15.5 m^2 per person. Most units have adequate circulation patterns, although some units seem to devote too much space to corridors and halls.

In the Pingshan Road project, a 2,000-m^2 commercial market was built, and transferred to the local district authorities, for which the TREDC received no funds. The actual amount of community facilities is regulated by the municipality, but apparently this is negotiable. In new areas, the amount of the project's constructed area that is to be devoted to community facilities is 7 percent. In the older areas, where most of the services exist, redevelopment projects negotiate with the local district officials.

The total cost of the Pingshan Road redevelopment project was Y 11,004,000. A detailed breakdown is provided in Table A2.10. In terms of total constructed area, the average cost is Y 324/m². However, since a considerable portion of the site was returned to former residents as replacement housing (14,813 m²), total project costs needed to be spread over the marketable commodity housing (17,154 m²). As a result, the break-even sales price of the housing was Y 641/m², about double the actual cost per m².

Tianjin: Wujaiyao Project

Wujaiyao was also developed by the Tianjin Real Estate Development Corporation. *Started in 1985, the project took approximately 1.3 years to complete.* The Wujaiyao site is 3.35 hectares. Before redevelopment, there were 15,715 m² of buildings, reflecting an FAR of 0.47. The site had 612 housing units and, like Pingshan Road, the structures were one-story unreinforced brick structures averaging less than 50 m² each. Based on an average household size of 4.7 persons, the project was home to 2,540 persons, with an average of 6.1 m² per capita. Housing contained no toilets and had only simple kitchen facilities. The site also contained a small factory and recycling center used for turning plastic scraps into usable products. There were no on-site community facilities.

The relocation process was generally the same as for Pingshan Road, and 700 households returned to Wujaiyao (actually, the 700 households come from 583 prior housing units, as 29 households did not return). Those that did move back paid the same rent per m² per month as before, despite the fact that they now live in a vastly improved environment. Rents paid per m² are about Y 0.2/m²/month, the same as for Pingshan Road.

Private housing owners received Y 105,089 in compensation for their old dwelling units, about Y 6.69/m² of preredevelopment constructed area. Total relocation payments to all tenants were Y 1,208,989, an average of Y 1,975/unit.

The redevelopment plan called for the construction of 61,319 m². The Floor Area Ratio after redevelopment was 1.77, an increase of nearly three times. Of this amount, 59,319 m² was for housing and 2,000 m² was for community facilities. Of the 59,319 m² of housing, most, 39,697 m², was for replacement housing.

The total cost of the redevelopment project was Y 23,744,00, an average of Y 387/m² of total constructed space (see Table A2.11 for a breakdown). However, since the replacement housing generates no revenue for the TREDC, the project's total costs must be recouped from the sale of commodity housing. For Wujaiyao, this meant that the commodity units had to be priced at Y 1,210/m²—over three times the actual cost of construction.

Baseline Simulation Case

In Chapter V, various simulations are presented to gauge the likely impacts of changes in relocation policies. These simulations are based on a common prototypical

Table A2.10: TIANJIN: PINGSHAN ROAD REDEVELOPMENT PROJECT

Site area (m²)	13,500
Total built area	33,987
Residential area	31,967
Marketable area	17,154

Construction costs	Cost (Yuan)	Cost/ site (m²)	Cost/ TCA (m²)	Cost/ RCA (m²)	Cost/ MRA (m²)
Preconstruction					
Relocation payments	162,000	12.00	4.77	5.07	9.44
Temporary rentals	82,000	6.07	2.41	2.57	4.78
Site preparation	29,000	2.15	0.85	0.91	1.69
Survey & design	63,000	4.67	1.85	1.97	3.67
On-site services	31,000	2.30	0.91	0.97	1.81
Fees & taxes	15,000	1.11	0.44	0.47	0.87
Subtotal	382,000	28.30	11.24	11.95	22.27
Construction					
Housing	8,710,000	645.19	256.27	272.47	507.75
Public facilities	50,000	3.70	1.47	1.56	2.91
Management fees	0	0.00	0.00	0.00	0.00
Contingencies	50,000	3.70	1.47	1.56	2.91
Interest	0	0.00	0.00	0.00	0.00
Subtotal	8,810,000	652.59	259.22	275.60	513.58
Infrastructure					
Water	100,000	15.11	6.00	6.38	11.89
Sewer & drainage	113,000	8.37	3.32	3.53	0.00
Gas	25,000	1.85	0.74	0.78	1.46
Electric	204,000	15.11	6.00	6.38	11.89
Roads	1,370,000	101.48	40.31	42.86	79.86
Other	0	0.00	0.00	0.00	0.00
Subtotal	1,812,000	134.22	53.31	56.68	105.63
Total Cost	11,004,000	815.11	323.77	344.23	641.48

TCA = Total Construction Area.
RCA = Residential Construction Area.
MRA = Marketable Residential Area.

Table A2.11: TIANJIN: WUJAIYAO PROJECT

Site area (m^2)	33,500
Total built area	61,319
Residential area	59,319
Marketable area	19,622

Construction costs	Cost (Yuan)	Cost/ site (m^2)	Cost/ TCA (m^2)	Cost/ RCA (m^2)	Cost/ MRA (m^2)
Preconstruction					
Relocation payments	580,000	17.31	9.46	9.78	29.56
Temporary rentals	629,000	18.78	10.26	10.60	32.06
Site preparation	130,000	3.88	2.12	2.19	6.63
Survey & design	225,000	6.72	3.67	3.79	11.47
On-site services	1,000	0.03	0.02	0.02	0.05
Fees & taxes	102,000	3.04	1.66	1.72	5.20
Subtotal	1,667,000	49.76	27.19	28.10	84.96
Construction					
Housing	17,455,000	521.04	284.66	294.26	889.56
Public facilities	670,000	20.00	10.93	11.29	34.15
Management fees	201,000	6.00	3.28	3.39	10.24
Contingencies	100,000	2.99	1.63	1.69	5.10
Interest	0	0.00	0.00	0.00	0.00
Subtotal	18,426,000	550.03	300.49	310.63	939.05
Infrastructure					
Water	853,000	22.72	12.41	12.83	38.78
Sewer & drainage	39,000	1.16	0.64	0.66	0.00
Gas	646,000	19.28	10.54	10.89	32.92
Electric	761,000	22.72	12.41	12.83	38.78
Roads	406,000	12.12	6.62	6.84	20.69
Other	946,000	28.24	15.43	15.95	48.21
Subtotal	3,651,000	108.99	59.54	61.55	186.07
Total Cost	23,744,000	708.78	387.22	400.28	1,210.07

TCA = Total Construction Area.
RCA = Residential Construction Area.
MRA = Marketable Residential Area.

redevelopment case, which reflects characteristics common to most of the 11 projects outlined above.

The project has a site area of 50,000 m². It had a preredevelopment constructed area of 40,000 m² (an FAR of 0.8). The site housed 1,086 households in a total residential constructed area of 38,000 m² (approximately 35 m²/unit). It also contained 2,000 m² of public facilities. The post-redevelopment simulation (baseline case) assumes that the site is redeveloped to an FAR of 2.0 and contains 100,000 m² of constructed space. Reflecting practices in many cities, the simulation assumes that all households are resettled on site and that each household receives an average of 50 m² of constructed area for a total area of 54,300 m². Additional public facilities are constructed to reach 5,000 m². After these allocations are made, there is an additional 40,700 m² of commodity space. Total average construction costs (both hard and soft costs) are assumed to average Y 1,000/m². Table A2.12 provides a breakdown of the costs of the baseline redevelopment project.

Table A2.12: BASELINE ASSUMPTIONS FOR SIMULATIONS

New FAR	2.00
Site area (m²)	50,000
Total built area	100,000
Public facilities	5,000
Residential area	95,000
% On-site replacement	100%
On-site replacement	54,300
Commodity housing	40,700

Construction costs	Cost (Yuan)	Cost/ site (m²)	Cost/ TCA (m²)	Cost/ MCA (m²)
Hard Costs				
Commodity housing	28,490,000	569.80	284.90	700.00
Public facilities	2,250,000	45.00	22.50	55.28
Water	500,000	8.00	4.00	12.29
Sewer & drainage	300,000	6.00	3.00	7.37
Gas	300,000	6.00	3.00	7.37
Electric	400,000	8.00	4.00	9.83
Roads	250,000	5.00	2.50	6.14
Other	350,000	7.00	3.50	8.60
Subtotal	32,840,000	656.80	328.40	806.88
Soft Costs				
On-site relocation	38,010,000	760.20	380.10	933.91
Off-site relocation	0	0.00	0.00	0.00
Temporary rentals	781,920	15.64	7.82	19.21
Site preparation	250,000	5.00	2.50	6.14
Survey & design	300,000	6.00	3.00	7.37
On-site services	200,000	4.00	2.00	4.91
Fees & taxes	15,000,000	300.00	150.00	368.55
Management fee	3,058,367	61.17	30.58	75.14
Contingencies	4,926,000	98.52	49.26	121.03
Interest	4,728,960	94.58	47.29	116.19
Subtotal	67,255,247	1,345.10	672.55	1,652.46
Total Cost	100,095,247	2,001.90	1,000.95	2,459.34

TCA = Total Construction Area.
MCA = Marketable Construction Area.

ANNEX 3

RESIDENTIAL RELOCATION POLICIES IN SELECTED CITIES

Tianjin's Relocation Policies

Some Chinese cities, Tianjin in particular, have followed a policy which grants very favorable relocation rights to tenants of redevelopment projects. When the Tianjin REDC redeveloped its Pingshan Road and Wujiayao projects, all of the residents were granted rights to return to the new project. In the case of Pingshan Road, 253 households were temporarily resettled and then returned to the site. For Wujiayao, only 29 of 600 households elected not to return.

During the site clearance and redevelopment phase, households are provided with temporary relocation assistance. If they stay with relatives or friends, they receive a monthly allowance of between Y 15 and Y 30. If they are housed by the REDC, they receive no cash compensation unless they are housed in a remote location, and then they receive a transportation subsidy.

Upon project completion, the households are provided with new units. In the case of both Pingshan Road and Wujiayao, the physical condition of the new units is vastly superior to preredevelopment housing. The new housing has individual toilet and kitchen facilities and is constructed with better materials and finishes. While tenant living conditions are vastly improved through the upgrading of the quality of construction, each resettled household receives additional space. The construction area of a typical flat was increased from 34 m² to between 50 and 60 m², so that households would be brought into alignment with the current living area standards promulgated by the Tianjin Urban and Rural Construction Commission.

Another facet of improved living conditions is the usual upgrading of public facilities. Most cities require that an additional 6 to 10 percent of the residential constructed area be developed for public facilities. In the older urban areas, there is usually far less space devoted to these activities and they obviously add to the quality of the new residential environment.

Despite the significant improvement in housing conditions and public facilities, the policy in Tianjin is to only marginally increase rents. In both projects, preredevelopment rents were extremely low, averaging about Y 0.2/m² of living area per month, an amount that does not even cover maintenance costs, let alone capital cost recovery. After redevelopment, rents were marginally increased from Y 0.20 to Y 0.25/m² of living area per month. While it is true that the increase in rents is 25 percent per m², the absolute rent level is still well below the actual capital costs of the new units. In fact, at a construction cost of Y 333/m² of constructed area, the new rents are less than one tenth the required break-even rent per month to cover operating and capital costs.

In Tianjin and to a lesser extent in Hangzhou, redevelopment projects are structured to provide for the almost complete on-site resettlement of affected households. In both cities, very little attempt is made to encourage residents to locate to lower-cost suburban projects. The tendency is to interpret the property rights of the tenants to include the right to return to the site and to continue to pay the same low level of rent. As illustrated below, this policy is extremely expensive and burdensome. The World Bank's project work, however, is encouraging a new pattern of behavior to emerge (Box A3.1).

Relocation in Guangzhou's Jin Hua Project

In Guangzhou, redevelopment and relocation laws are strict and costly to follow. In the process of structuring the massive 29 hectare Jin Hua project, the REDC met with each and every household and negotiated with them a precise settlement in terms of temporary relocation, compensation, and the provision of a new unit. While the project is still under construction and will not be completed for at least another year, planners estimate that 6,712 of 7,492 households will be resettled on-site—90 percent. Each household will receive 13 m^2 of constructed area per person (8 m^2 of living area per capita). Households electing not to return to the area will be paid approximately Y 10,000 in compensation, an average of Y 227/m^2.

All returning households will be allocated Y 400 for moving expenses. If they temporarily move in with relatives, they will receive Y 65 per person per month. If they are housed in other facilities, the redeveloper will pay the rent, plus an additional Y 12 per person per month. The developer expects that 50 percent of redevelopment site occupants will relocate with relatives and 50 percent will be housed in rented accommodations. Temporary relocation costs for the project are estimated to be Y 13,155,000, slightly less than Y 2,000 per resettled household.

The process of negotiation is especially difficult because there were essentially three kinds of housing accommodations on the 29 hectare site: approximately 2,400 units were owner-occupied; 2,400 units were publicly owned and managed (by the municipality) and 2,400 were owned by overseas Chinese.

Most owner-occupied private housing is very old, in poor condition and small—averaging 20 m^2. Most units lack toilet and kitchen facilities. In line with government policy to improve housing conditions, redevelopment policies and practices call for the provision of at least 13 m^2 of constructed area per person. On average, each household in the redevelopment area is allocated 42 m^2 of living area. However, unlike the practices in Tianjin, private owners will have to pay for the additional space, being required to pay Y 650/m^2 for the additional 22 m^2 allocated per household). For those living in the public housing, the relocation compensation will be the same. All households will be provided with 13 m^2 per person, an amount that is close to what most households residing in new public housing have at present. For overseas Chinese, owners receive replacement housing, and then they pay for the additional space, provided at Y 650/m^2. If the unit is rented to a third party and the owner wishes to take over the unit, the REDC will provide the tenant rental accommodation, usually in municipally

__Box A3.1__: TIANJIN URBAN DEVELOPMENT PROJECT: INNOVATIVE RESETTLEMENT SCHEMES

Many of the transport and drainage improvement components of the project serve dual purposes, not only to improve the particular subsector assets but also to improve land use and housing conditions in the central city areas. In particular, provision of better housing for the 4,046 households involved is one of the most important aspects of these investment components, consistent with Tianjin Municipal Government's (TMG) ongoing program of land use and housing improvements. Under the resettlement program, involving 17 hectares, the residents will move from the central city "pingfang" houses which are extremely crowded, dilapidated and lack kitchens or sanitary facilities to larger, adequately equipped ones in six new residential developments, on average about 4 km from current locations. Recognizing the importance of the housing improvement objectives, the project will support residential resettlement as an explicit component, while introducing improvements in resettlement procedures.

TMG has extensive experience in demolition and resettlement operations and has established effective regulatory and organizational arrangements. The displaced households receive new permanent housing units in compensation whose sizes are determined on the basis of the size of the housing they vacate and the household size and characteristics, according to well-established guidelines. Residents relocating under the project will get new housing which will be, on average, about 2.5 times the size of the old units, as well as small cash compensation for moving and other expenses. The new locations will, on average, be 4 km away from the original ones. While these arrangements have proven effective and well accepted by the resettling families, the existing practice of district governments allocating apartments for households does not allow residents freedom of choice nor foster competition among housing developers.

Under the project, TMG agreed to introduce new procedures to permit essentially market transactions for the new housing units, by allowing the resettling households to choose their new housing among a much larger number of apartments in six different locations offered by different housing companies, whose supply of units (7,200 apartments) far exceeds the number required by the relocating households. The transaction would be conducted through the use of resettlement vouchers bearing the value equivalent to the average cost of replacement housing of the size to which the relocating households would be entitled as determined under the standard practice. The households will be allowed to choose units that are more expensive than their voucher values, due to size or location, by making additional payments. On the other hand, they would also be allowed to choose smaller or otherwise less-expensive apartments than their entitlement and take cash compensation. However, these variations would be limited to within 20 percent of the voucher values. The verification procedures by the housing companies and the resident registration system would act as a check against outright transfer of the vouchers. TMG would redeem the vouchers tendered by the housing development companies and the IDA credit will be applied toward part of the construction cost of the new housing chosen by the resettling households.

The resettlement initiative has an added macrospatial advantage: at present, Tianjin's city center has very high residential population densities (500 to 700 persons per hectare), while densities in the Socialist suburbs, 3 km to 10 km away, drop off rapidly to 200 persons per hectare. An efficient land use strategy would call for high-density, high "value-added" uses in the city center, a densification of residential districts in the near suburbs, and a concentration of industrial jobs in the outer belts of the city. The project will promote all of these objectives, allowing commercial and institutional uses to grow in the city center; enabling the residential densification of the near suburbs, and improving overall access to jobs both in central and peripheral locations. The project's infrastructure components, unlike examples cited elsewhere, actually support this land use strategy, with transport, sewer, and drainage schemes appropriate for this new style city.

Source: Tianjin Urban Development and Environment Project (Report No. 10284-CHA), February 20, 1992.

managed units. This is the so-called two-for-one replacement problem when there is an overseas Chinese landlord.

Relocation Policy in Shanghai

In Shanghai, relocation is governed by the Shanghai City Housing Demolishing and Relocation Administration Implementation Detailed Regulation, dated July 19, 1991. The regulation states that the actual terms of relocation are to be negotiated by the party carrying out the redevelopment project and the household or affected unit. The terms of what constitutes appropriate compensation should include the following: the population to be resettled; amount of compensation; area of house; location; process for transition; time period of relocation; responsibilities and remedies for nonperformance. Relocation policies are more stringent for public works projects than for residential redevelopment projects (Box A3.2).

Box A3.2: SHANGHAI: RELOCATION POLICIES FOR PUBLIC WORKS PROJECTS

In Shanghai's City Housing Demolishing and Relocation Administration Implementation Detailed Regulation, Chapter 5 sets out specific rules for demolition and relocation related to municipal infrastructure. Article 60 of the chapter states that demolition and relocation should be guided by the principle of "vacate land first, deal with dispute second." Those affected by infrastructure projects should submit to the need for the project and accept relocation. In the case of important projects, procedures pertaining to negotiations with affected parties can be suspended. Permission for demolition and relocation for important construction projects can be granted without negotiations between the municipal infrastructure agency and affected parties.

Compensation for such projects is less generous than for residential redevelopment. In the case of nonresidential uses, employees of collective-owned enterprises may receive up to one year's wages (based on last year's levels). State-owned enterprises receive no compensation for idling. No compensation is paid for public facilities such as police stands, traffic signals, trees, green spaces and firehouses that are demolished.

Nonresidential buildings that were financed through local budgets (including everyday service facilities, schools, hospitals) must be replaced (in-kind compensation) with the same space, without free upgrading. Temporary buildings should be provided. No compensation is to be paid to tenants of these locally financed nonresidential buildings. No compensation is to be made for building decorations that are more than two years old. Facility damage caused by relocation and reinstallation will not be compensated. Equipment rendered unusable is not compensated, and higher authorities are called on to finance purchase and upgrading of new equipment.

The same standards of compensation are to be used for residential replacement in terms of in-kind contributions. There is, however, no protracted negotiation over the level of compensation, and standards are followed.

Source: Shanghai Construction Commission.

In principle, compensation for demolition and relocation should be the exchange of property rights, one unit for another. The regulation states that the area in the exchange should be based on the building area of the demolished house. Depending on the ownership of the previous house, the terms and conditions of resettlement compensation will vary. In the case of privately owned housing, the owner will receive compensation. The owner of the old unit is to surrender his property right and land use certificate to the Land Bureau and, based on negotiations, will receive a new property right certificate for a new unit. The negotiations for new units is based on the floor area of the demolished unit, and is to consider the variation in quality and cost of construction. If the average constructed area per person of the new unit offered to the affected household is below 24 m^2 per person, and if the new unit is smaller than the old unit, the new units are to be sold to the resettled household at one third the costs of the new construction, less the value of the old unit. If the new unit provides more than 24 m^2 per person but is still smaller than the demolished unit, the affected household must pay the full cost of the new unit which is above the 24 m^2 per person threshold. If the affected household still has housing difficulties (crowding), they can purchase additional space at full cost. The affected household can get ownership of the new unit only after the full price differential has been paid. Certificates of occupancy are obtained from district and county housing registration offices.

The law provides the option for private owners to relinquish their property rights and move into municipal housing. In such cases, the REDC will provide compensation to the household based on an evaluation of the demolished unit. If the household relinquishes its housing rights and does not request any form of housing, they will receive 150 percent of the set compensation for the loss of the unit. In the case of publicly owned properties, the law calls for the exchange of property rights. For nonresidential public properties, no compensation needs to be made if the redeveloper provides new facilities of the same nature and character and the resettled party is provided with new property rights for the use of the new facility. Previous rental relationships are to be maintained. In effect, the law does not provide for increases in rental payments for the new, and usually improved rental accommodations.

A major difficulty arises in cases where private owners rent their units to other households. Shanghai's Demolishing and Relocation Law provides for the resettlement and compensation of both landlord and tenant. If a landlord rents the entire unit and does not wish to maintain property rights, he is entitled to receive compensation and tenants should be resettled. This policy is particularly taxing to real estate developers since they end up having to provide two new units for each one unit demolished. In Guangzhou, where a significant portion of the inner-city housing stock is owned by overseas Chinese, this two-for-one compensation is common in redevelopment projects.

In cases where the landlord rents out part of the unit and lives in the other, and is willing to relinquish property right of the rented part, he will receive compensation for the part relinquished and the tenant will be relocated. If the landlord wishes to keep all property rights, the relationship between landlord and tenant should be maintained, and a new lease executed between the parties, which is in conformity with Shanghai Regulation for Renting of Private Houses.

Overall, in most cities in China, the occupants of redevelopment project area housing enjoy extremely secure and substantial property rights. In most cases, private owners of housing are provided with replacement housing that is vastly superior to their original units. Enterprise and municipal landlords receive the same treatment and are provided with new units without having to pay for them. The cost of such in-kind compensation is considerable.

Cash Versus In-Kind Compensation for Demolished Housing

While in-kind compensation is normally the rule, demolition and relocation regulations specify procedures and standards for payment of compensation. In most instances, the level of compensation paid for a building is based on the materials used to construct the structure, less some estimate of depreciation for age and condition. Table A3.1 presents residential compensation ranges for various types of structures in Tianjin and Fuzhou.

Table A3.1: FUZHOU AND TIANJIN REDEVELOPMENT
COMPENSATION SCHEDULES

City	Building material	Depreciated value (%)	Compensation (Y/m^2)
Fuzhou	High-quality concrete and brick	80	320
	High-quality concrete and brick	50	200
	High-quality concrete and brick	20	80
	Medium-quality brick	80	208
	Medium-quality brick	50	130
	Medium-quality brick	20	52
Tianjin	Steel and concrete		267-413
	Brick and concrete		187-333
	Brick and wood		158-351
	Simple		85- 99

Source: Redevelopment project surveys, 1989, 1992.

Apparently these schedules are indicative and the actual level of compensation varies, subject to negotiation over the building condition. For example, in the Jin Hua project, the payment of Y 227/m^2 is probably well above the depreciated value of the old private structures. However, the mechanism most often used to compensate for the loss of property is in-kind replacement. In Tianjin, for example, sitting tenants are provided with units in new redevelopment projects and, therefore, neither they nor their landlord (the municipality, an enterprise or a private property-owner) receive any cash contribution. In situations where sitting tenants receive new units, the level of compensation typically exceeds the actual value of the property taken through the redevelopment process. In the case of Pingshan Road and Wujiayao, the actual construction cost of the project, is Y 324 and Y 387, respectively, as compared to the residential schedule for compensation for brick and wood structures of between Y 158 and Y 351/m². Since the age and physical conditions of housing in both of these redevelopment areas was quite poor, the lower end of the range is assuredly the most applicable. This suggests that the level of compensation provided by the direct replacement of housing units exceeds what is required by statute.

The degree to which in-kind compensation of housing and property located in redevelopment areas exceeds the actual value of the demolished property obviously depends on the cost of producing the replacement units. Unless there is careful financial account of these costs, it is only by chance that there is some equivalence. Such an approach is followed in Fuzhou. In Fuzhou, as will be more fully elaborated below, all redevelopment project housing is commodity housing, and all purchasers must pay the commodity price. Sitting tenants of old areas to be redeveloped are compensated for the loss of their unit. This means that the various owners of rental properties—the municipality, enterprises and private individuals—receive compensation for units, according to the type of construction and conditions. As presented in Table A3.1, medium-quality brick structures are assessed at Y 260/m², and high-quality concrete and brick units are scheduled at Y 400/m². Depending on the age of the building and its condition, these assessments are reduced for depreciation.

The Fuzhou approach is novel and it merits serious consideration by other urban and rural construction commissions. It establishes a mechanism for decoupling the compensation for taking properties from the provision of new housing units. Such an approach makes the financial aspects of compensation for taken property more transparent. Another very important implication of the Fuzhou approach is that it shifts the burden of rent reform from the real estate developer onto the owner of the properties. In cases where redevelopment properties are owned by municipalities or enterprises, they must directly confront the financial implications of continuing to offer low rents to tenants after redevelopment.

The financial implications of in-kind contributions are enormous and greatly determine the financial feasibility of redevelopment projects. Because of the emphasis on in-kind contributions and the concept of exchanging property rights as opposed to financial compensation, resettlement and relocation payments are biased heavily in favor of the sitting tenant. Instead of structuring redevelopment and relocation benefits around the concept of in-kind compensation, it is far more efficient to provide financial compensation. A vast economics literature reporting on research on the value housing concludes that housing is best viewed as a bundle of services provided to the user. This flow of services includes areas for sleeping, entertaining and socializing, food preparation and storage, personal hygiene, and storage. The services also include access to employment, family, friends, shops and governmental and institutional activities. Given the complexity and extreme variation in levels of service exhibited by these physical and nonphysical attributes, it is clear that dwelling size alone is not the best measure of housing services.

Accordingly, demolishing and relocation policies should not be based only on the physical size of the unit. The proper method of compensation should be based on the current economic value of the unit. The evaluation should be based on estimates of the costs to physically reproduce the unit, given current construction cost, taking into account the material and technology used to build it. This estimate should be reduced for depreciation. Assuming that residential owners should receive no compensation for land, payment should be made for housing based on its replacement cost less depreciation, with the same levels of payment made to private owners, enterprises and government. For enterprise- and government-owned units, replacement housing will need to be acquired in specific projects, and it should be the responsibility of the redeveloper to assist government or enterprises in finding suitable replacement units. Private owners should be free to purchase replacement units in any one of a variety of projects, taking into consideration access to jobs, family and other services.

Table A3.2 provides estimates of the depreciated value of old dwelling units, the actual construction costs of the replacement units (excluding land or infrastructure costs) and the net differences between the two costs, taking into consideration changes in the size of the new unit provided to the tenant. As the table illustrates, the typical cost of the old housing unit (assuming an average depreciated value of Y 200/m^2, which reflects the range of values presented in Table A3.1 above and discussions with numerous real estate developers) ranges from Y 3,000 to Y 12,000. Based on new construction costs, new units provided to resettled households range from Y 16,048 to Y 71,050. In some cases, the value of the new unit is nearly four times greater than the value of the unit replaced. In the case with the smallest ratio, Jin Hua, new units cost nearly 50 percent more than the old ones, despite the fact that the new units are smaller.

While the policies and procedures of the exchange of property rights are based on the notion of replacing a tenant's use rights, in-kind compensation actually provides the tenants with much more. Even though tenants do not own the land on which their apartment sits, they are, in fact, receiving some of the development gain generated by the site's redevelopment. The cumulative effect of making these substantial in-kind payments results in high relocation costs. Table A3.3 illustrates the total in-kind compensation costs for the surveyed projects, and the percentage these costs are of total project redevelopment costs. The costs associated with merely replacing the demolished housing is considerable, ranging from 18 to up to nearly 70 percent of the total cost of redevelopment. An alternative approach would be to credit owners the value of the demolished unit and let them either apply the credit to the purchase of a new unit constructed on the site or use the credit to purchase another units elsewhere. This approach as been adopted in Fuzhou.

Fuzhou's Compensation Approach

The case of Fuzhou is important in that it provides a useful model for structuring a market-based system of redevelopment compensation. In Fuzhou, redevelopment is market-driven: REDCs find sites for redevelopment and negotiate with occupants for acquisition. Based on the site and the current market conditions, the REDC prepares a development proposal for the site.

Virtually all of the redevelopment activity in Fuzhou is for the construction of commodity housing. None of the former residents are relocated to the site. In theory,

Table A3.2: COMPARISON OF THE ECONOMIC VALUE OF OLD DWELLING UNITS
AND NEW IN-KIND REPLACEMENT UNITS

| Project | Households | Housing size | | Value Old Unit /a (Yuan) | Value Replaced Unit (Yuan) | Ratio Old/ New |
		Original (m²)	New (m²)			
An Deng	108	60	85	12,000	26,010	2.17
Jin Hua	7,492	44	42	8,800	12,852	1.46
Xiao Fuqing	120	50	79	10,000	24,174	2.42
Jian Guo	1,394	15	60	3,000	18,360	6.12
Hu Lang	553	14	48	2,800	14,688	5.25
Hui Yi	264	30	49	6,000	14,994	2.50
Ordinary	3,620	28	55	5,600	16,830	3.01
Tian He	204	60	83	12,000	25,398	2.12
Ying Xiang	1,400	22	71	4,400	21,726	4.94
Pingshan	253	35	59	7,000	18,054	2.58
Wujiayao	612	26	57	5,200	17,442	3.35

/a The economic value of the old unit is based on an estimated value of Y 200/m² of constructed area. The economic value of the new unit is based on the actual construction cost of the housing and excludes costs for land, infrastructure and fees and charges.

Source: Redevelopment Project Surveys, 1991, 1992.

households and businesses located in redevelopment areas have two options: (i) they can cash out and move to a new area, or (ii) they can cash out and purchase a new unit in the completed redevelopment project, should there be available housing units. The ultimate owners of the new units must pay the going rate for them.

Sitting tenants in redevelopment areas are compensated for the demolition of their units. Private tenants receive payment according to the type of construction of the unit (concrete and brick, brick or wood), the age of the unit and its condition. At the present time, high-quality concrete and brick units in excellent condition are compensated at Y 320/m², reflecting a value of 80 percent of the current replacement cost (see Table A3.1 for current compensation levels in Fuzhou). The actual amount of compensation is negotiated between the REDC and the tenant. The REDCs negotiate directly with private owners and payments go to them. In the case of units owned by enterprises or the municipality, negotiations are with the owner, not the tenant, and the payments go to the owner. After resettlement, the enterprises are free to set new rents. In most cases, these new rents increase to reflect the higher costs of the units. For municipally owned units, the developer negotiates with the government over the level of compensation. Rental rates for the tenants usually remain the same on a per m² basis.

Table A3.3: TOTAL REDEVELOPMENT AND RESETTLEMENT COSTS

Project name	Original house-holds	Total relocation cost (Yuan)	Total project cost (Yuan)	Relocation as a % of total cost
An Deng	108	2,809,080	8,025,000	35.00
Jin Hua	7,492	125,865,600	741,224,028	16.98
Xiao Fuqing	120	2,559,600	6,992,956	36.60
Jian Guo	1,394	89,076,600	265,209,200	33.59
Hu Lang	553	30,525,600	186,332,000	16.38
Hui Yi	264	18,757,200	46,291,500	40.52
Ordinary	3,620	179,190,000	257,470,000	69.60
Tian He	204	6,349,500	14,619,093	43.43
Ying Xiang	1,400	34,094,200	153,458,000	22.22
Pingshan	253	4,060,144	11,002,948	36.90
Wujiayao	612	10,255,896	23,742,829	43.20

Source: Redevelopment Project Surveys, 1991, 1992.

Affected tenants who were private owners can choose to relocate to other housing projects, using their compensation. They can purchase larger units if their prior space standards were below government-set targets. However, to encourage relocation, tenants going to suburban areas can also purchase up to 40 percent more space (even if it exceeds policy levels). The actual amount of the bonus varies according to the location of the suburban project (the more remote, the higher the bonus) and the site of the former house. Six zones are used to set the bonus system.

In the case of tenants living in enterprise housing that is to be redeveloped, the enterprise makes the decision on whether to resettle, presumably in consultation with their worker/tenants. Here, the enterprises are also eligible to obtain "bonus" space if they agree to relocate their workers to suburban projects. In the case of municipally owned housing, the government purchases additional units and relocates tenants, offering them limited choices. These tenants will also get more space, as an inducement to move to less accessible suburban areas. The rents paid by the tenants living in municipally owned buildings do not increase after redevelopment.

Regardless of the type of tenant, if redevelopment area occupants choose to return to the site after completion of the project, they will not be able to purchase "bonus" space. They will, however, be able to acquire some additional space if their per capita living space was below municipal targets. Currently, the typical price paid by the returning residents is on the order of Y 305/m^2 of construction for brick buildings and Y 365/m^2 for concrete and steel (high-rise) buildings.

The actual prices for the commodity housing are the subject of negotiation between the developer and the Fuzhou Housing Administration. Similar negotiations take place between the developer and the sitting tenants over the price to be paid for the units to be demolished. In cases where negotiations between sitting tenants and REDCs break down, the government can insist on and force tenants to relocate. This apparently does not happen very often. If the compensation for replacement housing provided in redevelopment projects was modeled on the principles followed in Fuzhou, redevelopment project cost savings would be substantial.

On-Site and Off-Site Replacement of Demolished Housing

The second most important determinant of the costs of housing compensation is whether affected households are provided with on-site replacement. Clearly, in the context of in-kind compensation and the notion of the exchange of use rights, many argue that tenants of demolished housing should be provided with new housing built on the redevelopment site. Such an approach makes it difficult to feasibly build new projects, since so much of the new construction is diverted to former tenants at no cost. In this section, we review the various policies taken in several cities in regards to on-site replacement housing.

In Tianjin, Guangzhou and Hangzhou, policies support and encourage the on-site resettlement of redevelopment-area households. Four of the 11 projects we surveyed provided 100 percent on-site relocation of households. Another three projects provided on-site replacement of demolished units for over 85 percent of households. Only four cases called for substantial off-site resettlement. In one case, this was because the site was used for a park (An Deng in Fuzhou). In the other three cases, new projects were developed which made it difficult to rehouse everyone on-site. The incidence of on-site redevelopment is a critical determinant of redevelopment feasibility because of the following reasons:

(a)   all redevelopment projects are financed through the sale of new commodity housing and commercial space produced on the site;

(b)   most redevelopment policies provide for the in-kind replacement of demolished housing with no payments provided from the existing owners;

(c)   redevelopment projects are constrained by limitations on increases in FAR and, as a result, the total floor area that can be constructed in a redevelopment project is limited;

(d)   redevelopment projects are required to build and transfer substantial new public facilities at no cost to local and district governments; and

(e)   most replacement housing has more constructed area per unit than originally existed on the site.

If affected households were compensated with cash for the demolition of their units and were then permitted to purchase commodity housing on-site, REDCs would be indifferent to on-site relocation. However, as has been described above, replacement units are provided at no cost to these tenants and this imposes substantial costs on the redeveloper.

With limitations on the potential floor area that can be constructed, requirements for new public facilities and increased living areas for occupants of replacement housing, the potential amount of commodity housing or space is limited. As a result, the break-even price of the commodity housing is frequently very high, and REDCs have difficultly selling space. In 9 of 11 cases, new development on the cleared sites occurred at higher densities. Despite efforts by planners to hold back development densities in inner-city areas, the average FAR for the 10 projects increased from 1.11 and 2.79, a 150 percent increase. In terms of constructed area, these 10 projects increased from an average of 57,581 m^2 to 156,037 m^2. Thus, on average, each redevelopment project provided an additional 98,456 m^2 of space.

However, not all of the additional space was marketable. In the new redevelopment projects, where nearly all former residents were relocated on-site, a substantial amount of the additional space was allocated to these households. Table A3.4 illustrates the prior and replacement housing construction levels for seven projects which resettled more than 85 percent of the residents on site. Before redevelopment, the seven projects had 501,547 m^2 of residential space, an average of 71,650 m^2 per project. There were 14,050 households living on-site, and each had an average of 35.7 m^2 of constructed space. With redevelopment came the construction of 630,540 m^2 of on-site residential replacement housing, an average of 90,077 m^2 per project. After redevelopment, 12,742 households returned to the seven projects, an average of 91 percent. Each household received 49.5 m^2 of constructed area.

In all but one project, households received considerably more housing space, as the redevelopment planners endeavored to increase living space in inner-city areas to policy standards for per capita minimums. In some cases, space per dwelling unit more than doubled. This substantial increase in the size of on-site replacement units averages 18,437 m^2 per project. For the seven projects, the total constructed area was increased from 527,100 to 1,446,723 m^2, a gain of 919,623 m^2. Of the gain, approximately 130,000 m^2, 14 percent, went to increasing the size of the replacement units.

In addition to using a portion of the net increase in redevelopment constructed area to increase the average size of replacement housing, real estate projects are frequently required to provide space for community facilities at no cost. Table A3.5 tabulates the net increase in total constructed area, constructed area for increasing the size of replacement housing and constructed area for public facilities. These tabulations illustrate that not all of the incremental space provided through redevelopment actually can be sold as commodity housing. As it illustrates, only between 43 and 71 percent of the marginal increase in floor area can be sold as commodity housing. Only in the case of Guangzhou's Jin Hua project, where replacement housing units are smaller than original units, was a high level of net new construction devoted to commodity housing.

Table A3.4: PREVIOUS AND NEW ON-SITE REPLACEMENT HOUSING IN
SEVEN REDEVELOPMENT PROJECTS WITH OVER 85 PERCENT
ON-SITE RESETTLEMENT

Project name	Previous residential constructed area (m²)	Average unit size (m²)	On-site replaced housing (units)	Average unit size (m²)	On-site replacement as a percent of total construction (%)
Jin Hua	329,648	44	282,000	42	38.3
Xiao Fuqing	6,000	50	9,530	79	61.8
Hu Lang	7,809	14	26,500	48	31.5
Ordinary Citizen	103,040	28	178,000	55	54.5
Ying Xiang	30,800	22	80,000	71	42.1
Pingshan	8,756	35	14,813	59	43.6
Wujiayao	15,494	26	39,697	57	64.7

Source: Redevelopment Project Surveys, 1991, 1992.

On-site replacement housing can account for significant portion of the net increase in total construction. In the seven surveyed projects with over 85 percent of the households were resettled on-site, replacement housing accounted for between 32 and 62 percent of total new construction. Devoting one to two thirds of a redevelopment project constructed area to replacement housing, for which no revenues are generated, imposes a series financial drag on project feasibility. On the other hand, when the replacement housing is provided off-site, the portion of net new construction going to commodity housing is much greater and can routinely exceed 100 percent of net new construction.

If these replacement units could be sold as commodity housing, considerable revenues could be generated. As long as the revenues generated per square meter from the sale of commodity housing exceed the per meter cost of off-site replacement housing, REDCs would benefit from resettling project-area residents to new areas. There is widespread awareness of the cost implications of guaranteeing on-site replacement housing. In some cities, such as Chengdu, policies have been adopted which require all residents of redevelopment projects to be relocated to suburban areas. There, virtually all residents of redevelopment areas are required to relocate to new areas. Before 1991, Chengdu private-owner households were allocated the same amount of space as previously held and made no payment. Starting in 1991, these households were required to pay a differential of between Y 30 and Y 100/m² of constructed area, which reflects to differential between the cost of the new unit and the value of the old. This policy is similar to that used in Fuzhou. If they desire, private owners can purchase additional living space by paying the actual construction cost of the additional space. In the case of public rental housing, the municipality makes no additional payments for the

Table A3.5: BREAKDOWN OF NET NEW CONSTRUCTED SPACE
IN DEVELOPMENT PROJECTS

Project name	Net increase constructed area (m²)	Increase size of replaced housing (m²)	Provide additional public facilities (m²)	Net area commodity sales (m²)	Percent of net increase (%)
Projects with High On-Site Resettlement					
Jin Hua	402,000	-47,648	163,648	286,000	71.1
Xiao Fuqing	9,417	3,530	1,402	4,485	47.6
Hu Lang	71,411	18,691	7,500	45,220	63.3
Ordinary Citizen	208,960	74,960	36,000	98,000	46.7
Ying Xiang	157,000	49,200	17,000	90,800	57.8
Pingshan	25,231	6,057	2,020	17,154	68.0
Wujiayao	45,604	24,203	2,000	19,401	42.5
Projects with Low On-Site Resettlement					
Jian Guo	62,179	0	4,300	57,879	93.1
Hui Yi	-380	0	0	-380	-
Tian He	3,320	-4,600	0	7,920	138.6

Source: Redevelopment Project Surveys, 1991, 1992.

replacement housing assigned to it by the REDCs. Rents for units, in new buildings remain at the same level as before, and currently average Y 0.13/m² per month.

While policies of mandatory off-site relocation might work in small- and medium-sized cities where impacts of relocation on trip patterns is likely to be small, in the larger cities it may not be politically feasible. Instead, there is apparently a trend towards providing a variety of space and financial inducements to encourage redevelopment-area households to relocate to suburban areas. Recognizing the special difficulties of redeveloping old areas, Shanghai's new relocation law provides for a differential payment for new housing constructed in redevelopment areas. In cases where commercial housing is to be developed on the cleared site, former users may purchase housing there, but they must pay a differential rent or price which reflects the cost differential between housing provided on the fringe of the city and the actual cost of the new commercial housing. Table A3.6 provides a breakdown of the differential rent "surcharges" for the seven delimited zones in Shanghai.

Another mechanism to facilitate the relocation of households to outlying areas is the stipulation in the act that regulates the amount of space that can be allocated to resettled households, providing more space to those who agree to resettle outside of the city center. In

Table A3.6: SHANGHAI'S DIFFERENTIAL
RENT SURCHARGES
(Applied to the Sales of Commodity Housing)

Zone	Percent Increase
1	50
2	45
3	30
4	15
5	10
6	5
7	0

Source: Mission interviews, August 1991.

either case, the amount of space allocated to residents of former slum areas is reduced. The justification for this policy is that the new housing units are better equipped with private toilets and kitchens (which are not included in the calculation of living area), and that the quality of construction is better.1/

Table A3.7 illustrates Shanghai's allocation standards. In addition to the standards outlined in the table, households choosing to locate in one of Shanghais several new towns would receive an additional one to two square meters per person of living area. While the intent of the law is commendable, reflecting the increased quality of construction and the provision of toilets and kitchens, the allocation differential between central and fringe space allocations is not pronounced enough to provide sufficient incentives for relocation. It is analogous to asking a New Yorker to choose between 5 m in Manhattan or 6 m in Queens, or maybe 7 m in Jersey City—the differential is not likely to alter people's tendencies toward central locations, especially given transit congestion.

In Beijing, redevelopment companies have been experimenting with price and space incentives to encourage sitting tenants to relocate to less costly suburban projects. Three recent redevelopment projects in Beijing, De Bao, Ju'er Lane, and Xiau Hau, are experimenting with incentives to encourage relocation. Households wishing to purchase a unit will pay lower prices in suburban projects. If they wish to continue leasing housing, they will be required to pay the full cost of maintenance, either by paying more for rent or by paying a rent deposit. Since the rental rates and maintenance costs are considerably lower in suburban projects, Beijing planners anticipate that more redevelopment households will opt for suburban areas.

1/ None of the Shanghai redevelopment cases examined in this study provided on-site resettled households with less space. In Guangzhou's Jin Hua project, the amount of space allocated to returning residents declined from an average of 44 to 42 m².

Table A3.7: SHANGHAI STANDARDS FOR THE REPLACEMENT OF
DEMOLISHED HOUSING

Original living area (m^2/person)	Living area allocations (m^2/person) if	
	Resettle on or near site	Resettle to fringe
under 4	maintain previous amount	4
4- 7	4- 5	5- 6
7-10	5- 6	6- 7
10-13	6- 7	7- 8
13-16	7- 8	8- 9
16-19	8- 9	9-10
19-22	9-10	10-11
22-25	10-11	11-12
25-30	11-12	12
30+	12	12

Source: Shanghai City Housing Demolishing and Relocation Administration Detailed
Implementation Regulation, July 19, 1991.

While initiatives aimed at providing incentives to households who choose to relocate to suburban areas should be encouraged, a major overhaul of the compensation framework is needed. It would be vastly easier for redevelopment corporations to compensate existing tenants for the depreciated value of their units and then require them to pay the full commodity price of new units developed on the cleared site. This policy should be applied to all classes of property ownership: municipal, enterprise and private. The last section of this report looks at the financial performance of redevelopment projects and assesses alternative strategies for improving project feasibility.

ANNEX 4

INSTITUTIONAL STRUCTURE OF LAND ADMINISTRATION 1/

Introduction

Like the administrative structure for the urban sector as a whole, the organization of land administration in China is also very complicated, and is shown in Figure A4.1. The land administration institutions can be divided into two layers; one involves the central state-level apparatus, operating directly under the State Council. The other involves the relevant departments at both the provincial and municipal government levels. In terms of land administration, the more direct control belongs to the municipal governments and their functioning departments.

State-Level Organizations

State Planning Commission

The State Planning Commission (SPC) was founded in June 1988 through the amalgamation of the former State Planning and State Economic Commissions. It operates as a large comprehensive management agency in charge of national economies and social development. Although it has much less involvement in actual land administration, its department of comprehensive development and state land use planning is responsible for providing macro-level policy guidance on land resources development and utilization, planning regional distribution of productive forces, determining the location of large-scale industry, and analyzing its effect on land resources. Since it still controls much of the state investment budget and planned materials supply, and since only approved projects will receive land allocations, its impacts on the land administration is important.

State Land Administration

The State Land Administration (SLA) was set up in August 1986 in order to provide overall management of urban and rural land administration. Its main functions is to take overall responsibility of executing the laws, regulations and policies on land administration; conducting land surveys, registration and statistics; and preparing the country's comprehensive planning of land use. In addition, it is also responsible for administering the national land expropriation and appropriation of agricultural land; inspecting, supervising, and resolving disputes involving land use in different places and between different departments; and

---

1/   Most of the descriptive materials are based on Cai Qiang and Cai Jiliang, *The Current Situation and Development of China's Real Estate Sector* 1989, Economic Research Institute, Ministry of Construction (in Chinese); J. Ratcliffe, S. Tsui, and H. Yu, 1990, *Land Management in the People's Republic of China*, Department of Building Surveying, Hong Kong Polytechnic; and information collected during the sector missions.

Figure A4.1: ORGANIZATION OF AUTHORITIES RELATED TO
LAND ADMINISTRATION

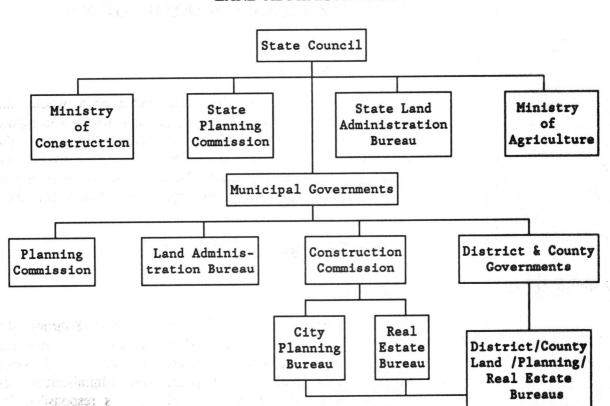

investigating and prosecuting illegal land use cases. From 1990, the Administration and its local bureaus took responsibility for all land lease activity. SLA and its local departments is the most active institution in addressing various land administration issues.

Under the Bureau there are six departments, two offices and three academic or professional institutes: Department of Land-Use Planning; Department of Cadastral Management; Department of Management on Land Use for Construction; Department of Supervision; Department of Science, Technology, Publicity and Education; Department of Policies and Laws; General Office; Foreign Affairs Office; China Land Surveying and Planning Institute; Council of China Land Society; and China Land Economy Research Association.

Ministry of Construction

Ministry of Construction (MoC) was set up in 1987 to replace the Ministry of Urban and Rural Construction and Environment Protection. The main task of MoC is to be responsible for the overall administration of the nation's construction work, including civil engineering, urban and rural development, the building industry, and the real estate industry. Its main objective is to turn the building industry into one of the mainstays of national economy. MoC has 15 bureaus, departments or associations. They include: Real Estate Administration;

Urban Planning;, Urban Construction; Construction Administration; Designing Administration; Rural Development; International Cooperation; Construction Supervision; Scientific and Technology Development Administration; Laws and Regulations; Standards, Norms Administration; Overall Planning for Financial Affairs; Qualified Personal Development; China Urban Housing Research Association; and China Real Estate Association. In addition, there are also some corporations and research institutions under the direction of MoC: China Building Technology Development Center (CBTDC); China Academy of Building Research (CABR); China Academy of Urban Planning and Design (CAUPD); China State Housing and Real Estate Development Company (CSHREDC); and China State Construction Engineering Company (CSCEC).

In terms of land administration, the more relevant departments are the Department of Urban Planning and the Department of Real Estate Administration. The main functions of the Department of Urban Planning include developing planning guidelines; supervising the implementation of urban development plans; planning and administering urban construction and land use; and participating in feasibility studies of large construction projects that will greatly affect city development.2/ The Department of Real Estate Administration is mainly responsible for administering the national real estate industry.

Ministry of Agriculture

The Ministry is responsible for regional agricultural planning administration. Currently, its role in land management is small compared with the three state organizations discussed above. Before the creation of SLA, the Agricultural Commissions at the provincial and municipal levels used to control vast rural areas within both the city proper and in suburban counties, which created many conflicts with local urban construction administrations.

<u>Local-Level Institutions</u>

At the provincial and autonomous regional level, real estate administration is the job of relevant construction commissions and the land administration bureaus. Their functions correspond to those of Ministry of Construction and State Land Administration Bureau.

At the city level, urban-rural construction commissions, real estate administration bureaus, city planning bureaus and land administration bureaus are all responsible for land and real estate administration. The city's construction commission, which is directly under a deputy mayor, is the main institution in charge of urban construction matters. While bureaus such as city planning and real estate administration are all under the leadership of construction commission, the land bureau usually reports directly to a deputy mayor.

2/   Both MoC and SLA claim responsibility for managing and planning urban land use; this causes continuous conflicts between these two departments and their local counterparts. A recently issued State Council Decree (No. 31, 1990) was designed to finally resolve this issue.

Land Administration Bureau

The municipal land administration bureau mirrors the SLA and acts as its executive arm in relation to the overall administration of land within its own administrative area. It is responsible for land title registration, land requisition approval, and land use rights transfer administration, as well as the collection of land use taxes and fees.

City Planning Bureau

The city planning bureau is responsible of drafting and executing the city master plan, approving land use proposals for state construction, project designs, and the issuance of state construction land use planning permits within the urban planning area, as well as acting as an administrative authority for urban planning and building design at local level.

Real Estate Administration Bureau (REAB)

Its responsibilities include: executing policies of the national Department of Real Estate Administration; controlling the public housing stock; collecting rent and maintaining public properties; administering the sale or transfer of public buildings; allocating new public housing to enterprises and individuals; selling public housing to individuals; registering the building stock in the urban area; as well as administering the urban demolition and relocation process.

Since the actual control over land and real estate affairs rest at municipal level, institutional arrangements at the city level are very complicated; and conflicts among different bureaus or departments often occur. Among these, perhaps the most visible conflict is over the issue of urban land management, where all three departments claim certain kinds of control. Both the No. 31 Decree of the State Council in 1990, and newly approved the City Planning Law of the People's Republic of China (May 1990) have, in principle, clarified the different roles of these three agencies in regard with urban land administration. According to these documents, the city planning bureau is responsible for approving the size and location of the land uses for any projects within the city planned area, and issuing state construction land use planning permits. The land administration bureau is responsible for handling various land administration issues, including the actual land requisition process, land titles registration, land use rights transfers and so on. And the real estate administration bureau is responsible for managing the existing building stock, arranging building registration, and supervising real estate activities, as well as overseeing urban demolition and relocation process.[3]

---

[3] The land registration and building registration will be divided between the land administration bureau and the real estate administration bureau. The implication of this separation could be serious, since there is no common base covering building and land registrations, and little information sharing between these two bureaus occurs. In recent years, some cities, such as Beijing and Guangzhou, have decided to reintegrate these two functions into one institution. In the case of Beijing, land administration functions were transferred back to the real estate administration bureau. In the case of Guangzhou, the two bureaus have simply merged into one bureau.

Given the above institutions structure, it is not difficult to imagine that the actual land allocation involves an extensive administrative approval process.4/ Many of these procedures have recently been institutionalized through the newly adopted City Planning Law. Article 31 of the new law explains the urban land allocation procedure:

> "A construction project in the urban planned area that needs to apply for urban land shall apply to the city planning department by presenting the relevant documents indicating the state approval of the project. The urban planning department shall approve the location and boundary of the site to be used by the project, provide conditions for designing and planning, and approve and issue the state construction land use permit. The unit or individual undertaking the project may apply to the land administration department at or above county level for use of land only after receiving the construction land use permit. After the application has been examined and approved by people's government at or above the county level, the land administration department will then allocate the land to the unit or individual undertaking the project."

The following is a case study on Shanghai's land administration institutions, which provides a more detailed description of the functional departments within the Land Administration Bureau, and the structures and roles of county- and district-level land administration bureaus.

Shanghai Land Administration Institutions: A Case Study

Shanghai Municipality has provincial status and is directly under the supervision of the State Council. Under the Shanghai Municipal Government, there are 12 urban district governments and 9 county governments. The urban districts are further divided into 139 subdistricts, whereas county governments supervise township and village governments.

Organizations related to land management are listed in Figure A4.2. Shanghai Municipal Land Administration Bureau (SHMLAB) is administratively under the supervision of the vice mayor of the Municipal Government. It is directly supervised by the State Land Administration Bureau. Similar to the Shanghai Municipal Planning Bureau and Shanghai Municipal Real Estate Administration Bureau, SHMLAB is coordinated by the Shanghai Municipal Construction Commission. A level down from the Municipal Government are the District Planning and Land Administration Bureaus in the urban districts, responsible for both land management and planning. County Land Administration Bureaus are solely responsible for land management in the counties. The lowest level of land management rests with street land

---

4/   For a detailed discussion of project approval procedure, please see Annex 2.

administration stations in the urban districts, and the township and village land administration stations in townships and villages.

Figure A4.2: GOVERNMENT STRUCTURE AND LAND MANAGEMENT INSTITUTIONS IN SHANGHAI MUNICIPALITY

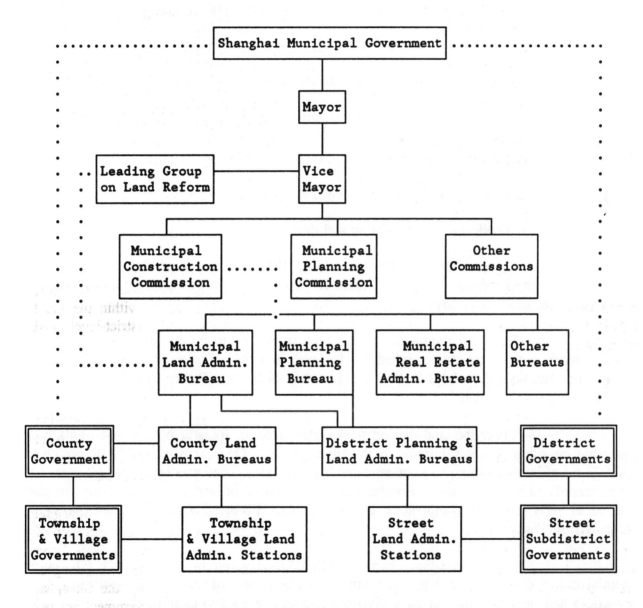

Note: The subordination of the Land Bureau to the Construction Commission is atypical, though the same arrangement exists in Guangzhou. In most cities, the Land Bureau reports directly to the relevant Vice Mayor or indirectly through other commissions.

Prior to 1985, land management in Shanghai was fragmented. The Land and Housing Office of REAB was responsible for land management in the urban built-up areas, while the Land Use Office of the Planning Bureau took care of land in new areas in the urban district. The Land Office of the Agriculture Bureau, on the other hand, managed land in the rural counties. In 1985, a year before the SLA in the central government was established, Shanghai unified land administration by setting up the Shanghai Municipal Land Administration Bureau (SHMLAB). Its main functions are:

(a)   to implement state land policies, regulations, and related guidelines;

(b)   to formulate municipal land policies and regulations;

(c)   to organize unified land acquisition;

(d)   to approve and issue land use certificates;

(e)   to collect land use fees;

(f)   to mediate land-related disputes; and

(g)   to collect land information and data.

A year later, in 1986, the role of SHMLAB was expanded to include land management system reform. Since then, extensive work has been done on land registration and issuing of land use certificates.

Land registration has almost been completed in the 12 urban districts, while similar work in the 9 counties is scheduled to finish in 1992. The work of issuing land use certificates has been completed in 8 of the 12 urban districts. The rest of the districts will complete their tasks in 1992.

Under the land management system reform, transfer of land use rights with valuable consideration was introduced in August 1988. On August 8, 1988, a parcel of 12,973 m^2 of land in Hongqiao Economic and Technological Zone was leased for 50 years for commercial and residential uses. Another parcel of 3,614 m^2 of land in the same zone was also leased in early 1989 for comprehensive development. Further progress on land leasing is discussed in Chapter III.

The organization chart of SHMLAB is given in Figure A4.3. It has 9 administrative divisions and 3 business units and an established staff of 170 persons. The functions and responsibilities of these divisions and units are given as follows:

(a)   **General Office.** This office provides general administration to other divisions. It coordinates and supervises the works of other units. It also handles disputes, complaints, reception and other day-to-day office management work.

Figure A4.3: ORGANIZATION CHART OF SHANGHAI MUNICIPAL LAND
ADMINISTRATION BUREAU (SHMLAB)

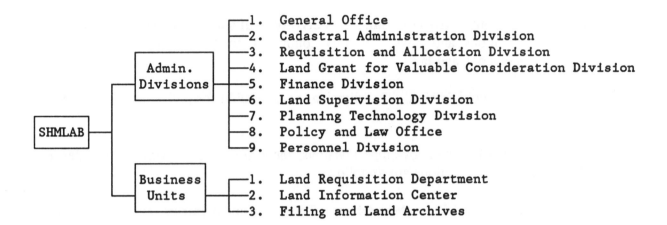

(b) **Cadastral Administration Division.** This division implements policies and regulations related to land registration and surveying. It issues land use rights certificates. It plans to issue a total of 1.57 million certificates (about 270,000 in the urban districts and 1.30 million in the rural counties). This division also determines survey methods, standards, codes and grades of land in the urban district.

(c) **Requisition and Allocation Division.** This division handles all land allocation and requisition, including approving land transfer, land supply planning, supervising district and county land requisition.

(d) **Land Grant for Valuable Consideration Division.** This division was established in 1987 directly under the director of the SHMLAB and works closely with the Leading Group on Land Use System Reform Office. It provides support services to the Leading Group. Auction and tender negotiation of land leases are also handled by this division. It publishes a Real Estate Market Report annually.

(e) **Finance Division.** This division sets the Bureau's budget and standards on land taxes and fees. It also collects taxes and fees on land.

(f) **Land Supervision Division.** It supervises all land use units, land regulations and laws. It also prosecutes unlawful and unauthorized land uses. In addition, this division supervises all land grants approved by district and county authorities in order to prevent unauthorized land allocation.

(g)   **Planning Technology Division.** This division conducts studies on land use planning policies and land resources utilization. It also coordinates disposal of land.

(h)   **Policy and Law Division.** This division drafts and formulates land policies, regulations and laws. It also comments on other bureaus' land-related regulations and laws.

(i)   **Personnel Division.** This division is responsible for personnel matters of the Bureau.

Apart from the above nine divisions, there are three business units under the Bureau. Their names and functions are as follows:

(a)   **Land Requisition Department.** This department carries out the actual land requisition work by negotiating with existing and future land users on the amount of compensation. It sets standards and requirements on compensation and supervises agreements reached by existing and future land users. It also resolves disputes between the two parties. This department charges a management fee of 1.5 percent of the cost of requisition.

(b)   **Land Information Center.** The center collects and keeps land information.

(c)   **Filing and Land Archives.** This unit was removed from the Land Information Center and became an independent unit in 1990. It manages all land registration and supervises lower-level, i.e., district and county, land registration.

District and County Land Management Organizations

As pointed out earlier, land administration in the urban districts in Shanghai has been combined with planning, in the form of District Planning and Land Administration Bureaus, whereas county land administration bureaus are solely responsible for land management. In order to illustrate the differences in land management between districts and counties, Changning District Planning and Land Administration Bureau and Shanghai County Land Administration Bureau are used as case studies.

Changning District is located at the southwestern part of Shanghai Urban District. It has a land area of 28.2 km² and a population of 560,000 and 13,800 households. Administratively, it is divided into 10 streets and one rural town government. Hongqiao Airport, Hongqiao Economic and Technology Development Zone, and Gubei New Area are all located in this district.

Before 1987, land administration was under REAB. State land was managed by the Planning Bureau. In August 1990, the District Planning and Land Administration Bureau was established. The structure of the Bureau is given in Figure A4.4.

Figure A4.4: CHANGNING PLANNING AND LAND ADMINISTRATION BUREAU

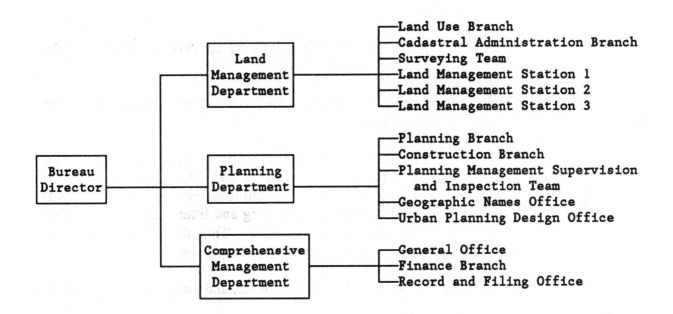

Shanghai County is located at the southwestern edge of the urban district. It has a land area of 374.44 km² and a population of 412,000. It has 19 towns and townships, 237 village committees, 24 resident committees and 2,197 village groups. The area of the County has been reduced from 453.79 km² to 374.44 km² since 1981, largely due to expansion of the urban area.

Planning and land management in the border areas between the urban districts and rural counties is different from that in other areas. Agriculture production of collective-owned farmland, which has been transferred to the urban district, is managed by the county, while land use is under the unified management of the municipal government. State land or collective-owned land that has been acquired by the state and transferred to the urban district is under the management of district government.

Shanghai County Land Administration Bureau (SHCLAB) was established in July 1987. It is responsible to the county government on all land matters. Its functions include management of land allocation, implementation of state/municipal land policies and regulations, supervision of land use, and provision of land-related services such as requisition and registration. The Bureau has the following seven branches: General Office; Finance Branch; Land Use Branch; Cadastral Branch; Land Requisition and Services Department; Supervision Branch; and Records and Information Office. Apart from these units, there are 19 land management stations in 19 townships under the Bureau. These stations are responsible for local land management.

Land Disposition Process in Shanghai

Similar to other parts of China, Shanghai has two types of landownership, i.e., state-owned and collective-owned land. State-owned land may be obtained through administrative allocation or through grant for valuable consideration. If land use rights are obtained by means of administrative allocation, they cannot be transferred or traded in the property market. Contrarily, land use rights obtained through grant for valuable consideration can be transferred, traded or inherited within the time limits stipulated in the lease. Collectively owned land can also be reverted to state-owned through legal requisition but not the other way around (Figure A4.5).

Figure A4.5: LAND OWNERSHIP TYPES IN SHANGHAI

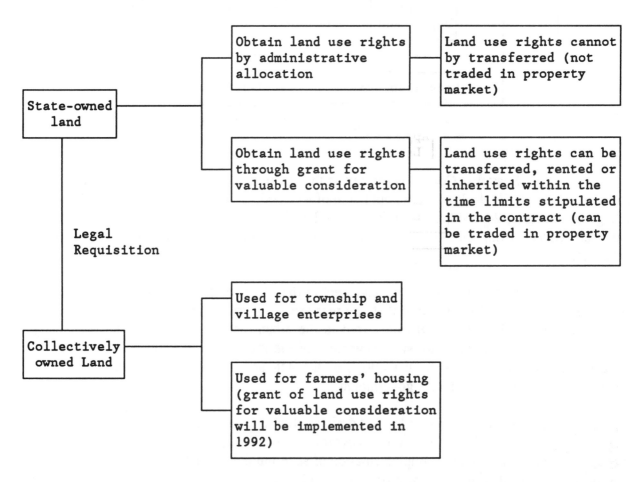

For collectively owned lands in rural counties in Shanghai, they are mainly used for enterprises and farmers' housing. The granting of land use rights for valuable consideration of collectively owned land has not yet been introduced but it will be implemented in 1992.

Figure A4.6 shows the administrative land allocation process. An enterprise or work unit seeking land for its expansion may submit an investment plan to the Shanghai Municipal Economic Planning Commission for approval. After the approval, the applicant prepares a site plan and sends it to the Shanghai Municipal Planning Bureau. Having obtained all the approvals from various concerned authorities, the applicant will be issued a construction permit by the Shanghai Municipal Land Administration Bureau. The applicant then begins land requisition and pays compensation to the affected residents. Construction work starts after the site has been cleared.

Figure A4.6: SIMPLIFIED LAND USE APPLICATION PROCEDURES IN SHANGHAI MUNICIPALITY

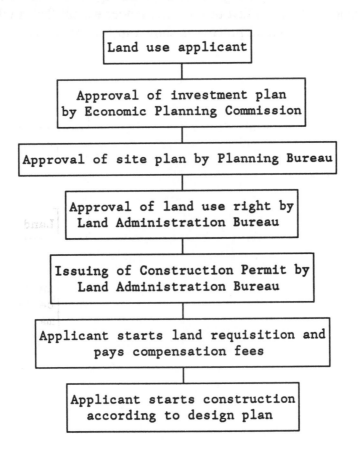

The process for granting and transferring of land use rights for valuable consideration is more complex. There are two forms of land grant, i.e., open tender and negotiated agreement (Figure A4.7). For open tender which was introduced in 1988, the Shanghai Municipal Land Administration Bureau (LAB) first publishes a tender notice and tender documents to invite bids. Tenderers submit tender forms together with deposits to a specified agency and location within the prescribed time limit. Tenders are opened, assessed and selected before the Shanghai Public Office by LAB. The successful tender will be issued an acceptance notice by the LAB and shall be required to sign a grant contract within a prescribed time. After the Grantee pays the premium in accordance with the grant contract, the Grantee receives a land use certificate and registers with the Registration Office of REAB within a prescribed time. The Grantee then uses the grant contract and land use rights certificate to apply to (1) the Foreign Investment Committee for a foreign investment enterprises certificate, (2) the Industry and Commerce Administration Bureau for registration and a license, and (3) the Customs and Tax Bureaus for related certificates. After obtaining all the above certificates and licenses, the applicant then makes an application to the Planning Bureau for a construction permit and then starts construction according to the design plan. There is no time limit for the above process. It might take several months to a couple of years depending on the size and complexity of the project.

The process for the grant of land use rights for valuable consideration under negotiated agreement is similar to that of the open tender except that it takes fewer steps and a relatively shorter time. The actual process is shown in Figure A4.7.

Figure A4.7: THE PROCESS OF THE GRANT AND TRANSFER OF LAND USE RIGHTS FOR VALUABLE CONSIDERATION IN SHANGHAI MUNICIPALITY

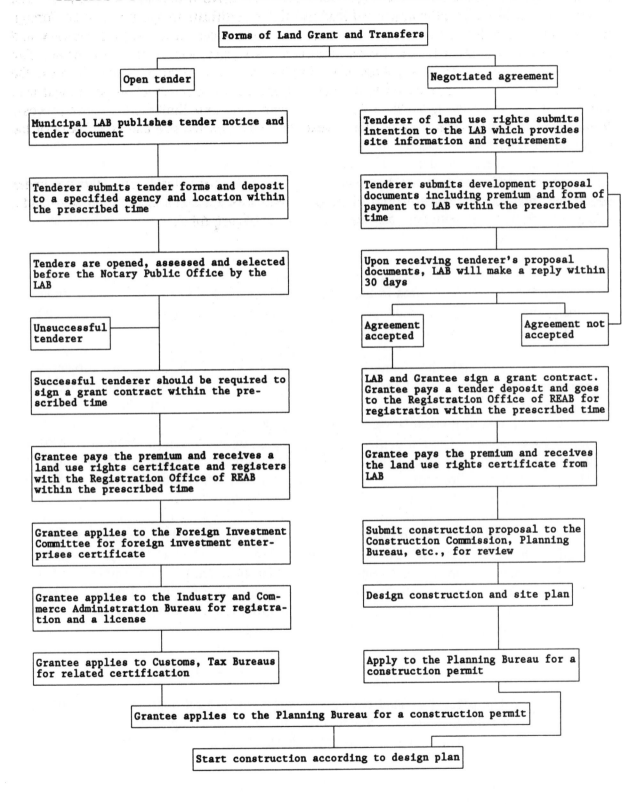

ANNEX 5

PROCEDURES AND COSTS OF LAND REQUISITION 1/

Nature of Land Requisition

In China, under the Constitution, there are only two types of land ownership: state ownership and collective ownership. In general, the land in cities and towns is state-owned, and the land in the countryside is collective owned. In the public interest, the state can requisition collectively owned land. In general, the process of urban expansion is also associated with a parallel process of converting collectively owned rural land into state-owned urban land. Land requisition for state construction is equivalent to "eminent domain" expropriation. There is limited room for negotiation on compensation terms, but the affected collectives and individuals have to comply.

This forced land requisition practice to accommodate state construction started in the early 1950s, and is codified in the "Land Administration Law of the People's Republic of China" (1986), which governs the process of land requisition and compensation, and divides authority over these activities among the central, provincial, and city government.

Although the "Land Administration Law" specifies that any project with cultivated land requisition above 1,000 mu (or 66.67 hectares) or noncultivated land above 2,000 mu (or 133.33 hectares) has to be authorized by the State Council (through the State Land Administration Bureau), no details were given regarding authorization limits applicable to local municipal governments. Their authorization limits are set by provincial governments. Most of municipal governments are given approval authorization of cultivated land requisition no more than 15 mu (1 hectare). For provincial governments, land requisition authorization for cultivated land could ranges from 15 mu to 1,000 mu (1 to 66.67 hectares).

Actual procedures involving project approval and land requisition are also governed by the "City Planning Law of the People's Republic of China" (1990), as well as by detailed implementation measures adopted by provincial and municipal governments. Under these two laws, any state-sponsored projects have to go through an approval procedure before any land requisition work can start. This approval procedure is designed to ensure proper implementation of city's investment and land use plans.

Approval Procedure of State Construction Projects

The process of land requisition starts with project approval, which includes approval from the local planning commission, the city planning bureau and the land administration bureau. The first step is to obtain local planning commission approval, which

---

1/   Most of the descriptive materials is based on Ye Xiaowei, *Land Requisition and Transfer in Shaoxing and Zhejiang*, World Bank, processed (1992), and data collected during the sector study missions.

puts the project into the local "investment" plan. The second step is to get approval from the city planning bureau. According to the City Planning Law, there are two functions within the city planning bureau. One is to select a site for the project, or confirm a site already selected. The other is to approve the size of the site. When this step is completed, a construction land use permit will be issued by the city planning bureau. Box A5.1 involves a project in Shanghai, and illustrates the relationship among various city bureaus regarding project approval and implementation.

The process of land requisition cannot begin until each project passes three key approval steps, including (1) project investment approval from the Planning Commission; (2) project site selection and site approval from the City Planning Bureau; and (3) project land use rights application approval by the Land Administration Bureau.

Land Requisition

Once a project is approved, the process of land requisition can begin. There are two different approaches to arranging for land requisition. One approach is to have the individual construction unit directly deal with collective farmers at the village or township level, to settle various compensation issues concerning land requisition. Although this approach has been adopted for many years, and it is still practiced in many Chinese cities, it is becoming increasingly inadequate to accommodate the needs of rapid urban expansion. Under this approach, negotiation on various compensation issues resembles a market trading process, in spite of extensive regulations and rules governing the supposed level of compensation. As a result, rising expectation from farmers and increasing new compensation items often lead to rapid increases in requisition costs and prolong the land requisition process. In some cases, the land requisition may take several years.

In order to deal with this problem, a different unified approach to land requisition was recommended by the "Provisional Regulation Concerning System Reform of Building Sector and Basic Construction Administration System," adopted by the State Council in 1984. According to this regulation, local governments were encouraged to take full responsibility for arranging land requisition for state projects. Under this approach, the City Land Administration Bureau (or any similar agency before the Land Administration Bureau was established) authorizes the construction unit and the local county Land Administration Bureau to sign a land requisition contract. The county land administration bureau will be responsible for implementing the actual land requisition steps on behalf of the construction unit, including: arranging compensation according to adopted rules and policies; evaluating rural labor resettlement requirements; and so on. Within the City Land Administration Bureau, the Land Requisition Department supervises the overall process.

Under this approach, because various rules and regulations are easier to implement, rapid increases in land requisition costs are avoided, and the whole process is completed within a relatively short period. In recent years, more and more cities have adopted this approach. Shanghai adopted this unified approach in 1986; this has resulted in shortening

---

Box A5.1: ZHONG YUAN ROAD HOUSING PHASE I

Step 1. Project Inception

On January 11, 1989, the Agricultural Commission approved the project sponsored by its Real Estate Development Company.

Step 2. Project Approval

On January 26 and January 28, two applications were sent out by the Real Estate Company: one was an application to the Shanghai Planning Commission for housing construction investment; the other, an application to the Shanghai City Planning Bureau for planning approval of a housing project, with a detailed design and site plan attached.

On April 15, 1989, the general design of the housing project was approved by the City Planning Bureau.

On June 19, 1989, the construction plan for housing was approved by the City Planning Commission.

Step 3. Land Allocation

After project investment and general site design approval, a construction land use permit certificate was issued by the City Planning Bureau. Based on these documents, the construction unit involved sent an application for construction land use to the City Land Administration Bureau. On July 5, 1989, state land allocation for the project was approved by the Shanghai Land Administration Bureau.

Step 4. Land Requisition

Once these approvals are completed (Steps 1 through 3), the project requires that land be requisitioned (if it is located in new area) or that developed urban land be expropriated and its occupants resettled (if the project is located in an existing built-up area). In general, the land requisition process would be carried out by local county or district land administration bureaus. Demolition and relocation in the built-up area would involve local district or county real estate bureaus. In this case, land was requisitioned from a suburban farm community. After the land requisition, a temporary construction land use certificate was issued by the City Land Administration Bureau on July 21, 1989.[1]

Step 5. Construction

Once the site was obtained and final designs were approved by the City Planning Bureau, construction permits were issued. The project started on August 5, 1989.

---

[1] In this case, since the site was already there, no actual land requisition procedure was required, which explains why it took only two weeks between the land allocation approval and the issuance of a temporary construction land use certificate.

---

the average requisition time to only two to three months (normally several months, for some key state construction projects), while also reducing the total requisition cost.

By having local governments in charge of all land requisition, it is much easier to enforce the various rules concerning the cash or in-kind payments. In some cities, such as Shenzhen, land requisition contracts are signed long before a project is ever conceived. The farmers are provided with a down payment, and allowed to farm until relocation is necessary. This allows the city to ensure that land is available at a relatively low cost.

Components and Cost of Land Requisition

Here, the cost of land requisition refers to the payment made by a potential land user during the process of expropriating land from collective villages under relevant regulations and laws. The ownership of expropriated land belongs to the state, while the land user only has land use rights. The following is a description of all land requisition items in Shanghai, and is broadly illustrative of the various fees paid and negotiation involved during the process. Table A5.1 provides a cost breakdown for two Shanghai projects.

Government-Collected Taxes or Fees

There are two such fees and taxes: one is the Cultivated Land Conversion Tax, which is collected by the local land administration bureau. The tax rate is Y 6,000/mu, or Y 9/m^2. For other cultivated land, the tax rate is set at Y 4,500/mu, or Y 6.7/m^2.

The second is the Vegetable Land Rebuilding Fund. The rate ranges from Y 12,000 to Y 20,000/mu, or Y 18 to Y 30/m^2. For vegetable land within the vegetable land protection zone, Y 20,000/mu, or Y 30/m^2, is collected. For vegetable land outside the protection zone, Y 120,000/mu, or Y 18/m^2, is collected.

Land Compensation

For current landowners, i.e., collective farmers, there are three types of payments directly related with land compensation. One is land compensation, which ranges from Y 3,700 to Y 5,000/mu, or Y 5.5 to Y 7.5/m^2, for vegetable land; and Y 2,500 to Y 2,800/mu, or Y 3.7 to Y 4.2/m^2, for other cultivated land.

The second is compensation for young crops, which ranges from Y 600 to Y 900/mu, or Y 0.9 to Y 1.3/m^2, for vegetable land, and Y 380-470/mu, or Y 0.6-0.7/m^2, for other cultivated land.

The third type is agricultural and nonagricultural grain and oil price subsidies. In China, urban residents are provided with subsidized grain and oil. Such subsidies are also required for those farmers who have been displaced by the project. The rate for such compensation is set at Y 2,500/mu, or Y 3.75/m^2, for vegetable land, and Y 1,800/mu, or Y 2.7/m^2, for other cultivated land.

Table A5.1: LAND REQUISITION COST FOR TWO PROJECTS IN SHANGHAI
(Yuan/mu)

Items	Shanghai Yongxin Factory		No. 3 Housing Project	
	Cultivated	Total	Cultivated	Total
Cultivated Land Tax	4,000	3,175	6,667	4,542
Vegetable Land Fund	12,000	10,550	20,000	15,220
Land Compensation	2,100	2,100	3,500	2,839
Young Crop Fee	5,576	4,425	700	450
Grain and Oil Price Subsidy	(not implemented yet)			
Farmer Houses	6,217	4,933	7,750	5,280
TVE Relocation	5,576	4,425	17,429	11,875
Farming Facilities	1,782	1,414	2,894	1,972
Public Housing	24,618	19,540	34,364	23,413
Labor Resettlement	none required		8,281	5,642
Administration Fee and Others	892	708	1,108	755
Total	57,915	47,369	102,693	71,988
Unit Price (Yuan/m^2)	87	71	154	107

Notes: 1. Yongxin Factory required 409.5 mu, or 27.3 hectares of cultivated land and 78.72 mu or 5.25 hectares of noncultivated land in 1988.
2. No. 3 Housing Project required 1,226.9 mu, or 81.8 hectares of total land area, of which 836.07 mu, or 55.7 hectares were cultivated land.

Source: Shanghai Land Administration Bureau.

Property Compensation Fees

The property compensation fees cover a range of collective-owned and private-owned structures or other farming facilities, including fishponds, water irrigation projects, and buildings. Compensation is paid to the collectives or individuals depending on who owns the property. There are four types of compensation:

(a)   one is compensation for relocating township and village enterprises, which averages Y 9,000/mu, or Y 13.5/m^2;

(b)   the second is compensation for demolished farming facilities, which is set at Y 2,000/mu, or Y 3/m^2;

(c)   the third type of compensation provides for public housing for relocated farmers, and averages Y 25,000/mu, or Y 37/m^2. The cost of providing public housing is based on 24 m^2 of floor space per person at 1.3 persons per mu, with a maximum total housing compensation cost set at Y 800/m^2; and

(d)   the last type is compensation for demolished farmers' houses. This averages Y 5,500/mu, or Y 8.2/m^2. This compensation is based on one family per 3 mu, and 130 m^2 per family, which reflects the price of demolished houses. If farmers choose to rebuild their houses, the compensation will be set at Y 8,000/mu, or Y 12/m^2. As a result, there will be no need to provide public housing for those farmers.

Compensation of Displaced Laborers

The potential land user will be responsible for the employment of displaced farmers. If the new users cannot absorb them into their enterprises, they must pay a resettlement fee to an enterprise that can absorb them. The total labor resettlement compensation is set at Y 15,000/mu, or Y 22.5/m^2.

In addition, social security support for the elderly is also required. The number of such elderly is based on 1.8 persons per mu, assuming an 8:2 ratio between qualified labor and elderly. The compensation for elderly individuals averages Y 20,750/person, with Y 17,845/person for males, and Y 23,716/for females. The combined total labor resettlement cost averages Y 29,000/mu, or Y 43.5/m^2. If the new land user can absorb the surplus laborers, there will be no labor resettlement cost.

ANNEX 6

PROCEDURES AND COSTS OF URBAN RESETTLEMENT

The Nature of Urban Resettlement in China

Unlike land requisition procedures, which change land ownership from collectively owned rural land to state-owned urban land, urban resettlement caused by urban redevelopment projects or infrastructure upgrading does not involve any landownership change. Instead, it often results in change of land use rights between existing land users and potential land users. Such differences, however, seems to have little impact on actual implementation of projects. In fact, if a proposed urban redevelopment is a state-sponsored construction project, it has the same "eminent domain" effect as in a land requisition case. Since most urban projects are sponsored or approved by the local government, in theory, most of these projects should be able to proceed unhindered.

According to newly adopted State Council regulations on urban resettlement—Urban Building Demolition Administration Regulation (March 1991)—if relocation is required under the general urban construction program, all affected units or individuals, who either use or own properties on the state-owned urban land, have to comply with the resettlement process. The relocator or developer is required to provide compensation for individuals and units being relocated.

Preconditions to Resettlement

The process of resettlement starts with the project approval, which includes approvals from the local planning commission, the city planning bureau and the land administration bureau. The first step is to obtain local planning commission approval, which puts the project into the investment plan. When the project is within the investment plan, the second step is to get approval from the city planning bureau. According to the City Planning Law, there are two functions assigned to the city planning bureau. One is to select a site for the project, or confirm a site that has been selected. The other is to approve the size of the site. When this step is completed, a construction land use permit is issued by the city planning bureau. Based on these documents, the construction unit sends an application for construction land use to the city Land Administration Bureau.

Once these approvals were granted, the project entered the land requisition phase. In general, the land requisition process is carried out by local county or district land administration bureaus. (Demolition and relocation in the built-up area would involve local district or county real estate bureaus.) Once the land is obtained, a temporary use of construction land certificate will be issued.

The process of urban resettlement or land requisition process will not begin until a project passes three key approval steps, including (1) project investment approval from the local Planning Commission; (2) project site selection and site approval from the City Planning Bureau; and (3) project land use rights application approval by the Land Administration Bureau. To some extent, we can view land requisition and urban resettlement as following the same overall project cycle approval process. Their main purpose is to acquire land in order to implement the approved project. However, because of many different issues involved during the process of land requisition and urban resettlement, a separated discussion of the procedures and costs involved in urban resettlement is necessary.

Procedures for Resettlement

Obtaining a Demolition and Relocation Permit

According to new resettlement regulations, both state and local, only those construction units or individuals who hold demolition permits will be allowed to carry out actual relocation and demolition. In order to obtain this permit, a construction unit has to submit the following documents, along with demolition and relocation applications, to local district or county real estate bureaus:

(a)   a project investment approval document;

(b)   a construction land use permit from the city planning bureau;

(c)   a land use authorization document from the land administration bureau; and

(d)   a relocation and resettlement plan.

If the application is granted, a certificate of relocation and demolition will be issued, which will authorize the unit or individual to carry out the resettlement. The permit will specify the boundary and time limit of the resettlement process. Normally, the demolition and relocation cannot exceed approved boundary and resettlement time limits.

In some cities, such as Shanghai, if a redevelopment project meets certain conditions, then the demolition and resettlement permit requires city-level real estate bureau approval. These conditions include:

(a)   if more than 300 households are to be relocated, or more than 100 households are to be temporary sheltered;

(b)   if more than 10 households must live in self-arranged temporary shelters; and

(c)   if foreign institutions and individuals are involved.

Given these conditions, it seems that most urban redevelopment projects will require city-level real estate bureau approval regarding demolition and relocation. In general, the city real estate bureau has to respond within 20 days, once an application is received.

Public Dissemination of Information

Once the demolition and relocation permit is issued, the real estate bureau must inform the public within the affected neighborhoods regarding the boundary of the redevelopment area, relocation timetables, and building demolition plans.

In addition, the real estate bureau is also responsible for informing relevant departments to stop activities within the boundary of the redevelopment project. This includes:

(a)   informing relevant departments to stop any sale, lease, or exchange of buildings within the demolition boundary;

(b)   informing the public security office to stop processing household registrations;

(c)   informing the commerce bureau to stop issuing business licenses within the area.

Resettlement Contract

The last and perhaps the most important step in the resettlement process is to arrange for a compensation and resettlement contract between the construction unit and affected residents and enterprises. Once the demolition and relocation permit is issued and the announcement is made, both the construction unit or developer and residents or units to be relocated are required to develop detailed compensation and resettlement arrangement plans. In this regard, newly adopted national and local regulations concerning demolition and relocation provide extensive details on how compensation for demolished buildings should be determined, and how resettlement arrangements must be made for both private building owners and tenants of public housing, as well as affected enterprises. Once a contract is signed between these two parties, the actual process of demolition, site preparation, and construction can begin.

Contents of Compensation and Resettlement

For any redevelopment project, such contracts often include two parts: one covers compensation made to owners of demolished properties; the other provides for resettlement arrangements for both tenants and private homeowners, as well as displaced enterprises or shops.

Compensation for Demolition

There are several ways of calculating proposed compensation: one is to provide replacement structures for building owners, either on-site or off-site. The second approach is to provide cash payment for demolished properties. The third approach is to combine the first two approaches. The amount of compensation made to replace structures and any additional cash compensation will be based on the amount of existing building floor space. Cash compensation, however, is often based on depreciated replacement value. In some cities, like in Shanghai, a separate cash payment schedule for different kinds of structures is formulated by the Construction Commission and the Price Bureau.

According to demolition and relocation regulations, for different types of users and different owners, different guidelines will be followed:

(a)   If the demolished building is a public service building, then the developer must rebuild this structure according to its original use, and size, or provide a replacement cash payment to the city for other arrangements. This approach also applies to other publicly owned nonresidential structures, except that public institutions have to pay the price difference resulting from any improved structure quality or increased floor space.

(b)   For public residential structures, the developer is required to provide replacement structures on-site or at different locations for the owner. The owner will not pay for the price difference resulting from any increased floor space and improved housing conditions. Original rental relationships involving public housing tenants will remain in place; no higher rents will be imposed.

(c)   For private housing owners, if they elect to receive cash compensation instead of a replacement structure, both their property ownership certificates and their land use certificates will be canceled. For those who want to keep their ownership, they will have to pay any price difference caused by improved quality and increased floor space. If the new per capita floor space is below 24 m^2, and the size of the new housing unit does not exceed the old one, the owner can buy additional floor space at one third of the construction cost. If the new per capita floor space is above 24 m^2, and the new unit size is smaller than the old one, the owner has to pay the cost-recovery price for any additional floor space. This additional price has to be paid in full before the owner can obtain the unit.

(d)   The last and often the most expensive compensation involves relocating industrial or commercial enterprises. In order to relocate a factory, the following costs have to be met:

   (i)   cash compensation for demolished properties and nonrelocatable equipment;

   (ii)   land requisition costs for providing a site of similar size;

   (iii)   moving and costs related to the installation of factory equipment;

   (iv)   wage compensation for employees during the period of temporary unemployment.

Compensation is paid in several parts. During the project preparation stage, 30 percent of total compensation has to be paid. When construction begins, the remaining 70 percent is then paid. They could also be paid in full at one time, if all old structures are to be demolished immediately. If the relocated factory allows the developer to build a new structure for it, no compensation will be paid to the original owner. In addition, price differences that result from an increase in land area, floor space and improved structures will be paid by the enterprise.

Resettlement Arrangement

The construction unit or developer is also required to provide replacement housing for those relocated from the proposed sites. If there is insufficient housing to accommodate all current users, both temporary shelter or self-arranged accommodations are permissible options. Temporary shelters are required to have "normal living conditions," and "basic housing facilities."

Here, "current property users" refers only to those who have permanent residency permits in the city and live within the redevelopment area. However, since one of the main purposes of redevelopment is to improve the housing conditions for existing residents, certain types of residents will not be eligible for resettlement. For example, if one family has an additional housing unit outside the redevelopment site, this family will not be given a new housing unit after redevelopment.

One complicated issue is determining those who are eligible for resettlement, and what kind of household "separation" will be allowed in order to calculate the total number of residents to be resettled. In order to deal with this, local regulations, particularly detailed implementation measures, include all possible conditions for determining who will be included in resettlement arrangements, and what kind of household "separation" will be allowed for resettlement purposes.

Once the number of persons and households to be relocated is determined, the next step is to figure out the exact amount of new housing space that each family will get, which is often linked to the different locations where replacement housing is provided. If the new project is not a residential project, all current residents will have to relocate to new suburban areas. If the new project is a commodity housing project, most of the residents have to relocate to the urban fringe; only those who want to pay the price differential between housing in the urban fringe and at the redevelopment site will be allowed to return to the original location. In order to encourage residents to move to suburban locations and improve the feasibility of the redevelopment project, incentives are given to people who choose to relocate to suburban locations (Table A6.1). This standard also applies to those private owners who want to give up their ownership rights and become renters of public housing units.

Table A6.1: SHANGHAI STANDARDS FOR THE REPLACEMENT OF DEMOLISHED HOUSING
(m²/person)

Original living area	Living area allocation in the same or near site	Living area allocation to fringe area
under 4	maintain previous amount	4
4- 7	4- 5	5- 6
7-10	5- 6	6- 7
10-13	6- 7	7- 8
13-16	7- 8	8- 9
16-19	8- 9	9-10
19-22	9-10	10-11
22-25	10-11	11-12
25-30	11-12	12
30+	12	12

Source: Shanghai City Building Demolition and Relocation Administration Detailed Implementation Regulation, July 19, 1991.

Cost of Resettlement

During the process of urban redevelopment, the major cost involves resettlement. In many cases, the resettlement cost is several times greater than that of the actual project cost (such as road expansion, and so on). Table A6.2 provides a detailed cost analysis of a redevelopment project in Hangzhou, the Xiao Fuqing Xiang Redevelopment Project.

Table A6.2: HANGZHOU: XIAO FUQING XIANG REDEVELOPMENT PROJECT

Items	Land area (ha)	Floor space ('000 m²)	FAR	Percent of total	Date
Total	0.74	14.02	1.91		1988-90
Of which:					
Resettlement Space		9.53		68.00	
Commodity Space		4.49		32.00	

Source: Hangzhou Building Development Corporation.

Several items need emphasizing. One is the ratio of commodity housing to total completed floor space. Since all resettlement space has to be financed by commodity housing sales, the higher the ratio of commodity to "free" housing, the more feasible or more profitable the redevelopment project. In this case, this ratio is only 32 percent, which is considered low by Chinese standards. In other words, almost 70 percent of the completed floor space will be used to accommodate current users or owners at virtually no cost. Table A6.3 illustrates the relatively high share of resettlement cost in terms of overall project costs.

Table A6.3: COST BREAKDOWN OF XIAO FUQING XIANG PROJECT

Items	Total cost (Yuan)	Unit cost (Yuan/m^2)	Percent of total
A. Planned Cost	4,791,211	1,068.27	70.65
Resettlement	3,014,974	672.24	44.46
Building compensation	161,426	35.99	2.38
Temporary shelter	242,863	54.15	3.58
Moving expense	3,588	0.80	0.05
Wage loss	110,780	24.70	1.63
Building residual value	(67,634)	-15.08	-1.00
Resettlement cost	2,563,951	571.67	37.81
Design & site preparation	154,328	34.41	2.28
Survey fee	13,365	2.98	0.20
Design fee	31,888	7.11	0.47
Site use fee	13,948	3.11	0.21
Water fee	8,073	1.80	0.12
Electricity	34,445	7.68	0.51
Land leveling	52,609	11.73	0.78
Construction	1,206,644	269.04	17.79
Construction	991,634	221.10	14.62
Installation	143,385	31.97	2.11
Other facilities	71,625	15.97	1.06
On-Site infrastructure	249,327	55.59	3.68
Water connection	130,507	29.10	1.92
Electricity	58,176	12.97	0.86
Sewage	25,349	5.65	0.37
Road	35,295	7.87	0.52
Administration cost	80,446	17.94	1.19
Loan interest	85,492	19.06	1.26
B. Planned Profit	146,036	32.56	2.15
C. Tax	321,084	71.59	4.73
D. Subtotal (A + B + C)	5,258,331	1,172.43	77.54
E. Price Difference	630,815	140.65	9.30
F. Surcharges	524,581	116.96	7.74
Off-site fee	496,551	110.71	7.32
Park fee	28,030	6.25	0.41
G. Construction Tax	368,034	82.06	5.43
H. Total (D + E + F + G)	6,781,761	1,512.10	100.00

Notes: 1. Total cost (H) is also the approved price for commodity housing.
2. Unit cost is obtained by dividing total cost by the 4,485 m^2 of commodity housing floor space.

Source: Hangzhou Building Development Corporation, 1991.

ANNEX 7

REDEVELOPMENT REGULATIONS IN SELECTED ASIAN CITIES

Introduction

This annex summaries the redevelopment experiences in three Asian cities: Hong Kong, Seoul and Singapore. The three cities share many common features and offer some lessons for the design of redevelopment policies and programs in the People's Republic of China. First and foremost, the three cities all experienced tremendous population and economic growth between 1950 and 1980, and the urban areas of these cities were virtually rebuilt. In the 1980s, urban growth declined as population pressures subsided, but rising incomes and fundamental structural economic change generated enormous demands for residential, commercial and industrial space.

In the early years of redevelopment, government played a critical role in slum clearance and urban renewal. In Hong Kong, Singapore and Seoul, vast areas of land were redeveloped, and government was quick to exercise its powers of eminent domain to assemble land to carry out its projects. Most attention was targeted on squatter settlements in these cities. In Singapore in 1959, over 250,000 people lived in dilapidated prewar housing and 300,000 occupied shacks and huts. In Seoul, over 32 percent of the housing stock in 1970 was classified as slums. In Hong Kong, massive slum clearance took place in the 1960s and 1970s. In both Hong Kong and Singapore, public housing was constructed at unprecedented levels and by 1990, such housing accounted for over 50 percent in Hong Kong and 87 percent in Singapore.

In the 1980s, middle-class resistance to heavy-handed public urban renewal emerged in Hong Kong and Seoul. In response, both governments altered their policies. In Seoul, the Korea Land Development Corporation (KLDC) and the Seoul Municipal Government (SMG) no longer initiate urban renewal projects; instead, they rely on private landowner associations (unions) to prepare redevelopment schemes. In Hong Kong, urban redevelopment is now handled by a quasi-governmental agency, the Land Development Corporation (LDC). Much like a private sector developer, the LDC is charged with the responsibility of redeveloping key districts. The LDC does not have direct powers of eminent domain; it must assemble land through negotiations. Only in extreme cases (there have not been any yet) can the LDC request assistance from the government to compulsorily acquire land. Since the LDC is an independent agency, it receives no special treatment from the Hong Kong Housing Authority to resettle households from redevelopment project areas.

In the Hong Kong case, redevelopment is still very much private sector-driven and the government, through the LDC, is now playing a limited role in promoting and carrying out urban redevelopment. To date, only one project has been completed since the LDC's inception in 1988. In Seoul, the pace of urban redevelopment has slowed, but there is still activity. The SMG has taken a position different from Hong Kong and it provides public housing for tenants displaced from redevelopment areas.

Singapore, in contrast to Hong Kong and Seoul, continues to pursue a highly aggressive redevelopment agenda, and is now quite active in the renovation and, in some cases, demolition and redevelopment of older housing projects. While there are some concerns over failure to preserve historic areas, by most accounts both the Urban Redevelopment Authority and the Housing Development Board are well-regarded by Singaporeans.

Given the pressing conditions faced in most cities in the People's Republic of China and the public ownership of land in urban areas, Singapore's practices seem to be the most relevant and appropriate for consideration for possible adaptation in China. Further assessments of the Singapore model of redevelopment should be considered. In the following sections, brief sketches of each city's redevelopment activities are presented.

Hong Kong

In the past 46 years, Hong Kong has experienced rapid population growth and urban development. The population of Hong Kong has grown from 1.6 million in 1946 to the present 5.8 million. During the first two decades after the Second War World, the annual population growth rate averaged 5 percent, causing tremendous demand for land to support housing and other economic activities.

After the late 1960s, the population growth of Hong Kong fell to 2 to 3 percent per year. Apart from the surge of illegal migration from China in the late 1970s that added near 400,000 newcomers, population pressure has greatly eased. At present, the annual population increase is around 1 percent. However, the slow growth of population has not decreased development pressures or the demand for land. Pent-up demand and rising incomes continue to spur development, especially in the core areas of Central, Wanchai and Kowloon. The high concentration of population, employment and other activities in these areas has resulted in continuing rebuilding and densification.

Redevelopment in Hong Kong is driven by an efficient and dynamic land and property market. In the inner city, different uses are competing with one another and the bidding for offices, hotels and other commercial floor spaces displaces the existing uses such as residential, manufacturing related and other activities. Rising land values in the center provide strong incentives to convert existing uses to higher and more profitable uses, and the private sector has led the way in rebuilding much of Hong Kong over the past 20 years.

Private urban redevelopment is guided by the market. When the shortage of housing reached its apex in the late 1950s, the private sector replaced the prewar tenements with high-rise residential blocks. Between 1957 and 1965, the whole city was practically rebuilt. When office and hotel demand was excessive in the late 1970s, buildings in Central, Wanchai and Causeway Bay were pulled down for commercial, financial and tourist purposes. The trend was later intensified by the construction of the Mass Transit Line. The waterfront has received attention too. Traditional port facilities such as dockyards, warehouses, rail depot, oil depots have been relocated to the outer areas, making way for housing estates and commercial uses.

Private redevelopment is supported by a range of agents such as landowners, developers, financial experts, legal professionals, real estate professionals and contractors. Development is competitive, specialized, professional, and coordinated. Nonetheless, the property market is highly cyclical as construction booms of one type of property follow another until a major readjustment halts the boom.

Guided by the market, private urban redevelopment is essentially profit-driven. Such redevelopment rarely takes social and environmental objectives into consideration unless these concerns are capitalized into market demand, and there are few examples of large-scale redevelopment projects by the private sector that incorporate community facilities landscaping.

From the supply side, the government acts as the sole supplier of land to private sector for development. The government also regulates redevelopment intensity and land use conversion through its dual capacity as the ultimate land lessor and land use regulator. Though the supply of land is always criticized as monopolistic and a "high land price" policy is adopted, the government seems to function in accordance to market forces. It is undeniable that land, particularly at prime locations, is short of supply because of the physical constraints. Yet the property market responds to excessive supply or demand by price fluctuation, as any other functioning market.

In some cases, private developers have difficulty assembling land for redevelopment. Despite poor building conditions and excellent locations, fragmented ownership and lengthy negotiations often make redevelopment projects unfeasible. In such circumstances, government can play an important role in facilitating urban redevelopment. In Hong Kong, as well as in Singapore and Seoul, governments were proactive in the 1960s and 1970s to promote redevelopment. However, in the 1980s, the Hong Kong Government shifted strategy to a more laissez faire policy, establishing the Land Development Corporation.

Hong Kong Land Development Corporation

In the early 1980s, the government commissioned a series of consultant studies to identify a future integrated, spatial development strategy for Hong Kong. Several developments led to this action. After a decade of massive commitment in new town programs, some policymakers began to reconsider whether alternative development strategies could make investment more cost-effective. While government programs have eased housing shortages (producing units for 41,366 households between 1972 and 1985), continuing economic prosperity called for higher-quality housing and amenities, more community facilities and higher environmental standards. The restructuring of the economy has imposed different type of land demand on nonresidential uses such as prime office floor space, commercial and hotel accommodation, and large-scale infrastructure.

In formulating the Territorial Development Strategy, the government divided Hong Kong into several subregions and conducted detailed studies in each area. Taken together, the studies' findings revealed that Hong Kong has the capacity to meet future land requirements associated with demographic and economic growth. In particular, the Study on Harbor

Reclamation and Urban Growth (SHRUG) concluded that the whole urban core could hold at least half a million additional persons if the development potential of all areas were fully exploited. The study's findings led to a policy shift away from new town development to initiatives aimed at promoting more centralized development, because of the latter approach's superiority over decentralized new town developments in terms of energy conservation and infrastructure cost-effectiveness. These studies would be of obvious interest to Chinese urban planners, especially those in Shanghai who have assumed that a decentralized land development strategy is the most appropriate means to accommodate future urban growth.

In March 1982, the Special Committee on Land Supply (SCLS) initiated a review of the effectiveness of the government's action toward urban renewal and redevelopment policies. The SCLS concluded that rehousing and consolidation of landholdings in amalgamating properties and in obtaining vacant possession appeared to be the major difficulties impeding redevelopment. In response to these conclusions, the SCLS established a Working Group on Urban Renewal to consider and recommend the broad principles and possible actions the government should take to expedite urban redevelopment. The Working Group outlined the following principal objectives: (a) to speed up private sector development in selected areas; (b) to encourage the participation of landowners; (c) to improve the quality and economic benefits of developments by assembling larger sites; (d) to ensure equitable treatment of the tenants; (e) to provide improved community facilities, including better traffic circulation; and (f) to minimize the need for direct government subsidies and the application of compulsory acquisition powers.

After considering several alternatives, the Working Group recommended the formation of an independent Land Development Corporation (LDC) as an effective means to encourage the private sector participation in land development. A feasibility study on the LDC was commissioned in 1983 to determine the scale, scope, and geographical coverage of the LDC. The consultant reported that the LDC was feasible, and it should focus on the redevelopment of the inner city. Three working groups were subsequently set up to examine the planning, land assembly, clearance, rehousing, organizational, legislation and financial aspects of the proposal.

In 1984, the Land Development Policy Committee accepted the recommendations of the consultancy report and announced its decision to establish the LDC as an statutorily independent public corporation to carry out redevelopment projects by utilizing private resources. The government then took the necessary steps to establish the LDC. The Executive Council approved starting of advanced activities connected with the formation of the LDC in June 1985. As a first step, a Coordinating Urban Renewal Team (CURT) within the Town Planning Division was set up to provide initial technical and professional support to the LDC. The CURT focused on providing planning inputs such as reviewing past urban renewal proposals, identifying sites for redevelopment, recommending priority areas, setting planning parameters and drafting action area plans. It also served as a coordinator among government departments regarding the programming of community and recreational facilities in relation to the redevelopment proposals. Parallel to these efforts, the Lands Division also set up teams at the district level to assess resumption cost (acquisition of leasehold interests in leased crown land) and to prepare for land clearance and other related duties.

Between 1984 and 1988, CURT compiled a priority list of districts in need of redevelopment. The Secretary of Lands and Works designated these districts as Urban Renewal Areas within which redevelopment proposals will be prepared. On the legislative side, the government prepared a bill to establish the LDC in mid-1987. In December 1987, the Legislative Council enacted the LDC Ordinance and the LDC was formally established in January 1988. The government provided a HK$100 million loan with the LDC as initial working capital.

As of 1992, apart from the conservation project of the government-owned Western Market, there has not yet a redevelopment scheme completed in the first four years of the LDC. In this period, the LDC has spent much of its effort in negotiating the purchase of properties in identified redevelopment areas, striking joint-venture deals with private developers, and getting the necessary planning permission or zoning amendments from the government.

Progress has been slow for a number of reasons, including a soft real estate market between 1989 and 1991. But apparently a major problem is LDC's difficulty in assembling land for projects. Despite the fact that between 1986 and 1988 many small developers and real estate agents acquired land in targeted redevelopment areas in anticipation of the creation of LDC, the agency has not attempted to structure joint ventures with landowners. Because of the decade-long deadlock between two groups of owners of residential and commercial properties in formulating an acceptable profit-sharing formula in the Four-Street comprehensive redevelopment proposal in Tsim Sha Tsui, LDC has ruled out the option that affected property owners can participate as partners or shareholder in redevelopment schemes. Rather, LDC prefers to purchase the properties by negotiation and pay cash. This obviously is not what many developers and owners have in mind.

Relocation and resettlement of affected tenants and owners is also a continuing problem for LDC. One problem is that there are few opportunities for resettling residents in nearby housing sites, and most households are offered units in distant new town areas. Relocation of shop-operators is extremely difficult, especially when vibrant street activities are demolished and replaced with modern high-rise housing and mixed-use blocks. Unlike China, households are not provided with in-kind replacement of units. Tenants renting units are expected to pay market rents if they relocate to new housing redeveloped on site. Since LDC has been set up as an independent agency outside the government, it receives no support from the Housing Authority in terms of finding replacement housing. Displaced tenants merely go to the end of the Hong Kong Housing Authority waiting list. This seems like an obvious problem, and it sharply contrasts with the redevelopment practices in Singapore, and the role played by the Seoul Metropolitan Government to assist displaced tenants in private redevelopment projects.

In Hong Kong, redevelopment policies have apparently gone too far toward a laissez faire posture. LDC has limited powers in terms of land acquisition, and relocation.

Instead, it must operate much like a private developer. In Seoul, a similar evolution of redevelopment has taken place, with the government getting out of the business of active redevelopment.

Seoul

Urban redevelopment in Korea has been extensive, reflecting the tremendous rates of urbanization experienced in the country. Between 1950 and 1983, Korea's urban population increased from 26.7 percent of the total population to 72.1 percent. Land readjustment has been used extensively in Seoul since 1937 as a means of modernizing urban spatial structure. Between 1937 and 1984, 13,984 hectares of land in the city of Seoul have gone through land readjustment. This accounts for 40 percent of the total urbanized land area in the metropolitan area in 1985.

In the early years, before the Korean Conflict, projects were financed largely through government budget and by allotments from landowners. Projects typically were smaller than 100 hectares. After the war, projects were restarted and massive redevelopment of damaged areas took place. Up until the 1960s, the focus of redevelopment centered on restructuring the central city area. In the 1970s, redevelopment focus shifted toward the production of large-scale housing to accommodate massive urbanization.

In Korea, major cities over 1,000,000 in population are required to prepare comprehensive redevelopment plans. In actual practice, only Seoul complies with the law, having prepared detailed planning studies for redevelopment and carried out redevelopment. According to researchers at the Korea Research Institute on Human Settlements (KRIHS), the national law of redevelopment is vague and does not precisely define blight, but surveys of urban areas which examine physical conditions, public health and safety conditions, and building densities and ratios of land to building values are required before establishing redevelopment districts.

The redevelopment law defines six criteria for designating a renewal district:

(a)   more than two thirds of buildings in the district are under the height of the lowest-height limit in the district;

(b)   more than two thirds of buildings in the district do not follow fire prevention codes;

(c)   more than two thirds of buildings in the district are below two stories and not constructed of fireproof materials;

(d)   land parcels are too small and/or irregular and difficult to utilize;

(e)   buildings are worn out or deteriorated; and

(f)   dense residential areas are intermixed with industrial areas.

According to national law, cities are to prepare and follow annual implementation plans and city government agencies are responsible for implementation. Once the city government has designated a redevelopment district, redevelopment projects can be executed by either: (a) district associations or unions; (b) municipal government; and (c) public development corporations such as the Korea Land Development Corporation or the National Housing Corporation. In the past, the municipal government and the Korea Land Development Corporation were extremely active in redevelopment, using their powers of condemnation to acquire land and buildings. In recent years, there has been considerable public backlash to urban redevelopment and both the local government and KLDC have backed away from initiating redevelopment programs, especially controversial ones. While the government still prepares plans for urban redevelopment, it relies on property owners to actually implement the plans.

To implement redevelopment programs, property owners form a landowner's association or union. If two thirds of the property owners in the area agree to participate in the redevelopment, then the union is given the power of eminent domain. However, these powers are not often used and owners negotiate with reluctant neighbors to join the scheme. Apparently, it is common practice for these reluctant owners to be compensated so that they support redevelopment projects. When there is full support for the redevelopment, the union submits a redevelopment scheme to the local government for approval. The front-end cost for preparing these schemes and compensating reluctant owners is often paid for by a developer or contractor who will actually carry out the project. In most cases, low-rise buildings, either squatter settlements or single-family dwelling units, are demolished and new apartment buildings constructed. Most plans call for significant increases in building densities. In older areas of Seoul where typical FARs are below 1:1, redevelopment schemes generally call for increasing the FAR to 1:1.5 to 1:2.0 and higher. In addition, they must follow statutory requirements regarding determination of housing allotment, management plan and provision of public facilities.

In exchange for the contribution of land, owners are allocated new units, and the precise level of compensation depends on the value of their property. In some cases, owners receive more than one unit. However, in other cases, owners of very small plots or squatter houses must pay additional monies to make up the difference between the value of their contributed land and the full development cost of the new unit. If the owners cannot afford to make this payment, they are cashed-out and move to a new area, usually in the suburbs.

Owners of properties normally are able to return to the site and during the construction phase, the developer pays them compensation for temporary relocation (in 1991 the typical payment was 600,000 Won ($770) per household member). Project financing is the responsibility of the union. However, if demolished units are occupied by nonowner tenants, the owner must negotiate with the tenant and pay some form of compensation. This is evidently where difficulties arise.

The redevelopment law provides that compensation be paid to qualified tenants who are forced to relocate. The compensation can take two forms: dwelling unit expense payment or a permanent tenant housing ticket. The local government currently has 6,167 housing units available in 13 suburban districts which may be allocated to displaced residents. Tenants not allocated municipal receive a dwelling settlement expense payment. Based on the average monthly per capita housing expense of Seoul residents, each household member is to receive three months' compensation. In addition, each household receives compensation for moving expenses.

Since 1976, 423 projects have been targeted for redevelopment nationwide. To date, 99 sites have been redeveloped, 50 sites are under way, and 274 sites have not been started. The lack of progress on the 274 sites is due to a lack of money, no developer or contractor interest and conflicts between owners.

In Seoul, as of May 1991, a cumulative total of 140 projects have been targeted for redevelopment. As of the date, 37 projects have been completed covering a total 930,016 m^2 of constructed area. Forty projects are currently under redevelopment, covering 1,843,177 m^2 of constructed area. Another 63 projects covering 4,180,539 m^2 are targeted for future redevelopment. Considerable redevelopment took place prior to the Olympics, and between 1984 and 1987, 42 areas were designated for redevelopment. The total number of redevelopment housing units planned for Seoul (in the 140 projects) is 68,874. Between 1984 and 1987, 15,897 units were produced.

Most of the completed redevelopment areas were areas with a high percentage of government landownership; in areas with high incidence of private ownership, difficulties developed in obtaining agreement to proceed with redevelopment. Areas with higher rates of squatter housing are more likely to be redeveloped than others. Completed redevelopment project areas had an average of 82 percent squatter housing. In areas which have not advanced, the average is 65 percent. Incidence of tenants also affects the likelihood of redevelopment. In completed areas, tenancy averaged 40 percent; in areas not started, 75 percent of residents are tenants.

In Seoul, redevelopment activities have brought about a marked decrease in slum housing. In 1970, 187,554 dwelling units were located in slum areas and accounted for 32.1 percent of the total housing stock in the metropolitan area. By 1985, the total number of slum houses had been reduced in absolute terms to 125,439 units, accounting for 10.6 percent of the housing stock.

Housing conditions in areas targeted for redevelopment are similar to those found in other Asian cities: high housing densities, poor housing conditions, lack of facilities and overcrowding. The living area per capita is low, ranging from 5 to 10 m^2 per person. Most slum area housing conditions are poor and units lack kitchens and indoor toilet facilities. Units average between 1.5 to 2.3 rooms, and many lack separate entrances.

After redevelopment, housing conditions for those households returning are vastly improved. In the completed areas, typical units are 109 m^2, about three times the size of original units. In 1991, SMG passed a new ordinance reducing the size of replacement housing units in order to lower costs and housing prices.

Creation of property owner unions to carry out urban redevelopment projects is novel and warrants further consideration. However, it is not without limitations or problems. A recent assessment of the Housing Renewal Program conducted by KRIHS recommends a number of modifications to the program:

(a)   provide replacement housing before demolition starts and more directly link union activities with those of public housing authorities;

(b)   the central government should subsidize the provision of public housing for displaced tenants;

(c)   redevelopment schemes should be required to provide small-sized affordable housing units for low-income residents;

(d)   all cities over one million in population should be required to prepare a master plan for housing renewal;

(e)   standards for designating renewal areas should be more precise and clear;

(f)   separate laws for residential and nonresidential redevelopment should be enacted;

(g)   a fund should be established to support union renewal activities; and

(h)   a time limit should be set for the designation of a renewal area.

Singapore

In 1963, with support from the United Nations Development Program, Singapore prepared its first master plan. The plan noted the dangerous and insalubrious conditions of older central areas, and called for redevelopment of these older areas. This marked the beginning of redevelopment in the City.

Large-scale redevelopment in Singapore began during the 1960s and it still continues, in modified form, today. The process of redevelopment can be divided into three phases: I (1960s), II (1970s), and III (1980s to present). The key element in the redevelopment process is that sitting tenants are relocated and are rarely offered the opportunity to return to redeveloped properties.

Control of land is obtained through Singapore's Compulsory Land Acquisition powers. Under the law, Urban Redevelopment Authority (URA) can acquire land for public purpose; owners of the to-be-acquired properties cannot challenge the acquisition process. They can, however, challenge the level of compensation offered for the properties.

Tenants of acquired properties are subject to relocation. This includes residential, commercial and industrial uses. The process of relocation is complicated by the fact that the British enacted rent control in 1947, with rents based on 1939 rents. This placed the rents of sitting tenants at very low levels and created a broad differential between pre- and post-relocation rents.

Commercial and Industrial Relocation

In the initial stage of relocation, the government built "transit facilities" around areas to be redeveloped. For commercial (shophouse) activities, these facilities were rows of new, but temporary wooden buildings. Small businesses targeted for relocation were offered space in the transit facilities. Because of the hardships caused by the relocation (principally the loss of "street presence"), merchants were offered below-market rents. Before relocation, tenants paid rents of below S$1/m²/month—reflecting the rent control policies. After relocation, they were offered a five-year subsidy on rents. Table A7.1 illustrates the pattern of rent subsidies offered to commercial tenants in the 1960s, 1970s and 1980s. Note the basic market rent is reduced by 10 percent before the subsidy is calculated.

Table A7.1: COMMERCIAL RENT SCHEDULES FOR MARKET, AND SUBSIDIZED
TENANTS, 1960, 1970 AND 1980 LOCATING IN " TRANSIT FACILITIES"
(S$/m²)

	1960	1970	1980
Market Rent	2.00	5.00	8.00
Basic 10% Discount	1.80	4.50	7.20
Gradual Discount:			
1st year	0.90	2.25	3.60
2nd year	1.08	2.70	4.32
3rd year	1.26	3.15	5.04
4th year	1.44	3.60	5.76
5th year	1.62	4.05	6.48
6th year	1.80	4.50	7.20

In the 1970s, the transit facilities became permanent and were constructed of concrete, although lacking air conditioning and escalators. They were multistory (5) and were sited near redevelopment areas. The same gradual rent subsidy was offered, but the market base rent was S$5.00. In the early 1980s, the third stage of transit facilities was developed: these were essentially shopping centers, equipped with escalators and air conditioning. The market rents for these facilities was S$8.00/m²/month.

In 1985, transit facilities were no longer provided; instead, shopkeepers were provided with a cash grant compensation. In 1985, the amount per shophouse structure (for permanent structures of under 200 m²) was S$58,000. In 1987, this amount was raised to S$76,000, where it remains. Permanent structures of over 200 m² now receive S$101,000. Currently, small shops in transit facilities receive S$26,000. According to URA staff, the cash compensation system is well received by shopkeepers. There are few complaints with the payment and the shopkeepers can relocate to any building they wish.

Industrial Uses

First, it is important to point out that Singapore developed as a trading center and it did not have the massive industrial base that is common to Shanghai, Tianjin or Guangzhou. Consequently, there was little industrial relocation in Singapore. For the industrial development taking place, the government built industrial estates on the outskirts of the city and relocated firms to them, using exactly the same process and subsidy arrangement as outlined above for commercial uses. In 1985, the government ceased constructing industrial estates for redevelopment relocation purposes and instead offered cash compensation for industrial enterprises being relocated. In 1985, the cash grant was S$26,000 per facility, and was raised to S$34,000 in 1987, where it remains.

Residential Uses

In 1960, the Singapore government commenced its program of public housing construction, building 10-story elevator-serviced buildings. Back then, rents were S$20 a month for a one-room unit, S$40 for a two-room unit, and S$60 a month for a three-room unit. In addition, tenants paid S$3-6 a month for services. In the old rent-controlled residential areas, tenants normally paid about S$10 per month rent for a one-room unit of low quality. These units averaged 10 m² in size. The new units that households moved into averaged 60-70 m². For relocation hardships, tenants receive S$3,000 per family and S$750 per individual.

Virtually no one returns to the area after redevelopment. Under the current system of homeownership and the Central Provident Fund, those tenants that are relocated can "jump the queue" and gain access to the Housing and Development Board (HDB) housing being sold.

On financing of infrastructure, all off-site services are provided by the URA, not the developer. The developer is responsible for all on-site infrastructure. In addition, the government authorizes the levying of a development charge on privately held lands that is to be used in a way that is essentially different from the purposes for which the ground was originally used.

Between 1971 and 1980, 3,464 farmers were resettled. Of these, 1,983 received units, 574 received land, and 341 found their own accommodation and received cash compensation. The remainder, 566, received cash compensation. In the central area, between 1974 and 1985, 6,007 nonresidential users were relocated (300 in 1975/76, 941 in 1984/85). Most found their own relocation—4,075—and half received a cash grant. The rest received HDB compensation. Table A7.2 provides a good indication of relocation activities in Singapore. It compares cleared relocation cases, for both residential and commercial users, with total constructed units. Up until 1982, the total is based on HDB output (it excludes units produced by the Housing and Urban Development Corporation). After 1982, the total construction output reflects both the HDB and the URA. The level of activity is considerable, and it clearly surpasses what took place in US cities. It certainly is far above redevelopment activity in West European cities from the 1970s onward. It might equal activities in the immediate post-war period.

Housing Development Board, Government of Singapore

Singapore's HDB is in its second generation of redevelopment. The initial period, starting shortly after it was granted independence in 1959, was directed toward the rapid redevelopment of slum and squatter areas in and around the city center. In the initial stages, the units were mostly occupied by tenants without title or they were rented from landlords.

In 1960, Singapore had a quarter of a million persons living in slum areas, and another 330,000 living in squatter areas. Most of the slum areas were in and around the central area and were covered by rent control. Most units were severely dilapidated and slum landownership was highly fragmented, making land assembly difficult. Furthermore, rent control provided no incentive. In short, private redevelopment was impossible.

In response, the government amended its compulsory land acquisition powers and began taking steps to acquire land for redevelopment. Under the 1973 Land Acquisition Act, the compensation for acquired land as provided for in the Act is the market value of land as of November 30, 1973 or at the date of Gazette Notification, whichever is lower, to ensure that the cost of compensation will not fluctuate too widely. Market value is determined on the basis of the existing use or the zoning of the land, whichever is lower. The potential future value of the land in some more intensive use is not considered. These strict measures were imposed to curb speculation and to curtail the rising cost of land acquisition the government was experiencing in the 1970s as it aggressively purchased land.

In 1981, the Land Acquisition Act was again modified, and now owners of private property are paid up to the market value of the property or S$600,000 which ever is less. (This is in sharp contrast to Hong Kong's policy that LDC must negotiate the purchase of land in designated redevelopment areas, and only if all avenues have been exhausted will the government step in to compulsorily acquire land.)

The process of compulsory land acquisition begins with a proposal for acquisition, which is made by the HDB or other government authority. These proposals are

Table A7.2: SINGAPORE REDEVELOPMENT RELOCATION ACTIVITY

Year	Total units		Percent cases/constructed
	Cases cleared	Constructed	
1961	294	7,320	4.0
1962	817	12,230	6.7
1963	1,181	10,085	11.7
1964	3,643	13,028	28.0
1965	6,510	10,085	64.6
1966	6,018	12,659	47.5
1967	5,984	12,098	49.5
1968	5,863	14,135	41.5
1969	6,519	13,096	49.8
1970	6,125	14,251	43.0
1971	3,882	16,147	24.0
1972	4,060	20,252	20.0
1973/74	12,067	23,224	52.0
1974/75	10,980	26,169	42.0
1975/76	12,011	28,027	42.9
1976/77	11,015	30,024	36.7
1977/78	15,018	30,406	49.4
1978/79	16,443	30,176	54.5
1979/80	18,052	27,189	66.4
1980/81	15,033	19,875	75.6
1981/82	12,665	16,366	77.4
1982/83	14,855	20,918	71.0
1983/84	17,868	42,400/a	42.1
1984/85	21,958	70,345/a	31.2
1989/90	2,107	11,979/a	17.6
1990/91	3,151	13,805/a	22.8

/a Includes units from URA built after 1982.

carefully scrutinized by government and go through multiple reviews. After the approval is given by the President, it is gazetted. Next, the acquisition proceedings commence. Owners can appeal, and take their case to the Appeals Board.

The acquisition process is complemented by a resettlement program. In principle, every household requiring relocation is offered alternative accommodation. In 1957, a Resettlement Department was established to handle relocation and resettlement. Since its inception in March 1985, 230,000 resettlement cases have been cleared.

Second-Stage Redevelopment—Upgrading Old HDB Projects

Starting in 1980, HDB began redeveloping some of its older rental projects which do not measure up to present housing estate standards. Specific projects are those that have a high portion of three-room units and have high vacancy rates. The process of redevelopment of these areas is programmed over a 140-week cycle.

In these outdated projects, many tenants have moved out to purchase larger flats, and in some cases the vacancy rate is 50 percent. Those who remain are typically the elderly and have low incomes. Since these sitting tenants have week-to-week tenancy, they are served notice of the intention of HDB to redevelop the area. They are offered the choice of moving to another rental flat, or purchasing a new unit. There is never any guarantee that the sitting tenant will be permitted to return to the site.

Of the sitting tenants, approximately 50 percent opt to purchase a flat. They are provided some incentives: they can obtain 95 percent financing as opposed to 80 percent when purchasing a three-room unit (90 percent financing for four- to five-room units). They pay the going rate for the unit; they do not get a price discount; and the interest rate and the term of the mortgage is the same as for other qualified Singapore citizens.

Given that the typical price of a three-room unit ranges from S$22,700 in new towns to S$36,200 in the city center, that the interest rate is 4.64 percent, and that the term of the mortgages is 25 years, these low-income elderly households would need to pay between S$121.60 and S$193.89 per month for new three-room units. While these mortgage terms are attractive, they are well above the current rents for three-room units—S$26.00 to S$33.00 per month. Consequently, about half of the sitting tenants choose to relocate to other rental accommodations.

Commercial shops located in HDB projects to be redeveloped are not provided with relocation assistance. Instead, they receive a cash compensation of S$38,000 per shop. They receive modest preferential treatment in seeking new locations in HDB new towns or in other redeveloped areas. While they must complete with other businesses in the normal tender process used to secure space, their tender bid is increased by a 10 percent "preferential margin."

In the 1960s, when the redevelopment of slum and squatter areas was in full swing, many shops were relocated to HDB projects. This turned out to be problematic and many of the shops failed because they were inappropriate for the neighborhood-oriented centers or simply because too many shops were programmed into the early HDB centers.

In light of these failures and recognition of serious design problems resulting from the programming of retail activities into ground-floor apartment blocks, HDB restructured the planning and programming of commercial spaces. First, in reflection of the changing patterns of shopping behavior, where households go to large shopping centers to do their comparison and fashion goods shopping, commercial space in neighborhoods has been down-scaled to include only convenience goods stores. Second, because of design problems related to user conflicts, commercial activities in HDB centers have been consolidated into stand-alone centers. This redesign has solved space usage conflicts, and it also allows for these commercial centers to be located on the edges of projects to attract patrons traveling on arterial streets.

Resettlement Policy

Of the three cities surveyed, Singapore has the most effective program of resettlement. Affected households in HDB housing redevelopment projects are provided with the option of taking either replacement rental housing, or the purchase of a new unit. Households having huts and improvements are provided with cash compensation of for the loss of their assets, and they receive a disturbance/transportation allowance. The system of compensation seem to be well received, and there is a high incidence of households opting for purchase of new units. Between 1974 and 1985, the percentage of all redevelopment resettlement households opting to purchase new units increased from 69 to 92 percent (however, the current rate in the old HDB project redevelopments is lower—50 percent).

By combining a effective resettlement program with an aggressive housing delivery system, Singapore's HDB and URA have made impressive strides in urban redevelopment. They have been able to skillfully balance public and community interests with those of the private sector. Such a model is worthy of further in-depth assessment to gauge its potential applicability in the People's Republic of China.

ANNEX 8

ASSESSING THE FINANCIAL PERFORMANCE OF RESIDENTIAL REDEVELOPMENT PROJECTS

Introduction

The redevelopment of residential areas in Chinese cities is closely regulated by local and provincial authorities. In virtually all cities surveyed, redevelopment corporations must have the prices of newly constructed housing units targeted for the domestic market approved by the local price bureaus. These price reviews are very thorough and, in most cities, the prices of new units are set on a cost plus profit basis. Thus, the actual profitability of a typical redevelopment project is regulated. However, in virtually all cases, the sales price of the domestically sold housing is set at that level which will generate enough revenues to fully finance the redevelopment project.

The policy followed in most redevelopment projects is to set the price of commodity housing at that level where costs are recovered, including a modest markup for profit. In cities where generous on-site replacement of demolished housing is the norm, the markup is enormous, and can reach 300 percent. As illustrated in Table A8.1, the break-even prices of commodity housing vary considerably across redevelopment projects, ranging from a low of Y 641 for Tianjin's Pingshan Road project, to Y 5,611 for the overseas-oriented Hui Yi project in Shanghai. The average break-even sales price, excluding the Hui Yi project, is Y 1,974/m^2. The average cost of construction for these same 10 projects is Y 1,072/m^2. Thus, the break-even price for these 10 projects is 1.84 times above the actual cost of construction and profit. The markup to recover total project costs implies that the purchasers of commodity housing units pay an average of 84 percent over the average cost (plus profit) of redevelopment projects.

The typical approach to pricing and cost recovery reflects the absence of long-term financing for real estate development and the failure of rents to cover the real capital costs of new construction. The only way to pay for replacement units, given the government policies outlined in Annex 9, is for the REDC to recover the costs from those who can pay—the purchasers of commodity housing. This strategy produces two serious problems which limit its long-term sustainability. First, there are enormous distributional questions associated with the cost recovery. Should purchasers of new units pay inflated prices for their units in order to finance replacement for existing residents of these redevelopment areas? What are the implications of having enterprises (the dominant purchasers of commodity housing in redevelopment projects) finance the replacement of old municipal and privately owned housing in inner-city areas? Why should the workers of one enterprise subsidize the housing of other enterprises?

The second problem generated by the pricing strategy is that, in some cases, enterprises or individuals are not willing to pay the inflated prices. This is because they can

Table A8.1: BREAK-EVEN PRICES FOR COMMODITY HOUSING IN REDEVELOPMENT PROJECTS

Project name	Percent on-site resettlement (%)	Break-even price of housing/m² (Yuan)	Average construction cost/m² (Yuan)	Ratio of break-even price to cost (%)
An Deng	0	877	473	185
Jin Hua	90	2,592	1,006	258
Xiao Fuqing	100	1,559	454	343
Jian Guo	0	3,154	3,000	105
Hu Lang	100	3,727	2,218	168
Hui Yi	0	5,611	5,611	100
Ordinary Citizen	90	2,320	1,200	193
Tian He	45	1,924	850	226
Ying Xiang	86	1,744	808	216
Pingshan	100	641	324	198
Wujiayao	100	1,210	387	313
Average		2,305	1,485	155
Average without Hui Yi		1,974	1,072	184

Source: Redevelopment Project Survey, 1991, 1992.

avoid the costs by purchasing housing in greenfield areas where there are no redevelopment costs to shoulder. In some cases, they may even build their own housing. In market economies, it would be extremely difficult for the developers of inner-city redevelopment projects to simply pass on the costs of replacement housing, because they face price and product competition from other developers.

In Shanghai, there are four channels of housing supply: apartments built by property development companies which are put directly on the market (typically these units are located in suburban and "greenfield areas"); apartments invested in by the government which will be allocated as welfare or sold to government employees; apartments built by government bodies which will be allocated to employees of government and the apartment construction company building the project; commodity housing produced in redevelopment projects which can sold to individuals and enterprises. Government agencies can clearly avoid paying higher prices by developing their own projects. Enterprises have the option to purchase units in either redevelopment or new-area projects. The current price differential for units in inner urban areas is nearly 100 percent, and as a result, unless the redevelopment project is extremely well-located, enterprises and individuals will opt for lower-cost suburban housing.

Why is there such tremendous variation between the average cost of redevelopment projects and the break-even sales prices of these redevelopment projects? In this section, we will assess price cost variations and describe what factors influence high commodity housing prices. The focus of the assessment is on FAR, replacement space standards, on-site versus off-site replacement, provision of public facilities and payment of fees and taxes.

Floor Area Ratio and Redevelopment Cost and Financing

Based on a review of redevelopment projects and the financial simulation of redevelopment project cost and potential revenue generation it is apparent that the floor area ratio of new redevelopment projects is the single-most important determinant of redevelopment project feasibility. The greater the increase in FAR, the more commodity housing and commercial space can be built on a redeveloped site. Using data for 10 of the 11 surveyed redevelopment projects, Figure A8.1 illustrates this relationship. As it shows, the percentage of a new redevelopment's constructed area going to commodity sales space increases with the increase in postredevelopment FAR. The more additional space that can be built, the more commodity space a developer will have to sell. With more space, the break-even commodity housing price can be reduced and brought closer to the actual cost of the project.

Figure A8.1: RELATIONSHIP BETWEEN INCREASE IN FAR AND THE PERCENT OF NEW CONSTRUCTION THAT IS SOLD AS COMMODITY HOUSING OR COMMERCIAL SPACE

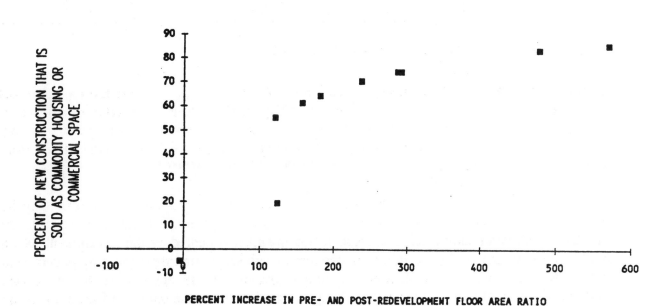

Figure A8.2 illustrates the impact of increasing FAR on the break-even price of commodity space. This figure is based on simulation test results of a financial model developed for a typical redevelopment project. The project has a site area of 50,000 m², had a preredevelopment constructed area of 40,000 m² (a FAR of 0.8). The site housed 1,086 households in a total residential constructed area of 38,000 m² (approximately 35 m² per unit). It also contained 2,000 m² of public facilities. The postredevelopment simulation (baseline case) assumes that the site is redeveloped to a FAR of 2.0 and contains 100,000 m² of constructed space. Reflecting practices in many cities, the simulation assumes that all households are resettled on-site and that each household receives an average of 50 m² of constructed area for a total area of 54,300 m². Additional public facilities are constructed to reach 5,000 m². After these allocations are made, there is an additional 40,700 m² of commodity space. Total average construction costs (both hard and soft costs) are assumed to average Y 1,000/m².

Figure A8.2: BREAK-EVEN SALES PRICE BY FLOOR AREA RATIO FOR PROTOTYPICAL REDEVELOPMENT PROJECT

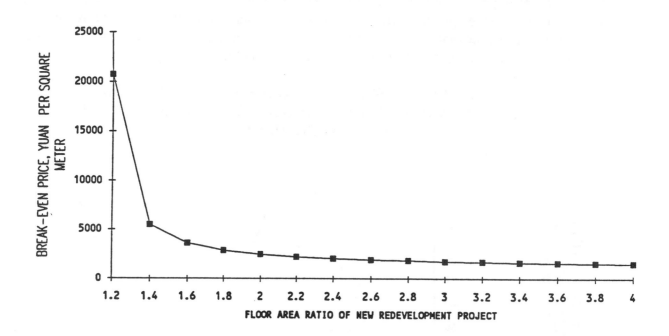

In Figure A8.2, it is assumed that the FAR of the redevelopment project varies from 1.2 to 4.0. As the graph illustrates, the break-even sales price from the project declines as the FAR increases. This decline reflects the fact that increases in FAR raise the portion of constructed area that can be sold as commodity space. However, the overall price structure of a typical project is also determined by other factors as well. In the next section, we consider the replacement policies of government in terms of the area of new space provided for each square meter of sold area.

Replacement Space Standards

Discussions with housing planners and government official across China reveal a preoccupation with the per capita living area and constructed area. In most cities, housing policies are targeted on goals aimed at increasing per capita residential areas. As described above, in most redevelopment areas per capita space is limited and there is considerable overcrowding. For projects where most households were resettled on-site, the size of preredevelopment dwelling units ranged from 14 to 50 m², averaging about 31 m² per unit. After redevelopment, on-site space allocations increased to an average of 59 m², a 90 percent increase. Only in the case of Guangzhou's Jin Hua redevelopment project were space allocations reduced after redevelopment from 44 to 42 m².

The degree to which more space is allocated to tenants receiving on-site replacement housing will significantly effect the break-even prices of commodity housing. For a given level of total constructed area (set by planning and development controls), there will be less commodity space for sale as the amount of replacement housing space increases. Figure A8.3 illustrates the relationship between space allocation standards and the portion of net new space sold on the commodity market. As the graph illustrates, as the ratio of replacement space for old housing space increases, the percentage of a redevelopment project's net new constructed area which can be developed decreases. The rate of decrease is faster with lower levels of FAR.

Figure A8.3: RELATIONSHIP BETWEEN REPLACEMENT SPACE STANDARDS AND THE PORTION OF NET NEW CONSTRUCTION SOLD ON COMMODITY MARKET

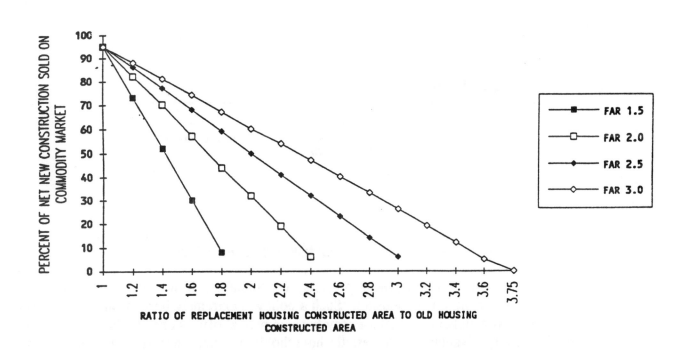

The impact of space allocation policies on the portion of commodity space in a project directly effects the break-even sales price of the commodity housing. In Figure A8.4, simulations of variations in break-even prices are provided for a range of replacement of housing policies. The prices have been normalized, with the break-even price set to equal 100 when the replacement ratio is 1:1. The figure vividly illustrates the price implications of offering generous replacement space standards, assuming that all replacement housing is to be financed through commodity sales. Depending on the FAR of the redevelopment project, prices rise dramatically when the replacement ratio increases beyond 1.6, 2.2, 2.8 and 3.4 for FARs of 1.5, 2.0, 2.5 and 3.0, respectively. In cases where considerable additional housing needs to be provided and resettlement is to occur on-site, the FAR will need to be increased, probably doubled or tripled. In cases where such increases in FAR are not feasible, then redevelopment planners should consider relocating households to other sites. The next section assesses the cost implications of off-site relocation.

<u>Figure A8.4</u>: RELATIONSHIP BETWEEN REPLACEMENT SPACE STANDARDS AND BREAK-EVEN SALES PRICE OF COMMODITY SPACE FOR VARIOUS FARs

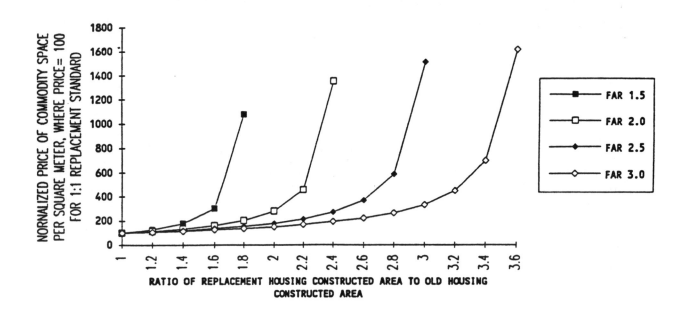

<u>On-Site Versus Off-Site Housing Replacement</u>

In most redevelopment projects, considerable, if not all, households are provided with on-site replacement housing. Such a policy is extremely burdensome for several reasons. If a site has a higher potential use, say for commercial offices or retail facilities, it will always be financially advantageous to resettle households off-site, since all space in the new project could be sold at considerably higher prices. But even under circumstances where the housing units are replaced and where the sales price of commodity housing in such projects is strictly limited to a price which achieves cost recovery, it may still be advantageous for most households to be resettled off-site. By shifting the replacement housing to off-site locations, redevelopment projects can increase the percentage of new construction devoted to commodity sales. On the other hand, off-site replacement housing requires the purchase of land and buildings for resettlement and it may or may not be less expensive to provide than on-site units.

If off-site replacement housing can be provided for sitting tenants less expensively than on-site provision, it will always be financially advantageous for redevelopment area households to be relocated off-site. Off-site replacement costs are usually lower per square meter than on-site cost because the housing is usually of lower density (six-story versus high-rise) and built with lower-cost materials. Another reason is that off-site relocation does not require the provision of temporary housing or relocation benefits. On pure cost terms, off-site relocation can be less expensive if it avoids building high-rise structures and if suburban land costs are low.

In the Shanghai Jian Guo redevelopment project, all households were relocated off-site. The 1,394 households, which had an average of 15 m² of constructed area were allocated 60 m², a total of 83,640 m². The cost of the relocation was Y 79,458,000, an average of Y 950/m². The total cost of constructing new space on the site was Y 176,091,200, an average of Y 1,992/m². In inner-city redevelopment projects, like Jian Guo, households are relocated to suburban projects and housed in six- to eight-story walkup buildings.

However, in order to successfully implement off-site relocation, REDCs must offer a variety of inducements to encourage relocation. The most common form of inducement is to increase the allocation of replacement space to households electing to relocate. For example, in Shanghai and Guangzhou, households agreeing to relocate to suburban areas will be provided with an additional 20 to 30 percent more space, depending on household size, crowding and the initial amount of space. These additional inducements can reduce the financial benefits of promoting off-site relocation by increasing the size and, thus, the cost of off-site housing. While these inducements are appropriate, under the current form of pricing and allocation, they may completely offset the economic benefits of increased off-site relocation.

To assess the benefits and costs of off-site versus on-site relocation, the baseline redevelopment project outlined above was used to simulate the effects of variations in the percentage of on-site replacement housing provided. A number of simulations were prepared, reflecting differing assumptions regarding on-site versus off-site construction costs, and how much additional space is provided to those agreeing to relocate to off-site locations. Twelve separate simulations were run, and their results are presented in Figures A8.5 and A8.6. Figure A8.5 assumes that residents agreeing to relocate off-site will receive a space allocation bonus of 25 percent. Figure A8.6 assumes that off-site resettlers receive a 50 percent space bonus. Both figures provide break-even price estimates for three overall housing replacement policies and two different cost differentials between on-site and off-site housing construction. The three replacement policies assume a replacement ratio of 1:1, 1:2 and 1:3. Six of 12 simulations assume that the costs of housing replacement are the same for both on-site and off-site locations, and six assume that off-site costs are 50 percent of on-site housing construction costs.

Figure A8.5: BREAK-EVEN PRICES BY PERCENT OF ON-SITE RESETTLEMENT, ASSUMING 25% OFF-SITE BONUS FOR VARIOUS HOUSING REPLACEMENT POLICIES AND COSTS (Yuan/m²)

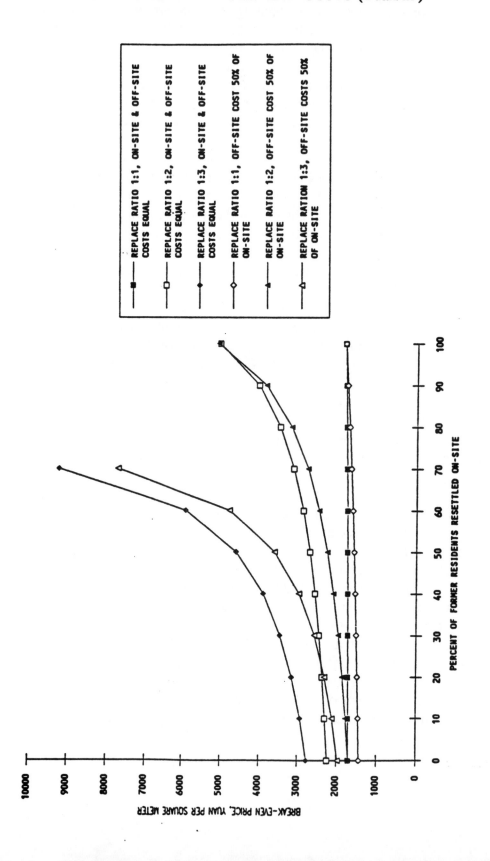

Figure A8.6: BREAK-EVEN PRICES BY PERCENT OF ON-SITE RESETTLEMENT,
ASSUMING 50% OFF-SITE BONUS FOR VARIOUS HOUSING
REPLACEMENT POLICIES AND COSTS (Yuan/m²)

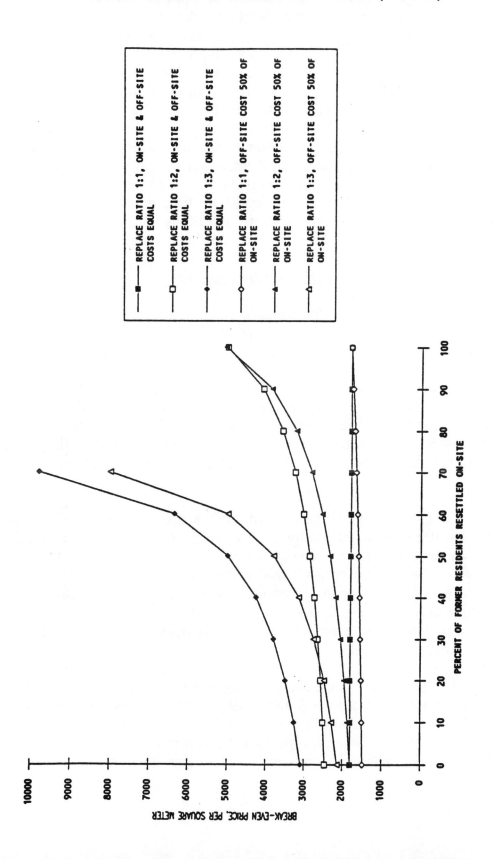

The results of the simulations reveal that, in all cases, the break-even prices of commodity space increase with the percentage of residents resettled on site. Redevelopment projects, which provide generous replacement benefits to sitting tenants, can achieve the greatest cost savings by lowering the percentage of residents resettled on site. This suggests that when existing tenants are to be provided with two to three square meters of new floor area for each square meter demolished, redevelopment projects should provide little on-site resettlement.

These results hold even when the those agreeing to resettle off-site receive a space bonus of 25 to 50 additional space. If the overall replacement ratio is 1:2 or more, redevelopment projects should encourage off-site resettlement. The overall patterns illustrated in Figures A8.5 and A8.6 suggest that cost differentials between on-site and off-site housing construction modestly affect the impacts of on-site versus off-site resettlement. In cases where the construction costs between on- and off-site construction are similar, the benefits of shifting replacement housing off-site are less that when off-site costs are lower. It is important to point out that of the three factors assessed in the simulation, the overall replacement ratio is the critical factor determining the potential impacts of shifting replacement housing off-site. Construction cost differentials and off-site bonuses have far less impact on break-even prices.

Provision of Public Facilities

In many of the redevelopment projects assessed, district and municipal governments require significant contributions of public facilities. Since, in virtually all cities we assessed, these facilities are turned over free-of-charge to the local government, they represent a significant cost of redevelopment. As illustrated in Figure A8.7, in some of the redevelopment projects, a substantial portion of the net new space constructed went to public facilities. Of the 10 redevelopment projects, seven were required to provide public facilities. Of those projects providing public facilities, between 1,402 and 163,648 m² of space were provided, representing between 4 and 41 percent of the total net new construction. The greatest contribution both in terms of square meters and as a percent of net new space was Guangzhou's Jin Hua project.

In some cities, public facilities are required according to planning standards and vary between 5 and 10 percent of the constructed residential area. Planning standards for shops, clinics, schools and other facilities are somewhat greater than found in other countries, but they are not excessive. What typically occurs is that redevelopment projects are viewed as "golden geese" which can be squeezed to produce citywide services such as markets, clinic and cultural facilities. This is clearly the case in the Jin Hua project, where government planners have loaded numerous facilities onto the project. This pattern exists because the space is provided at no cost to the local government.

Instead the cost is shouldered by the purchasers of commodity housing. To illustrate the cost impacts of excessive public facility dedication requirements, Figure A8.7 illustrates the results of a simulation of break-even prices for various public facilities. Using the baseline model discussed in Annex 9, Figure A8.7 illustrates the change in break-even prices as the percentage of public facilities in increased. The figure reveals that break-even sales prices

Figure A8.7: NORMALIZED BREAK-EVEN PRICES BY PERCENT OF TOTAL CONSTRUCTED AREA DEVOTED TO PUBLIC FACILITIES

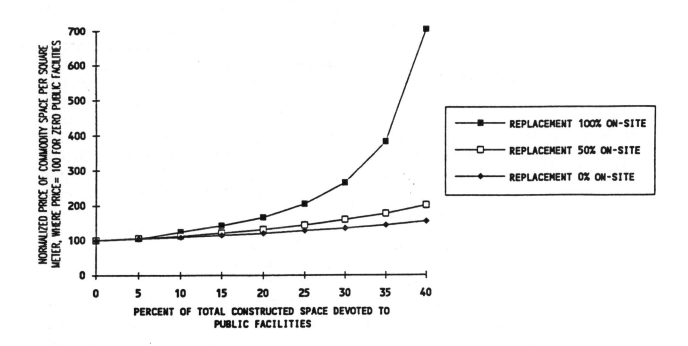

of commodity space increase as the percentage of public facilities required in a project increases, especially when all housing is replaced on-site.

Policy reforms are needed to curb the practice of redevelopment projects having to shoulder the costs of public facilities that are used by citywide residents. When such facilities are needed, the local government should pay for them and not attempt to extract the costs out of the redevelopment project. In other countries, space used for shops and markets is either sold or leased to private operators. In the case of public space, land is usually dedicated for facilities and the government is the one who actually pays for and builds the space. Most of the developers we talked to suggested that they be able to sell space for shops and markets instead of giving it over to district authorities. This is obviously an issue worth considering.

Fees and Taxes

All redevelopment projects are required to pay a variety of taxes and fees. In some cases, these fees and taxes are extraordinary, amounting to over 15 percent of total redevelopment costs. Table A8.2 presents estimates of total fees and taxes levied for the redevelopment projects surveyed in this report. As revealed in the table, the incidence of taxes and fees varies considerably across cities. In Tianjin, only token fees and taxes are charged on projects and, instead, redevelopment projects are required to provide substantial off-site infrastructure. In Fuzhou, modest taxes and fees are charged for redevelopment. In the An

Deng project (the off-site resettlement project), fees and taxes amounted to about 9 percent of project costs.

Table A8.2: FEES AND TAXES PAID BY REDEVELOPMENT PROJECTS

Project name	Fees & taxes (Yuan)	As a percent of total project cost (%)	Per m² of marketable area (Yuan)
An Deng	750,000	9.3	82
Jin Hua	115,988,000	15.6	546
Xiao Fuqing	1,213,699	17.4	271
Hu Lang	12,250,000	11.0	348
Hui Yi	4,575,000	6.6	245
Ordinary Citizen	35,500,000	7.1	320
Tian He	2,090,000	12.6	275
Ying Xiang	18,800,000	12.3	214
Pingshan	14,504	0.1	1
Wujiayao	101,693	0.4	5

Source: Redevelopment Project Survey, 1991, 1992.

In Guangzhou and Shanghai, there are a variety of taxes and fees which redevelopment projects must pay. In the Jin Hua project, in addition to the onerous public facility requirements, the redevelopers must also pay out nearly Y 116 million in fees and taxes, a staggering Y 546/m² of marketable area, accounting for 16 percent of total project costs. In Shanghai, all redevelopment projects are required to pay Y 95/m² to the Shanghai Municipal Government as an off-site infrastructure fee. Other fees and taxes increase total payments to between Y 213 to Y 555/m² of marketable space. In percentage terms, fees and taxes range from a low of 6.6 percent of total project costs to 17.4 percent.

It seems clear that taxes and fees account for a considerable portion of redevelopment costs. While these fees and taxes are used to support the construction of capital plant and to provide services of benefit to redevelopment area residents, it is often the case that redevelopment activities are used to finance projects which benefit a wider audience. Similar to arrangements for the provision of public facilities, redevelopment projects should not be pressed upon to fund projects providing citywide benefits.

ANNEX 9

STRATEGIC PLANNING IN HONG KONG AND SINGAPORE

Hong Kong

Hong Kong's Strategic Plan is divided into three tiers: a territorial strategy plan; seven subregional planning statements; and local, district-level plans. Applicable to each of the three levels, there is an accompanying "Hong Kong Planning Standards and Guidelines" government manual, which is revised periodically and is not statutory in nature.

The Strategic Plan, at the territorial level, was first introduced in 1984 after examining four development scenarios, and their associated implications. It is citywide in scale, and multisectoral in nature, covering investment plans, financial resource requirements and institutional details needed to implement a 10-15 year land use scenario that is associated with the achievement of various socioeconomic and environmental objectives. The Plan is subject to periodic monitoring and "feedback," allowing revisions to be incorporated from time to time.

The subregional development statements provide land use plans and accompanying texts that detail planned land use zones, and necessary sectoral policies and plans raised by key issues encountered in elaborating the recommended plans. These statements have a "shelf life" of 10 years, and are meant to translate territorial goals into concrete regional plans, while helping district planners pay heed to the larger picture as individual developments are executed. The statements cover such areas as assumed population and employment targets, general land use plans, transportation and environmental problems to be tackled, the phasing of major public works, building height and urban design guidelines, principal implementing agencies and coordinating mechanisms. Special "action plan areas" meriting particular attention are also highlighted.

Local or district plans involve the development of statutory outline zoning plans. These plans are prepared for existing and potential urban areas and show areas zoned for specific purposes, based on existing and forecasted uses. Each plan is subject to public inspection for two months, then reviewed at the highest level of government, where all objections are examined and appropriate changes are made. The plans are then issued as laws.

Attached to each statutory plan is a schedule of notes that set out uses which are always permitted in a zone, those that require permission from local authorities, and those that are banned. As noted, government agencies have nonstatutory development and layout plans that accompany the district statutory plans; these are used to help facilitate needed infrastructure development.

The whole process of urban land use planning is overseen by the Governor, assisted by the Executive and Legislative Councils. Various executive agencies are involved in the process, including a land development policy committee, a land building advisory committee, a transport advisory committee, and an environmental pollution advisory committee, the financial secretary, as well as the various executing authorities or boards.

Singapore

Singapore began with a conventional statutory Master Plan, which was completed in 1955 and adopted in 1959. It was meant to be a statutory instrument used to regulate land use through zoning, density, and plot ratio controls; while reserving land for public facilities, open space and infrastructure. It had a decidedly decentralization bent, and included a broad greenbelt around the central city and plans for new towns and other designated urban areas. Maps were prepared for the Central Area, other city and town development zones, and the rural parts of the island. The Plan was flexible enough to allow for ad-hoc rezoning based on new plans or planning reevaluations of any specific area. Each Map was accompanied by written statements that elaborated on the Maps, and outlined uses that were automatically allowed, those that would be considered, and those that were banned.

Soon the Master Plan was declared inadequate to deal with the changing pace of development, and the redirection of the local economy. Instead, it has been retained as a document, revised every five years, that controls private development and legalizes the charging of exactions from developers who are granted favorable rezoning decisions that increase the profitability of their development by removing certain Master Plan constraints.

As a legal document, the Master Plan was set aside for the statutory agencies that are responsible for much of Singapore's development, including the Housing and Development Board, the Urban Redevelopment Authority, and the Jurong Industrial Corporation. The new instrument guiding development was labeled the Concept Plan, and its elaboration coincided with a shift to a strong center-city development strategy, setting many decentralization objectives aside.

The first Concept Plan was issued in 1971 and revised in 1987-91. Its aim was to set strategic directions for more detailed local planning, while laying out a transportation plan to guide land use trends over time. That transport plan was centered on the Central Area and radiated out along three corridors, with associated circumferential ring roads.

The Concept Plan sets goals for the year 2000, 2010, 2030, and a final year "x". It is linked to a set of associated plans covering not only transport, but also parks and waterways, the natural habitat, and plans related to leisure, culture, and sports facilities.

The broad vision plans provide the basis for 50 development guide plans, one for each of the island zones. The plans lay out land use, control parameters and urban design guidelines. They are based on existing conditions and forecasts, but are meant to be flexible and developer-friendly. All plans are subject to public inspection and review, and various objections lead to modifications before plans are finalized. These plans are accompanied by urban design plans that provide greater detail concerning the guidelines to be followed in designing the height, mass, and form of buildings, while providing for pedestrian and vehicular access, plus open spaces. More recently, conservation plans, covering an initial 100 hectares of the Central Area, have been introduced to control urban renewal, in recognition of the historic fabric and economic value of historic preservation.

Obviously, all private developers must obtain the requisite approvals. Local allocation of land for public sector uses is, however, vetted at the highest level by a Master Plan Committee, headed by the chairman of the Urban Redevelopment Authority; these plans are subject to detailed review meant to conserve land.

ANNEX 10

REGISTRATION OF PROPERTY INTERESTS

An appropriate and functional registration system would record, in one location, all the potential and multiple rights associated with a single parcel of land. Potential rights include:

(a)   Above-Ground Rights

    (i)   Air-use rights
    (ii)   Building ownership
    (iii)   Stratified building ownership (for multiple dwelling and multiple use buildings)
    (iv)   Occupation rights (through allocation system)
    (v)   Residence leases (for compensation)
    (vi)   Commercial leases (for compensation)
    (vii)   utility easements
    (viii) road rights-of-way

(b)   Ground-Use Rights

    (i)   Land ownership
    (ii)   Land-use rights (through allocation)
    (iii)   Land-use rights leases (for compensation)

(c)   Below-Ground Rights

    (i)   Mineral extraction rights
    (ii)   Oil and gas extraction rights

(d)   Foundation Financing

Financial instruments:
    (i)   Mortgages using ground leases as collateral
    (ii)   Mortgages using building or apartment ownership as collateral
    (iii)   Liens on property

Public access to determine what rights have been granted and to whom is essential to engendering the confidence required to promote financing of urban development.

An accurate legal description of a parcel of land is the foundation for an orderly registration of all related property rights.

ANNEX 11

CADASTRAL MAPPING

Cadastral Mapping and Geographic Information

The key to management of a market-oriented land use control system lies in the effectiveness of monitoring and adjustment mechanisms. The availability of information technologies offer urban planners and administrators a powerful tool with which to exercise more dynamic planning techniques, anticipate changes in the social and economic objectives of the community, and reduce negative regulatory impacts.

The cadaster is supported by a cadastral map prepared by the local land administration bureau. The map is prepared according to national standards set by SLA and shows the location, reference numbers and features of contiguous land parcels as defined by the certificate diagrams in relation to the local topographic survey control system (often linked to the national survey control system). This enables the pinpointing of any parcel of land and the precise identification of its boundaries on the ground. In dense urban areas, the maps are prepared at a scale of 1:500 and each map covers an area of 5 hectares. In suburban and rural areas, where densities are low and collective parcel sizes are large, scales of 1:1,000 and 1:2,000 are used. A city such as Shanghai requires some 16,000 maps to cover the entire municipality (6,340 km²), an exercise which is expected to cost about Y 6 million; this is probably a serious underestimate. Updating is expected to occur at five-year intervals. Production of the cadastral maps is carried out where possible in conjunction with topographic mapping obtained from aerial photography. The cadastral information is generally obtained separately by ground survey methods and is overlaid on the topographic map base. This separate activity is relatively expensive since the ground survey methods used are relatively slow and manpower-intensive.[1] Some cities have created their own cadastral surveying capacity for this purpose; others have hired survey contractors (usually the provincial survey bureau), sometimes using competitive bidding (e.g., Chengdu). Methods of cadastral surveying by cheaper aerial surveying means have been developed by the NBSM (e.g., the Xi'an cadaster was produced in this way), but accuracy in locating the corner points remains a stumbling block.[2] A discussion of some alternative cadastral mapping methodologies is provided below.

---

[1] According to SLA estimates, land ownership investigation currently costs about Y 100,000/km², and land registration about Y 42,000/km². It is proposed to recover these costs through increases in the registration tariffs.

[2] Conventional aerial photography enables a point on the ground to be located with an accuracy of about 50 cm compared to the SLA standard of 5 cm in urban areas and 20 cm in suburban areas.

Cadastral Mapping in Selected Urban Areas

The absence of a cadaster renders efficient land management well nigh impossible. Progress in the case study cities surveyed is mixed. Cadastral mapping of Shanghai's urban area, containing some 273,000 plots, is allegedly 82 percent complete. It was carried out over four years.[3] Current cadastral map production in Guangzhou Municipality is not only proceeding slowly, but also in a form which limits its usefulness and inhibits rapid processing of the leases or land use rights certificates. Mapping to date has covered about 180 km^2 of the 1,443 km^2 city proper area of Guangzhou. Plot diagrams relating to 57,000 plots have been prepared, compared to an estimated required total of 600,000. The diagrams are based on individual ground surveys for the most part, because the cadastral mapping does not denote boundaries with adequate precision. The cadastral mapping is adapted from low-order accuracy, topographic mapping which dates from 1978 and is due to be updated or resurveyed. In Chengdu, although 40 percent of the estimated 150,000 urban plots have been surveyed; cadastral mapping has barely begun elsewhere except for six county towns (1,387 km^2 from a total area of 12,390 km^2). A low-cost means for rapid cadaster production is clearly desirable.

Topographic surveys are a common basis for cadastral mapping in cities. Urban areas contain a lot of detail compared to rural areas and require maps of relatively large scale to convey the information. Cadasters in dense areas typically require a "large" scale of 1:1,000 or even 1:500 (which is also a convenient working scale for construction planning and utility mapping). Low-density or undeveloped areas can be mapped at 1:2,000. Maps can contain details covering about 5 ha at a scale of 1:500, or 25 ha at 1:1,000; hence, a large city with a built-up area of, say, 200 km^2 would require 4,000 map sheets at 1:500 or 800 sheets at 1:1,000. A ground survey would be the most critical component in time and cost terms, especially in urban areas with restricted sight distances. In order to minimize costs, surveys of large areas such as a city are usually carried out by mass-production techniques using

---

[3] Shanghai's 5,965 km^2 of suburban area contain an estimated 1.5 million plots. The cadaster, begun in 1988, is only 9 percent complete.

photogrammetric methods based on large-format aerial photography.4/   Although once controversial, large-scale aerial photography is now accepted as a suitable basis for 1:500 mapping in urban areas, but supplementary ground survey work may be required in very dense areas. Images from remote-sensing satellites, while capable of covering very large areas, do not yet yield a sufficiently detailed basis for larger-scale mapping.

A much lower cost alternative to large-format aerial photography has emerged in recent years in the form of small-format aerial photography. This technology uses a light aircraft and a 53 mm camera flying at, for example, 1,000 m above ground, to produce 1:20,000 scale negatives (i.e., covering 1 km^2); these can be enlarged to 1:1,000 scale prints. The prints can be digitized to create a database and generate maps of reasonable accuracy.5/

Where ground survey methods are essential in order to supplement information which cannot be determined from aerial photography, a system of digital field data collection is available. In this system, survey data are obtained by automatic surveying instruments (eliminating the need for tape measurements) and then entered in a field recorder. The data can be downloaded into a portable computer (PC) which is programmed to generate the cadastral

---

4/   Photogrammetry involves deducing ground measurements (horizontal and vertical distances) from aerial photographs. Producing maps by photogrammetry involves four steps: (a) aerial photography; (b) ground control point surveying; (c) photo rectification; and (d) cartography. The *photographs* are taken with a large-format (23 cm) aerial camera mounted in a specially equipped aircraft that is flown along a series of parallel flight lines at a constant height (depending on the detail required) to provide the coverage required and to provide adequate overlap between the photos. China's civil aviation authorities provide most aerial photography services in China. Accurately surveyed *control* points located on the ground and visible in the photographs are used to position the photos either individually or in blocks and help adjust them to an appropriate planimetric accuracy. The ground control points are often linked through either major and/or minor control surveys to the national geodetic survey network (established in China by the NBSM). The adjustment process is known as *rectification* which helps eliminate the natural distortions in the print image. Rectification is carried out by large precision instruments (analog plotters or the more modern analytical plotters). The investment in the plotters is considerable and these are typically available at the provincial-level survey and mapping bureaus, and some larger municipalities. Traditionally, information from the rectified photograph could either be selectively plotted automatically (usually in pencil) to the scale required and checked (by field surveys where necessary), or transformed as a whole directly into a reproducible orthophoto map. Plotting from analog plotters must then go through a *cartographic stage* to produce the final reproducible map. The resulting line map is usually traced by hand, in ink, on sheets of stable, transparent plastic film that have been preprinted with borders, title blocks, grids, scale, etc. More recently, analytical plotters have been developed which digitize the required information for inclusion in a computer database as well as automatic line-map plotting or orthophoto presentation.

5/   As noted, the technology was developed by the International Institute for Aerospace Survey and Earth Sciences, Netherlands. Wuhan Technical University of Surveying and Mapping is equipped to carry out this form of aerial photography and mapping in China.

map, parcel or plot diagrams and descriptions, as well as the information for a digital information system database.6/

Many municipal departments require maps for the performance of their day-to-day duties in planning, construction, and operations and maintenance (O&M). Many of China's cities have a 1:2,000 scale topographic map series and many have 1:1,000 and/or 1:500 maps of their denser areas. Such mapping is theoretically updated at five-year intervals, but budget constraints often prevent this. While each department might wish to obtain its own map series, there are considerably economies of scale in jointly obtaining a suitable map, although not all agencies' specifications are the same and some compromises must usually be made.7/ The advent of digitizing, however, has not only improved the ease and quality of mapping but, equally important, it has also provided an easy means of assembling a database for use in Land Information (LIS) or GIS. Such data must be coordinated, either by measurements from the map (i.e., rough coordinates, i.e., within 5 m) or directly from field measurements, if high precision is necessary (e.g., plot boundary corner points). It has become relatively easy and useful, therefore, to incorporate the high survey accuracy standards for a cadastral map into joint mapping program specifications.

The significance of a cadastral map lies partly as a tool for land management and partly in its role in registration of land titles. Many title systems use extracts from the cadaster plan as diagram inputs attached to deeds or certificates, e.g., Guangzhou's counties. Guangzhou City, however, currently uses a specially drawn diagram compiled from field measurements obtained from a unique site visit. Considerable time could be saved by using a cadastral plan extract. Although some field measurements would still be required, these could be obtained as part of a mass-survey program, as described above. The digitized information obtained could be used to produce the cadastral map and parcel diagrams.

6/   Such a system (Field Data Collection and Computer-Aided Mapping System) has been developed and is in use by the Research Institute of the Guangdong Provincial Land Administration Bureau.

7/   Planning Departments, for example, might have use for maps at 1:2,000 scale with a relatively low degree of accuracy (i.e., a 1 mm distortion on hard-copy media is equivalent to 2 meters on the ground). Engineering departments would generally wish to have maps accurate to within 50-100 mm on the ground (i.e., 0.1 to 0.2 mm on hard copy). Such accuracy is difficult to obtain in reality and key points are generally given x,y coordinates in order to locate them on the ground accurately. Cadastral maps should also incorporate a high degree of accuracy, and boundary corner points should be given coordinates obtained from field surveys or high-precision photogrammetry.

ANNEX 12

GEOGRAPHIC INFORMATION SYSTEMS (GIS)

Hardware and Software

The elements of a GIS configuration are:

(a)   data acquisition, i.e., a means of entering data in a digitized form into data storage such as by keyboarding (from written lists, for example), interaction with other compatible electronic databases, or scanning (from plans, photographs, remote-sensing images);

(b)   data storage, i.e., a database which stores information in a classified and interrelated way for future retrieval;

(c)   data management, i.e., tools for organizing, manipulating and analyzing the information;

(d)   data retrieval, i.e., means of transforming and visually presenting information in tabular or graphical output form and generating hard copies; and

(e)   data application software, i.e., programs which use the stored information for specific purposes (e.g., transport network modeling, terrain modeling, infrastructure maintenance planning, feasibility analysis, etc.).

Because of the immense data storage needed, early GIS were generally supported by costly mainframe or minicomputers. The computing power required is now available in inexpensive desktop 386- and 486-type microprocessor-based PCs. Even with the addition of essential hardware such as scanners, data storage devices, monitors, printers and plotters, a PC-based GIS workstation is still a relatively inexpensive option. Through network linking, several workstations can be served by a single computer. Software programs with various degrees of capability are readily available 1/ and Chinese-language versions are under development. Compatibility among the hardware and software (and information) components is of paramount importance, which in turn requires careful thought to the design of the GIS. Selection of equipment and software, however, will have much to do with the applications envisaged.

1/   PC-based GIS programs vary in capability and price from $1,000 to $3,000 each. Under current supplier terms for the software, one program is required for each user or workstation. Software for larger systems with greater capability, such as may be required by advanced municipal users, varies from $5,000 to $10,000. Such systems are often modular and can be built up progressively. Lower-priced software tends towards thematic or pin map production capability, whereas the larger systems include analytical features and applications programs and tend to have better data management capabilities.

Information Management

Basic Information

Through its unifying influence, the benefit of wide-scale GIS architecture to municipal operations is potentially very large. The systems development, engineering and training requirements are, however, considerable and implementation can take several years to complete. Moreover, information gathering and updating costs can be high. However, many applications can proceed on the basis of small-scale but powerful, "mixed technology" or Strategic Information Systems (SIS) that combine existing maps and hard-copy information with digital technology to confront immediate problems. The introduction of GIS-based methodologies and applications, therefore, need not (nor should not) wait for the development of a full-scale database. SIS development can proceed in a parallel fashion. The two versions would, over time, naturally converge into a single system.

In the approach to design of the full-scale database, it is also important to remembers that much information is available in sectoral agency files and databases, and need not necessarily be centrally stored or available to all. Hence, a modular, incremental development approach is possible. However, a fundamental information base is of common interest. The cadastral plan, if available, or an equivalent topographic plan, can provide this fundamental framework.

Since integration is an important strength of the GIS, the information stored in a GIS must be interrelated in order to serve this purpose. It is important that data be classified rationally and entries coded and addressed systematically to facilitate comparability. Currently, classification and coding standards are not available in China, although the NBSM is attempting to prepare draft standards. The basic relationship is positional; ideally, all data should be referenced to a common *cartesian coordinate* system. Most cities uses a cartesian or plan coordinate system (similar to a rectilinear grid) referenced to latitude and longitude for city maps. In China, the NBSM has established a system of geodetic control points accurately positioned with respect to latitude and longitude, which can be used as the origin for a local grid.2/

In designing the database, consideration of the scales of maps that may be required as output is important. The detail that can be shown at a large scale of 1:500 (a common scale for construction planning purposes) would be difficult to display at 1:2,000 (useful for small-area planning) or even more so at 1:5,000 or smaller (for large-area planning).

2/   A plan coordinate system or rectilinear grid has sides which are parallel and perfectly horizontal, in contrast to lines of longitude which converge on the Poles and like lines of latitude conform to the circular shape of the Earth. The local grid may be based on a North-South orientation or may be rotated to some degree for local convenience. The grid will, therefore, usually have a single reference to latitude and longitude as its origin. Latitude and longitude coordinates can be transformed to the local grid coordinates and vice versa, using a suitable orthogonal Mercator projection (e.g., Universal Transverse Mercator projection). Local coordinates are usually designated in x,y form.

Thus, the database management system must either be designed to suit a particular scale or include some sifting or screening feature to ensure that an appropriate level of detail is presented.

Physical Information

Physical information such as building corners, road center lines, or other prominent points can, through precise (cadastral) surveying methods, be referenced to the coordinate system and, hence, plotted in relation to one another, which provides the basis for an accurate map drawn to scale, as well as the computation of precise areas and distances. Coordinates can be inferred from existing maps, but obviously with limited and uncertain accuracy. Land or plot boundaries, administrative boundaries, census area boundaries, etc. can all be represented geometrically as *polygons* and accurately positioned on the map. Similarly, *lines* such as pipelines or roads, or *points* such as buildings or lampposts can be positioned. Information based on coordinate positioning is known as "vector data" and the point location coordinates must be established for this purpose. It can be stored in a GIS database or sometimes in common proprietary database files. Information obtained by automatic scanning of photographs or remote-sensing images is stored as "raster data." These data consist essentially of a mosaic of colored points (pixels) and are not compatible with vector data. It is, however, easy to acquire such data, which are often useful for specific applications but of limited value to a comprehensive, relational database. Software programs are available (including Chinese-designed programs) to convert raster data into vector data.

Thematic Information

Thematic information related (or attributable) to the polygons can be stored, such as population, or property areas, ownership and values, or quality of water supply services, or incidence of disease, pollution or flooding, etc. Attributes related to "lines" such as the volume of traffic (or incidence of traffic accidents), or the size, depth and condition of the pipeline or cable and its maintenance records, can also be stored. Common proprietary spreadsheet programs can be used to store attribute data. Frequent updating of such information is possible, which can then be monitored and analyzed to alert planners and decisionmakers of emerging trends and problems such as, e.g., shortages, capacity constraints or overcrowding. Such up-to-date information can facilitate the planning of appropriate, just-in-time solutions, which minimize the need for excess capacity and idle investment.

Issues and Constraints

The development of GIS systems is a widespread activity in many municipalities and research institutes throughout China. Many are facing similar obstacles as well as local constraints. The major issues are:

(a)   **Technology**. The GIS must draw upon many different data sources and support many different users. Each of these sources and users will likely have an information system in place or under development. Many subsystems have similar data needs and a common layer (or layers) of information such as topography, cadaster, population, etc. is called for. Unified, digital surveying and mapping technology, as well as systematic cooperation, should be used to facilitate topographic and cadastral survey work and the creation of a digitized, coordinated database. The specialized information needs to be stored in a compatible form and referenced in a manner that can be understood by others. The data structure, its classification and coding should be standardized. Hardware and software interfaces are needed to allow exchanges of information. Database programs should be relational and data acquisition and entry simplified. Software should be powerful, versatile, user friendly and inexpensive. Hardware should be as inexpensive and reliable as possible. An interagency central clearinghouse for technology development and evaluation would be a useful measure to avoid duplicate or redundant research.

(b) **Municipal Information Systems Policies.** Such policies are lacking, particularly in the area of data sharing and exchange, as well as updating and archiving. Local practices and security concerns affect this issue. Linkages among various commissions and bureaus information systems (Planning, Finance, Construction) are desirable in order to have the necessary economic, financial and physical data needed for integrated planning purposes. Guidelines on "best" practices in data sharing and exchange are needed. As mentioned above, data structure, classification and coding should be standardized to facilitate exchanges.

(c) **Applications.** Most effort to date has been applied to the information engineering aspects of GIS. Little effort has been spent on identifying applications for the data or integrating the use of the database into routine work such as macrospatial planning, sectoral planning, annual planning and budgeting, project analysis, operations and maintenance planning and management, or program and project evaluation. User requirements must be surveyed, and processes and procedures spelled out and their data needs and reports identified.

GIS Development Strategy and Costs

A strategy for building a wide-scale GIS in conjunction with the cadaster production could be as follows:

Phase I:

(a) form a municipal user task force and working group to (i) survey and review potential user information needs and commonalities, and (ii) define objectives, system concept, standards and engineering (including rough benefit/cost analysis), phased implementation plans and budgets (6-12 months);

(b) speed up cadaster map production; engage surveying contractors; **equip the land administration or mapping agency with the capacity to digitize maps and train staff** (12 months);

(c) develop, test and operationalize mini-GIS ("mixed technology") **applications** (3 months);

(d) develop cost-recovery mechanism options;

Phase II:

(e) review large-scale GIS hardware and software system **options; select** appropriate vendors and establish pilot-scale information **centers in selected** users' offices (6 months);

(f) build a fundamental database from the cadaster and/or topographic maps (**along** with cadaster mass production) and supply this to all user information centers (12 months);

(g) encourage users to build compatible sectoral database files **and acquire or** develop applications programs (12 months);

(h) train users; internalize applications into spatial and sectoral planning, **and** investment planning and budgeting procedures (12 months);

Phase III would expand the scope of pilot system and training **program to other** potential users.

Phase I would benefit from participation of national and other **municipal** agencies or research institutes in order to establish standards and norms **and exchange** experience. A development plan for disseminating the technology and experience **throughout** China to a network of GIS-related institutions could be included also as a Phase I objective.

Notional estimated costs (in US$) for the Phase I pilot city program, **excluding** national exchange network costs, could equal $500,000 equivalent (including **the cadastral** mapping), or somewhat less, if cadasters are already available. Phase II cannot **be realistically** costed at this time, but an indicative amount would be $1 million for cadaster **production,** $500,000 for GIS workstations and software, and $250,000 for training and development, **or** say, about $2 million in total for a medium-sized city. A fully developed GIS system, **covering** a large built-up area such as Shanghai, would be much more expensive, and cost $25-35 **million** to implement, requiring 3-5 years to complete.

Distributors of World Bank Publications

ARGENTINA
Carlos Hirsch, SRL
Galeria Guemes
Florida 165, 4th Floor-Ofc. 453/465
1333 Buenos Aires

**AUSTRALIA, PAPUA NEW GUINEA,
FIJI, SOLOMON ISLANDS,
VANUATU, AND WESTERN SAMOA**
D.A. Books & Journals
648 Whitehorse Road
Mitcham 3132
Victoria

AUSTRIA
Gerold and Co.
Graben 31
A-1011 Wien

BANGLADESH
Micro Industries Development
   Assistance Society (MIDAS)
House 5, Road 16
Dhanmondi R/Area
Dhaka 1209

   Branch offices:
   156, Nur Ahmed Sarak
   Chittagong 4000

   76, K.D.A. Avenue
   Kulna 9100

BELGIUM
Jean De Lannoy
Av. du Roi 202
1060 Brussels

CANADA
Le Diffuseur
C.P. 85, 1501B rue Ampère
Boucherville, Québec
J4B 5E6

CHILE
Invertec IGT S.A.
Americo Vespucio Norte 1165
Santiago

CHINA
China Financial & Economic
   Publishing House
8, Da Fo Si Dong Jie
Beijing

COLOMBIA
Infoenlace Ltda.
Apartado Aereo 34270
Bogota D.E.

COTE D'IVOIRE
Centre d'Edition et de Diffusion
   Africaines (CEDA)
04 B.P. 541
Abidjan 04 Plateau

CYPRUS
Center of Applied Research
Cyprus College
6, Diogenes Street, Engomi
P.O. Box 2006
Nicosia

DENMARK
SamfundsLitteratur
Rosenoerns Allé 11
DK-1970 Frederiksberg C

DOMINICAN REPUBLIC
Editora Taller, C. por A.
Restauración e Isabel la Católica 309
Apartado de Correos 2190 Z-1
Santo Domingo

EGYPT, ARAB REPUBLIC OF
Al Ahram
Al Galaa Street
Cairo

The Middle East Observer
41, Sherif Street
Cairo

FINLAND
Akateeminen Kirjakauppa
P.O. Box 128
SF-00101 Helsinki 10

FRANCE
World Bank Publications
66, avenue d'Iéna
75116 Paris

GERMANY
UNO-Verlag
Poppelsdorfer Allee 55
D-5300 Bonn 1

HONG KONG, MACAO
Asia 2000 Ltd.
46-48 Wyndham Street
Winning Centre
2nd Floor
Central Hong Kong

INDIA
Allied Publishers Private Ltd.
751 Mount Road
Madras - 600 002

   Branch offices:
   15 J.N. Heredia Marg
   Ballard Estate
   Bombay - 400 038

   13/14 Asaf Ali Road
   New Delhi - 110 002

   17 Chittaranjan Avenue
   Calcutta - 700 072

   Jayadeva Hostel Building
   5th Main Road, Gandhinagar
   Bangalore - 560 009

   3-5-1129 Kachiguda
     Cross Road
   Hyderabad - 500 027

   Prarthana Flats, 2nd Floor
   Near Thakore Baug, Navrangpura
   Ahmedabad - 380 009

   Patiala House
   16-A Ashok Marg
   Lucknow - 226 001

   Central Bazaar Road
   60 Bajaj Nagar
   Nagpur 440 010

INDONESIA
Pt. Indira Limited
Jalan Borobudur 20
P.O. Box 181
Jakarta 10320

IRELAND
Government Supplies Agency
4-5 Harcourt Road
Dublin 2

ISRAEL
Yozmot Literature Ltd.
P.O. Box 56055
Tel Aviv 61560

ITALY
Licosa Commissionaria Sansoni SPA
Via Duca Di Calabria, 1/1
Casella Postale 552
50125 Firenze

JAPAN
Eastern Book Service
Hongo 3-Chome, Bunkyo-ku 113
Tokyo

KENYA
Africa Book Service (E.A.) Ltd.
Quaran House, Mfangano Street
P.O. Box 45245
Nairobi

KOREA, REPUBLIC OF
Pan Korea Book Corporation
P.O. Box 101, Kwangwhamun
Seoul

MALAYSIA
University of Malaya Cooperative
   Bookshop, Limited
P.O. Box 1127, Jalan Pantai Baru
59700 Kuala Lumpur

MEXICO
INFOTEC
Apartado Postal 22-860
14060 Tlalpan, Mexico D.F.

NETHERLANDS
De Lindeboom/InOr-Publikaties
P.O. Box 202
7480 AE Haaksbergen

NEW ZEALAND
EBSCO NZ Ltd.
Private Mail Bag 99914
New Market
Auckland

NIGERIA
University Press Limited
Three Crowns Building Jericho
Private Mail Bag 5095
Ibadan

NORWAY
Narvesen Information Center
Book Department
P.O. Box 6125 Etterstad
N-0602 Oslo 6

PAKISTAN
Mirza Book Agency
65, Shahrah-e-Quaid-e-Azam
P.O. Box No. 729
Lahore 54000

PERU
Editorial Desarrollo SA
Apartado 3824
Lima 1

PHILIPPINES
International Book Center
Suite 1703, Cityland 10
Condominium Tower 1
Ayala Avenue, Corner H.V. dela
   Costa Extension
Makati, Metro Manila

POLAND
International Publishing Service
Ul. Piekna 31/37
00-677 Warzawa

For subscription orders:
IPS Journals
Ul. Okrezna 3
02-916 Warszawa

PORTUGAL
Livraria Portugal
Rua Do Carmo 70-74
1200 Lisbon

SAUDI ARABIA, QATAR
Jarir Book Store
P.O. Box 3196
Riyadh 11471

**SINGAPORE, TAIWAN,
MYANMAR, BRUNEI**
Information Publications
   Private, Ltd.
Golden Wheel Building
41, Kallang Pudding, #04-03
Singapore 1334

SOUTH AFRICA, BOTSWANA
For single titles:
Oxford University Press
   Southern Africa
P.O. Box 1141
Cape Town 8000

For subscription orders:
International Subscription Service
P.O. Box 41095
Craighall
Johannesburg 2024

SPAIN
Mundi-Prensa Libros, S.A.
Castello 37
28001 Madrid

Librería Internacional AEDOS
Consell de Cent, 391
08009 Barcelona

SRI LANKA AND THE MALDIVES
Lake House Bookshop
P.O. Box 244
100, Sir Chittampalam A.
   Gardiner Mawatha
Colombo 2

SWEDEN
For single titles:
Fritzes Fackboksforetaget
Regeringsgatan 12, Box 16356
S-103 27 Stockholm

For subscription orders:
Wennergren-Williams AB
P. O. Box 1305
S-171 25 Solna

SWITZERLAND
For single titles:
Librairie Payot
1, rue de Bourg
CH 1002 Lausanne

For subscription orders:
Librairie Payot
Service des Abonnements
Case postale 3312
CH 1002 Lausanne

TANZANIA
Oxford University Press
P.O. Box 5299
Maktaba Road
Dar es Salaam

THAILAND
Central Department Store
306 Silom Road
Bangkok

**TRINIDAD & TOBAGO, ANTIGUA
BARBUDA, BARBADOS,
DOMINICA, GRENADA, GUYANA,
JAMAICA, MONTSERRAT, ST.
KITTS & NEVIS, ST. LUCIA,
ST. VINCENT & GRENADINES**
Systematics Studies Unit
#9 Watts Street
Curepe
Trinidad, West Indies

TURKEY
Infotel
Narlabahçe Sok. No. 15
Cagaloglu
Istanbul

UNITED KINGDOM
Microinfo Ltd.
P.O. Box 3
Alton, Hampshire GU34 2PG
England

VENEZUELA
Libreria del Este
Aptdo. 60.337
Caracas 1060-A